LEADERSHIP-AS-PRACTICE

This book develops a new paradigm in the field of leadership studies, referred to as the "leadership-as-practice" (L-A-P) movement. Its essence is its conception of leadership as occurring as a practice rather than residing in the traits or behaviors of particular individuals. A practice is a coordinative effort among participants who choose through their own rules to achieve a distinctive outcome. It also tends to encompass routines as well as problem-solving or coping skills, often tacit, that are shared by a community. Accordingly, leadership-as-practice is less about what one person thinks or does and more about what people may accomplish together. It is thus concerned with how leadership emerges and unfolds through day-to-day experience. The social and material contingencies impacting the leadership constellation—the people who are effecting leadership at any given time—do not reside outside of leadership but are very much embedded within it. To find leadership, then, we must look to the practice within which it is occurring.

The leadership-as-practice approach resonates with a number of closely related traditions, such as collective, shared, distributed, and relational leadership, that converge on leadership processes. These approaches share a line of inquiry that acknowledges leadership as a social phenomenon. The new focus opens up a plethora of research opportunities encouraging the study of social processes beyond influence, such as inter-subjective agency, shared sensemaking, dialogue, and co-construction of responsibilities.

Joseph A. Raelin holds the Asa S. Knowles Chair of Practice-Oriented Education at Northeastern University, USA.

ROUTLEDGE STUDIES IN LEADERSHIP RESEARCH

LEADERSHIP-AS-PRACTICE

Theory and Application

Edited by Joseph A. Raelin

Routledge
Taylor & Francis Group

NEW YORK AND LONDON

First published 2016
by Routledge
711 Third Avenue, New York, NY 10017

and by Routledge
2 Park Square, Milton Park, Abingdon, Oxon OX14 4RN

Routledge is an imprint of the Taylor & Francis Group, an informa business

© 2016 Taylor & Francis

The right of the editor to be identified as the author of the editorial material, and of the authors for their individual chapters, has been asserted in accordance with sections 77 and 78 of the Copyright, Designs and Patents Act 1988.

Trademark notice: Product or corporate names may be trademarks or registered trademarks, and are used only for identification and explanation without intent to infringe.

Library of Congress Cataloging in Publication Data
Leadership-as-practice : theory and application / edited by Joseph A. Raelin.
    pages cm. – (Routledge studies in leadership research ; 2)
Includes bibliographical references and index.
1. Leadership–Study and teaching. 2. Organizational behavior. I. Raelin, Joseph A., 1948- editor.
    HD57.7.L431645 2016
    658.4'092–dc23
            2015029509

ISBN: 978-1-138-92485-7 (hbk)
ISBN: 978-1-138-92486-4 (pbk)
ISBN: 978-1-315-68412-3 (ebk)

Typeset in Bembo
by Taylor & Francis Books

CONTENTS

LIST OF ILLUSTRATIONS

Figures

Tables

Boxes

LIST OF CONTRIBUTORS

Joseph A. Raelin holds the Asa S. Knowles Chair of Practice-Oriented Education at Northeastern University where he is also Professor of Management and Organization Development in the D'Amore-McKim School of Business. Joe's recent work has focused on collective leadership and collaborative learning and the merger between the two. He is a prolific writer and among his books are the classics: *The Clash of Cultures: Managers Managing Professionals, Work-Based Learning: Bridging Knowledge and Action in the Workplace*, and *Creating Leaderful Organizations: How to Bring Out Leadership in Everyone*.

Brigid J. Carroll is an Associate Professor in the Department of Management and International Studies and Research Director of the New Zealand Leadership Institute both at the University of Auckland. Her research interests closely focus on identity, discourse, and power in leadership and the development of leadership practice. She is also involved in the development and design of leadership development interventions and programs in organizations across New Zealand. In this way, along with the Institute, she tries to intentionally live a theory/practice relationship.

Lucia Crevani is senior lecturer at Mälardalen University in Västerås, Sweden. Her research is focused on the study of leadership, entrepreneurship, project management, and gender and ethnicity as social processes taking place in and between organizations. Her work has been published in international journals as *Scandinavian Journal of Management, Service Business, Ephemera: Theory & Politics in Organization*, and *Project Management Journal*. She is also co-organizer of the After Method workshops, a series of workshops focusing on the methodological challenges of studying a world of change.

Ann L. Cunliffe is 50th Anniversary Professor of Organization Studies at the University of Bradford, UK, and Visiting Professor at Escola de Administraçâo da Fundaçâo Getulio Vargas, Brazil. Ann's current research addresses how leaders shape responsive and ethical organizations and she publishes on qualitative research methods and reflexivity. Her recent publications include *A Very Short, Fairly Interesting and Reasonably Cheap Book about Management* (2014) and articles in *Organizational Research Methods, Human Relations,* the *Journal of Business Ethics,* and the *Journal of Management Inquiry.* She is Co Editor-in-Chief of *Management Learning,* and organizes the biennial Qualitative Research in Management and Organization Conference.

David Denyer is Professor of Leadership and Organizational Change and Director of Research at Cranfield School of Management. His research interests include complexity leadership, organizational change and resilience, evidence-based management, and new approaches to leadership development. David helps senior leaders in a wide range of organizations to establish strategic direction and deliver sustained performance improvement. He has published a large number of important and highly cited articles and book chapters. His latest edited book is on *Managing Change in Extreme Contexts* (Routledge).

Nada Endrissat is a lecturer at Bern Business School, Switzerland. She has a Ph.D. in Management from Basel University and has spent research visits at HEC Montreal and MGSM Sydney. Her current research interests include processes of (creative) projects, aesthetic practices, and the interplay between branding and identity construction. Her research has been published in *Leadership* and is forthcoming in *Organization Studies* and the *Journal of Business Research* special issue on creative industries.

Jackie Ford is Professor of Leadership and Organization Studies at the University of Bradford, with former Professorial roles since 2008 at the Universities of Leeds and Bradford. Her research interests include the exploration of working lives, with a particular interest in studying leadership, gender, ethics, and management practices through critical, post-structural lenses. She has co-authored a monograph entitled *Leadership as identity: Constructions and deconstructions* (Palgrave Macmillan, 2008); co-edited *Making public services management critical* (Routledge, 2010); co-edited a textbook entitled *Leadership: Contemporary critical perspectives* (Sage, 2015); and has published in a range of journals including *British Journal of Management, Human Relations, Journal of Management Studies, Leadership, Management Learning, Organization, Sociology,* and *Work Employment and Society.*

Kenneth J. Gergen is a Senior Research Professor in Psychology at Swarthmore College, and the President of the Board of the Taos Institute. He is also the Associate Editor of *Theory and Psychology,* a position in which he has also served for the *American Psychologist*. He is internationally known for his contributions to social constructionist theory, technology and cultural change, and relational practices. Among his most notable books are *Realities and Relationships, The Saturated Self, An Invitation to Social Construction*, and *Relational Being: Beyond Self and Community*. Gergen has received numerous awards for his work, including honorary degrees in both the US and Europe.

Lone Hersted (M.A.) is a lecturer and Ph.D. fellow at the Department of Learning and Philosophy at the University of Aalborg (Denmark). Her teaching and research is concerned with leadership, organizational development, coaching, and creative change processes. At Aalborg she is coordinator and lecturer for the Masters program in Organisational Coaching and Learning. Lone has also worked as a consultant since 2003 and was earlier educated at the Nordic Theatre School. Among her publications, she is the co-author of the books, *Behind the scenes of artistic creativity, Relationelle perspektiver på Ledelse*, and *Relational leading: Practices for dialogically based collaboration*.

Paul Hibbert is Professor of Management at the University of St Andrews School of Management, Associate Editor of *Management Learning* and Associate Editor of *Management Teaching Review*. Paul's recent work has focused on collaborative and relational processes of organizing and learning. His work appears in a wide range of international journals, such as: *Academy of Management Learning and Education, Journal of Business Ethics, Journal of Management Education, Management Learning, Organizational Research Methods*, and *Organization Studies*.

Brad Jackson is the Head of School of Government and Professor of Public and Community Leadership at Victoria University of Wellington. Prior to this he was the Fletcher Building Education Trust Chair in Leadership and Co-Director of the New Zealand Leadership Institute at The University of Auckland Business School. He is a former co-editor of the journal, *Leadership*, the former Vice-Chair of the International Leadership Association, a Fellow of the Australian and New Zealand Academy of Management, the Leadership Trust, and the Lancaster Leadership Centre.

Stephen Kempster is Professor of Leadership Learning and Development and Director of the Lancaster Leadership Centre at Lancaster University Management School. With a Ph.D. in leadership learning, Steve has published articles, chapters, and books that explore leadership learning, entrepreneurial leadership development, purpose, and responsibility in leadership. His work on research methods includes examining critical realism and developing grounded theory and auto-ethnography. Journals he has published in include: *International Journal of Management Reviews, Leadership Quarterly, Management Learning*, and *Leadership*. Steve has been a Board Director of the International Leadership Association and is on the Editorial Boards of *Management Learning* and *Leadership*.

Ken Parry is Professor of Leadership Studies at Deakin University. He is a Fellow of four professional academies. He was Founding Director of the Centre for the Study of Leadership, a joint venture with private industry, and Founding Editor of the journal of the Australian and New Zealand Academy of Management. He has won awards for qualitative and quantitative research, and is a regular keynote speaker at industry conferences.

Caroline Ramsey is a senior lecturer and director of the Doctor of Business Administration program at the University of Liverpool, UK. Most of her writing in management learning and organizational studies has been about practice-based learning, but research projects have included developing practices for the management of innovation, judgment, and conversations within and across organizational boundaries. It is this interest in talk and conversation that has led Caroline to research leadership as a relational process worked out in the day-to-day practice of organizing.

Viviane Sergi is assistant professor at the Management and Technology department at ESG UQAM, Canada. She is a member of the Strategy as Practice Study Group (GéPS) at HEC Montréal. Her research interests include leadership, materiality, project organizing, performativity, and methodological issues related to qualitative research. Her work has been published in *Academy of Management Annals, Human Relations, Scandinavian Journal of Management, Qualitative Research in Organizations and Management*, and in the *International Journal of Managing Projects in Business*.

John Shotter is Emeritus Professor of Communication in the Department of Communication, University of New Hampshire, and a Research Associate, Centre for Philosophy of Natural & Social Science (CPNSS), London School of Economics, London, UK, and also a Visiting Professor at the Open University and Leeds University Business Schools. His long-term interest has been, and still is, in the social conditions conducive to people having a voice in determining the conditions of their own lives, that is, in the development of participatory democracies and civil societies. He is the author of: *Social Accountability and Self-hood, Cultural Politics of Everyday Life, Conversational Realities: The Construction of Life through Language, Conversational Realities Revisited: Life, Language, Body, and Word, Social Construction on the Edge*, and *Getting It: Withness-Thinking and the Dialogical … in Practice.*

Barbara Simpson is Professor of Leadership and Organisational Dynamics at Strathclyde Business School in Glasgow. Her Ph.D. in Management, which was awarded by the University of Auckland in 1998, marked a sea change from her earlier career as a physics-trained geothermal scientist, traces of which nevertheless remain evident in her work today as she brings the principles of action, flow, and movement to bear on the processes of creativity, innovation, leadership, and change. Her current research is deeply informed by the philosophies of the American Pragmatists, especially George Herbert Mead's thinking on process and temporality. She has published in a variety of journals including *Organization Studies*, *Human Relations*, *Organization*, *R&D Management*, and *Journal of Management Inquiry*.

Kim Turnbull James is Professor of Leadership and Executive Learning at Cranfield School of Management. Her research interests include new approaches to leadership development, collaborative learning for leadership, organization politics, and the impact of group and organization dynamics in organizational leadership. Kim is on the editorial boards of *Management Learning* and *Leadership*, international journals in this field, and her latest edited books are *Leadership Perspectives: Knowledge into Action* and *Leadership Learning: Knowledge into Action*, both with Palgrave. Executive coaching, consulting to teams, and leadership development are all part of Kim's portfolio.

Philip A. Woods is Professor of Educational Policy, Democracy and Leadership at the University of Hertfordshire, UK, and Chair of the British Educational Leadership, Management and Administration Society (BELMAS). Author of over 120 publications, his work particularly focuses on distributed and democratic leadership, governance, equity, and change towards more democratic and holistic learning environments. Awards include best conference paper at the International Philosophy of Management Conference in Oxford, published in 2010 as 'The Geography of Reflective Leadership: The inner life of democratic learning communities' (co-authored with Dr Glenys Woods) in *Philosophy of Management*. His books include *Transforming education policy: Shaping a democratic future*.

London.

oned Beth Faig   ed.
dny), 1293. 283.
., Stap   Hodi ngpea

1

INTRODUCTION TO LEADERSHIP-AS-PRACTICE

Theory and application

Joseph A. Raelin

Overview

Welcome to our research volume on *Leadership-as-Practice*, a new movement in leadership research and practice destined to shake the foundations of the very meaning of leadership in the worlds of both theory and application. Its essence is its conception of leadership as occurring as a practice rather than residing in the traits or behaviors of particular individuals. The book seeks to assemble what we know about the leadership-as-practice (L-A-P) movement and extend its conceptualization through a number of critical themes that have not been sufficiently explored or, in some cases, not explored at all.

The editor and authors of this volume sincerely hope that this work will provide an indispensable resource for scholars working in the more progressive domains of leadership studies. As an authoritative text on leadership as a social, material, and jointly accomplished process, it seeks to offer greater insights into the realities of leadership than texts focusing on the role of individual leaders. In this way we hope to create momentum for a new movement in the field of leadership that is ripe for a more critical perspective that incorporates the emerging practice view. We refer to our approach as a movement because we are observing some of the attributes of social mobilization from social movement theory (see, e.g., James & van Seters, 2014). In particular, those of us working in the broadly defined practice domain have formed a collective identity that has assumed a normative orientation for changing the conventional view of leadership. In the end, we hope that our collective efforts will continue across time as other adherents join us to advance our agenda of change.

In the current volume, we seek to present an integrated and coherent thematic assemblage of chapters that build on one another and fill out a needed conceptualization in leadership-as-practice. In places, readers will notice that authors approach our movement from somewhat different perspectives, but it is thought that any exposition of contentions and variations (some of which will be referred to below) will only serve to enrich the movement by encouraging continuing research and development in a spirit of transparency. Among the themes that we will explore are:

- The distinctions between L-A-P and other collective and relational perspectives of leadership as well as between L-A-P and other "as-practice" approaches;
- The historical, philosophical, critical, and ideological foundations of L-A-P that make it exigent in understanding the contemporary organization and workforce;
- The complex site where activity and its representation embodied in leadership practices intersect;
- The artifacts, symbols, material, and language games that establish identity and achieve leadership in L-A-P;
- The nature of agency including the inter-active and trans-active agency underlying L-A-P;
- The dialogic patterns that produce sustainable collective practices;
- The methodologies that in attempting to capture L-A-P change the tools, methods, and technologies underlying the study of leadership and leadership development; and
- The change in leadership development when conceived as a practice rather than as a psychological parameter within the consciousness and behavior of particular individuals.

Finally, we hope you will find that the selected authors of this book are among the most prominent and highly cited progressive scholars in the world undertaking critical studies in the field of leadership. What is also compelling about these authors is that none of them is merely a transcriber of thoughts, rather each is actively involved in the practice world through their own empirical studies, although most indicate a preference for qualitative ethnographies over a priori theory construction and quantitative testing. The chapters thus combine the authors' applications with theory. As the editor, it will be my pleasure to introduce these chapters later in this Introduction. At this point, I will provide a brief introduction to leadership-as-practice to orient the reader to this emerging and what we hope you will find exciting movement in leadership research and practice. Following a preamble to the "practice view," I will cover some of the basic parameters of the L-A-P movement: its prior traditions, the problem of structure and agency in L-A-P, its enumerated activities, and end with its development orientation, research, and ideology.

Introducing the "practice view"

The foundation of the leadership-as-practice approach is its underlying belief that leadership occurs as a practice rather than from the traits or behaviors of individuals. A practice is a coordinative effort among participants who choose through their own rules to achieve a distinctive outcome. Accordingly, leadership-as-practice is less about what one person thinks or does and more about what people may accomplish together. It is thus concerned with how leadership emerges and unfolds through day-to-day experience. The social and material-discursive contingencies impacting the leadership constellation—the people who are effecting leadership at any given time—do not reside outside of leadership but are very much embedded within it. To find leadership, then, we must look to the practice within which it is occurring.

The practice view may consequently upend our traditional views of leadership because it does not rely on the attributes of individuals, nor does it focus on the dyadic relationship between leaders and followers, which historically has been the starting point for any discussion of leadership. Rather, it depicts immanent collective action emerging from mutual, discursive, sometimes recurring and sometimes evolving patterns in the moment and over time among those engaged in the practice. This definition suggests an ecumenical approach to practice because at times it refers to routine activities; at other times, it suggests a more perpetually unfolding dynamic. Perhaps the simplest way to account for this difference is to compare the concepts of practices and practice.

Practices, as per the definition of Pickering (1995), refer to specific sequences of activities that may repeatedly recur, whereas practice refers to emergent entanglements that tend to extend or transform meaning over time. In Chapter 8 of this volume, Simpson links practices to an inter-actional mode of activity in which pre-formed entities—be they people or discourses or institutions—vie for influence over other "inter-actors." Practice, on the other hand, is associated with a more trans-actional mode characterized by a continual flow of processes where material-discursive engagements produce meaning that is emergent and mutual. Practices, therefore, as Crevani and Endrissat point out (Chapter 2, this volume) rely on an entitative ontology of subject-object or subject-subject relations in which individuals may be viewed within fields of relationships. Practice, on the other hand, is processual and thus considered more situated and recursive. Another way to differentiate these two forms of activity is to use the philosophical language employed by Cunliffe and Hibbert (Chapter 3, this volume) in which practices may be considered objectivist or subjectivist, depending on whether the practices in question are studied as objects separate from the people engaged in them or whether they are subject to the intentions and interpretations of the actors who experience them. Practice, meanwhile, may be considered intersubjective in character because it is interwoven not between people but "within" the dynamic unfolding of their becoming (see Shotter, Chapter 7, this volume).

When we associate leadership with practice, we think of it as not only material-discursive but shared or collective (Bolden, Petrov & Gosling, 2008; Pearce &

Conger, 2003; Spillane, 2006). The parties to the practice engage in semiotic, often dialogical, exchange, and in some cases for those genuinely committed to one another, they display an interest in listening to one another, in reflecting on new perspectives, and in entertaining the prospect of changing direction based on what they learn (Raelin, 2013). Gronn (2002) refers to the engagement as a conjoint agency characterized by reciprocal dependence. In effect, the parties look to coordinate with one another to advance their individual or mutual projects. In the integrated professional services realm, for example, individual contributors may seek to work inter-professionally in aligning their thoughts and actions with others to interpret problems of practice and to respond to those interpretations (Edwards, 2005).

The activity of leadership is at times orderly; at other times, it will be irregular and provisional. As people within an enterprise work together, they may develop a sense of mastery not only in accomplishing the daily mundane work of the organization but in surmounting unexpected challenges and disruptions. At times, the practices become so obvious that they are no longer questioned and begin to represent an objectified context for members of a community (Endrissat & von Arx, 2013). At this point, actions become pre-determined until system perturbance pulls people out of their contextual patterns. Unfamiliar stakeholders may be invited to contribute their knowledge. New or forgotten resources may be solicited to add to the knowledge base. Eventually, familiar routines may be broken or familiar relations may even end in unresolved conflict as new structures, material, and relations become salient. Activity may resume, however, as participants decide whether or not to continue the effort. A casual observer to the action may see the activity as an organized effort leading to a planned conclusion, but if paying close attention, it may actually resemble a jazz improvisation in which, as Hatch explains (Hatch, 1999: 85): "The directions [the tune] will take are only decided in the moment of playing and will be redetermined each time the tune is played."

The practice of leadership is not dependent on any one person to mobilize action on behalf of everybody else. The effort is intrinsically collective. However, in the process of engagement, leadership may emanate from the actions of particular individuals who, often because of historical reasons, may be able to suggest meaning with a high degree of insight, such as by extracting or providing critical cues, by suggesting behavioral patterns, or by transmitting cultural norms to minimize the range of choices available (Dawkins, 1989; Pye, 1993). These "meaning makers" may be serving in managerial roles, but anyone within the team can be responsible provided they have astute awareness of the perspectives, reasoning patterns, and narratives of others (Jordan, Andersson & Ringnér, 2013).

Prior traditions

Although characterized here as a movement, the leadership-as-practice approach resonates with a number of closely related traditions, such as collective, shared, distributed, and relational leadership. What these approaches have in common is their push for a line of inquiry that differentiates from a focus on traits, behaviors, abilities, or competencies in a way to gain a deeper knowledge of leadership as a social phenomenon. On the other hand, leadership-as-practice is able to release leadership from a role-driven, entitative influence relationship that is still characteristic of many of the aforementioned perspectives. Nor does it pre-establish the occupants of leadership roles. Heeding the warning from Alvesson and Sveningsson (2003) that the sheer act of naming someone a leader may in some cases over-emphasize and in other cases undermine reports of leadership practice as it is occurring, L-A-P pursues and seeks to understand leadership activity wherever and however it appears.

Agency and structure

Leadership becomes evident when agency appears as a constraint to structure. At times, it may even transform it. Using such resources as self-consciousness or deliberation, agents can use individual and collective reflexivity to overturn the historical contexts and expectations imposed on people and institutions (Archer, 2000; Blumer, 1969; Gherardi, 2000; Giddens, 1984; Herepath, 2014; Rose, 1998). Although agency may be exhibited during normal everyday routines, it often takes place during moments of crisis or indeterminacy or when there is inadequate knowledge about what to do. Yet, in this liminal space, someone may have a "felt sense" about how to proceed (Gendlin, 1964). He or she may propose an idea or a thought or demonstrate a particular approach. The initiative may not prevail but it may spur other members of the group to demonstrate "their own way out." In due course, as people build on each other's moves, a collaborative endeavor may ensue that might re-orient the practice toward a resolution, temporary though it may be. So leadership would emerge not necessarily out of individual intentionality but within the flow in its intra-action when a project would become other than what it was before (Barad, 2003).

As an agentic relationship among parties to an activity, L-A-P is not necessarily focused on the initiator or even on the recipient of the activity. Others often become involved. By focusing only on the initiator, we promote a fallacy that one party is active and the others passive, the latter awaiting the fateful message that will abruptly thrust them into action. But people tend to already be in motion and are not necessarily static until activated by others.

Practice theory thus has a connection to the social but not through rational purpose and markets nor through the norms of culture. Rather it situates the social through shared or collective symbolic structures of knowledge that establish social order. In this process that arises from everyday actions and interactions rather than from mental capacities or texts, patterns of bodily behavior are established via certain routinized ways of understanding and knowing (Reckwitz, 2002). Leadership is consequently embodied through language and through other semiotic manifestations and in conjunction with the material, structural, and aesthetic resources within the actual workings of practice rather than through individual a priori intentions. Leadership as a practice becomes ecumenical as anyone may participate in leadership as he or she engages in agentic activity. Practice becomes the engine of collaborative agency (Raelin, 2014). Participants (to the activity) constitute but are also constituted by the discursive and intersubjective practices of participants within a nexus of activity (Davies, 1991). During the activity, leadership might ensue as people decide what to do and how to do it. As Crevani, Lindgren and Packendorff (2010) explain, it is a matter of constructing and reconstructing positions and issues as those engaged produce the boundaries of their own action.

The activities of leadership-as-practice

Constructing positions and issues, as cited above, form some of the specific activities that animate the parties engaged in leadership-as-practice. In addition to the construction of issues would be a corresponding co-construction of responsibilities for particular tasks and of identities shared by interacting actors. Besides Crevani et al. (2010), other authors from such fields as organizational discourse, innovation, and complex systems, suggest other unique practices that speak to the task activity of leadership, in other words, getting the job done (Carroll & Simpson, 2012; Goldstein, Hazy & Lichtenstein 2010; Hazy & Uhl-Bien, 2014). Augmenting these are those from the affective dimension that are designed to support and sustain team or organizational members while performing their work. These are often referred as maintenance, socioemotional, or reflective functions (Bales, 1950; Marsick, 1990). Here, then, are seven additional activities to be found in leadership-as-practice (Raelin, 2014):

1. scanning—identifying resources, such as information or technology, that can contribute to new or existing programs through simplification or sensemaking;
2. signaling—mobilizing and catalyzing the attention of others to a program or project through such means as imitating, building on, modifying, ordering, or synthesizing prior or existing elements;
3. weaving—creating webs of interaction across existing and new networks by building trust between individuals and units or by creating shared meanings to particular views or cognitive frames;
4. stabilizing—offering feedback to converge activity and evaluate effectiveness, leading, in turn, to structural and behavioral changes and learning;
5. inviting—encouraging those who have held back to participate through their ideas, their energy, and their humanity;
6. unleashing—making sure that everyone who wishes to has had a chance to contribute, without fear of repercussion, even if their contribution might create discrepancy or ambiguity in the face of decision-making convergence; and

7.   reflecting—triggering thoughtfulness within the self and with others to ponder the meaning of past, current, and future experience to learn how to meet mutual needs and interests.

Leadership development

The conduct of leadership may be mundane or what Chia and Holt (2006) refer to as "non-deliberate practical coping" rather than "planned, intentional action" (p. 643). In the day-to-day practice of leadership, much activity may therefore be unspoken or unconscious (Chia & MacKay, 2007). In thinking about how to develop leadership, we may need to find ways to bring more of the unconscious and unreflective into the conscious and explicit domain. We also need to study instances of failure, dissonance, crisis, obstruction, or even surprise that spur interventions (Carroll, Levy & Richmond, 2008). Leadership development thus requires an acute immersion into the practices that are embedded within social relations and between people, objects, and their institutions. It needs to be a learning associated with lived experience that occurs within specific historical, cultural, and local contexts (Nicolini, Gherardi & Yanov, 2003). Using such models as cognitive apprenticeships (Lave, 1988), understudy (Dreyfus, 2001), communities of practice (Wenger, 1998), or reflective communities (Bohm, 1985), learners would observe and experiment with their own collective tacit processes in action.

There are also development approaches from what we might refer to as the "action modalities" or interventions that have as their commonality a commitment to work with people where they are as they engage with one another on mutual problems, and offering them a means of collective reflection on their experience so as to expand and even create knowledge while at the same time serving to improve practice (Raelin, 2009). Among these modalities would be such strategies as action learning, action research, action science, cooperative inquiry, cultural-historical activity theory, developmental action inquiry, and participatory (critical) research. They each tend to adopt a dialectic epistemology that sees knowledge as arising from a contested interaction among a community of inquirers rather than from a single source of expertise. It is thus not representational. It arises from local interactive engagement that is emergent before the need for representation (Bakhtin 1986; Chia & Holt 2006; Schatzki 1997). In the case of action learning, for example, managers are not sent away to training, rather the learning experience is brought to them as they are in the midst of engaging with their colleagues on their own problems (Marquardt, 1999; Yorks, O'Neill & Marsick, 1999; Boshyk, 2002; Raelin, 2008; Pedler, 2011).

Leadership development in a practice world would also recognize the experiential and embodied nature of leadership and adjust its methods accordingly. In addition, as pointed out by Denis, Langley and Rouleau (2010), learning about leadership would require the examination of four other qualities—that leadership be considered:

1. dynamic (leadership at one time can affect subsequent leadership actions);
2. collective (leadership depends on a constellation of complementary co-leaders in interaction);
3. situated (leadership is found in specific contexts and is both a cause and consequence of immanent activity); and
4. dialectic (negotiated practices can produce conflicted outcomes).

Research

L-A-P offers researchers the opportunity to study leadership at multiple interacting levels beyond the individual level of analysis. For example, it would be interested in probing into interpersonal and intercultural relationships inclusive of the material artifacts, the technologies, the physical arrangements, the language, the emotions, and the rituals, each brought out to understand the meaning of the practice in question. The methodological preference would be for more process-oriented studies and those that consider cultural, historical, and political conditions embedded within the leadership relationship (Knights & Willmott, 1992; Wood, 2005). Process-oriented dynamics would be rich in power dynamics and human relations and would privilege emergence and ambiguity over control and rationality, and thus would resist closure on the familiar categories of leadership that are often individualistic and directive. At the same time a process approach, in which leadership is seen as a continuous social flow, would of necessity require slowing down the action sufficiently to study the discernible practices and interactions. Further, L-A-P methodology would be interested in the collective beliefs and co-constructions that arise to guide subsequent individual and collective action.

The research of leadership under a L-A-P lens, then, would take advantage of more narrative forms of inquiry, such as ethnographies using thick description that attempt to capture the dialogical and practice activity concurrently in process (Weick, 1989). The role of the researcher would not so much be to inquire from outside the activity but rather to provide tools to encourage the observed to become inquirers themselves (Clot, 1999; Jarzabkowski & Whittington, 2008). These tools would not serve merely as mirrors for "looking in" to the activity but actually constitute the activity in all its rich dialogic interaction (Tsoukas, 1998).

Ideology

Along with the focus on the activities of leadership, it is important to distinguish whether there are values within a movement such as L-A-P that guide the quality, relevance, and outcomes of its practices. We also might submit that compared with other models of leadership that emphasize individual sovereignty, linearity, influence, and agreement, L-A-P emphasizes collective engagement, divergence, intersubjectivity, and ambiguity. L-A-P privileges the value of social interactions, but it would be trivial to point to such interactions ideologically without a corresponding emphasis on reflective emancipatory processes to scrutinize their taken-for-granted assumptions and meanings. We might also argue in the tradition of Spicer, Alvesson and Kärreman (2009) that a practice approach to leadership engage in critical dialogue in which we seek to question the language and practices that bear the imprint of social domination. Indeed, L-A-P potentially represents an alternative critical discourse to the mainstream personality approach to leadership which tends to incarnate the individual leader as a beacon of prosperity and moral rectitude.

On the other hand, in our era of so-called "post-bureaucracy" and "post-heroic" leadership, characterized by flexible peer decision-making processes, less routinization, enhanced discretion, and distributed authority, recentralization may ensue because of a focus on visibility, predictability, and accountability (Heckscher, 1994). As managers make greater use of sophisticated methods of unobtrusive appraisal using such means as electronic surveillance and monitoring, there is a chance of a resumption of the iron cage of standard bureaucracy, characterized by individual responsibility and vertical accountability (Hales, 2002; Heydebrand, 1989; Hodgson, 2004).

Popular accounts of executive misdeeds notwithstanding, hierarchical decision making is still dominant, and albeit the emerging concerns with global warming and other non-sustainable practices, the ultimate aim of such decision making is on productivity. We also must recognize that participatory spaces are imbued with power relations that in some cases cause suppression of voices and self-muting among those disenfranchised from the dominant discourse, thus thwarting critical review (Cleaver, 2007; Kesby, 2005). Nevertheless, by focusing our attention on the group in practice, we encourage the formation of community within which members through social critique may have a better chance to resist oppression and other forms of inequitable social arrangements compared with conditions of sole individual intervention (Crevani et al., 2010; Raelin, 2014). Further, the practice approach may, in the end, be more critical than critical leadership studies (see, e.g., Collinson, 2011) because it does not take as its starting point a critique of the ultimate hegemonic relation—the leader-follower dyad. Rather, in double-loop tradition, it challenges the very assumption of the necessity of this relationship in the ontology of leadership (Argyris & Schön, 1974). Not requiring pre-specified outcomes, practice can actually precede agency while focusing on a process that can be inclusive of participants' own communal, shared, and exploratory discourses.

The chapters of this volume

The volume is presented in four parts and 13 chapters in total. The chapters are dedicated to specific themes carefully selected to present a new movement—in this case, of leadership-as-practice. The editor, Joe Raelin, has already provided the current introductory chapter to orient readers to the emerging L-A-P field, distinguishing it from the individualist paradigm while offering its intrinsic features. To follow are three chapters that constitute Part I representing the background to the movement.

In Chapter 2, Lucia Crevani and Nada Endrissat provide a comparative explanation of the leadership-as-practice movement to help frame the book as well as to enable prospective researchers to understand the promise and challenge of conducting research from a L-A-P perspective. After digesting this chapter, readers will have obtained a thorough orientation to the field, including a perspective on how leadership itself is viewed when conceived from a practice point of view; in particular, the authors advance it as providing direction for organizing processes and as re-orienting the flow of practice through collaborative agency. Their take-off point is to distinguish between two very different ontological positions in leadership studies: an entitative vs. a relational approach; the first giving priority to social states and pre-existing entities, whereas the second giving priority to unfolding relations and processes. From here, they draw comparisons between the leadership-as-practice movement and both the leadership styles and the relational leadership approaches, focusing on the unit of analysis that produces the necessary knowledge about leadership. They then compare L-A-P with two other so-called "as-practice" approaches: strategy-as-practice and coordination-as-practice. They show in the second instances that the difference is based on the social accomplishments on which each of the approaches focus.

The next foundation chapter looks at leadership-as-practice from the philosophical tradition of phenomenology, and especially from "Hermeneutics." According to Ann Cunliffe and Paul Hibbert, hermeneutic inquiry as a contestation to standard scientific inquiry is receptive to multiple interpretations of text to include an interrogation of ways of being, that is, what it means "to be." This form of inquiry is fundamental to our understanding of practice because it incorporates a range of unique dynamics, such as grounding, detaching, and composing, which are contextualized and make sense only within specific spaces of intelligibility. From Gadamer, for example, we learn that intersubjective inquiry occurs through both diachronic (between ourselves and text) and synchronic (between ourselves and another) dimensions. Ultimately, many of our L-A-P traditions are thought to fall within an intersubjective "problematic" such that practice is interwoven between people in which meanings, actions, and interpretations shift in and through time and across relationships.

Chapter 4, written by Philip Woods, continues the focus on the need for philosophical grounding of the L-A-P movement by examining the vital question of whether leadership, and leadership-as-practice in particular, should pay particular attention to their "Democratic Roots." His answer is that as an emergent social process, it must do so because leadership needs to honor the individual's development of his or her human capabilities to its full holistic extent. Each individual, furthermore, needs to be counted in this consideration, not just the senior-most leaders. Leadership-as-practice accordingly observes a philosophy of co-development because of its consideration of co-dependent parties interacting to create their own practice and meaning which they share through dialogue. They engage freely not as directed by an authority or by rule as in the instance of what Woods refers to as performative governance. Woods acknowledges that L-A-P, however, must be analyzed across multiple distributions, such as in its structures and practices. Leadership-as-practice qualifies contingently as a democratic process as long as it promotes a critical reflection by participants in actively understanding their selves and of others in the practice of everyday relationships.

Part II of the volume considers the embodied nature of L-A-P, suggesting that it is not cognition in its isolated condition located within the mind of a prime instigator, call him or her the leader, that mobilizes leadership. Rather, leadership occurs from an interaction with the environment through both individual and collective sensorimotor processing.

Brigid Carroll in her "Leadership as Identity" unveils at the outset of her chapter the critical distinction between talking about leadership and doing leadership. When equated, there is always the tendency for the subject to create a fantasy leadership identity. This is because those designated leaders have a need to represent themselves with coherence and distinctiveness although they may be involved in work that is often fluid, precarious, and filled with contradiction and fragmentation. Identity is accordingly seen as a mediator between the self and the surrounding social structure that is created as actants use and move through organizational spaces. It is not a quality existing prior to the context in which it is organized. According to Carroll, in spaces, such as the IT environment that she employs in her case example, leadership identity is established through the artifacts, conversations, and routines on which participants rely in responding to and reacting to the choices they are making in accomplishing their work.

In the second chapter of Part II, Viviane Sergi in "Who's Leading the Way?" explores some of the undiscovered elements of leadership practice, looking in particular at how the design of material elements contributes to the achievement of leadership, defined in terms of directing, shaping, and ordering activities. She joins the authors of this volume in challenging the individual paradigm of leadership by focusing on three specific orientations: leadership's processual dynamics which occur *in situ*, unfolding over time; its collective orientation that emerges from its view as an interactional joint performance; and its mundane character that speaks to its occurrence in banal situations and interactions. Viviane prods the leadership-as-practice movement to not overlook how materiality intervenes in agency to co-generate leadership. In a case study of a software development project, she illustrates how a key document generated direction, shape, and order during key moments in the project's life and also stabilized what had been negotiated during prior times and what options might be available in the project's subsequent development.

In the last chapter of this Part, John Shotter delves further into the hermeneutical nature of the leadership relationship (introduced in Chapter 3 by Cunliffe and Hibbert) by, in his words, "Turning Leadership Inside-Out and Back-to-Front!" In this provocative account, John offers an alternative to familiar Cartesian-Newtonian forms of thought. Using primarily a philosophical line of reasoning, he argues that we need to discover not only what we are before our representations but also what "kind of world we take it for granted that we are living in." We need to become more aware of our "before-the-fact" common sense that characterizes our spontaneous activities as a social group. What John accomplishes in this chapter is to give us a special and deep insight into the world of practice to help us "notice" our connectedness with others as well as, as he calls it, "the othernesses" around us. The process is hermeneutical in that no preconceived framework is available; rather, each particularity in the situation stands on its own while being linked with other particularities. John's account reminds us that to find and study leadership, we need to conduct more than scientific explorations. We need to mount philosophically structured inquiries into how leadership may emerge in each successive episode in practice.

In Part III of the volume, the social interactions that underlie the practices of leadership are fully developed in three chapters. The authors are careful to distinguish the nature of the interaction that occurs in leadership practice as an activity which is more than an exchange between individuals; it is often an in-the-moment intra-action out of which dynamic unfolding may be some form of leadership agency. Barbara Simpson in her chapter seeking to find this "Agency" in L-A-P invokes a framework from the collaborative work of Dewey and Bentley. The framework distinguishes three modes of inquiry: self-action, inter-action, and trans-action and each mode invokes a distinct orientation to leadership: the leader-practitioner, leadership as a set of practices, and leadership in the flow of practice. By clarifying the focus of each mode, Barbara argues against their conflation as their means of inquiry are largely incommensurable. In the self-action mode, agency tends to reside in the free will of individual leaders; in the inter-action mode, agency is distributed among entities engaged in discrete predictable practices. It is in the trans-action mode that we may find leadership-as-practice as a perpetually unfolding dynamic in which it is the action itself that re-orients the flow of practice towards new directions.

Ken Gergen and Lone Hersted in their chapter continue to refine our understanding of the transactional nature of leadership-as-practice by characterizing leadership as a "Dialogic Practice." They join other post-structuralist critics who have begun to question the entitative approach to leadership and organization behavior based on fixed attributes or structures. Rather, the authors take a relational view enriched through the medium of dialogue to consider leadership as an emergent outcome of interlocking practices. As they explain at the outset of their chapter, "there are no leaders independent of the relational patterns of which they are a part." At the outset, the authors become very technical about the mechanics of dialogue, examining it as the basis for coordinated action rather than as a representation of the speaker's mind. They show that the meaning of any utterance, for example, depends on its functioning within a relational matrix. Unfortunately, the outcome of relational leading may lead to degenerative as well as generative scenarios. Our understanding of this dynamic allows us to structure leadership development activities and rehearsals to offset some of the ill-effects of degeneration, such as animosity, silence, or even severance of the relationship. The chapter illustrates some prospective interventions in dialogic training, using skilled facilitation and what is called the "polyphonic" reflecting team. These vehicles take advantage of the practice approach to coordinated action potentially resulting in productive leadership relationships.

Caroline Ramsey concludes our coverage of social interactions with a novel chapter on what she refers to as "Conversational Travel," in which she advocates conversational dynamics as the most propitious method to discern the emergence of leadership as a practice. However, rather than have the conversation analyst preconceive the occurrence of leadership within the leader-follower relation, she proposes that conversational travel can identify leadership without the need to identify specific individual roles. In particular, she proposes building a new vocabulary of leadership moments through three shifts in conversational analysis. First, she would have us treat talk as invitational rather than as only constitutive. Second, she recommends that we enhance the chance for leadership through an act + supplement discourse that allows for enhanced mutual activity. Third, she recommends reliance on improv theatre as a means to construct a performative approach to conversation. Using several case extracts, she demonstrates how the *intra*-action among the players can lead to a change of trajectory that constitutes leadership in the moment—a leadership that arises from the social process rather than from the recognition of individual performers.

The authors in the last section of this volume, Part IV, dedicate themselves to a series of critical applications of the L-A-P approach. The L-A-P movement requires, in particular, an accounting of its treatment of the subject of diversity in organizations as well as its manner of study and method. It also likely requires an alternative consideration of the very application of leadership development. Jackie Ford begins this coverage by critically assessing the treatment of "gendered relationships" in L-A-P. It has not been clear yet that L-A-P has shed the traditional "phallocentric" view of the world unless its scholars show a sensitivity towards concerns about power in the form of knowledge, language, and subjectivity. By focusing on gender, Jackie exposes the myth of the self-determining, autonomous individual that L-A-P seeks to decenter with its focus on practice. But Jackie warns us that a practice-oriented approach still needs to contend with the political dimension that may reproduce scripted lives without attention to emancipatory discourses.

Stephen Kempster, Ken Parry, and Brad Jackson in their chapter focus on the subject of methodology and undertake the difficult task of describing how to conduct studies of leadership-as-practice given that the practice of leadership is in continual emergence and shaped by antecedents and ongoing recursive interactions. Further, it poses additional dilemmas to researchers who rely on theory to develop their methodology. The authors respond that theory is important in L-A-P research, but more as an outcome than as an antecedent. Relevant research needs to begin with what they refer to as ontological thinking along with imaginative techniques to provide the necessary rigor to describe, illuminate, and help explain leadership practice. In particular, the authors call for pursuing holistic methodologies and multiple techniques to produce triangulation and stimulate theory illumination. They contend that the processual nature of leadership-as-practice, in particular, lends itself to qualitative methodologies. Illustrated in the chapter are narrative and conversational analysis, content analysis, critical incidents, ethnographies and autoethnographies, and activity theory.

In our last chapter, Chapter 13, David Denyer and Kim Turnbull James argue that although most leadership development programs address the topic of leadership, they tend to focus almost inclusively on the individual leader in position. Even when there is strategic attention to leadership, the authors contend the focus is traditionally on leader competencies or personal development that is often detached from the very site in which the skills and competencies are to be applied. They then describe some specific interventions that incorporate what they refer to as an alternative "leadership-as-practice development" or LaPD. Their examples make full use of collaborative leadership learning groups that achieve learning in practice through three forms of knowledge: knowledge that learners bring, knowledge available through public sources, and knowledge that is collaboratively constructed and developed. Although they are fervent spokespersons for LaPD, they caution against dispensing with any attention to individual development because any transition from hierarchical organization and traditional leadership comes with emotional costs that need to be addressed.

References

Alvesson, M., & Sveningsson, S. (2003). Managers doing leadership: The extra-ordinarization of the mundane. *Human Relations*, 56(12), 1435–1459.

Archer, M. S. (2000). *Being human—The problem of agency*. Cambridge: Cambridge University Press.

Argyris, C., & Schön, D. A. (1974). *Theory in practice: Increasing professional effectiveness*. San Francisco: Jossey-Bass.

Bakhtin, M. M. (1986). *Speech genres and other late essays* (V.W. McGee trans.). Austin, TX: University of Texas Press.

Bales, R. F. (1950). A set of categories for the analysis of small group interaction. *American Sociological Review*, 15, 257–263.

Barad, K. (2003). Posthumanist performativity: Toward an understanding of how matter comes to matter. *Signs: Journal of Women in Culture and Society*, 28(3), 801–831.

Blumer, H. (1969). *Symbolic interactionism*. Englewood Cliffs, NJ: Prentice-Hall.

Bohm, D. (1985). *Unfolding meaning*. Loveland, CO: Foundation House.

Bolden, R., Petrov, G., & Gosling, J. (2008). *Developing collective leadership in higher education—Final Report*. London: Leadership Foundation for Higher Education.

Boshyk, Y. (Ed.) (2002). *Action learning worldwide: Experiences of leadership and organizational development*. New York: Palgrave.

Carroll, B., & Simpson, B. (2012). Capturing sociality in the movement between frames: An illustration from leadership development. *Human Relations*, 65, 1283–1309.

Carroll, B., Levy, L., & Richmond, D. (2008). Leadership as practice: Challenging the competency paradigm. *Leadership*, 4(4), 363–379.

Chia, R., & Holt, R. (2006). Strategy as practical coping: A Heideggerian perspective. *Organization Studies*, 27(5), 635–655.

Chia, R., & MacKay, B. (2007). Post-processual challenges for the emerging strategy-as-practice perspective: Discovering strategy in the logic of practice. *Human Relations*, 60(1), 217–242.

Cleaver, F. (2007). Understanding agency in collective action. *Journal of Human Development*, 8(2), 223–244.

Clot, Y. (1999). *La fonction psychologique du travail*. Paris: Presses Universitaires de France.

Collinson, D. (2011). Critical leadership studies. In A. Bryman, D. Collinson, K. Grint, B. Jackson, & M. Uhl-Bien (Eds.), *The Sage Handbook of Leadership* (pp. 181–194). London: Sage.

Crevani, L., Lindgren, M., & Packendorff, J. (2010). Leadership, not leaders: On the study of leadership as practices and interaction. *Scandinavian Journal of Management*, 26, 77–86.

Davies, B. (1991). The concept of agency: A feminist poststructuralist analysis. *Social Analysis: The International Journal of Social and Cultural Practice*, 30, 42–53.

Dawkins, R. (1989). *The selfish gene* (2nd edition). Oxford: Oxford University Press.

Denis, J.-L., Langley, A., & Rouleau, L. (2010). The practice of leadership in the messy world of organizations. *Leadership*, 6(1), 67–88.

Dreyfus, H. L. (2001). *On the internet*. London: Routledge.

Edwards, A. (2005). Relational agency: Learning to be a resourceful practitioner. *International Journal of Educational Research*, 43, 168–182.

Endrissat, N., & von Arx, W. (2013). Leadership practices and context: Two sides of the same coin. *Leadership*, 9(2), 278–304.

Gendlin, E. T. (1964). A theory of personality change. In P. Worchel & D. Byrne (Eds.), *Personality change* (pp. 100–148). New York: John Wiley & Sons.

Gherardi, S. (2000). Practice-based theorizing on learning and knowledge in organizations. *Organization*, 7, 211–223.

Giddens, A. (1984). *The constitution of society: Outline of a theory of structuration*. Berkeley and Los Angeles, CA: University of California Press.

Goldstein, J. A., Hazy, J. K., & Lichtenstein, B. (2010). *Complexity and the nexus of leadership: Leveraging nonlinear science to create ecologies of innovation*. New York: Palgrave Macmillan.

Gronn, P. (2002). Distributed leadership as a unit of analysis. *Leadership Quarterly*, 13(4), 423–451.

Hales, C. (2002). 'Bureaucracy-lite' and continuities in managerial work. *British Journal of Management*, 13(1), 51–66.

Hatch, M. J. (1999). Exploring the empty spaces of organizing: How improvisational jazz helps redescribe organizational structure. *Organization Studies*, 20(1), 75–100.

Hazy, J. K., & Uhl-Bien, M. (2014). Changing the rules: The implications of complexity science for leadership research and practice. In D. V. Day (Ed.), *The Oxford handbook of leadership and organizations* (pp. 709–732). Oxford: Oxford University Press.

Heckscher, C. (1994). Defining the post-bureaucratic type. In C. Heckscher & A. Donnellon (Eds.), *The post-bureaucratic organization* (pp. 14–62). Thousand Oaks, CA: Sage.

Herepath, A. (2014). In the loop: A realist approach to structure and agency in the practice of strategy. *Organization Studies*, 35(6), 857–879.

Heydebrand, R. (1989). New organizational forms. *Work and Occupations*, 16(3), 323–357.

Hodgson, D. E. (2004). Project work: The legacy of bureaucratic control in the post-bureaucratic organization. *Organization*, 11(1), 81–100.

James, P., & van Seters, P. (2014). Global social movements and global civil society: A critical overview. In P. James & P. van Seters (Eds.), *Globalization and politics, vol 2: Global social movements and global civil society* (pp. vii–xxx). London: Sage.

Jarzabkowski, P., & Whittington, R. (2008). A strategy-as-practice approach to strategy research and education. *Journal of Management Inquiry*, 17(4), 282–286.

Jordan, T., Andersson, P., & Ringnér, H. (2013). The spectrum of responses to complex societal issues: Reflections on seven years of empirical inquiry. *Integral Review*, 9(1), 34–70.

Kesby, M. (2005). Retheorising empowerment through participation as a performance in space: Beyond tyranny to transformation. *Signs: Journal of Women in Culture and Society*, 30(4), 2037–2065.

Knights, D., & Willmott, H. (1992). Conceptualizing leadership processes: A study of senior managers in a financial services company. *Journal of Management Studies*, 29(6), 761–782.

Lave, J. (1988). *Cognition in practice: Mind, mathematics, and culture in everyday life*. Cambridge: Cambridge University Press.

Marquardt, M. J. (1999). *Action learning in action*. Palo Alto, CA: Davies-Black.

Marsick, V. J. (1990). Action learning and reflection in the workplace. In J. Mezirow (Ed.), *Fostering critical reflection in adulthood* (pp. 23–46). San Francisco: Jossey-Bass.

Nicolini, D., Gherardi, S., & Yanow, D. (2003). *Introduction in knowing in organizations*. Armonk, NY: M. E. Sharpe.

Pearce, C. L., & Conger, J. A. (2003). *Shared leadership: Reframing the hows and whys of leadership*. Thousand Oaks, CA: Sage.

Pedler, M. (Ed.) (2011). *Action learning in practice* (4th edition). Farnham: Gower.

Pickering, A. (1995). *The mangle of practice: Time, agency, & science*. Chicago, IL and London: University of Chicago Press.

Pye, A. (1993). "Organizing as explaining" and the doing of managing: An integrative appreciation of processes of organizing. *Journal of Management Inquiry*, 2(2), 157–168.

Raelin, J. A. (2008). *Work-based Learning: Bridging knowledge and action in the workplace*. San Francisco: Jossey-Bass.

Raelin, J. A. (2009). Seeking conceptual clarity in the action modalities. *Action Learning: Research and Practice*, 6(1), 17–24.

Raelin, J. A. (2013). The manager as facilitator of dialogue. *Organization*, 20(6), 818–839.

Raelin, J. A. (2014). Imagine there are no leaders: Reframing leadership as collaborative agency. *Leadership*, Online First, 25 November 2014.

Reckwitz, A. (2002). Toward a theory of social practices: A development in culturalist theorizing. *European Journal of Social Theory*, 5(2), 243–263.

Rose, N. (1998). *Inventing ourselves: Psychology, power, and personhood*. Cambridge: Cambridge University Press.

Schatzki, T. R. (1997). Practices and actions: A Wittgensteinian critique of Bourdieu and Giddens. *Philosophy of the Social Sciences*, 27(3), 283–308.

Spicer, A., Alvesson, M., & Kärreman, D. (2009). Critical performativity: The unfinished business of critical management studies. *Human Relations*, 62(4), 537–560.

Spillane, J. P. (2006). *Distributed leadership*. San Francisco: Jossey-Bass.

Tsoukas, H. (1998). The word and the world: A critique of representationalism in management research. *International Journal of Public Administration*, 21(5), 781–817.

Weick, K. E. (1989). Theory construction as disciplined imagination. *Academy of Management Review*, 14(4), 516–531.

Wenger, E. (1998). *Communities of practice: Learning, meaning, and identity*. Cambridge: Cambridge University Press.

Wood, M. (2005). The fallacy of misplaced leadership. *Journal of Management Studies*, 42(6), 1101–1121.

Yorks, L., O'Neil, J. & Marsick, V. J. (Eds.) (1999). *Advances in developing human resources: Action learning: Successful strategies for individual, team and organizational development*. San Francisco: Berrett Koehler.

PART I
Background

2

MAPPING THE LEADERSHIP-AS-PRACTICE TERRAIN

Comparative elements

Lucia Crevani and Nada Endrissat

Introduction

Inspired by the practice turn in organization and social theory (Schatzki, Knorr-Cetina & von Savigny, 2001), there has been increasing recognition of the value of theorizing about and studying leadership from a practice perspective (Denis, Langley & Rouleau, 2005, 2010; Carroll, Levy & Richmond, 2008; Crevani, Lindgren & Packendorff, 2010; Raelin, 2011; Endrissat & von Arx, 2013). The resulting notion of "leadership-as-practice" gives rise to high expectations but may also cause misunderstandings among leadership scholars and practitioners alike. To recognize its potential we believe it is important to bring to the fore some of its underlying assumptions and outline its similarities and differences to other relatively close concepts. Hence, this chapter provides an introduction to the leadership-as-practice perspective by means of two central comparisons (see Figure 2.1): First, we probe into leadership studies and consider the similarities and differences of a leadership-as-practice perspective with related leadership approaches such as the leadership style approach (and the subsequent situational leadership and contingency models) and the relational leadership approach. We highlight the consequences of doing research from each one of these three perspectives, mainly with respect to the underlying understanding of reality (ontology) and, consequently, the "*unit of analysis*" (i.e. what is studied and focused on to produce knowledge about leadership). We include examples of typical research questions and exemplary studies in each of the three domains to support our reasoning. Naturally, the comparison is not complete by considering just two other approaches. However, the two seem most relevant because they share several similarities with the leadership-as-practice approach that need closer examination to define the specific contribution of leadership-as-practice. The style (and the situational/contingency) approach is widely known, entitative in character, but with a similar focus on leadership actions to the practice approach. By making the differences between the two approaches explicit, we hope to inspire the broad range of scholars familiar with the style approach to consider the practice perspective as a potential alternative that allows them to enrich understanding of the accomplishments of leadership. The relational approach, on the other hand, is the closest to the practice approach, and this is sometimes even used synonymously. However, differences exist and we believe that it is important to make them explicit to better understand the critical contribution of leadership-as-practice.

In the second comparison we look outside leadership studies and focus instead on the "as-practice" approach, outlining the similarities and differences between leadership-as-practice and other practice approaches in organization studies, namely strategy-as-practice and coordination-as-practice. As we will show, although the underlying assumptions are the same, they differ with respect to the *social accomplishment* on which they focus, that is the consequences of organizing processes that they try to explain and understand. Because of space restrictions, we had to limit our comparison to those organizational phenomena that we consider most relevant for defining leadership-as-practice. Both coordination and strategy work share similarities with leadership that sometimes make it difficult to distinguish among them. We hope that the focus on "social accomplishment" will help the reader to better understand what the unique contribution of each of these organizational constructs is.

The overall aim of these comparisons is to "map the terrain" of a leadership-as-practice perspective and to sketch its boundaries in relation to other constructs and approaches to make more explicit its particular potential and promise. We

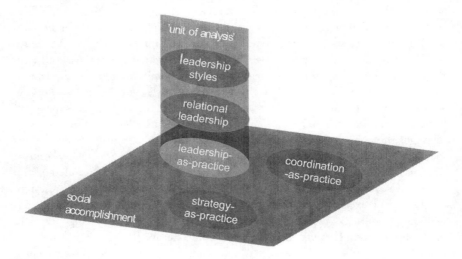

FIGURE 2.1 A comparative framework of leadership-as-practice

believe that too often these comparisons are not explicitly discussed, and that they are especially useful for researchers and students who are new to the field and who take an interest in understanding the consequences of doing research from a leadership-as-practice perspective.

Before developing our comparisons, we want to provide the reader with a definition of what leadership-as-practice means to us. We will go back to such a definition during the chapter and fill in more details, but to start with we can say that "leadership" in leadership-as-practice is about producing direction for organizing processes (Crevani, 2011; Packendorff, Crevani & Lindgren, 2014), re-orientation of the flow of practice (see Simpson, Chapter 8, this volume), and emergent co-construction through collaborative agency (Raelin, 2014).

One important distinction that we need to introduce at this point is one between *entitative* and *relational ontologies*—a distinction that maps onto other distinctions as *weak* and *strong process* studies (Langley & Tsoukas, 2010), *practice as a perspective* versus *practice as a philosophy* (Orlikowski, 2010), or *leadership as a set of practices* versus *leadership in the flow of practice* as described by Barbara Simpson (Chapter 8, this volume). Although there is no complete overlap between such distinctions, they are related to each other. For the purpose of this chapter, we will refer to the distinction between *entitative* and *relational ontology* as well as between *practices* and *practice*. Put briefly, an entitative approach gives ontological priority to entities or social states that pre-exist relations and processes. A relational approach gives ontological priority to unfolding relations; they are what "makes the world"—people and other entities are made and remade in such unfolding processes as we become in relations (cf. Dachler & Hosking, 1995). Such a distinction between entitative and relational mirrors the difference between the concept of *practices* and *practice* (see Raelin, Chapter 1, this volume; Simpson, Chapter 8, this volume). *Practices* may describe routinized sequences of activities or building blocks of organizing. If practices are thought of as mobilized by actors, then this view resembles an entitative approach. This means that even *processual* approaches focusing on the doings and practicing (such as leadership-as-practice as well as relational leadership) may be entitative in character. We will refer to this approach as *entitative-soft* (to differentiate it from individual-centric entitative approaches as advocated in the leadership style approach). *Practice*, on the other hand, may be understood as an unfolding emergent dynamic and thus follows a *relational* ontology. We will come back to these distinctions as we compare the different approaches.

Leadership styles, relational leadership, and leadership-as-practice: The "unit of analysis"

To highlight what is specific to leadership-as-practice (e.g. Crevani *et al.* 2010, Crevani, 2011; Denis *et al.*, 2010; Endrissat & von Arx, 2013), we have chosen two other leadership approaches to compare it with: leadership styles and relational leadership. The leadership styles approach represents one of the "classical" leadership approaches, but, contrary to other approaches defining leadership as a property of the individual (i.e. the leadership trait approach), the style approach focuses on what leaders do, their behaviors (cf. Grint, 2005). Thus, the idea of a recurring pattern of behavior at first sight may be considered similar to leadership-as-practice. It is all the more so if looking at the situational leadership and contingency approaches, evolutions of the style approach in which the importance of the context is foregrounded. For the purpose of comparison we focus on the style approach as the one that introduced *patterns of behaviors* as relevant for doing leadership. We believe that taking the step from a style (or the following above mentioned approaches) to a practice approach may be natural just because of the attention paid to patterns in what is done. Relational leadership, on the other hand, is chosen because of its many similarities with a leadership-as-practice perspective. In fact, some of the authors of chapters in this book have themselves written other texts under the "relational leadership" label, hence the need for discussing what difference exists between the two. There are also other approaches that are close to leadership-as-practice, for instance the growing body of literature on shared leadership (cf. Pearce & Conger, 2003; Döös, Backström, Melin & Wilhelmson, 2012), which highlights the collective nature of leadership. In this chapter we focus on relational leadership as it, along with leadership-as-practice, shares many of the underlying assumptions about the nature of reality and about how to produce knowledge about the phenomenon of leadership.

We compare the leadership style, the relational, and leadership-as-practice approaches with respect to their "*unit of analysis*." By unit of analysis, we refer to what produces knowledge about the phenomenon of leadership. We use "unit of analysis" well aware that it suggests the idea that such a unit can be singled out and studied separately, an assumption based on a non-relational ontology that we do not advocate. However, we hold on to this notion to reach those scholars unfamiliar with relational perspectives.

Leadership style: A leader-centered approach

The general discourse around leadership still tends to grant primacy to the notion of the single, heroic, masculine leader as a norm for modern and effective leadership (e.g. Alvesson & Sveningsson, 2003; Crevani *et al.*, 2010; O'Reilly & Reed, 2010; Holgersson, 2013). This resonates well with the general development in the field of leadership studies, which has traditionally been leader-centered, that is focused on individual leaders and their traits, abilities, and actions (Wood, 2005), placing the abstract phenomenon of "leadership" into distinct individuals who are detached from their cultural context (Barker, 2001). Similar to the traits and skills approach, the *leadership style approach* (cf. Blake & Mouton, 1964, 1978; Eagly & Johnson, 1990) has a long tradition in the leadership field and represents one of the "foundations of modern leadership research and theory" (Schedlitzki & Edwards, 2014: 24). The idea is that the leader's behavior is crucial for leadership and that certain behaviors are better than others. Classical examples include the Boys Club Experiment (Lewin, Lippitt & White, 1939), the Ohio (Stogdill & Coons, 1957) and Michigan (Katz & Kahn, 1951; Likert, 1961) State Studies, as well as the Managerial Grid by Blake and Mouton (1964, 1978). The studies typically involved the comparison of either task versus people or directive versus participative leadership styles (Wright, 1996). The unit of analysis is thus a person's unique leadership style, his or her routinized, relatively stable patterns of leadership behavior, which supposedly leads to superior performance outcomes. Despite some scholars pointing out that leadership styles vary across hierarchical levels in organizations (e.g. Oshagbemi & Gill, 2004), the leadership styles approach generally tends to advocate a single best way of leading, and does not consider situational variance in theory. Yet, empirical research was never able to confirm a universal style for all situations (Northouse, 2007) and the assumption led to criticism and the development of situational and contingency leadership approaches. In these approaches, the possible influence of the context on which style is most effective is studied—an enterprise that is not void of difficulties (Graeff, 1997). Still, the idea that the situation in which leadership is enacted is important for leadership has rooted itself in the literature and compares to the assumptions on which leadership-as-practice relies.

The fundamental difference compared with the leadership-as-practice approach is that the underlying ontology is based on a classical entitative perspective: the individual actors act in isolation and are separated from the world on which they act. They are seen as autonomous, independent selves ordered in a subject–object relation (Hosking, 2011). This understanding of reality assumes rationality and linearity from intention to intervention. Leadership is about influencing people to follow a course of action that is set by the leaders—influence stems from one individual and affects others. Studies focus on formal leaders, their patterns of behavior, and the effects of their styles. Typical research questions include exploration of the leader's typical leadership behavior and the assessment about which leadership style is the most effective (in a particular situation, across cultures, etc.). The method of choice in this approach is the standardized questionnaire (see below). These assumptions differ from a leadership-as-practice approach in which individuals are not foregrounded as they are not seen as the primary source of leadership. Rather than focusing on patterns of individual behavior, leadership-as-practice emphasizes the patterns of connected actions. Hence, despite both approaches focusing on the "doings" rather than on innate characteristics, they provide very different accounts and analysis of such doings.

To more clearly illustrate the differences between the approaches, we present brief examples of what such approaches result in. Below, we therefore provide one example of a leadership styles questionnaire that outlines the typical empirical approach in analyzing a person's leadership style—for example, whether his or her leadership style is focused on task accomplishment or relationships (see Box 2.1).

BOX 2.1 THE LEADERSHIP STYLES APPROACH

The following statements are typical examples of items in a leadership style questionnaire (Northouse, 2010). For each item the respondent is asked to think of how often s/he engages in the described behavior on a scale from "never" to "always."

1. Tells group members what they are supposed to do.
2. Acts friendly with members of the group.
3. Sets standards of performance for group members.
4. Helps others in the group feel comfortable.

(Northouse, 2010, p. 85)

The respondent's reaction to the statements provides information on whether his/her leadership behavior is task or relationship oriented.

To conclude, the leadership styles approach focuses on the leader's typical (routinized) behavior and is therefore leader-centered with an emphasis on the practitioner. The behaviors can be measured according to definite scales. The leadership style approach is, in other words, strongly entitative and in this respect fundamentally different from leadership-as-practice.

Relational leadership: A focus on "becoming" in relationships

Having examined an entitative construct, we now turn our attention to a construct that has the potential for being a relational (ontology) construct: relational leadership. This is a broad construct that is currently used both in entitative and relational ways, depending on the scholar and his or her understanding of "relational." Uhl-Bien (2006), and subsequently Uhl-Bien and Ospina (2012), provide a collection of research contributions that range from seminal work stemming from relational constructionism (cf. Dachler & Hosking, 1995) to LMX approaches to leadership (Graen & Uhl-Bien, 1995), that represent relational and entitative ontologies, respectively (the latter focusing on individuals in relation rather than on relations shaping individuals and realities). The challenge is that processual approaches may have an entitative character when it comes to the ontology, which means that some of the contributions studying relational leadership as a process are entitative rather than relational.

Following a process perspective (both weak and strong), the "unit of analysis" in relational leadership is the emergent relational dynamic that is often found in the form of local, momentary interaction. Talk and language are foregrounded when studying how leadership is co-constructed in interactions and how this construction shapes further interactions and developments. In fact, the emphasis in this approach is on *becoming in relation*—which takes place in interactions and relationships. Broadly speaking, in relational leadership approaches people are involved "in a co-construction of each other and the leadership process" (Schedlitzki & Edwards, 2014: 115). Those scholars subscribing to a relational ontology further claim that relations are subject-to-subject relationships, which means that influence is necessarily mutual and all subjects are constantly (partially) reconstructed as relations are established, intensified, and interrupted (Dachler & Hosking, 1995). The main claim of relational leadership is thus that the self is a relational construction made in relational processes, a dialogical self (Hosking, 2011)—compared with a singular independent (leader) self, trying to control "others," which is the typical Western conception of leadership (see leadership style approach above). Leadership is thus about influential acts of organizing that affect the structuring of relations and interactions, in which definitions of social order are negotiated, constructed, and enacted (Dachler & Hosking, 1995). Attention is often concentrated on language and conversation, as relating is conceptualized as a language-based process (Hosking, 2011) and language is treated as the most important resource used to accomplish social reality (cf. Barge, 2012). Everything that is said in conversations is in relationship to "others": "other people, other ideas, other conversations"; and each conversation is both old and new (see, especially Cunliffe & Eriksen, 2011, p. 1434, in reference to Bakhtin). The past is thus constitutive of the present, although not determining the present (Langley & Tsoukas, 2010). In other words, "current conversations draw on past conversations; past 'voices' are mobilized in current utterances" (ibid., p. 5). This does not necessarily mean that the conversation results in shared understanding and that such understanding is recalled in the "right" way in the coming conversations, but that current utterances are resourced by past utterances. This means that certain constructions are decisive for which actions and talks may become actual and which not, which talks become possible to supplement, which paths the process of constructing reality takes and which not (Crevani, 2011). Or, in other words, different constructions resource and constrain "how processes 'go on' and the realities that are made" (van der Haar & Hosking, 2004, p. 1023). Hence, for those scholars mostly influenced by a relational ontology (not only a process perspective), the "responsibility" for leadership lies with the collective, throughout the organization, not with individual leaders, and a larger number of relationships are legitimized as having to do with leadership.

Hence, theoretically, the unit of analysis is the *interactional dynamic* that unfolds throughout the organization. But empirically, the focus is still often on leaders as they relate. The main preoccupation is, in fact, to de-centralize leadership from "individuals" to "relations," in particular, co-constructive (subject-to-subject) relations, rather than to fully explore the potential to de-centralize leadership to "the activity of doing work," something that may be more fully explored by scholars adhering to leadership-as-practice.

To be acknowledged at this point, however, is that both the relational leadership approach and leadership-as-practice are aimed at producing less individualistic and more processual accounts of leadership in which entitative/relational ontologies co-exist. In the case of relational leadership this means that constructionist approaches may see "relational" as an epistemological position (for instance, see Cunliffe and Hibbert, Chapter 3, this volume) in which *inter-actions* (see Simpson, Chapter 8, this volume) are central for how meaning is created and in which the lived experience of people is central (for example by building on a phenomenological tradition). Other scholars are closer to a relational (strong process) ontology, in which relational processes are foregrounded in the form of *trans-actions* (see Simpson, Chapter 8, this volume) in which people and the world are in constant becoming, which means that the lived experience is not focused on to the same extent. Moreover, in the leadership-as-practice movement we have a range of positions on the scale entitative-relational, as the chapters in this book make evident and as we will discuss below. Here it is important to notice that even outside relational leadership discussions (e.g. Hernes, 2008), and outside organization theory at large, there are scholars arguing for relational ontologies (for instance, Massey 2005) that enable processual understandings of phenomena. We will develop such a discussion later in the chapter.

We conclude by providing examples of research questions and of empirical studies related to relational leadership to make the comparison with leadership-as-practice clearer. Typical research questions focus on what is done in relations and include: How do relational dynamics contribute to structuring (entitative-soft if the focus is on individuals in relations, relational if the focus is on the dynamics)? How do we relate to each other and what is the consequence for leadership (entitative-soft if the focus is on how leaders/followers relate to each other, relational if the focus is on how people and leadership emerge from the relationship)? How can we recognize the primacy of relationships in everything we do (Gergen and Hersted, Chapter 9, this volume)? How are organizational realities and identities constructed in relations (entitative-soft if the focus is on individual's identities, relational if the focus is on how the relationship constitutes identities and realities)? But also, how do leaders talk about their relationships and what do they see as being important in those relationships (entitative-soft) (Cunliffe & Eriksen, 2011)? As mentioned above, this is one of the tensions within the relational leadership literature: to what extent are we analyzing leaders in relation and acting through relations compared with unfolding relations achieving leadership? Also, although theoretical conceptualization is ample, empirical studies based on a relational ontology are rather limited.

To make more visible for the reader the character a relational leadership study may have, we refer to two examples. The first example, Box 2.2, comes from the constructionist side of relational leadership informed by an entitative view of reality in which the focus is on exploration of the way in which leaders and followers relate to each other. As the text makes explicit, the idea of the hero-conductor is challenged by de-centering leadership to the relational dynamics between the conductor and the followers—hence its entitative character. The dimensions that Koivunen and Wennes (2011) examine are also described as practices in their article, in the sense of how a leader can practice leadership relationally (the leader as practitioner as in Simpson, Chapter 8, this volume), suggesting that studies of relational leadership on the constructionist entitative-soft side may inform normative accounts of the leader as a practitioner.

BOX 2.2 A FIRST EXAMPLE OF RELATIONAL LEADERSHIP

Koivunen and Wennes (2011) provide an example of relational leadership by looking at leadership in orchestras (p. 58).

"We claim that symphony orchestra conductors engage in a specific form of leadership that consists of relational, aesthetic and embodied processes. Based on our data analysis and the reading of theory we label these three dimensions (1) relational listening (relational activity in the theoretical section), (2) aesthetic judgment, and (3) kinaesthetic empathy (embodiment). [...]

This leadership approach examines the sophisticated interaction processes between the conductor and the musicians. The process involves nonverbal communication and is based on the craft of playing an instrument, knowledge of repertoire and skillful sense perception, listening in particular. Collective virtuosity in an orchestra takes place through hearing the sounds with skillful listening. At the core of interaction lies the music. The conductor is part of the orchestra who helps the musicians in their work and receives the music and listens to the quality of the music. The conductor listens to the sound produced by musicians, and based on that auditive material helps them to play together by directing solo parts, showing phrasing and articulations, and estimating the balances between different instrument sections. In this approach to leadership, the conductor does not force the orchestra to play according to her pre-existing idea of music interpretation but first listens to the orchestra and then works from that on. This marks a distance to the dominating view of the conductor as the leader with full control and authority (task-oriented and rational) (Hosking, 1988)".

The second example, Figure 2.2, is an analysis one of us (Crevani, 2011) made of conversations at work, in which formal leaders may or not be involved. These conversations are presented in the form of comic strips to reproduce interactions that retain some of the elements that are so easily lost when writing dialogues.

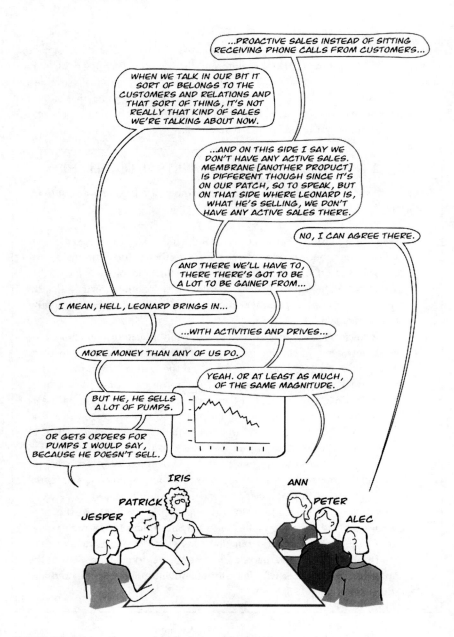

FIGURE 2.2 A second example of relational leadership

For example, it becomes graphically apparent that conversations are not ordered as people interrupt each other or finish each other's sequences. What is emphasized is the conversation, the interaction in terms of the words said. Figure 2.2 gives an example of one short part of one of these conversations. Of course it is not possible to give the reader enough information to motivate why this interaction is doing leadership in the limited space at our disposal (for such an analysis, please refer to Crevani, 2011). The idea is instead to give the reader a feeling of what the "unit of analysis" is, namely the conversation or the interaction as it unfolds. We propose that the example in Figure 2.2 provides an instance of those studies that contribute to both relational leadership and leadership-as-practice by adhering to a relational ontology and de-centering leadership to situations in which work is carried out.

Leadership-as-practice: A practice centered approach

Leadership-as-practice emphasizes the importance of practices, not the practitioner (leader). It follows exactly the other way around from the style approach. The practice approach does not ask what style is typical for a particular leader, but what kind of practice enables a specific identity or agency (Nicolini, 2012). Leadership, seen from this perspective, is co-constructed by actors in certain practices/practice; the "unit of analysis" is thus not a single "unit," but bundles of related actions or "the work of leadership" as it takes form in patterns of action and interaction (which are routinized when looking for practices, respectively emergent when looking for practice). Leadership-as-practice is based on a *process* perspective, which means considering the world as "an ongoing routinized and recurrent accomplishment" (Nicolini, 2012, p. 3.) In addition, practice approaches acknowledge relationality by conceptualizing "the world as a seamless assemblage, nexus, or confederation of practices" (ibid., p. 3) and rejecting the "idea that the world comes nicely divided into levels and factors" (ibid., p. 8) as advocated by the leadership style approach. Practice theories also highlight the critical role of the body and material things in all social affairs. They respect the importance of discursive practices for the constitution of organizational life, but stress that language and discourse alone cannot account for all organizational aspects (e.g. Endrissat & von Arx, 2013; Sergi, Chapter 6, this volume).

The leadership-as-practice approach hence acknowledges the importance of everyday activity, performances, and interactions, that is the *doings* of leadership. Whereas the leadership-as-practice studies that are grounded in a strong process focus on *practice as it unfolds* (which is very similar to relational leadership, see above), the entitative-soft strand looks for *patterns of action* (which we refer to as practices, see above). The latter is similar to the leadership style approach in that both focus on what is done (the actions, behavior). The difference is that attention is not centered on the behavior of one person but on more distributed patterns of action. Therefore, looking for leadership practices means looking not only at actions performed by one person in a formal leadership positions but, more generally, at how actors get on with the work of leadership. Thus, it also includes the "un-heroic" work of practitioners. However, this does not suggest that *any* activity is a practice. Instead, practices are seen as "configurations of actions which carry a specific meaning" (Nicolini, 2012: 10). The focus is on the *routinized* ones that occur repeatedly and represent a form of *social knowledge* that only members of a specific community recognize and understand. It is in this sense that practices represent collectively shared knowledge (Denis *et al.*, 2010).

Although both foci (practices and practice) are possible within an "as-practice" perspective, empirical research in the latter instance is still scarce. So far, most studies follow an entitative-soft understanding and focus on the practices of leaders as they do leadership and, hence, do not fully explore the possibilities opened up by a practice perspective that actually foregrounds action and emergence rather than individuals. This book gathers a number of scholars that dig deeply into some crucial aspects of what leadership-as-practice has meant and may mean, thus providing grounds for further studies that more fully embrace the relational practice view.

The idea of leadership-as-practice has thus informed rather different empirical studies that contribute to processual understandings of leadership by conceptualizing leadership as socially constituted, by examining in a finely graded manner micro-level activities and their effects (Denis *et al.*, 2010), by highlighting the time dimension when accomplishing work (Holmberg & Tyrstrup, 2010), by trying to perform leadership development programs promoting leaderful practice (Raelin, 2011), by taking into consideration everyday actions as leadership and seeing individuals as "fields of relationships" (Carroll *et al.*, 2008), and by analyzing leadership as stretched over leaders, followers, and the material and symbolic artifacts in the situation (Spillane, Halverson & Diamond, 2004).

Possible research questions include: What is leadership work? How is leadership achieved? Where and how is leadership work done? What are the recurring patterns of action that we can observe? (For all questions, consider them: entitative-soft if the focus is on the practices of official leaders/humans/non-humans; relational if the focus is on emergence; e.g. how "influence" is being produced or "direction" changed).

Methodologically, leadership-as-practice means researching leadership as a "lived" experience rather than a "reported" experience in standardized questionnaires (see the example provided in Box 2.1). It requires paying attention to the specific context in which the phenomenon takes place including possible contradictions and ambiguities. To come close to the practice(s), often (non-)participant observations have been the method of choice (Crevani, 2011) and so have narrative interviews (Rouleau, 2010). The aim is to study people in their "natural" context and to explore the nature of a social phenomenon over time/space; to study mundane activities in organizations as they take shape on a daily basis to capture the lived experiences of individuals and working dynamics (Nicolini, 2012).

Other chapters in this book, in particular Chapter 12 by Kempster, Parry, and Jackson, lend further insight into these methodological challenges.

To illustrate the leadership-as-practice approach, we provide an example from the work of Endrissat and von Arx (2013), which describes how leadership is achieved during a large-scale strategic change in a university hospital (Box 2.3). The excerpt gives an illustration of the entitative-soft perspective on leadership-as-practice, that is the perspective in which a number of practices, or repeated patterns of action that constitute leadership, are identified. In this example, one of such practices is *relying on the self-organization of the professionals (physicians)*, a pattern that was repeatedly witnessed. Consequently, leadership was achieved in the interplay among the official project leader's actions and the professionals' values and norms, which were re-created in their daily actions. What we want to illustrate with this short excerpt is the focus on situated acting, involving a number of actors, that gives direction to organizing, something typical of this kind of leadership-as-practice approach.

BOX 2.3 A FIRST EXAMPLE OF LEADERSHIP-AS-PRACTICE.

Excerpt taken from Endrissat and von Arx (2013: 293):

> Leadership practice: relying on the self-organization of the professionals (along hierarchies and patient-paths). The physicians' work practices are highly standardized and largely pre-structured by the patient. The ethical rule to always act for the patient's well-being is deeply anchored in the physicians' practice. This provides a frame of reference regardless of the work structures or organizational chart in place. As a consequence, the physicians' everyday practices remain the same on the day that the new structure finally comes into force. The main concern is less about how the initiative is implemented than about whether all the patients will receive correct treatment. The physicians therefore cope relatively well with the reorganization. The self-organization is supported by typical 'patient pathways'. The physicians seem to switch to an emergency mode, in which they all work with enormous dedication. Each of them 'adopts' their patients (personalization) and, step-by-step, steer them past the system problems.

The other example illustrates the focus on practice with a stronger relational ontology (Box 2.4). The emphasis here is on interactions and the kinds of conversational movements taking shape in the flow of the interactions.

BOX 2.4 A SECOND EXAMPLE OF LEADERSHIP-AS-PRACTICE.

This example is taken from Carroll and Simpson (2012). The researchers have analyzed an online conversation and categorized the different statements according to which frames were mobilized. In their analysis the researchers focus on the different kinds of movements between frames to produce knowledge about ongoing processes from which leadership emerges.

Example of frames mobilized are "school," "expedition," "performance," "intermediary." For instance, the expedition frame is clear in this statement: "I don't believe we should be addressing what their expectations are at all. How about taking them on a journey?" (p. 1295); and the school frame in "THEY CANNOT SHUT DOWN THE DISCUSSION! (yes I meant to shout) ... from where I sit I feel he was lecturing us like naughty kids ... (Puhlease) ... give us some credit for getting the real game ... the meeting is not a student council meeting!" (p. 1298).

The interesting dynamics are then how movements between such frames take place—the researchers focus on three: kindling, stretching, and spanning. Each movement has different implications for the emergence of new direction (leadership).

Given the focus on dialogue and emergence, this example (similar to the example in Figure 2.2) provides an illustration of an empirical study that can contribute to both the leadership-as-practice and the relational leadership literatures. Thus, whether it is a study informing relational leadership or leadership-as-practice is not a question of data collection but of interpreting the data and theoretical framing.

Discussion of comparative element I: "Same same, but different"

While the comparison between leadership styles and leadership-as-practice approaches is not particularly challenging given that the ontological premises, and thus the unit of analysis, are clearly different, the comparison with relational leadership proves more difficult. As anticipated, both relational leadership and leadership-as-practice approaches apply a process perspective to reality and leadership. Leadership is thus a phenomenon taking place as work is done, in space and time. What makes a distinction hard is that in both approaches we have some studies that follow a relational ontology and some that are more entitative (entities involved in processes) that we have characterized as entitative-soft to distinguish them from approaches that are purely entitative (as for the leadership style approach or the leader-as-practitioner position in Simpson, Chapter 8, this volume). In other words, our first comparison involves one entitative approach (leadership styles) and two approaches that include entitative-soft and relational positions. As outlined above, leadership-as-practice and relational leadership overlap to a large extent, particularly when the empirical focus is grounded in a relational (strong process) ontology. Subscribing to a relational ontology (relational leadership and leadership-as-practice) means to try to understand and name emergent processes of production of direction, thus foregrounding the momentary, the co-evolving, and the flow. The difference between relational leadership and leadership-as-practice studies in this case is, we propose, a question of focus. Relational in relational leadership is often conceptualized in terms of human dialogue and thus often concerned with discursive practices, such as in the form of text or language (Dachler & Hosking, 1995). With a practice perspective, which builds on post-humanist approaches among others, relational often means interactions, which may include both humans and non-humans. Hence, the leadership-as-practice perspective is concerned with language but also offers more conceptual means to include other elements such as the body, objects, and the "form" of leadership other than just talk (Endrissat & von Arx, 2013). In both cases, empirical studies focusing on relational processes are still relatively rare, which makes it rather difficult to see the consequences of such positions when doing research.

Concerning more entitative-soft studies in leadership-as-practice, that is those identifying a set of "practices" in which leadership goes on, and more entitative-soft positions in relational leadership, that is those attending to how people are in relations, we propose that both approaches contribute to de-center leadership as a phenomenon from individuals to processes, but in different ways. Relational leadership de-centers from independent individuals to beings-in-relation, whereas leadership-as-practice approaches identifying leadership practices de-center leadership from individuals to patterns of action. Hence, relational leadership provides the means to focus on the construction and re-construction of human relations (whether by focusing on conversations or on long-term developments), whereas leadership-as-practice is interested in *recurring patterns of action*, that is on *already stabilized patterns of action*. Figure 2.3 illustrates these distinctions.

On a more critical note, one could argue that the leadership-as-practice studies have moved our attention to leadership as activity accomplished in interactions, whether in particular situations or over longer periods of time. But, when doing empirical research, scholars tend to grant actors some degree of intentionality and individual motivation (for instance, Denis *et al.*, 2010). Actors choose which practices to deploy and the effects of such practices can be observed and classified. And despite leadership-as-practice principally acknowledging that leadership can be achieved by actors other than formal leaders, many empirical studies still focus on formal leaders (e.g. Carroll *et al.*, 2008), with some notable exceptions that more clearly foreground practice (e.g. Carroll & Simpson, 2012). Thus, while interactions gain in significance, the step to making the practice as what "comes first," and not actors, is not completely taken. Even in the case of relational leadership, empirical studies continue to largely focus on the leaders (e.g. Cunliffe &

Eriksen, 2011). In this sense, both the relational leadership and leadership-as-practice approaches have an ambition to re-focus research from individuals to "the social," but there is a need for further empirical studies to make this shift complete. This is no easy endeavor as discussed by Kempster, Parry, and Jackson (Chapter 12, this volume), also given the multiplicity of perspectives in leadership-as-practice (see the chapters in this volume)—a quandary also to be found in other "as-practice" approaches (as in strategy-as-practice; see, e.g., Golsorkhi, Rouleau, Seidl & Vaara, 2010). This book therefore aims at pointing the reader towards the richness of the leadership-as-practice movement and to provide the ground for developing it further.

To conclude, despite having shown more or less strong similarities between the three different leadership approaches, we propose that the "unit of analysis," or the focus of empirical interest, differs, at times greatly, at times more slightly. The leadership style approach focuses on the leader and his or her typical behavior in an entitative fashion. This clearly differentiates such an approach from the other two approaches we selected. Whereas Figure 2.3 illustrated the overlaps and differences between relational leadership and leadership-as-practice, Table 2.1 demonstrates the common points and differences in more detail.

FIGURE 2.3 A conceptual comparison between relational leadership and leadership-as-practice.

TABLE 2.1 Comparison between three leadership approaches by unit of analysis.

	Leadership styles	Relational leadership		Leadership-as-practice	
	Entitative	*Entitative-soft (weak process)*	*Relational (strong process)*	*Practices: Entitative-soft (weak process)*	*Practice: Relational (strong process)*
Ontology					
Characteristics	Leader-centered Individual actors acting in isolation, separated from the world on which they act Linearity from intention to intervention Performance is supposedly determined by purpose Dualism—distinction subject-object—influence stems from one person (the leaders) and affects another person (the follower)	Decentering the leader Focus is on individuals and how they relate to each other, how they construct relationships with each other, how they (re)construct their identities in relationships Subject-subject relationships	Decentering the leader Focus is on the relationship and how it enables leadership to emerge and for people/subjectivities to become Subject-subject relationships	Decentering the leader Practices are building blocks of organizing Practices as sources of meaning and identity Practices are governed by "habitus," by a modus operandi rather than from conscious intent Subject-subject relationships	Decentering the leader Logic of practice influences processes of becoming Practice is a recursive encounter Subject-subject relationships
Empirical focus	Individuals in leadership positions (leader centered) Typical/routinized behavior Patterns of behavior that can be generalized	Relationships Dialogue Mutual adjustment Collaborative learning Collective sensemaking		Situated activity, the "doing" of leadership Typical/routinized behavior Patterns of behavior that are reoccurring Emotions, embodiment, materiality	
Examples of research questions, e.g., if leadership is to be studied in professional organizations	What is the leader's typical leadership behavior in his/her interaction with professionals? Which leadership behavior is the most effective?	How is leadership co-constructed in relations between people belonging to different professions?	In what kind of relational dynamics are courses of action being set and how is the emergent construction of the professional boundaries related to such processes? How do relational dynamics contribute to structuring?	Which professional practices contribute to producing direction? How is leadership work achieved in the interaction between humans and non-humans?	How is leadership produced? How does the re-construction of professional norms intertwine with the emergence of leadership?

Strategy, coordination, leadership: Social accomplishments from a practice perspective

As the practice perspective is gaining in momentum among organizational scholars, it can be used to help understand different organizational phenomena, such as, technology-as-practice (e.g. Orlikowski, 2000); knowledge and learning-as-practice (e.g. Nicolini, Gherardi & Yanow, 2003; Raelin, 1997), strategy-as-practice (e.g. Chia & MacKay, 2007; Whittington, 1996; Golsorkhi *et al.*, 2010), and coordination-as-practice (e.g. Jarzabkowski, Lê & Feldman, 2012). In these contributions, the focus is often on practices (rather than "practice") that are mostly seen as "building blocks" that help understand organizing and organizational phenomena. However, the challenge of applying a practice perspective to these different areas is that various organizational outcomes might be achieved through the same *everyday actions and doings contributing to organizing*. That is, the question might arise how we can discern and differentiate *analytically* between the organizational phenomena when the "units of analysis" in all of them are *practices (or practice)*. To address this issue we follow Nicolini (2009), who suggests "zooming in" on the *social accomplishments* of practices. For our second comparison, we thus consider the similarities and differences among leadership, strategy, and coordination from a practice perspective. We chose strategy-as-practice as one field to which to compare leadership-as-practice given the lively community around this field which has, over the years, produced a number of interesting studies. Moreover, when adopting a practice perspective, it may no longer be obvious what is strategy and what is leadership, which makes such discussion necessary. We chose coordination-as-practice as a second field of comparison given that, although the field is not as established as strategy-as-practice, the possible overlap with leadership-as-practice is clear, for instance, leadership has been defined in terms of alignment (Drath *et al.*, 2008), which is also what coordination-as-practice is said to be about. Before delving into such a discussion, it seems necessary to comment on the consistency of the fields. For the sake of clarity in this chapter, we will simplify and summarize in a few sentences what each field is focusing on, but the reader should keep in mind that "practice" is not "one theory" but rather a number of theoretical approaches (Nicolini, 2012) and, consequently, also each "as-practice" field may include studies that are rather different. The recent handbook of strategy-as-practice, for example, organizes contributions to the field depending on whether they consider practice as a phenomenon (the focus is on what people actually do), a theoretical perspective (practice-centered theory is used in analyzing empirical situations), or an ontology (reality is fundamentally understood as constituted of bundles of practices) (Golsorkhi *et al.*, 2010).

Strategy-as-practice: Negotiating future directions

Common to studies of strategy-as-practice, coordination-as-practice, and leadership-as-practice is that they are concerned with how space of action in organizing is produced and the courses of action, or the development of interrelated trajectories, affected. Yet, we propose that the three fields shed light on different aspects of such processes. Unfortunately, such difference in focus and the relation between the fields is seldom discussed. What makes matters even more difficult is that concepts such as leadership and strategy are not always clearly defined. In particular, in the strategy-as-practice literature it may be difficult to find definitions of what "strategy" work is (for example, in Golsorkhi *et al.*, 2010). Our reading of such literature is that the *accomplishment of strategy* may be argued to be the ongoing negotiation of *future order* and an intentional path forward to such order, hence differing in this case from leadership in its temporality (which we argue, below, is about the present). Moreover, a number of scholars are also concerned with how such future order becomes inscribed and enacted in the present. Some strategy texts, for example, have performative effects (see, e.g., Vaara, Sorsa & Pälli, 2010). One could argue that the practice approach allows us to look at how paths forward are (re-)made real and relevant, rather than taking the "playground" and the "plan for the game" as given. As a consequence, focusing on practices suggests we move our attention from strategy as a finished text to what ordinary actors (including objects) do when they strategize/engage in strategy work. Such an enterprise may take different shapes, from very detailed analysis of individuals in conversation inspired by an ethnomethodological tradition (Samra-Fredericks, 2003) to critical discursive approaches of textual agency (Vaara *et al.*, 2010), two examples that illustrate the diversity of the strategy-as-practice field—and this is both an opportunity and a challenge (Golsorkhi *et al.*, 2010).

Box 2.5 reproduces a small excerpt from the work of Samra-Fredericks (2010), who tries to trace the shaping of strategic directions by highlighting the "facts" that are being accomplished (see Box 2.5). Again, the excerpt is too short for the reader to get an understanding of the full empirical situation (for this, please refer to Samra-Fredericks, 2010), but it helps to illustrate what kind of empirical material and data analysis can be employed within the strategy-as-practice perspective. As mentioned above, the example shows an ethnomethodological approach in which conversational dynamics are analyzed in detail. By means of such analysis, the researcher is able to say something about the process in which strategic direction is produced, or, in our own words, how future order is negotiated.

To conclude, strategy-as-practice is a broad approach that provides the opportunity for a variety of methods to study its social accomplishment: the negotiation or enactment of future order. Both the negotiation and enactment of future order intersect with the doings of leadership and may take place in the same interactions in which leadership emerges. However, different from strategy-as-practice, we propose, and discuss below, that leadership-as-practice has to do with the present and the emergence of premises for shaping new spaces of action and moving forward in certain directions rather than mobilizing notions of the future, in particular an organized future.

BOX 2.5 AN EXAMPLE OF STRATEGY-AS-PRACTICE

This excerpt comes from the reproduction of a conversation involving people working on strategic documents that Samra-Fredericks (2010) uses to illustrate how data interpretation from a strategy-as-practice perspective can be informed by ethnomethodology and conversation analysis. The dialogue is reproduced according to specific conventions of conversation analysis that make it possible to analyze also the form the conversation takes in terms of sequentiality and organization of talk.

5	strategist 1	what did you say on that (.) you said (.) when you say [name of division] do you mean [Group name]?
	strategist 2	er yeah [name of company] and the organization, the external market
	strategist 1	I'd think I'd call1 that recent trends [quietly speaks as reads]
10		survival' [reads] it's another bit that goes in there, I think you've got it somewhere else but the urm the dirt cheap asset prices need to go in there
	strategist 2	yeah I've got that in the main body of the report and the competition but yeah we can put that in there as well
15	strategist 1	I think its part of the (.) if you made that into market structure=
	strategist 2	=yes=
	strategist 1	= what that says is (.) here's a big consolidation piece [inaudible three words] its (.) consolidation [as he writes] (Samra-Fredericks, 2010, p. 236)

Coordination-as-practice: Alignment and co-orientation

The accomplishment of coordination-as-practice is the moment-by-moment achieving of *alignment* and *co-orientation*, which brings and increases order and stabilizes the collective course of action (e.g. Jarzabkowski *et al.*, 2012). Such an understanding of coordination moves our focus from formal coordination forms (e.g., roles or hierarchy) to more emergent forms: coordination is what ordinary people and objects achieve together—it is emergent and recursive. The coordination-as-practice field is not yet as established as in the case of strategy-as-practice or leadership-as-practice, but the recent work by Jarzabkowski and colleagues (2012) clearly indicates that coordination research has taken the "practice turn."

In their article, Jarzabkowski and colleagues (2012) analyze the dynamics between ostensive coordination mechanisms and the enactment of specific performances in the creation of new coordinating mechanisms. As leadership is also concerned with the emergence of order, we believe it is relevant to compare the two as-practice approaches with respect to their social accomplishment. We propose that the difference is, as is the case for strategy-as-practice and leadership-as-practice, the *analytical focus* of the organizational phenomenon in which we are interested and to which we are con-tributing, and what knowledge we are producing. In the case of coordination, the aim is to understand how collective action is achieved in practice by stabilizing the relation between different trajectories, such as courses of action, whereas in the case of leadership the aim is to understand how direction and movement are produced.

A recent study on perfume-making by Endrissat, Islam and Noppeney (2015) provides an example of approaching the study of coordination with a practice perspective (see Box 2.6).

BOX 2.6 COORDINATION-AS-PRACTICE—EXAMPLE.

The example is analyzed in detail in Endrissat, Islam and Noppeney (2015). Central to the coordination in the design process under study (i.e. perfume making) is an object, the so-called mood board. Mood boards are part of the "briefing" situation in which a creative director or a client communicates to the development team basic information about the new product. The mood board is able to communicate a "mood" or a theme through aesthetically enriched material such as visual images. In their study, the researchers analyze how the object plays a central role throughout the creative process of producing a new product (including the fragrance, the packaging, the advertising, etc.). The data analysis shows how the mood board is interacting with the people involved, who were physically placed in different locations and could not meet face-to-face on a regular basis. When focusing on practice, we can see that the mood board is able to balance the seemingly contradictory require-ments of coordinating and providing creative freedom in creative processes. It coordinates via practices of (a) setting the scene, (b) directing activities and aligning sub-products, and (c) establishing a point of reference. It pro-vides creative freedom via (a) leaving room for interpretation, (b) providing a source of inspiration, and (c) allowing self-expression and signature style.

The challenge in this case, as in many other settings, is to balance the need for coordination, which means aligning the actions performed by different actors with the need for creativity, which means leaving space for emergent and diver-gent trajectories. The researchers emphasize the role played by "mood boards," an object that is used for briefing the actors involved in the process regarding what the new product should be about. The mood board displays aesthetic rather than technical aspects of the product idea, and succeeds to maintain plurality while also directing and aligning. By means of this example, we want to illustrate how an analysis using coordination-as-practice may proceed. The focus is on practices enabling co-orientation of action, but also how the possibility of "bringing materiality in" is more fully explored than in a number of current leadership-as-practice empirical studies, a lack that is also addressed by Sergi (Chapter 6, this volume).

Leadership-as-practice: Producing direction and setting the course of action

The *accomplishment of leadership* may be said to be the moment-by-moment production of *direction*, or collective agency in changing *and setting courses of action* (e.g. Crevani, forthcoming; Carroll & Simpson, 2012; Drath *et al.*, 2008; Raelin, 2014). Whereas traditional leadership theory takes direction as a "given," as linear and as unproblematic, the concept of practice allows us to appreciate the "organic" nature of courses of action that change and/or intensify as people interact. Although there may be formal courses of action that have been sanctioned by the upper management, the courses of action that take form as people work may differ from those sanctioned, and are constantly under construction, contested, and changing. The formal leader has no chance to control such courses of action, which are the result of social interactions throughout the organization. Hence, leadership-as-practice refocuses our attention from what (extraordinary) individuals are, to what ordinary people and objects do as they engage in leading. Leadership-as-practice is about collaborative agency (Raelin, 2014) and about weaving together co-evolving trajectories in a movement toward the future (not the mobilization of future order in the present, as in strategy-as-practice).

To exemplify the focus a leadership-as-practice study may take, we refer to the work of Raelin, who briefly describes in Chapter 1 of this volume a number of activities that cannot be linked to single individuals but are rather inherently social and interactional in their nature. These are scanning, signaling, weaving, stabilizing, inviting, unleashing, reflecting (Raelin, Chapter 1, this volume). Another example may be found in the work of Carroll and Simpson (2012) who identify "framing movements" in conversations, which they label kindling, stretching, and spanning (see Box 2.5 above which illustrates Carroll and Simpson's (2012) analysis of the attention paid to the micro-interactions and dialogical dynamics that make up leadership). Thanks to such movements, new realities and rationalities, such as opening up or closing down the shared space of action, may emerge. Although the focus of this contribution is on direction and movement or a form of agency in flow (see Simpson, Chapter 8, this volume), there are also studies of an entitative character more traditionally focused on the practices mobilized by formal leaders. Denis *et al.* (2010), for instance, show the development of certain initiatives over time and the kind of practice that formal leaders develop.

Discussion of comparative element II: Blurred lines

The "as-practice" movement has rapidly grown in the last decade as the approaches that fall under such a label have helped scholars come closer to studying organizing while organizing is taking place, something that has both a theoretical relevance (filling a void in our understanding of "organization" as a phenomenon) and a practical relevance (coming closer to the experience people at work have of this phenomenon). Practices are by definition "bundled," and there is no practice that makes sense in isolation. Practice is also a construct that directs our attention to the ongoing, social nature of organizing and to its holistic character, opposed to other approaches that present static snapshots and single out the causes that lead to a certain result (Langley, Smallman, Tsoukas & Van de Ven, 2013). Hence, it is a fundamental characteristic of the practice idea that there are not different discrete practices leading to different discrete results. Rather, bundles of practices are studied to understand organizing—what we have called the "entitative-soft" approaches. Taking a relational approach and focusing on "practice," rather than "practices" means embracing even more the holistic nature of reality and organizing in particular. Moreover, acknowledging the active role of objects, representations, and materiality suggests that we take a fresh look at what happens in organizations.

Most of the studies that are available at the moment in strategy-as-practice, coordination-as-practice, and leadership-as-practice are extending a focus on practices (the entitative-soft perspective) and thus on the building blocks of organizing. However, although this brings many insights, one challenge of considering organizing activities from a practice perspective is that the formerly distinct categories and labels—such as strategy, coordination, leadership—might actually collapse; they all become *practices of organizing*. It can happen that the same building blocks (e.g., providing direction) can be part of leadership as much as it can be part of coordination or strategy work. The question arises as to whether the distinction among the fields of research (strategy, coordination, leadership) still makes sense or simply represents a remainder of an entitative approach. If so, the practice perspective would require an entirely new approach to studying organizational phenomena, an approach in which we do not reproduce the constructs that we have inherited from more traditional approaches but refer to all of them as "organizing in relation."

We believe that it is valuable to understand that people "do" several "things" at the same time; there is no sequentiality in our action in the sense that simple chains of cause-effect relations are not possible to identify. But we are also convinced that it may be fruitful to analytically differentiate between different kinds of social accomplishments and to consider them as complementary to each other,

all contributing to organizing processes from somewhat different angles. Our understanding is that the "as-practice" movement has a great potential to advance those fields that have focused on single individuals and discrete phases of complex processes (e.g. strategy, coordination, leadership), but to make such a contribution, the different fields might have to be addressed with their specific terminology. Moreover, from a practical point of view, when working with development in organizations, it may be easier to design and participate in development initiatives that have labels with which one is familiar, for example strategy. The challenge is to change how we are used to thinking about such familiar concepts so as not to get stuck in a static view of complex phenomena. In sum, for the researcher it is important to be familiar with the grounds of the practice approach, which are common across the fields. To which "as-practice" field one is contributing, will ultimately be a question of emphasis and empirical interest: What is our research interest? What are we trying to understand? Where do we put the empirical emphasis? What we have proposed is that strategy-as-practice has to do with the production and enactment of future order, coordination-as-practice with the stabilization of order by means of alignment of courses of action, and leadership-as-practice with the emergence of direction for courses of action. Put slightly differently, if, following Massey (2005), we conceptualize the world as a mesh of co-evolving trajectories (people, objects, physical places, etc.), we could say that strategy-as-practice has to do with the intentional production and enactment of future relational configurations, coordination-as-practice with the stabilization of relational configurations, and leadership-as-practice with the ongoing emergent shaping of relational configurations.

As regards similarities and overlaps between studies focusing on strategy-as-practice, coordination-as-practice, and leadership-as-practice, all three areas of research focus on the practice of *ordinary actors*, which includes actors who do not necessarily hold official positions or roles as leaders or strategists and which also includes non-human actors such as objects and materiality. The recognition that objects are central to practices is probably best established in the field of coordination research (see, e.g., Okhuysen & Bechky, 2009 for an overview) and strategy-as-practice (e.g. Golsorkhi et al., 2010), but is increasingly highlighted by leadership-as-practice scholars (Sergi, Chapter 6, this volume). Looking back at the "as-practice" examples we have provided, it is possible to see that the same examples might have been analyzed as instances of another kind of "as-practice" modality if the researchers had interpreted the processes from another angle. For instance, the study on the process of creative projects (Endrissat et al., 2015) focuses on coordination but could also be read as a study of how leadership is achieved in the interaction between human actors and materiality.

Although the presence of such overlaps may be surprising, even annoying, at first sight, one could argue that it is actually reasonable as reality does not come in discrete units but is—according to a practice perspective—entangled and complex. Knowledge produced about one aspect of the phenomenon, such as "organizing," enriches the understanding of other aspects of the phenomenon. This implies that we need to develop more arenas in which the different "as-practices" can meet. The fact that the boundaries are blurred provides scholars and practitioners with an intriguing opportunity to learn from each other's fields.

Finally, although the phenomena of strategy and coordination have concrete manifestations in the form of different kinds of documents, which often means that the study of practices is anchored, in one way or another, to such material manifestations (for instance the production of strategic texts), leadership has no such a material manifestations. This may be one reason for often anchoring the phenomenon to individuals in formal leadership positions. It requires scholars to more clearly define what they mean by "leadership" when taking a practice approach and to discuss how to study this phenomenon. On the other hand, the notion of leadership is also mobilized in organizations and such mobilization produces effects on the collective space of action—what Crevani et al. (2010) call the performativity of leadership. In this sense the three phenomena, strategy, coordination, and leadership, are different as these notions are mobilized in different situations and with different effects, emphasizing the multifaceted understanding of processes in organizations.

To sum up, although traditional studies of strategy, coordination, and leadership may be placed in clearly separated fields and provide distinctive results, taking a practice approach means that the boundaries between the empirical phenomenon of interest, the analytical framing, and, consequently, the fields of research themselves become blurred. One may even argue that phenomena, analyses, and fields collapse into one phenomenon (organizing), one analytical framework (practice), and one field of research (organization studies). We have put forward the argument that this is reasonable—we have bundles of practices contributing to organizing processes—but that there is a value in upholding the boundaries, although blurred, to make the largest impact on theory and practice.

Conclusion

This chapter tries to help orient newcomers to the leadership-as-practice field by comparing related constructs on two important dimensions: "unit of analysis" and "social accomplishment." To promote discussion, we have had to simplify some of the research positions and tried to emphasize (sometimes over-stressed) commonalities as well as differences, well aware that, in conducting research, some analytic distinctions get blurred and commonalities may not be obvious. Our hope is that the reader will benefit from our interpretation of the positions that we have sketched in this chapter and can more clearly see the contribution of leadership-as-practice, its uniqueness as well as its interdependence with other constructs. The two dimensions of comparison are important given that they are at the core of a research project, making it necessary to reflect on them when producing knowledge about leadership. This kind of reflection is, however, seldom made explicit and some of the constructs are at times used inter-changeably, as for instance in the case of leadership-as-practice and relational leadership. In a similar way, questions about "what is the difference?" when it comes to different "as-practice" approaches remain largely unanswered, poten-tially risking alienation of newcomers. We therefore saw the need to discuss these issues in this chapter. We want to be clear that with this chapter we do not claim to having defined the field once and for all, or that our distinctions are the only or "correct" ones. Rather, we want to put some relevant elements on the table and start a discussion about the need (or not) for different constructs and about how to trace (permeable and blurred) boundaries in a meaningful way that respects researchers' own convictions as well as helping a newcomer orient her/himself. This discussion is, thus, relevant for those who want to embark on the study of leadership by adopting a non-traditional approach. But it should also be relevant for those people "doing leadership" at work, as it has implications for how to proceed when trying to develop leadership. Depending on the "unit of analysis," the development effort will have to be tailored in a specific way, focusing on what the approach argues "leadership" is to meaningfully develop leadership competence, which may be either individual or collective.

References

Alvesson, M., & Sveningsson, S. (2003). Managers doing leadership: The extra-ordinarization of the mundane. *Human Relations*, 56(12), 1435–1459.
Barge, K. J. (2012). Systemic constructionist leadership and working from the present moment. In M. Uhl-Bien & S. Ospina (Eds.), *Advancing relational leadership research* (pp. 107–142). Charlotte, NC: Information Age.
Barker, R. A. (2001). The nature of leadership. *Human Relations*, 54(4), 469–494.
Blake, R. R., & Mouton, J. S. (1964). *The managerial grid*. Houston, TX: Gulf Publishing Company.
Blake, R. R., & Mouton, J.S. (1978). *The new managerial grid*. Houston, TX: Gulf Publishing Company.
Carroll, B., Levy, L., & Richmond, D. (2008). Leadership as practice: Challenging the competency paradigm. *Leadership*, 4(4), 363–379.
Carroll, B., & Simpson, B. (2012). Capturing sociality in the movement between frames: An illustration from leadership development. *Human Relations*, 65(10), 1283–1309.
Chia, R., & MacKay, B. (2007). Post-processual challenges for the emerging strategy-as-practice perspective: Discovering strategy in the logic of practice. *Human Relations*, 60(1), 217–242.
Crevani, L. (forthcoming). Is there leadership in a fluid world? Exploring the ongoing production of direction in organizing. *Leadership*.
Crevani, L. (2011). *Clearing for action: Leadership as a relational phenomenon*. Doctoral Thesis. KTH The Royal Institute of Technology, Stockholm.
Crevani, L., Lindgren, M., & Packendorff, J. (2010). Leadership, not leaders: On the study of leadership as practices and interactions. *Scandinavian Journal of Management*, 26(1), 77–86.
Cunliffe, A. L., & Eriksen, M. (2011). Relational leadership. *Human Relations*, 64(11), 1425–1449.

Dachler, H. P., & Hosking, D. M. (1995). The primacy of relations in socially constructing organizational realities. In D. M. Hosking, H. P. Dachler, & K. J. Gergen (Eds.), *Management and organization: Relational alternatives to individualism* (pp. 1–29). Aldershot: Avebury.

Denis, J. L., Langley, A., & Rouleau, L. (2005). Rethinking leadership in public organizations. In E. Ferlie, L. Lynn, & C. Pollitt (Eds.), *The Oxford handbook of public management* (pp. 446–467). Oxford: Oxford University Press.

Denis, J. L., Langley, A., & Rouleau, L. (2010). The practice of leadership in the messy world of organizations. *Leadership*, 6(1), 67–88.

Drath, W. H., McCauley, C. D., Palus, C. J., Van Velsor, E., O'Connor, P. M. G., & McGuire, J. B. (2008). Direction, alignment, commitment: Toward a more integrative ontology of leadership. *Leadership Quarterly*, 19, 635–653.

Döös, M., Backström, T., Melin, M., & Wilhelmson, L. (2012). Isolated cases or widespread practice? The occurrence of sharing managers in Swedish working life. *Economics and Business Letters*, 1(3), 23–36.

Eagly, A. H., & Johnson, B. T. (1990). Gender and leadership style: A meta-analysis. *Psychological Bulletin*, 108(2), 233.

Endrissat, N., & von Arx, W. (2013). Leadership practices and context: Two sides of the same coin. *Leadership*, 9(2), 278–304.

Endrissat, N., Islam, G., & Noppeney, C. (2015). Visual organizing. Balancing coordination and creative freedom via mood boards. *Journal of Business Research*, http://dx.doi.org/10.1016/j.jbusres.2015.10.004.

Golsorkhi, D., Rouleau, L., Seidl, D., & Vaara, E. (Eds.) (2010). *Cambridge handbook of strategy as practice*. Cambridge: Cambridge University Press.

Graeff, C. L. (1997). Evolution of situational leadership theory: A critical review. *Leadership Quarterly*, 8(2), 153–170.

Graen, G., & Uhl-Bien, M. (1995). Relationship-based approach to leadership: Development of leader-member exchange (LMX) theory of leadership over 25 years: Applying a multi-level multi-domain perspective. *Leadership Quarterly*, 6(2), 219–247.

Grint, K. (2005). *Leadership: Limits and possibilities*. Basingstoke: Palgrave Macmillan.

Hernes, T. (2008). *Understanding organization as process. Theory for a tangled world*. Abingdon: Routledge.

Holgersson, C. (2013). Recruiting managing directors: Doing homosociality. *Gender, Work & Organization*, 20(4), 454–466.

Holmberg, I., & Tyrstrup, M. (2010). Well then—what now? An everyday approach to managerial leadership. *Leadership*, 6(4), 353–372.

Hosking, D. M. (1988). Organizing, leadership and skilful process. *Journal of Management Studies*, 25(2), 147–166.

Hosking, D. M. (2011). Telling tales of relations: Appreciating relational constructionism. *Organization Studies*, 32(1), 47–65.

Jarzabkowski, P. A., Lê, J. K., & Feldman, M. S. (2012). Toward a theory of coordinating: Creating coordinating mechanisms in practice. *Organization Science*, 23(4), 907–927.

Katz, D., & Kahn, R. L. (1951). Human organization and worker motivation. In L. R. Tripp (Ed.), *Industrial Productivity* (pp. 146–171). Madison, WI: Industrial Relations Research Association.

Koivunen, N., & Wennes, G. (2011). Show us the sound! Aesthetic leadership of symphony orchestra conductors. *Leadership*, 7(1), 51-71.

Langley, A., Smallman, C., Tsoukas, H., & Van de Ven, A. H. (2013). Process studies of change in organization and management: Unveiling temporality, activity, and flow. *Academy of Management Journal*, 56(1), 1–13.

Langley, A., & Tsoukas, H. (2010). Introducing 'Perspectives on process organization studies'. In T. Hernes & S. Maitlis (Eds.), *Process, sensemaking, & organizing* (pp. 1–26). Oxford: Oxford University Press.

Lewin, K., Lippitt, R., & White, R. K. (1939). Patterns of aggressive behavior in experimentally created social climates. *Journal of Social Psychology*, 10, 271–301.

Likert, R. (1961). *New patterns of management*. New York: McGraw-Hill.

Massey, D. (2005). *For space*. London: Sage.

Nicolini, D. (2009). Zooming in and out: Studying practices by switching theoretical lenses and trialing connections. *Organization Studies*, 30(12), 1391–1418.

Nicolini, D. (2012). *Practice theory, work & organization*. Oxford: Oxford University Press.

Nicolini, D., Gherardi, S., & Yanow, D. (2003). *Knowing in organizations: A practice-based approach*. Armonk, NY: ME Sharpe Inc.

Northouse, P. G. (2007). *Leadership: Theory and practice*. Thousand Oaks, CA: Sage.

Northouse, P. G. (2010). *Leadership: Theory and practice* (5th edition). Thousand Oaks, CA: Sage.

Okhuysen, G. A., & Bechky, B. A. (2009). Coordination in organizations: An integrative perspective. *The Academy of Management Annals*, 3(1), 463–502.

O'Reilly, D., & Reed, M. (2010). 'Leaderism': An evolution of managerialism in UK public service reform. *Public Administration*, 88(4), 960–978.

Orlikowski, W. J. (2000). Using technology and constituting structures: A practice lens for studying technology in organizations. *Organization Science*, 11(4), 404–428.

Orlikowski, W. J. (2010). Practice in research: Phenomenon, perspective and philosophy. In D. Golsorkhi, L. Rouleau, D. Seidl, & E. Vaara (Eds.), *Cambridge handbook of strategy as practice* (pp. 23–33). Cambridge: Cambridge University Press.

Oshagbemi, T., & Gill, R. W. T. (2004). Differences in leadership styles and behavior across hierarchical levels in UK organizations. *Leadership and Organization Development Journal*, 25(1), 93–106.

Packendorff, J., Crevani, L., & Lindgren, M. (2014). Project leadership in becoming: A process study of an organizational change project. *Project Management Journal*, 45(3), 5–20.

Pearce, C. L., & Conger, J. A. (2003). *Shared leadership: Reframing the hows and whys of leadership*. Thousand Oaks, CA: Sage.

Raelin, J. (1997). A model of work-based learning. *Organization Science*, 8(6), 563–578.

Raelin, J. (2011). From leadership-as-practice to leaderful practice. *Leadership*, 7(2), 195–211.

Raelin, J. (2014). Imagine there are no leaders: Reframing leadership as collaborative agency. *Leadership*, Online First. Published online before print 25 November, doi:10.1177/1742715014558076.

Rouleau, L. (2010). Studying strategizing through narratives of practice. In D. Golsorkhi, L. Rouleau, D. Seidl, & E. Vaara (Eds.), *Cambridge handbook of strategy as practice* (pp. 258–270). Cambridge: Cambridge University Press.

Samra-Fredericks, D. (2003). Strategizing as lived experience and strategists' everyday efforts to shape strategic direction. *Journal of Management Studies*, 40(1), 141–174.

Samra-Fredericks, D. (2010). Researching everyday practice: The ethnomethodological contribution. In D. Golsorkhi, L. Rouleau, D. Seidl & E. Vaara (Eds.), *Cambridge handbook of strategy as practice* (pp. 230–242). Cambridge: Cambridge University Press.

Schatzki, T. R., Knorr-Cetina, K., & Savigny, E. (2001). *The practice turn in contemporary theory*. London: Routledge.

Schedlitzki, D., & Edwards, G. (2014). *Studying leadership: Traditional and critical approaches*. London: Sage.

Spillane, J. P., Halverson, R., & Diamond, J. B. (2004). Towards a theory of leadership practice: A distributed perspective. *Journal of Curriculum Studies*, 36(1), 3–34.

Stogdill, R. M., & Coons, A. E. (Eds.) (1957). *Leader behaviour: Its description and measurement*. Columbus: Bureau of Business Research, Ohio State University.

Uhl-Bien, M. (2006). Relational leadership theory: Exploring the social processes of leadership and organizing. *Leadership Quarterly*, 17, 654–676.

Uhl-Bien, M., & Ospina, S. (Eds.) (2012). *Advancing relational leadership research: A dialogue among perspectives*. Charlotte, NC: Information Age.

Vaara, E., Sorsa, V., & Pälli, P. (2010). On the force potential of strategy texts: A critical discourse analysis of a strategic plan and its power effects in a city organization. *Organization*, 17(6), 685–702.

van der Haar, D., & Hosking, D. M. (2004). Evaluating appreciative inquiry: A relational constructionist perspective. *Human Relations*, 57(8), 1017–1036.

Whittington, R. (1996). Strategy as practice. *Long Range Planning*, 29(5), 731–735.

Wood, M. (2005). The fallacy of misplaced leadership. *Journal of Management Studies*, 42(6), 1101–1121.

Wright, P. L. (1996). *Managerial leadership*. London: Routledge.

3

THE PHILOSOPHICAL BASIS OF LEADERSHIP-AS-PRACTICE FROM A HERMENEUTICAL PERSPECTIVE

Ann L. Cunliffe and Paul Hibbert

Why is an understanding of the philosophy of practice important to studying and theorizing practice?

It would be easy to think that a philosophical understanding and the study of practice are contradictory, because philosophy is often viewed as a discipline abstracted from lived experience. In this chapter we argue that an understanding of philosophy is crucial in highlighting the pluralism of practice as we both experience and study it. This pluralism is evidenced in practice-based studies in general, for example, Sandberg and Dall'Alba (2009) observe that practice-based approaches in Organization Studies draw on communities of practice, activity theory, socio-cultural theories, and actor network theory. Additionally, practice scholars utilize narrative (Fenton & Langley, 2011) and ethnomethodological (Samra-Fredericks, 2003; Nicolini, 2009) approaches. It is also evidenced in the range of philosophical positions utilized by leadership-as-practice authors in this book: for example, from Jackie Ford's critical (Chapter 11), Barbara Simpson's pragmatist (Chapter 8), and Ken Gergen and Lone Hersted's dialogic (Chapter 9) approaches. Although there is no unified approach to practice, as Schatzki (2001) notes, a central core is that practices are "embodied, materially mediated arrays of human activity centrally organized around shared practical understandings" (p. 2). The value of viewing the world in this way is that it draws attention to actual practices—to *what is done* in relation to leadership, work, strategy, organizing, etc.—by people in complex and open circumstances. In this way, practice-based studies also offer a way of bridging the theory-practice divide.

As a means of situating our chapter, we turn to Feldman and Orlikowski (2011), who identify three approaches to practice: empirical, theoretical, and philosophical.

- An *empirical* focus sees practice as the object of study by examining everyday activities in organizations (e.g., Bechky, 2003; Kellogg, 2011). One example using empirical data to illustrate leadership-as-practice is that of Crevani, Lindgren and Packendorff (2010, p. 204) who draw attention to the constructed nature of leadership practice by drawing on interactions within a meeting.
- A *theoretical* focus articulates the theoretical relationships and logic underpinning practices as a means of explaining them. For example, Engeström's (2004) activity theory identifies and explains the development, structure, and multiple relationships in activities and practices, while Feldman's work around routines and improvisations offers a different theoretical lens (e.g., Feldman & Rafaeli, 2002). Within the leadership-as-practice arena, Raelin (2011) has theorized leadership-as-practice as the emergent collective ordering of ideas and actions, and as a more ideologically democratic leaderful practice characterized by collectiveness, concurrency, collaboration, and compassion (p. 204).
- A *philosophical* focus addresses the ontology and epistemology of practice, particularly that practice is an ontological formation organized around notionally shared understandings. Schatzki (2005), for example, draws on Heidegger to propose an ontology of practice in which social life transpires in the connections between practices and materialities in a context. Similarly, Gherardi (2006, 2009) argues that practices are intimately interwoven in constructing social and organizational realities and that the many different understandings of "practice" relate to the epistemic position of the researcher. She offers an epistemology—an ecology—of practice in which practices are studied as practical, situated, unstable, and political activities.

From this we begin to understand that "practice" from both general and leadership-as-practice perspectives is a construct that is multiple and contested (Geiger, 2009). This diversity can be explained by the various philosophical assumptions that practice scholars work from.

The range of philosophies underpinning practice is vast: for a critical lens on practice we need to go to philosophers including Foucault (1976) and Lyotard (1979); for a reflexive lens on practice to scholars including Bourdieu (1972), Garfinkel (1967), and Schutz (1972); for pragmatist-driven approaches to Dewey (1938) and Mead (1938); for a socio-material lens to Latour (2005); and a complexity lens to Law and Mol (2002). Barad (2003), for example, developed a posthumanist performativity in which the world is "made" in intra-actions or material discursive practices. This range is reflected in the varying positions taken by authors in this book, whose work is based on the ontological and epistemological assumptions underpinning their work. Not least of these assumptions is what we might mean by *understanding*, which has implications for how we perceive the study of (and participation in) practice to be meaningful (c.f. Gadamer, 2013).

We suggest that an understanding of *how* philosophical assumptions influence the work of research is key to recognizing and valuing the insights that pluralism can bring to understanding particular phenomena (Cunliffe, 2011). The contrary, a single paradigmatic stance, can lead to paradigmatic defensiveness; conflict over definitions; debates about "validity" and "generalizability"; and whether "good" knowledge is universal or situated, abstractable, or immanent.

In this chapter, we will begin by addressing three main philosophical positions, and go on to explore how the various philosophies of practice relate to leadership-as-practice. In particular, we focus on phenomenological and hermeneutic underpinnings of leadership-as-practice, which incorporate the work of philosophers including: Heidegger (1962), Gadamer (2013/1975), and Ricoeur (1992). We then tentatively outline plausible articulations of the leadership practices that can be viewed through each philosophical lens, along with associated characterizations of leadership and its ethical stances. We conclude with suggestions for research that arise from our philosophical speculations.

Philosophical underpinnings of practice

In explaining the multiple approaches to practice-based studies, it is important to address the fundamental ontological and epistemological assumptions that underpin our work. Such assumptions influence how we view, study, and theorize the phenomena of interest. It is therefore important to ask:

- What is the ontological nature of practice?
- What does "good" knowledge about practice look like?
- What are the implications for studies of practice?

Elsewhere, in trying to answer these questions from a general organization studies perspective, the first author of this chapter has articulated three knowledge problematics: objectivism, subjectivism, and intersubjectivism (Cunliffe, 2011). Problematics are "a cross-disciplinary sense of where our questions come from, what is thinkable and not thinkable in the name of social inquiry in particular historical conjunctions" (Lather, 2006, p. 46), and are based on ontological and epistemological assumptions that lend each problematic an internal logic and differentiate it from others. A problematic influences how we view our topic of research, what we see as "data," how we collect, interpret, and theorize from that data, and how we write our research accounts. More recently, she has examined the implications for practice studies (Cunliffe, 2015). We briefly outline the philosophical assumptions underpinning each problematic and their implications for studying practice (Table 3.1).

From an objectivist ontology, practice and practices are studied as objects separate from the people engaged in them. Meaning lies within the practice itself (Schatzki, 2001) and they are studied in terms of patterns, generalizable

TABLE 3.1 Three problematics (Cunliffe, 2015, p. 444)

	Objectivism	*Subjectivism*	*Intersubjectivism*
Ontology	A real concrete social reality existing independently from us. Humans as socialized into that reality	Realities socially constructed in the interactions, discursive practices, language use, and conversations of people. Humans as actors and interpreters, shaping and shaped by understandings of "realities"	Shared, unique, and contested understandings of social "realities" created between people in and across moments of time and space. Humans embedded in relationships with others at many levels
Epistemology	Search for structures, laws, systems, rules, behavioral patterns, categories, processes, roles, generalized identities, and relationships between elements	Knowledge and knowing occurring in the mundane and indexical activities of people	A knowing in-situ from within the moment of interaction and conversation. Meanings and understanding created fleetingly between people
Practice	Practice is studied as an object or phenomenon—abstracted from the context, situated interactions and intentions of people. Generalizable characteristics, models and, theories of practice can be identified	Practice is embedded in the actions, interactions, and conversations of people in a particular context. We need to understand the actors' intentions, interpretations, and study how they talk about their experience to generate interpretive insights	Practice is complexly interwoven in responsive relationships between people, in which meanings, actions, and our sense of what's going on, shifts in and through time and across relationships. Insights and transitory understanding are shaped between people

characteristics, routines, and socio-material contingencies. This is encapsulated in Nicolini's (2011, p. 603) intention "to substitute the dominant belief that subjects are the ultimate source of meaning and knowledge with the view that knowledge and meaning reside in a nexus of practices … ."

From a subjectivist ontology, humans are very much involved in shaping practices and researchers study the meanings that people give to the "mundane" everyday work in which they are engaged, that is people's multiply interpreted lived experiences. Carroll, Levy and Richmond (2008) take a more subjectivist, social constructionist perspective to study the different ways in which participants on a leadership development program articulate their practice. Subjectivist scholars are also interested in the intentionality of people around their practices, as exemplified in the following quote from a Federal Security Director talking about why he holds meetings: "I have my weekly staff meetings with the staff. They have their individual team meetings ... I want them to tell me what they think needs to be done. So we do have this cross-dialogue back and forth in terms of what is going on out there" (Cunliffe & Eriksen, 2011, p. 1434).

An intersubjective ontology is based on the notion of "we-ness," that we are always selves-in-relation-to-others. As such, it draws on the work of hermeneutic phenomenologists such as Ricoeur (1992) and Merleau-Ponty (1964). Our practices and understanding of such practices are shaped between us (intentionally and otherwise), *in situ*, in our relationally responsive interactions and conversations (Shotter, 2008). Intersubjectivism differs from subjectivism in that it is not about individual subjects and their interpretations and actions (I's) but about the betweeness or "we's." There are few practice-based intersubjective studies. Working from a practice perspective, Küpers (2013) develops the related but different concept of inter-practices in leadership, which he says involves exploring: "the interplay of entwined embodied materialities, subjectivities, and intersubjectivities of practices of leading and following with its multimodal orchestration of bodies and material artifacts and discourses" (p. 342). We suggest that "inter-practices" fall within an objectivist problematic because the focus is not on the interpretations of people within their lived experience but on the inter-practices themselves. In the following section we move on to elaborate phenomenological approaches to practice, which begin to conceptualize our lived experience from a more intersubjective perspective.

Phenomenological approaches to leadership-as-practice

Phenomenologists are interested in understanding and explaining who we are in the lived world. For a number of hermeneutic phenomenologists, such as Ricoeur (1981), the hermeneutic task focuses on an interpretation of texts (which also includes discourse), the polysemy or multiple meanings of language, and a critique of the theory of knowledge in the human sciences. The three philosophers selected, Martin Heidegger, Hans-George Gadamer, and Paul Ricoeur, additionally have been concerned with extending the task of hermeneutics beyond an epistemological one to an ontological one, in other words from only addressing ways of knowing and developing a methodology to compete with scientific modes, to also include an interrogation of ways of being, that is what does it mean "to be." They question why, when studying the world, we classify, categorize, and code "objects," when in our lived moments we do not experience the world in that way. In the following discussion we outline the main arguments of each philosopher that relate particularly to leadership-as-practice, and briefly address their implications for leadership learning and development. These are summarized in Table 3.2 and explicated below. For a more general review of phenomenological thinking and leadership, see Ashman (2007) and Lawler (2005).

TABLE 3.2 The philosophical underpinnings of leadership-as-practice

	Heidegger	Gadamer	Ricoeur
Practice	We live in a world in which social interactions, actions, practices, and meanings are contextualized and make sense within specific spaces of intelligibility (life-world, entwinement, being-in-the-world)	An intrinsically hermeneutic means of enacting an event of understanding, that involves dialogue in two dimensions: synchronically with (others in) our social contexts and diachronically with our tradition(s)	Narrative emplotment of life and selves in lived experience. The nature of ethical selfhood
Leadership-as-practice	Leadership takes place in "everyday practical coping" activities. *Authentic* individuals recognize they are inseparable yet different; are sensitive to taken-for-granted conventions and norms	A fusion of horizons in which that towards which one is oriented, is situated in understanding through dialogue between individuals in which notions of leading and following are situated in the context of mutual influence	Individuals recognize and understand the importance of being ethical selves in relation to others. Also the nature of ethical practice
Leadership learning	Requires reflexive attunement within an unfolding world. May only occur with disruption to unnoticed practices	The development of: a rich awareness of the contextual breadth and the historicity of one's situation and a reflective return to tradition	Individuals are reflexively aware of how they narrate their own and others identities and worlds in joint action and interactions

Being and the entwinement of practice: A Heideggerian perspective

A number of practice-based scholars draw on the work of Heidegger (e.g., Sandberg & Tsoukas, 2011; Schatzki, 2005), in particular, Heidegger's conceptualization of *Being*, the *life-world, entwinement*, and *intelligibility*. In *Being and Time* (1962), Heidegger argues that to determine the nature of *Being*, we have first to inquire into our own mode of *Being* in the world, to "get provisionally articulated in [our] Being" (p. 27). Phenomenologists are particularly concerned with the given social nature of our immediate lived experience or life-world, and for Heidegger this means that *Being* cannot be conceptualized apart from the world and the context in which it is embedded: *Being* is nowhere and everywhere because it does not reside in an entity but in what is to hand—the many objects and understandings in our world. Our life-world has a *throwness* quality in that we are tossed into a world without choice or prior knowledge, a world that is difficult to fully grasp because we are inseparable (*entwined*) in a relational whole of people, objects, activities, culture, history, and so on. In this relational whole are specific ways of being (*being-in-the-world*) which help us make sense because we live within spaces of *intelligibility*, social interactions, actions, practices, meanings, etc. What this means is that because we are preoccupied with our everyday practices, with getting on with whatever we are doing, be it leading, nursing, driving … , we don't notice or think about them.

Therefore, Heidegger's (1962) argument is that everyday experience is about primordial, non-deliberate ways of being and doing. We dwell, or are caught up in a world in which we instinctively incorporate objects and materialities. Chia and Holt (2006) draw on Heidegger's work to argue that strategy unfolds in "everyday practical coping actions" (p. 637)—based on strategists' familiarity, and mundane and "absorbed involvement," with their world. In relation to leadership this means understanding the practice of leadership from within the practice and that the situation and site in which leadership is done will influence particular ways of behaving, saying, and engaging with the objects and people around. Leadership is reframed as a social practice inseparable from context, in which a "practice and its members are co-constituted; neither can exist without the other" (Sandberg & Dall'Alba, 2009, p. 1355). From a Heideggerian perspective it is only when individuals are in relationship with a meaningful totality that they can understand and be understood because the totality influences and orients the types of activities, behaviors, and identities that are significant and proper. A practice therefore becomes intelligible through distinctions about what matters: key activities, the tools to hand, and a "teleological structure" or purpose which gives the practice its defining features (Sandberg & Tsoukas, 2011, p. 343). Because we cannot take ourselves out of the world, understanding means seeing the possibilities that may emerge in our lived experience. Drawing on Heidegger's contrast of *building* (deliberate mental activity and motivated actions by individuals) and *dwelling* (unreflective, unfolding actions), Carroll *et al.* (2008) develop seven discourses of dwelling (habits, process, consciousness, awareness, control, everydayness, and identity) from the ways in which participants on a leadership development program articulated and rearticulated their practices. They propose that researchers could combine building and dwelling as a way of developing more knowledgeable and new practices out of previously unquestioned habits.

Also of relevance to leadership-as-practice is the attention Heidegger (1962) brings to the interplay of two ways of Being: *authentic* and *inauthentic*. Authentic relates to a way of Being that embodies care and commitment, whereas inauthentic refers to living in a way that may involve imposed, normative, and conventional modes of life that are pre-conceived, unexamined and care-less. We cannot escape the latter, nor can we overthrow it—but if we are not care-ful, we can lose ourselves in it. We therefore have to see what meaningful action we can take and how we may act in authentic ways. Authenticity is recognizing our Being is inseparable from others and our world, and also recognizing our differences.

Over the last 10–15 years, the notion of authentic leadership has gained popularity, but often in a more *building* than a *dwelling* sense. In leadership studies, authenticity is seen as improving profits and sustainable growth through self-awareness, self-development, leading through values, leading with head and heart, and being yourself (George, 2003; George, Sims, McLean & Mayer, 2007). Shamir and Eilam, for example, argue that

> authentic leaders can be distinguished from less authentic or inauthentic leaders by four self-related characteristics: 1) the degree of person role merger i.e. the salience of the leadership role in their self-concept, 2) the level of self-concept clarity and the extent to which this clarity centers around strongly held values and convictions, 3) the extent to which their goals are self-concordant, and 4) the degree to which their behavior is consistent with their self-concept.
>
> *(Shamir & Eilam, 2005, p. 399)*

We can even develop instruments to measure authentic leadership (e.g., Neider & Schriesheim, 2011). Sparrowe (2005) argues that constructing "authenticity" in these ways, is very leader-centric, narcissistic and does not recognize multiple views and selves. He is one of the relatively few leadership scholars (see also Jackson, 2005; Nyberg & Sveningsson, 2014) who draw on phenomenology (particularly the work of Ricoeur) to explicate authenticity as a form of narrative self: "When narrative recounts how an individual acts out of character yet, in time and through a succession of events, he or she comes to their senses, it portrays inauthenticity and then authenticity in the story of a life" (p. 430). Authenticity in a phenomenological sense is about understanding, being responsible, and being true to ourselves in relation to the pressures and influences around us (Cunliffe, 2009).

How might those involved in leadership then begin to learn and possibly change their practice? Zundel (2013) argues that from a Heideggerian perspective, because we are thrown into an undefinable world, we learn not by disengaged reflection, as common in many leadership courses, but by a whole body "walking around" and sensing possibilities in our worlds—a contemplative thinking. Phenomenology draws attention to embodied leadership practice (Ladkin, 2008; Sinclair, 2011), which connects with such a pre-reflective dwelling in and walking around. "Phenomenologically, practices and practising are embodied and as such inter-involve various bodily modes of belonging, relationships and practical engagements" (Küpers, 2013, p. 337). In other words, we live in a sense-world, we feel practices, and practices are inscribed in our bodies. Heidegger himself suggests that temporary breakdowns or disruptions offer moments for reflection within practice that involve questioning one's very being in the practice.

> Watch me unravel, I'll soon be naked
> Lying on the floor (lying on the floor)
> *(Weezer, Undone-The Sweater Song)*

Segal (2010) addresses the impact of such "unraveling" on our practical ways of coping. He argues that the "conditions in which the philosophical question of leadership becomes important is when we lose all sense of leadership" (p. 384): when old taken-for-granted practices and ways of being are questioned and need to be replaced with new. Breakdowns, such as a leadership crisis, and "unraveling," and feelings of self-doubt about our role, abilities, values, or relationships cause us to question our everyday ways of coping, how we are "existentially" in our practice, and require us to "feel our way" around the circumstances in which we find ourselves. Segal suggests that breakdowns can be an impetus for learning leadership, but that this requires a "reflexive attunement" in which we question our assumptions, ways of talking, and acting in our practices.

Interpretive practice as/for leadership: A Gadamerian perspective

In this section of the chapter we focus on Gadamer, and particularly on his principal work *Truth and Method* (Gadamer, 2013 [1975]; note that the revised edition has a useful afterword that directly addresses practice). This magnum opus has some roots in Heidegger's work, perhaps most directly in relation to Heidegger's *Ontology: The Hermeneutics of Facticity* (Heidegger, 1999 [1928]), although it clearly also shows connections to *Being and Time* (1962); Palmer (2010) provides further debate on these connections. Building on Heidegger, Gadamer focuses on the universality of hermeneutics, focusing on reflection on and within the everyday inescapability of interpretation, rather than situations of disruption that lead to moments of *particular* reflective awareness. In doing so, he offered distinct possibilities for how hermeneutics was to develop, both as an approach to method in the human sciences but more importantly as a way of framing *understanding* as ontology; or, combining both, as "the ontological grounding of the humanities' practices" (Davey, 2010).

Practice is then, for Gadamer, hermeneutic practice; interpretation is to be seen as intrinsic to human experience and practice and is effectively our way of being. Thus every interpretation (of a text, object, conversation …) is a "real" event, a *genuine* presentation of the "being" of the thing, an instantiation but not a summation of it. From this point of view interpretations are realities, but they are not *exhaustive* realities (c.f. Fristedt, 2010). How is this so? Gadamer approaches his ontological characterization of interpretive practice by arguing that humans are linguistic beings (partly through the idea that "being that can be understood is language"), whose every experience is *always already* interpretive.

Although Gadamer initially builds up his characterization through a consideration of engagement with works of art and texts, a picture of to-and-fro hermeneutic dialogue within a fusion of horizons is argued to apply to every event of interpretation/understanding. Thus a dialogue between persons takes (or at least can take) the same pattern (Hibbert, Siedlok & Beech, 2014). But it is important to understand what is meant by the fusion of horizons to make sense of this. To do so, we need to begin with an understanding of the particular situation, which is to say the horizon, of an individual interpreter. Every interpreter (that is every individual) is historically and linguistically situated. Thus on the one hand, one interprets diachronically from within a tradition as experience is grounded in encounters in which the world: "… is constantly being handed over to us—traditur—as an open totality. It is experience and nothing but experience. It is always co-present when the world is experienced, when unfamiliarity is cancelled, when something becomes clear, when insight happens …" (Gadamer, 2006, p. 48).

But on the other hand, one also interprets synchronically from within the current social context of debate. And these diachronic and synchronic dimensions (c.f. Vandevelde, 2010, who labels the dimensions "vertical" and "horizontal") constitute our horizons, tied together in language. What may be understood between ourselves and a text or ourselves and another happens within language in the interpretive space afforded by the fusion of horizons: " … the interpreter and the text each possess his, her, or its own horizon and every moment of understanding is a fusion of these horizons" (Gadamer, 2006, p. 45).

Thus the nature of experience is always interpretive, and represents an event of understanding into which we are drawn. From this view, practice is the effecting of interpretation, in relation to particular tradition(s) that characterize understanding within a particular context or sphere of human activity. But this is not limited to the unconscious workings of tradition nor is it, in the manner of the natural sciences, simply about the interpretive move between the presuppositions proper to that sphere, and the application of them in practice.

Instead, Gadamer (2013 [1975]) argued for the possibility of critical reflection within practice; and Prado (2010, p. 151) took this further by arguing that Gadamer's project was generative, as its intent was "to instill openness to intellectual diversity and possibility, rather than to inculcate intellectual practices and dispositions … " Malpas and Zabala (2010, p. xv) agree, arguing that: "Pluralism, engagement and conversation are three key consequences of hermeneutical thought and practice—and not only as it plays out politically, but also 'philosophically.'" That is, practice, from a Gadamerian philosophical hermeneutic perspective, therefore involves reflection and unforeseen possibilities emerging in understanding. This is because individuals can enter dialogue on the "horizontal" contextual dimension (Vandevelde, 2010), which potentiates new events of understanding that add to the historical "vertical" dimension of tradition—and vice versa.

Thus the dialogical nature (or at least potential) of interpretive practice allows the interpreter to use tradition to speak to context and context to speak to tradition. Over time, an individual's experience of (interpretive) practice further enriches their ability to engage in dialogue. For this reason Davey argued (Davey, 2011, p. 48) that "practices have their rules, but good practice is not a matter of blindly following them [instead, individuals develop through] a prolonged practice of discernment." Gadamer (2013 [1975]) and his followers see the dialogic development of the individual through the practice of interpretation—and the interpretation that *is* practice—as intrinsic to the character of our social life. Risser (1997, p. 115–116) puts it this way: "Hermeneutics as practical philosophy uncovers (in its theoretical attitude toward the practice of interpretation) the insight that practical rationality is unique to our social life as a natural human capacity."

Gadamer (2013 [1975]) also, following Aristotle, associated this intrinsic human capacity in the practice of interpretation with practical rationality (phronesis). He regarded practice as its own domain of knowledge that should not be displaced by the technical rationality of the natural sciences, and was scornful of the mis-understanding (or forgetting) of practice in the natural sciences: " ... since science views its purpose as isolating the cause of events—natural and historical—it is acquainted with practice only as the application of science. But that is a 'practice' that requires no special account. Thus the concept of technology displaced that of practice; in other words, the competence of experts has marginalized political reason" (Gadamer, 2013, p. 581)

Gadamer argued against the apparent triumph of technical rationality in "... an age credulous about science to the point of superstition" (2013, p. 577). Instead he suggested that the personal development of hermeneutic practice was not like the acquisition or refinement of some technique; this is because of the dialogic nature of understanding, in which that which we seek to understand (or through which we encounter understanding) speaks to us and addresses us in our historical situation:

> ... in hermeneutics history co-determines the consciousness of the person who understands. [...] On this depends the whole richness of the herme-neutic universe, which includes everything intelligible. Since it brings this whole breadth into play, it forces the interpreter to play with his own pre-judices at stake. These are the winnings of reflection that accrue from prac-tice, and practice alone. [...] In truth hermeneutic experience extends as far as does reasonable beings openness to dialogue.
>
> *(Gadamer, 2013, p. 592)*

What Gadamer (2013) is suggesting is that in understanding in genuine, dialogic interpretive practice (and he argued that anything less is inauthentic), our basis for understanding is in play along with that which we seek to understand. The stakes are maximal, as our ends are matters for reflection (perhaps for discovery) along with the means, in the same event of interpretation. This is because practice is not reflective in relation to some ultimate purpose, but instead in relation to a con-sistency in our practice, a consistency that is about historical continuity. Historical continuity is established through the series of events of interpretation through which we receive tradition and hand it on (c.f. Hibbert & Huxham, 2010). This is a continuity that, therefore allows for change through generations:

It is thus that the guiding image of the individual as of the society is formed, and in such a way that the ideals of a younger generation, precisely in differing from those of an older, determine them further—that is, establish them—through the concrete practice of their own behaviour within their own field of play and context of ends.

(Gadamer, 2013, p. 594–595)

Overall practice, from a Gadamerian perspective, is intrinsically hermeneutic, and involves dialogue that encompasses synchronic engagement with (others in) our social contexts and diachronic engagement with our tradition(s). Through this interpretive engagement, practice provides a continuity of understanding as tradition, in and through the events of understanding that we (co-)create.

From this Gadamerian view of practice we see leadership-as-practice as a situated event in dialogue; influence is in play in these events, but those interpreted as "leading" and "following" are both influenced. The situatedness of such events—in both the social context of current debate and the historical context of tradition—is important. Within this context the influence that enables leadership is rhetorical, and appeals to individuals reflectively and holistically:

It is the realm of practice and humanity in general [...] where controversial issues are decided by reasonable consideration. The arts of rhetoric and argumentation (and their silent analogue, thoughtful deliberation with oneself) are at home here. If rhetoric appeals to the feelings, as has long been clear, that in no way means it falls outside of the reasonable.

(Gadamer, 2013, p. 592)

But, critically, reason and reflection is argued to be open to participants in the dialogue, and this means that the *ends* that an individual seeks to advance are open to question, as well as the means (or desired action that is sought from others). The dialogic nature of the event of understanding means that the presumed ends are not necessarily given, as (as discussed earlier) individuals understand differently within the conceptual space opened up by the fusion of horizons. Gadamer's view of reasonable reflection is not a picture of a tidy and easily delimited process, but instead a situation in which everything is in play:

What role does reason play in the context of human practice? In every case it takes the general form of reflection. That means it does not merely apply reasonable, efficient means in order to achieve pregiven purposes and ends. It is not confined to the realm of purposive rationality. [...] Hermeneutic reflection makes ends conscious as well, and not in the sense of a knowledge of previously established ultimate ends, followed by reflection about the legitimacy of means.

(Gadamer, 2013, p. 593)

How can one engage in learning for leadership if one accepts that the dialogic nature of understanding means that both means and ends are in play (and therefore at risk)? For Gadamer (2013) this relates to grounding in tradition, and an *authenticity* that is rooted in consistency with the past. This grounding gives those-who-would-be-leaders some anchorage in their current social context, so that their practices can be both a new instantiation and a continuing of the history of interpretation.

This Gadamerian take on practice and leadership-as-practice leads to further questions: about how the creative, dialogic relationship of self and other is to be understood in hermeneutic experience; and about how the continuity of understanding between events in conversation and the long-term (hi)story of tradition is effected. For answers to these questions—on the relationship of self and other, and the relationships between conversational time and narrative time—we leave Gadamer and turn to Ricoeur.

Practice and narrative self: A Ricoeurian perspective

> Practice is activity considered together with its complex context and in particular with the social conditions which give it meaning in a world actually experienced.
>
> *(Granger, 1968 cited in Ricoeur, 1981, p. 136)*

Paul Ricoeur (1981, 1988, 1992) has written extensively on hermeneutics, narrative, and ethical selfhood. His work has rarely been taken up in the leadership arena, but has much to offer in relation to leadership identity and ethics (see Cunliffe & Eriksen, 2011; Nyberg & Sveningsson, 2014; Sparrowe, 2005, for examples).

Ricoeur (1988) argues that we make sense of and shape our lives and our identity as narrative: "To answer the question 'Who?' … is to tell the story of a life" (p. 246). He suggests that we do so by emplotting or constructing a coherent narrative from narratives we already know (e.g., narratives about those in leadership positions—what they do and what they are) and discordant events and situations we face. The narrative is never complete as situations are always open to further interpretations and new meanings. And while we might narrate the story from our own perspective, we do so from many intersecting narratives around us—other characters are involved. He therefore extends Heidegger's notion of *Being*, suggesting that *otherness* mediates between self and the world, not just another person separate from us but someone who is an integral part of who we are: we are selves-in-relation-with-others, that is intersubjectivity. Therefore our identity is a narrative identity, an "unending work of interpretation" (1992, p. 179), and because it is interpreted in interactions with others, it is also a way of connecting us to others (p. 117). Ricoeur also argues that human action is based on description, narration, and prescription (1992, p. 114) because narratives help us make sense of situations, evaluate them, and then decide what to do. As Sparrowe (2005, p. 426) states, "For Ricoeur, narrative is a bridge between what is lived and what is told, between tradition and innovation, between what was, what is, and what might be, and between an author of a narrative and a reader ... ." The "self" is created by constructing a coherent narrative around what it means to *be* in leadership. In this way, a person is both "a reader and the writer of his own life" (Ricoeur, 1988, p. 246).

Ricoeur also argues that narration and narrative identity bring an ethical responsibility because they are always in relation to others. "The actions refigured by narrative fictions are complex ones, rich in anticipations of an ethical nature. Telling a story ... is deploying an imaginary space for thought experiments in which moral judgement operates in a hypothetical mode" (1992, p. 170). Based on the work of Ricoeur, Cunliffe and Eriksen (2011) develop the notion of *relational integrity*: the need for those in leadership positions to be "sensitive, attuned and responsive to moments of difference, and feel responsible for working with those differences" (p. 1438). They argue that this shifts attention from individualistic forms of leadership to more relational ones, where those involved in leading recognize they are always speaking and acting in relation to others and in doing so narrating meanings, organizational "realities" and identities in lived experience. From Ricoeur's perspective, ethics are not just institutional but are also interpersonal, relating to ethical selfhood and how we treat others. This means individuals need to develop a reflexive awareness of themselves in relation to others and recognize their responsibility to act and relate in ethical ways.

A reflexive understanding of how we make sense of ourselves in relation to others can be accounted for and conceptualized through the Ricoeurian (1992) idea of emplotment. Sparrowe summarizes emplotment in this way: "The emplotment of the self is not a process of winnowing what is distinctively one's own from all that surrounds one; instead, it is a process of crafting a distinctive plot through which one's own character takes shape. It involves experimentation with provisional story lines, counterfactual pasts, and hypothetical futures" (2005, p. 432)

This process of emplotment provides for a distinctive approach to leadership learning. In particular, it offers four particular ways in which individuals may develop both their own sense of self in a relational context, and the rhetorical capabilities to use their sense and story of oneself as a means of working with others. The first of these approaches to leadership learning is through engagement with classic (in Gadamer's (2013) sense) narratives, especially those of a bio-graphical nature (c.f. Sparrowe, 2005), and even more particularly where these classics are seen as accounts of the enactment of virtue(s) (c.f. Schedlitzki, Jarvis & MacInne, forthcoming). The second approach is through practice in narrating—developing the ability to narrate one's own story—but importantly, in the context of life with others that are taken seriously and valued as oneself (Ricouer, 1992). The third is to be creative about narratives and narrative identity. Ricoeur suggests that engagement with literature can lead to more creative narratives (pp. 148, 162)—individuals can then re-story themselves through access to characters and stories in films and other media (Kelan, 2013; Schedlitzki, *et al.*, forthcoming).

Concluding discussion

We began by highlighting the philosophy underpinning practice-based studies in general, arguing that the contested nature of practice can be traced to the various ontological and epistemological positioning of practice-based scholars. We then examined the implications for leadership-as-practice. In particular, we focused on three hermeneutic phenomenological scholars and assessed how some of their ideas have influenced—and may influence—leadership-as-practice. Heidegger, Gadamer, and Ricoeur draw attention to the importance of social context and lived experience and how our experience helps us to make sense. Heidegger and Ricoeur particularly elaborate the relationship between *Being*/selfhood and our world. Gadamer also illuminates the horizons within which we understand that relationship: our historical situation which provides the ground of being and the dynamic social context that opens up the possibility of interpreting (and enacting) ourselves differently as relational beings. But these summary points should not mask the fact that there are some tensions and distinct differences between three philosophical perspectives in terms of their insights for leadership and leadership-as-practice. There are three particular areas that we wish to highlight, each of which could be a useful focus for further reflection and research. These three areas of tension are: if and how individuals might shape organizations through practices; how particular characterizations of "leaders" can be associated with each of these perspectives; and the alternative stances on leadership ethics that flow from these. Each of these is addressed in turn below.

Shaping "organizations" through leadership practices

Each of the three focal authors in this account offers quite distinct differences in our expectations of what leadership practices may achieve within organizations. From a Heideggerian perspective, leadership-as-practice is concerned with everyday coping through interrupting unawareness and enabling authenticity moment-by-moment. Care-ful (Heideggerian) practice thus aims at authenticity in a relational context, but does so by (aiming at) enabling individuals to avoid being subsumed in thoughtless practice in those contexts. Heidegger also argues that the sleeping consensus of a population needs to be questioned for there is no once-and-for-all, fixed idea of superiority or truth. Thus, the authenticity of *everyone* is crucial: it is the authenticity of Ginsberg's *Howl*:

> The bum's as holy as the seraphim!
> The madman is holy as you my soul are holy!
> *(Ginsberg, 2001 [1956])*

An authenticity that is at best tenuously understood, that can seem strange to those that are "going with the flow." And this kind of (leadership) practice casts its influence *constructively* in the turn of a conversation, but destructively/disturbingly perhaps much further. Care-ful, Heideggerian practice is not easily associated with the conventional idea of leadership, which aims at influencing a collective towards a determined purpose over any substantial scale. For the purpose is always at issue, because social interactions, actions, practices, and meanings are contextualized and make sense only within *specific* spaces of intelligibility.

Gadamer perhaps takes us further towards the conventional leadership of organizations by surrendering such an independent view of authenticity. Rightly associated with conservatism, Gadamer's (2013) appeal to tradition implies that our practices are always constructed from and judged against the historical context. A shared tradition (one accommodated to some degree in a fusion of horizons) thus provides a basis for this or that leadership practice as being understood. But rhetorical and linguistic practice that appeals to tradition is in some ways led by it—that which speaks from (with) tradition asserts itself in being understood—and thus leadership-as-practice is constrained to surrender not to others in the current social context, but to those in the past (c.f. Hibbert & Huxham, 2010). It is constituted in a fusion of horizons, in which that towards which one is oriented is situated in understanding through dialogue between "leader(s)" and "follower(s)," but the leader may be construed as the tradition as well as the individual. Nevertheless we can imagine skilful dialogic practice that deploys the content of tradition with a degree of imagination and rhetorical flair to offer some preferred sense of direction.

Ricoeur (1992) brings imagination to the fore in emplotment. Fiction (drawn from culture and tradition) provides a source of thought-experiments that allow for variations in the narrative template for organizing ourselves and our stories (Sparrowe, 2005). Although not totally detaching practices from the ground of tradition as the basis of intelligibility, this view allows for creative practices to reach beyond the established historical context of understanding. Leadership-as-practice is authorial when seen in this light; practices of narration and narrating are central.

Overall we see an interesting dynamic emerging between the perspectives and the practices that they foreground. Gadamer helps us to see the practices of *grounding* and *explaining*, in which connections to tradition and language are made and the possibility of understanding is enabled. Heidegger's work suggests practices of *disturbing* and *detaching*, in which the everyday practicing of lived experience under the sway of tradition is interrupted and observed. Ricoeur's insights show the practices of *composing* and *narrating*, in which an interrupted and somewhat shaken tradition is recognizable, but turned to new purposes. Holding all three of these views in tension seems to provide for a plausible understanding of what leadership as *hermeneutic, phenomenological practice*(s) may entail.

Leadership practices and leadership ethics

In the preceding discussion we set out different hermeneutical perspectives on leadership practices and offered related characterizations of leadership. In this section we offer a brief articulation of the ethical positions that can be associated with each characterization. The Gadamerian practices of grounding and explaining are associated with legitimating ends against the interpreted historical content of tradition(s) (Gadamer, 2013). As such they can be characterized as supporting deontological ethics. In contrast the Heideggerian practices lead to relational ethics of care (Segal, 2010), as the equality of all and our interdependence are highlighted (although there is also an effort to disturb the complacent acceptance of this). The Ricoeurian (1992) position also has been strongly associated with relational ethics (Cunliffe & Eriksen, 2011), but the imaginative and creative potential of narrative emplotment and engagement with ideal narrative figures suggests virtue ethics. Thus overall, there are different ethical stances and priorities associated with practices developed from each of the philosophical positions. Does this, then, make "balanced" leadership a state of moral relativism, or signify conditions in which someone is called to account in ways that are specifically associated with their current mode of practicing? These are issues yet to be debated.

Emerging possibilities for research

To conclude, we wish to offer three indicative suggestions for research that have emerged from our philosophical speculation. First, we have outlined a number of particular kinds of practices that are suggested by considering leadership from each of the hermeneutic perspectives we have explored in this chapter. Ethnographic research that walks alongside individuals in their contexts of practicing might illuminate the degree to which our picture is useful, suggest alternative conceptualizations, and perhaps provide an account of how the various practices are enacted and connected over time. Second, research within the same contexts might also show the degree to which individuals are fluent in the enactment of different sets of practices (that is, differing in scope and scale) and how we might better characterize them and the effects with which they are associated. Third, extensive interpretive conversational research with those identified as representing particular kinds of leadership practice would help us to understand the felt moral strengths, tensions, and dilemmas as they are experienced.

References

Ashman, I. (2007). Existentialism and leadership: A response to John Lawler with some further thoughts. *Leadership*, 3(1), 91–107.

Barad, K. (2003). Posthumanist performativity: Toward an understanding of how matter comes to matter. *Signs: Journal of Women in Culture and Society*, 28(3), 801–831.

Bechky, B. A. (2003). Sharing meaning across occupational communities: The transformation of understanding on a production floor. *Organization Science*, 14(3), 312–330.

Bourdieu, P. (1972). *Outline of a theory of practice*. Cambridge: Cambridge University Press.

Carroll, B., Levy, L., & Richmond, D. (2008). Leadership-as-practice: Challenging the competency paradigm. *Leadership*, 4(4), 363–379.

Chia, R., & Holt, R. (2006). Strategy as practical coping: A Heideggerian perspective. *Organization Studies*, 27(5), 635–655.

Crevani, L., Lindgren, M., & Packendorff, J. (2010). Leadership not leaders: On the study of leadership as practices and interactions. *Scandinavian Journal of Management*, 26(1), 77–86.

Cunliffe, A. L. (2009). The philosopher leader: On relationalism, ethics and reflexivity—A critical perspective to teaching leadership. *Management Learning*, 40(1), 87–101.

Cunliffe, A. L., & Eriksen, M. (2011). Relational leadership. *Human Relations*, 64(11), 1425–1449.

Cunliffe, A. L. (2011). Crafting qualitative research: Morgan and Smircich 30 years on. *Organizational Research Methods*, 14(4), 647–673.

Cunliffe, A. L. (2015). Studying strategizing through ethnographic methods. In D. Golsorkhi, L. Rouleau, D. Seidl & E. Vaara (Eds.), *Cambridge handbook of strategy-as-practice* (2nd edition) (pp. 435–450). Cambridge: Cambridge University Press.

Davey, N. (2010). Truth, method and transcendence. In J. Malpas & S. Zabala (Eds.), *Consequences of hermeneutics* (pp. 25–44). Evanston, IL: Northwestern University Press.

Davey, N. (2011). Philosophical hermeneutics: An education for all seasons? In P. Fairfield (Ed.), *Education, dialogue and hermeneutics* (pp. 39–60). London: Continuum.

Dewey, J. (1938). *Logic: The theory of inquiry*. New York: Holt.

Engeström, Y. (2004). *Developmental work research: Expanding activity theory in practice*. Vol 12. International Cultural-Historical Human Sciences. Germany: Docupoint Magdeburg.

Feldman, M. S., & Orlikowski, W. J. (2011). Theorizing practice and practicing theory. *Organization Science*, 22(5), 1240–1253.

Feldman, M. S., & Rafaeli, A. (2002). Organizational routines as sources of connections and understandings. *Journal of Management Studies*, 39(3), 309–332.

Fenton, C., & Langley, A. (2011). Strategy as practice and the narrative turn. *Organization Studies*, 32(9), 1171–1196.

Foucault, M. (1976). *The archaeology of knowledge*. New York: Harper Row.

Fristedt, P. (2010). Philosophical hermeneutics and the relativity of truth and meaning. *International Journal of Philosophical Studies*, 18(4), 473–492.

Gadamer, H.-G. (2006). Classical and philosophical hermeneutics. *Theory, Culture and Society*, 23(1), 29–56.

Gadamer, H.-G. (2013). *Truth and method*, revised second edition. London: Bloomsbury. (Original English edition: 1975, London: Bloomsbury.)

Garfinkel, H. (1967). *Studies in ethnomethodology*. Englewood Cliffs, NJ: Prentice-Hall.

Geiger, D. (2009). Revisiting the concept of practice: Toward an argumentative understanding of practicing. *Management Learning*, 40(2), 129–144.

Ginsberg, A. (2001 [1956]). *Howl and other poems*. San Francisco: City Lights.

George, B. (2003). *Authentic leadership: Rediscovering the secrets to creating lasting value*. San Francisco: Jossey-Bass.

George, B., Sims, P., McLean, A. N., & Mayer, D. (2007). Discovering your authentic leadership. *Harvard Business Review*, February, 129–138.

Gherardi, S. (2006). *Organizational knowledge: The texture of workplace learning*. Oxford: Blackwell Publishing.

Gherardi, S. (2009). Introduction: The critical power of the 'practice lens'. *Management Learning*, 40(2), 115–128.

Heidegger, M. (1962). *Being and time*. Oxford: Blackwell.

Heidegger, M. (1999). *Ontology: The hermeneutics of facticity*. Bloomington: Indiana University Press. (Assembled by his students from his 1928 lecture series and published posthumously.)

Hibbert, P., & Huxham, C. (2010). The past in play: Tradition in the structures of collaboration. *Organization Studies*, 31(5), 525–554.

Hibbert, P., Siedlok, F., & Beech, N. (2014). The role of interpretation in learning practices, in the context of collaboration. *Academy of Management Learning and Education.* Available online early, doi: 10.5465/amle.2014.0004.

Jackson, K. T. (2005). Towards authenticity: A Sartrean perspective on business ethics. *Journal of Business Ethics*, 58(4), 307–325.

Kelan, E. K. (2013). The becoming of business bodies: Gender, appearance, and leadership development. *Management Learning*, 44(1), 45–61.

Kellogg, K. (2011). Hot lights and cold steel: Cultural and political toolkits for practice change in surgery. *Organization Science*, 22(2), 482–502.

Küpers, W. M. (2013). Embodied inter-practices of leadership—Phenomenological perspectives on relational and responsive leading and following. *Leadership*, 9(3), 335–357.

Ladkin, D. (2008). Leading beautifully: How mastery, congruence and form create the aesthetic of embodied leadership practice. *Leadership Quarterly*, 19(1), 31–41.

Lather, P. (2006). Paradigm proliferation is a good thing to think with: Teaching research in education as a wild profusion. *International Journal of Qualitative Studies in Education*, 19(1), 35–57.

Latour, B. (2005). *Reassembling the social: An introduction to actor-network-theory.* Oxford: Oxford University Press.

Law, J., & Mol, A. (2002). *Complexities: Social studies of knowledge practices* (2nd edition). Durham, NC: Duke University Press.

Lawler, J. (2005). The essence of leadership? Existentialism and leadership. *Leadership*, 1(2), 215–231.

Lyotard, J. (1979). *The postmodern condition.* Manchester: Manchester University Press.

Malpas, J., & Zabala, S. (2010). Introduction: Consequences of hermeneutics. In J. Malpas & S. Zabala (Eds.), *Consequences of hermeneutics* (pp. xi–xviii). Evanston, IL: Northwestern University Press.

Mead, G. H. (1938). *The philosophy of the act.* Chicago, IL: University of Chicago Press.

Merleau-Ponty, M. (1964). *Signs* (R. C. McCleary trans.). Evanston, IL: Northwestern University Press.

Neider, L. L., & Schriesheim, C. A. (2011). The authentic leadership inventory (ALI): Development and empirical tests. *Leadership Quarterly*, 22(6), 1146–1164.

Nicolini, D. (2009). Zooming in and out: Studying practices by switching theoretical lenses and trailing connections. *Organization Studies*, 30(12), 1391–1418.

Nicolini, D. (2011). Insights from the field of telemedicine. *Organization Science*, 22(3), 602–620.

Nyberg, D., & Sveningsson, S. (2014). Paradoxes of authentic leadership: Leader identity struggles. *Leadership*, 10(4), 437–455.

Palmer, R. (2010). Two contrasting Heideggerian elements in Gadamer's philosophical hermeneutics. In J. Malpas & S. Zabala (Eds.), *Consequences of hermeneutics* (pp. 121–131). Evanston, IL: Northwestern University Press.

Prado, C. (2010). Gadamer and Rorty: From interpretation to conversation. In J. Malpas & S. Zabala (Eds.), *Consequences of hermeneutics* (pp. 147–160). Evanston, IL: Northwestern University Press.

Raelin, J. (2011). From leadership-as-practice to leaderful practice. *Leadership*, 7(2), 195–211.

Ricoeur, P. (1981). *Hermeneutics and the human sciences: Essays on language, action and interpretation.* Cambridge: Cambridge University Press.

Ricoeur, P. (1988). *Time and narrative*, Vol. 3. Chicago, IL: University of Chicago Press.

Ricoeur, P. (1992). *Oneself as another*. Chicago, IL: University of Chicago Press.

Risser, J. (1997). *Hermeneutics and the voice of the other*. Albany, NY: State University of New York Press.

Samra-Fredericks, D. (2003). Strategizing as lived experience and strategists' everyday efforts to shape strategic direction. *Journal of Management Studies*, 40(1), 141–174.

Sandberg, J., & Dall'Alba, G. (2009). Returning to practice anew: A life-world perspective. *Organization Studies*, 30(12), 1349–1368.

Sandberg, J., & Tsoukas, H. (2011). Grasping the logic of practice: Theorizing through practical rationality. *Academy of Management Review*, 36(2), 338–360.

Schatzki, T. R. (2001). Introduction: Practice theory. In K. Knorr Cetina, T. R. Schatzki & E. von Savigny (Eds.), *The practice turn in contemporary theory* (pp. 1–14). Abingdon: Routledge.

Schatzki, T. R. (2005). The sites of organizations. *Organization Studies*, 26(3), 465–484.

Schedlitzki, D., Jarvis, C., & MacInnes, J. (forthcoming) Leadership development: A place for storytelling and Greek mythology? *Management Learning*, doi:10.1177/1350507614560303.

Schutz, A. (1972). *The phenomenology of the social world*. Evanston, IL: Northwestern University Press.

Segal, S. (2010). A Heideggerian approach to practice-based reflexivity. *Management Learning*, 41(4), 379–389.

Shamir, B. & Eilam, G. (2005). "What's your story?": A life-stories approach to authentic leadership development. *Leadership Quarterly*, 16, 395–417.

Shotter, J. (2008 [1993]) *Conversational realities revisited: Life, language, body and world*. Chagrin Falls, OH: Taos Institute Publications.

Sinclair, A. (2011). *Body possibilities in leadership*. London: Sage.

Sparrowe, R.T. (2005). Authentic leadership and the narrative self. *Leadership Quarterly*, 16(3), 419–439.

Vandevelde, P. (2010). What is the ethics of interpretation? In J. Malpas & S. Zabala (Eds.), *Consequences of hermeneutics* (pp. 288–305). Evanston, IL: Northwestern University Press.

Zundel, M. (2013). Walking to learn: Rethinking reflection for management learning. *Management Learning*, 44(2), 109–126.

4

DEMOCRATIC ROOTS

Feeding the multiple dimensions of leadership-as-practice

Philip A. Woods

Understanding the understanding of leadership

What is good leadership? Is leadership about the exercise of power? What is the role of ethics in leadership? Such questions, and many others, are behind the drive to understand the concept of leadership.

Much attention, accordingly, is given to addressing the phenomenon of leadership analytically, that is to advancing how it can be understood and described in better ways that then inform practice and reflections on leadership. Both the movement to understand leadership as leadership-as-practice (L-A-P) and other approaches, such as moves to see leadership as distributed, have sought to do this. For example, L-A-P is concerned to learn more about "where, how, and why leadership work is being organized and accomplished" (Raelin, 2011, p. 196); Gronn (2002) argues that understanding leadership is better served by focusing on a "unit of analysis" that includes varieties and patterns of distributed leadership beyond the more familiar focus on the single leader or the senior elite.

I find it helpful to see these approaches to conceptualizing and describing leadership in the light of the sociological theory of analytical dualism (Archer, 2003). The debate about the agency/structure divide in sociology concerns the question of who, or what, makes society. Is it people (and their agency—a concept also addressed by Simpson, Chapter 8, this volume); or is it social forces such as social class, organizations, and culture? Both seem to be important. However, for many the idea of seeing the latter as forces distinct from people is to reify them: it is to render to them an ontological existence that they do not warrant. After all, if there were no people, there would be no social class, organizations, and other social structures. But if the view is taken that people are *the* sources of social life, this ignores the very real effects of social phenomena beyond individuals' control—factors such as social class, gender, ethnic inequalities, and the effects of different cultures and structural positionings within organizations that have tangible impacts on people. How can this divide be overcome? One way is to collapse the agency and structure into one entity—the "duality of structure"—that encompasses them both (Giddens, 1979). In this conception, the rules and structures of society are internal to the individual and only made real when people act and interact with others: they are "memory traces" (Giddens, 1986, p. 25). This, however, compresses everything into the individual. Archer (1995, 2003) makes a convincing case that to understand social life we need to recognize the power and real effects of both agency and structure. This means recognizing that agency and structure interact continuously over time and that the elements of structure are emergent phenomena of this process. Although there may be ontological arguments about how or whether structures can be conceived as "real" phenomena, it makes sense heuristically—because structure has recognizable consequences for people—to envisage agency and structure as separate dimensions of the ongoing flow of social life. To take this further, in my view, it helps to articulate the analytical frame as a *trialectic* process (Figure 4.1)—an ongoing interaction between structure, person, and practice (or action) (Woods, 2005). Within this

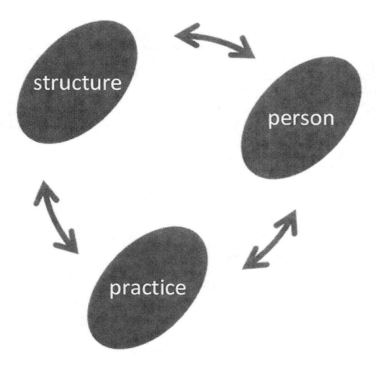

FIGURE 4.1 Trialectic process.

continuous interaction, social structures—cultures, institutions, and patterns of relationships—emerge.

There are implications for understanding leadership. Conceived as a social process in this trialectic framework, leadership is not reducible to individual actions, nor to personal capabilities, nor to social determinants such as institutional interests, cultures, and patterns of relationships. Leadership is, rather, a process that is emergent: leadership emerges from ongoing interactions between the person (the self's capabilities, motivations, values, intentions, etc.), practice (actions with and through other social actors), and structure (the patterns of relationships, cultural ideas and values, institutional structures, and resource dependencies within which the person and their practice are located).

It has to be asked, however, whether a framework that is analytical in intent is sufficient for a practice such as leadership. The answer rests in part on how we understand practice. One way is to understand practice as behavior, a pattern of activity and the carrying out of techniques and procedures. Practice in this perspective is defined by its outward features—that is, the actions and their consequences—and the surface intentions that guide and motivate the actions.

Another way is to understand practice as a process co-formed with others and through an interactive relationship with a well-spring of personal and social factors. These factors are an active part of practice, shaping and feeding the outward features of action and in turn affected by action and its consequences. In other words, practice is continuously interacting with and being formed by structural and personal factors as in the trialectic process illustrated in Figure 4.1. These factors include the ideas and values that ground the intention giving rise to action, and the meaning that action has or comes to have as it interacts with other people and their actions. Practice, from this perspective, is an unfolding activity that is co-constructed and involves enacting and creating knowledge, values, identities, and power relations (Gherardi, 2003).

In a study of interpretations of entrepreneurialism for educational purposes, my co-researcher and I found it helpful to recognize the layers of meaning that contextualize the interpretations (Woods & Woods, 2011), and in particular to recognize that these layers include "architectonic" principles, that is principles which "relate to the fundamental structuring elements of a person's overall view of life" (McLaughlin, 1996, p. 12). Architectonic principles can take different forms: religious, democratic, economistic, spiritual, secular, and so on. A person may be guided or influenced (explicitly or implicitly) by one or more of these kinds of architectonic principle. The principles will have a particular detailed content according to the cultural background, reflections, education, and ongoing dialogues of the person. Architectonic principles, although powerful, are not necessarily unchanging. They can be tested and altered through experience and interaction with other social actors. The "overall view of life" represented by these architectonic principles does not stand apart from practice, but imbues it with prefigured senses of what is good, appropriate, and feasible. Ideas on what is good, right, and to be valued are part of these worldviews. Hence, ethical view-points inform and are integral to practice.

In summary, two key points are apparent from the above discussion. Firstly, leadership is emergent. The practice of leadership takes place within a trialectic process of structure, person, and practice; and it is a continuous exercise of social construction between interacting parties (Raelin, 2011, pp. 197–198). Secondly, as well as knowledge, identities, and power relations, leadership carries, enacts, and constructs values and ethical viewpoints.

Two views of the ethical nature of human beings

The analytical drive of L-A-P places a premium on recognizing and studying what *is*. If it is accepted, however, that leadership carries, enacts, and constructs values and ethical viewpoints, it follows that any understanding of leadership that has nothing to offer concerning the ethical and values dimension of leadership practice will fall short. By its nature, study and research that are to be relevant to leadership practice have to address questions about the ethical aspects of leadership ends, processes, and consequences. They cannot suggest what is good leadership with-out having some stance on what is ethically good. That stance then provides a basis to consider whether any particular example of leadership is conducive or otherwise to the well-being and development of those affected by that leadership (which includes those who are designated as leaders). It is important to explore, therefore, with regard to any understanding of leadership its (stated or unstated) viewpoint concerning what is ethically good for people. This applies to L-A-P.

Arguably, certain ethical viewpoints are embedded in much of the writing around L-A-P. For example, a concern to understand how some people may be marginalized through processes of leadership practice suggests an ethical interest in disparities of power and patterns of unjust exclusion. If so, identifying and problematizing injustice implies an ethical view on the value of social justice and participation. L-A-P is viewed as possessing a "natural affinity" with democracy (Raelin, 2011, p. 195), which resonates with a recent focus on "collaborative agency" that involves "fair dialogical exchange" (Raelin, 2014, p. 7). Yet Raelin (2011, p. 204) also suggests that L-A-P can be considered more neutral than "leaderful practice," as the latter is explicitly based on democratic values and requires "the co-creation of a community by all who are involved interdependently in its development."

The practice in any particular context that is the focus of study by L-A-P as an analytical perspective is not of necessity or by definition fair and democratic. Practice is also "contestation" (Raelin, 2011, p. 197). The co-construction of practice can be the site of conflict, exclusion, the exercise of power and clashes of interest, which may challenge and undermine social justice and democratic values. People engaged in influencing the work and direction of an organization can equally be carriers of institutional and personal interests and of cultural ideas that position others hierarchically according to signifiers that may include gender, social class, and ethnic background. Research on the practice of distributed leadership provides examples of social positioning and power differences that emerge privileging, for example, one gender as against another (e.g. Scribner & Bradley-Levine, 2010; Woods & Roberts, 2015).

We have to dig deeper into the philosophical anthropology underpinning L-A-P to get a sense of its underlying ethical orientation in relation to democracy. While L-A-P is "consistent with democratic practices and outcomes" (Raelin, 2014, p. 14), is it in fact more closely aligned with or grounded in democratic values?

People are beings capable of the creative accomplishment of working together in ways that generate leadership as a practice. That includes creatively co-constructing the ethics and values in leadership practice which have ramifications within and beyond the organization (Western, 2013). From the L-A-P perspective, people in organizations are essentially relational beings. They do not act as individuals—that is, as the generators, each sufficient to itself, of their actions. They are communicative beings whose interactions are not confined to instrumental exchanges that seek to cause or influence change: their interactions include expressive exchanges about feelings, ideas, and knowledge, and conversations that share meanings and are part of making sense of their work, selves, and organizational contexts (Raelin, 2011, pp. 200–201). They are communicative beings who embody some kind of "overall view of life" and expression of architectonic principles that frame a perspective on what is good and right.

I want to focus on a particular aspect raised by the question of whether L-A-P is in fact more than consistent with democratic values but intimately aligned with or grounded in them. The aspect I am focusing on is the ethical nature of the person that comprises one element of the trialectic social process—that is, the way of being that will lead to living ethically, or which at least is most conducive to developing towards a life that is ethically good. What is it in the ethical nature of human beings that enables people in leadership practice to be co-creators of values and action that are ethically good?

To assist in answering this question, it is helpful to recognize two contrasting views of the ethical nature of human beings—a philosophy of dependence and a philosophy of co-development—and to show their connections with different understandings of leadership.

Philosophy of dependence

The first is the view that, to be ethically good, people need to be directed and to follow an authority and rules. The latter will curb and shape the imperfections of the human being. This is termed a philosophy of dependence here. The belief underlying this perspective is that ethical signposts can be discovered and ethically correct action established by following the principle, theory, or vision that expresses ultimate moral truths, *and that an authority (a leader or set of leaders) is necessary to show which is the right principle, theory, or vision and to translate this into rules for practical action that others may follow.* The choice of which principle, theory, vision, and rules is crucial. The key implication for the follower is that, to be part of the good, ethical direction of change, they need to find the right leader who can make this choice.

The dependence cultivated by this philosophy is upon rules and the authority of the leader. The nature of the foundation of those rules and the authority of the leader can take different forms. For example, one basis for such authority is the notion that the correct ethical signposts can be found in a fundamental set of ideas—such as a revelatory text, an ultimate ideology or a set of foundational principles—and a leader who knows what needs to be done to shape the world so that it moves in the direction required by those ideas. This leader is followed because they can identify the authoritative rules and "principle-based theory" (Fryer, 2011, Chapter 2) that show the true ways to be and act in the world and can work out the right action from these rules or principle. Another basis is the charismatic visionary who is taken to be the fount of true knowledge and sets out the path for people to follow. The charismatic visionary may be the leader; or a follower of the visionary may embody or interpret his or her beliefs convincingly enough to be the charismatic leader in the name of the visionary. Leaders setting forth fundamental ideas or visions as the lodestar of change are governed by an ethic of ultimate ends (Weber, 1970).

Another kind of leader could be firmly fixed to following a utilitarian or consequentialist principle: namely, the notion that "what happens to human lives" (Sen, 2009, p. 213) as a result of an action is the overriding criterion for decisions. In contrast with the ethic of ultimate ends, this is Weber's (1970) ethic of responsibility in which the political leader judges decisions according to their consequences. In a further variant, the leader may use his or her judgment to balance both the ethic of ultimate ends and the ethic of responsibility as the situation requires, on the grounds that neither in itself is sufficient: the leader, as Weber argues, has to face up to the tensions between these two ethics and come to a judgment informed by both. The challenge and difficulties of making practical judgments informed by an ultimate ethic such as duty and a consequential concern for suffering is illustrated by Sen's (2009, pp. 208–214) discussion of a warrior's dilemma in fighting a just war: Sen shows how Arjuna—the warrior in the Sanskrit epic *Mahabharata*—leans towards the need to minimize death and suffering while also recognizing the imperative to follow his duty.

My concern here, however, is not the virtues or otherwise of the different ethical orientations of leaders, but the relationship between followers and leader encapsulated by the philosophy of dependence. In this perspective, followers—to be able to choose the ethical way—are dependent on the leadership they are given. They do not choose ethical ends or wrestle with clashing ethical imperatives. They require "conditioning socialisation" (Hellesnes, 1976, p. 18, quoted in Moos, 2004, p. 7) which reduces them to objects that have to be shaped to serve the right aims. The key implication for the follower is the imperative to find, or to be given, the right leader.

One manifestation of this is the Messiah leadership discourse that grew to be particularly influential from the 1980s, in which the leader creates the vision that imbues organizational members with a sense of direction and enthusiasm (Western, 2013, p. 218). The idea of the Messiah leader is compelling and attractive for some, but it is also problematic. For example, it depends on heroic leaders being able to live up to the ethical demands of such powerful leadership. And, as Fryer (2011, pp. 53–56) argues, translating rules (as promulgated by the leader) into practice is not as straightforward as it might seem: followership requires degrees of interpretation and discernment. More fundamentally, relying on authority and abstract rules can have a deleterious effect on people's ethical sensibilities, as Montesquieu (among others) warned (Dallmayr, 2007, p. 110). If people are reliant on authorities for answers to problems, under the pressure of expectations those authorities can end up offering fake remedies or following avoidance strategies in an effort to take people's minds off the real problems (Heifetz, 1994, pp. 72–73).

The philosophy of dependence is consistent with performative governance. Or, we might say, there is an affinity between the two. This is because performative governance essentially encourages widespread followership, even though it is also associated with advocating and almost idolizing (heroic, transformational, Messiah) leadership. Performative governance promotes a nexus of institutional and cultural pressures that define priorities and values in terms of narrow, measurable, and economistic criteria, and neo-liberalism as the "common sense" way of understanding society (Ward *et al.*, 2015a,b; Woods, 2013). In relation to individuals, it promotes performative subjective autonomy. By this I mean a sense of having some freedom to bring about change through one's own volition and informed by one's self identity (subjective autonomy), but having also a predisposition to use any such discretion (such as that facilitated by distributed leadership) to act in ways consistent with a managed identity that is defined by the values and priorities of neo-liberal and competitive governance measured by narrow calculations of achievement (Woods, 2014). There is, then, an affinity between the philosophy of dependence and performative subjective autonomy (Figure 4.2).

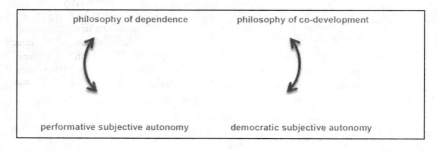

FIGURE 4.2 Affinities

This may involve strategies such as widening membership of committees, teams, and working groups so that those not in formal leadership roles are actively engaged in change, and allocating resources (financial and other forms, like time) that support engagement and development as co-leaders. Equally, some aspects of institutional structures may be designed or work in practice in ways that exclude or narrow opportunities for enabling people to be recognized, active, and effective participants in leadership.

Cultural: The kind of knowledge and values concerning leadership that are encouraged and become part of the organizational discourse are important. For example, an organizational culture in which leadership is viewed and valued as a phenomenon that emerges from ongoing flows of interactions across the organization and its hierarchy, and not one that arises simply from the actions of the single leader or small leadership elite, communicates a message of inclusion to organizational members. Seeing and valuing leadership in this way takes time to permeate an organization. And it may well be that such an inclusive organizational message plays out differently and is communicated less clearly in some parts of the organization than others. In other words, the knowledge and values that construct understandings of leadership may be differentially distributed across groups and sub-cultures within the organization.

Social: An open, inclusive social environment encourages participation in leadership and the sharing and testing of new ideas. This refers to the holarchic aesthetic rationality highlighted above in which relationships involve a valuing of people as individuals for themselves, and a sense of belonging, social equality, flexibility, fluidity, openness, respect, trust, and mutually affirming relationships. Such a social environment may not necessarily be a consistent feature across an organization. Organizational members' experience of relationships and interactions can vary according to the different groups, sub-cultures and departments within which they are located or identified with.

Person

A variety of capabilities and personal characteristics are important in influencing the degree to which people feel enabled and are prepared for being a contributor to leadership. These personal factors can include confidence, feelings of trust and respect, motivating values that encourage participation, and skills and experience in communication, co-leadership, and team-working. A rich democratic formulation of leadership, such as that provided by holistic democracy, suggests that the best leadership also entails a distributed capacity to exercise ethical judgment and to be responsive to a feel for social justice and fairness and to a sense of deep connectedness with people, nature, and spiritual sensibilities. Personal capabilities and characteristics are affected by the predispositions and the prior experience that the person brings to the organization, and also by the experience, personal reflections, and professional and personal development that the person undergoes as an organizational member. Personal capabilities and characteristics are therefore likely to differ between individuals, and although they are not fixed, their distribution is in some measure likely to be affected by structural variables such as position in the organizational hierarchy and professional and educational background. It is important to recognize, however, that it cannot be assumed that all such personal factors are more likely to be better developed among the more powerful and privileged: a capacity and feel for ethical matters and social justice, for example, may be more keenly developed among those with less power and without formal authority; and people may discover and develop previously unrecognized skills through new opportunities to engage in leadership practice. The range of capabilities and characteristics that people have and how these develop and emerge across the organizational membership will affect the distribution of engagement in leadership and innovative change.

Practice

Leadership practices comprise a complex and continuous stream of actions that constitute meetings (formal and informal), communication flows, decisions, ideas sharing, and myriad forms of interaction. The actions that make up this continuous stream of activity arise, as the trialectic process suggests, within a context in which the "inner workings" of persons interact with the structural features (institutional, cultural, social) of their organizational context. Leadership emerges from these day-to-day individual and collective leadership actions, which is to say that their (planned and unplanned) effects influence and shape the direction and nature of the organization and the efficiency and quality of organizational services and outcomes. The kinds of leadership actions and interactions that occur across the organization, how they vary in different contexts within the organization, and the ways in which organizational members and other stakeholders are included or excluded, are some of the factors important in understanding the distribution of leadership practice.

This section has suggested a richly democratic formulation (based on holistic democracy) of the philosophy of co-development. If such a formulation is accepted as underpinning L-A-P study and research, L-A-P can be said to have its roots in an understanding that the humanity of people is expressed through their collaborative development as ethical and democratic actors. This is more than saying L-A-P is consistent with democratic practices and outcomes. It is to assert that good leadership practice, from the L-A-P perspective, advances the values of a rich conception of democracy which includes the holistic well-being of people and social justice. This section has also suggested that the notion of multiple distributions is a helpful way of recognizing the breadth and challenges involved in making leadership more distributed and democratic. In the next section, I consider briefly some of the implications for L-A-P of these conclusions.

Implications for L-A-P

Firstly, the conclusions of the last paragraph do not mean abandoning the analytical drive of L-A-P. The analytical argument of L-A-P that the unit of leadership analysis should not be the single, designated leader remains a powerful one. Recognition of an explicit, democratic root, however, means that L-A-P is able to extend its reach into normative questions that are inescapably part of leadership practice.[2] Some studies within the L-A-P perspective may be more analytical in scope and purpose, whereas others may take a more normative and critical perspective.

Secondly, following from the latter point, it would be valuable to make sure that in these early times of the L-A-P movement an active strand of research is developed within L-A-P that critically interrogates leadership practices. This strand of research puts to the fore, for example, the investigation of conflict, power abuse, and social injustice. An indication of what one aspect of this strand of critical L-A-P research could look like is given by Ford (Chapter 11, this volume).

Thirdly, critical L-A-P research needs to reflect on, deploy and develop the appropriate conceptual tools and theories for its purposes. Ford (Chapter 11, this volume) connects L-A-P to the work of Critical Leadership Studies and reflects on gender and other bases for difference and exclusion in leadership practices. Consideration can also be given to the distinctive values-base of L-A-P as discussed in this chapter in terms of a democratic philosophy of co-development and to the question of what it means to critically interrogate leadership practices from this perspective.

Fourthly, the concept of multiple distributions provides an analytical framework for such critical interrogations. The multiple distributions framework poses the question: To what degree and in what ways are factors giving rise to leadership distributed in each of the elements of the trialectic process (structures, person, and practice)? This may be answered through a systematic audit of these elements. A systematic audit can be a means of investigating L-A-P in one setting or as a way of organizing the gathering of data in different cases to compare differing realities of L-A-P across those cases. An audit of multiple distributions may ask the kind of questions in Box 4.1, which can draw from a variety of conceptual tools: for example, the notion of distribution of capitals—the properties of people and groups, such as social and professional capitals, which influence perceived relative worth, social positioning, and the exercise of influence and power (Noordegraaf & Schinkel, 2011; Woods & Roberts, 2015); critical ideas such as the proposition that participation in performative cultures promotes "responsibilisation" rather than genuine involvement (Rose, 1999, p. 214); and the contrast between democratic subjective autonomy and performative subjective autonomy (Woods, 2014). The questions in Box 4.1 are by no means intended to be a definitive list, but are offered as illustrative.

BOX 4.1 MULTIPLE DISTRIBUTIONS FRAMEWORK

Structure

Institutional

What roles (formal and informal) exist to provide leadership opportunities?
What institutional mechanisms are there to facilitate collaborative working and the sharing of ideas and learning from innovations?
To what extent is formal authority distributed across the organization?
Are there institutional mechanisms to facilitate participation in setting the strategic direction and values of the organization?
Who allocates resources (not only financial, but also time for example)? To what degree is there devolved decision making about use of resources? Are resources allocated to support engagement and development as co-leaders?

Cultural

What assumptions, ideas, and values does the organization convey about what leadership means? Is greatest value placed on top-down leadership by senior leaders, or is a message sent out that participation in leadership is valued from across the organization?
To what extent is there a shared view among organizational members about leadership in their organization? Do they view leadership as hierarchical, or do they see and value leadership as a practice that occurs across the organization?

Social

How do organizational members perceive and experience relationships in the organization?
To what extent are belonging, respect, trust, and feelings of support distributed equally across the organization?
Is the organization's internal social environment experienced as open, fluid, and encouraging of boundary spanning by some, but as closed, fixed, and dominated by boundaries by others?

Person

Do people feel they are part of their organization's leadership practice? Is it part of their identity as organizational members?
What is the distribution of personal leadership capabilities and capitals across the organization?
Who has access to personal and professional development opportunities? Do these opportunities encourage critical reflection and the holistic development

of human capabilities that support participation in leadership practice and reduce inequalities in personal capitals?

Practice

In what ways are opportunities to initiate change and to work in genuinely collaborative ways distributed among organizational members? In what ways are organizational members included in or excluded from different kinds of leadership practices?

Who in day-to-day practice is most influential in initiating and influencing change? What are the scope and limitations for practicing democratic subjective autonomy in contrast to performative subjective autonomy?

Conclusion

This chapter has sought to argue that the L-A-P perspective on leadership should see itself as having a root in democratic values. The chapter has also introduced the notion of "multiple distributions" of leadership and put forward an analytical framework based on this to help in framing critical investigations of leadership as a distributed and democratic phenomenon.

It has been argued that the democratic root of L-A-P is best conceived as drawing from a rich conception of democracy (specifically holistic democracy). Democratic practice from this perspective involves working subjectively and inter-subjectively towards two aims that interconnect: development as whole human beings, with ethical, spiritual, cognitive, and other dimensions, and inclusive participation, which involves critically interrogating injustices and power abuses and changing these through practice. Explicit recognition of this rich democratic root would help L-A-P to extend its reach into questions of ethics, values, and human well-being that are inescapably part of leadership practice.

Notes

1 The concept of holarchic aesthetic rationality is discussed in more detail in Woods (2014).
2 See Woods and Woods (2013) for a discussion that makes a distinction between an analytical model of distributed leadership (DL) and an applied model of DL—the latter involving implications about how leadership should be conducted. The article argues that a deeper approach to the latter is needed, grounded in principles of holistic democracy and social justice.

References

Archer, M. S. (1995). *Realist social theory: The morphogenetic approach*. Cambridge: Cambridge University Press.

Archer, M. S. (2003). *Structure, agency and the internal conversation*. Cambridge: Cambridge University Press.

Benefiel, M. (2005). The second half of the journey: Spiritual leadership for organizational transformation. *Leadership Quarterly*, 16(5), 723–747.

Dallmayr, F. (2007). *In search of the good life*. Lexington, KY: University Press of Kentucky.

Fryer, M. (2011). *Ethics and organizational leadership: Developing a normative model*. Oxford: Oxford University Press.

Gherardi, S. (2003). Knowing as desiring: Mythic knowledge and the knowledge journey in communities of practitioners. *Journal of Workplace Learning*, 15(7/8), 352–358.

Giddens, A. (1979). *Critical problems in social theory*. London: Macmillan.

Giddens, A. (1986). *The constitution of society: Outline of the theory of structuration*. Oakland, CA: University of California Press.

Green, T. H. (1886). On the different sense of 'freedom' as applied to will and to the moral progress of man. In R. L. Nettleship (Ed.), *Works of Thomas Hill Green*, Vol. II (pp. 308–333). London: Longmans, Green & Co.

Gronn, P. (2002). Distributed leadership as a unit of analysis. *Leadership Quarterly*, 13, 423–451.

Habermas, J. (1987). *The theory of communicative action: The lifeworld and the system*. Boston: Beacon Press.

Hay, D. (1994). "The biology of God": What is the current status of Hardy's hypothesis?. *The International Journal for the Psychology of Religion*, 4(1), 1–23.

Heifetz, R. A. (1994). *Leadership without easy answers*. Cambridge, MA: Harvard University Press.

Hellesnes, J. (1976). *Socialisering og teknokrati* [*Socialisation and technocracy*]. Copenhagen: Gyldendal.

James, W. (1985 [1902]). *The varieties of religious experience*. Harmondsworth: Penguin Books.

Joas, H. (2000). *The genesis of values*. Cambridge: Polity Press.

Kinjerski, V. M., & Skrypnek, B. J. (2004). Defining spirit at work: Finding common ground. *Journal of Organizational Change Management*, 17(1), 26–42.

MacIntyre, A. (2007). *After virtue*. London: Bloomsbury.

McLaughlin, T. (1996). Education of the whole child? In R. Best (Ed.), *Education, spirituality and the whole child* (pp. 9–19). London: Cassell.

Moos, L. (2004). Introduction. In J. MacBeath & L. Moos (Eds.), *Democratic learning: The challenge to school effectiveness* (pp. 1–18). London: RoutledgeFalmer.

Noordegraaf, M., & Schinkel, W. (2011). Professional capital contested: A Bourdieusian analysis of conflicts between professionals and managers. *Comparative Sociology*, 10, 97–125.

Raelin, J. (2011). From leadership-as-practice to leaderful practice. *Leadership*, 7(2), 195–211.

Raelin, J. (2014). Imagine there are no leaders: Reframing leadership as collaborative agency. *Leadership*. Online First, 25 November 2014.

Rose, N. (1999). *Powers of freedom: Reframing political thought*. Cambridge: Cambridge University Press.

de Sanctis, A. (2005). *The 'Puritan' democracy of Thomas Hill Green*. Exeter: Imprint Academic.

Scribner, S. M. P., & Bradley-Levine, J. (2010). The meaning(s) of teacher leadership in an urban high school reform. *Educational Administration Quarterly*, 46, 491–522.

Sen, A. (2009). *The idea of justice*. London: Allen Lane.

Vincent, A., & Plant, R. (1984). *Philosophy, politics and citizenship*. Oxford: Blackwell.

Ward, S. C., Bagley, C., Lumby, J., Woods, P. A., Hamilton, T., & Roberts, A. (2015a). School leadership for equity: Lessons from the literature. *International Journal of Inclusive Education*, 19(4), 333–346.

Ward, S. C., Bagley, C., Lumby, J., Woods, P. A., Hamilton, T., & Roberts, A. (2015b) What is "policy" and what is "policy response"? An illustrative study of the implementation of the leadership standards for social justice in Scotland. *Educational Management Administration & Leadership*. Published online before print 6 March 2015, doi: 10.1177/1741143214558580.

Weber, M. (1970). Politics as a vocation. In H. H. Gerth & C. W. Mills (Eds.), *From Max Weber: Essays in sociology* (pp. 77–128). London: Routledge & Kegan Paul.

Western, S. (2013). *Leadership: A critical text* (2nd edition). London: Sage.

Woods, G. J. (2007). The "bigger feeling": The importance of spiritual experience in educational leadership. *Educational Management Administration & Leadership*, 35(1), 135–155.

Woods, P. A. (2003). Building on Weber to understand governance: Exploring the links between identity, democracy and "inner distance". *Sociology*, 37(1), 143–163.

Woods, P. A. (2005). *Democratic leadership in education*. London: Sage.

Woods, P. A. (2006). A democracy of all learners: Ethical rationality and the affective roots of democratic leadership. *School Leadership and Management*, 26(4), 321–337.

Woods, P. A. (2011). *Transforming education policy: Shaping a democratic future*. Bristol: Policy Press.

Woods, P. A. (2013). Drivers to holistic democracy: Signs and signals of emergent, democratic self-organising systems. In S. M. Weber, M. Göhlich, A. Schröer, H. Macha & C. Fahrenwald (Eds.), *Organisation und partizipation: Beiträge der kommission organisationspädagogik* (pp. 343–355). Berlin: Springer VS.

Woods, P. A. (2014). Hierarchy and holarchy: Leadership for equity and democracy in performative school culture. Paper presented at Oxford Education Research Symposium, University of Oxford, 11–13 December.

Woods, P. A., & Roberts, A. (2013). Distributed leadership and social justice: A case study investigation of distributed leadership and the extent to which it promotes social justice and democratic practices. In L. Moos & P. Hatzopolous (Eds.), *School leadership as a driving force for equity and learning: Comparative perspective* (pp. 148–170). European Policy Network on School Leadership. Available at www.leu.lt/download/14539/c3_ep nosl-2_del4.1.pdf (accessed 8 January 2015).

Woods, P. A., & Roberts, A. (2015). Distributed leadership and social justice: Images and meanings from different positions across the school landscape. *International Journal of Educational Leadership*. Published online before print, 1 June, 2015, doi: 10.1080/ 13603124.2015.1034185

Woods, P. A., & Woods, G. J. (2011). Lighting the fires of entrepreneurialism? Constructions of meaning in an English inner city academy. *International Journal of Technology and Educational Marketing*, 1(1), 1–24.

Woods, P. A., & Woods, G. J. (2013). Deepening distributed leadership: A democratic perspective on power, purpose and the concept of the self. *Vodenje v vzgoji in izobraževanju (Leadership in Education)*, 2, 17–40. (English version available at https://herts.academia.edu/PhilipWoods).

PART II

Embodied nature

5

LEADERSHIP AS IDENTITY

A practice-based exploration

Brigid J. Carroll

Introduction

Imagine going into an organization as a leadership researcher with a particular interest in identity and not being able to talk or communicate in any way. That means not being able to question anyone about how they define and understand leadership or identity and perceive how either and both occurs. All one can do is observe people going about their daily work, listen to their ongoing conversations, and attempt to identify what is done that appears to be recognized as leadership identity. That's the practice challenge in a nutshell: uncovering what constructs such as leadership mean in "whole" worlds where people in specific contexts, interconnected in their tasks, produce something we call work. A researcher cannot isolate their particular construct (in this case leadership identity), invite people to talk to it explicitly, exclude other constructs that wander into such discussions (such as management or teamwork or role), and rely on people's description of what they think or do. Such a researcher walks into the middle of multiple, ongoing, unfolding, processes where their privileged construct, if it is there at all, is intertwined with all manner of other social processes in the complexities of organizational life.

This chapter recounts such a scenario and attempts to explore how leadership and identity play out in pure practice. Of course pure practice is largely an ideal and researchers tend to be given a starting point. The starting point in this case was to shadow a team leader for a morning and learn about leadership in this organization from observing their interactions. Although this sounds like it could be a thoroughly conventional "follow a leader" study, this researcher assumed that the so-called team leader reflected a role more than an identity and could be doing any number of things (management, administration, human resources, specialist IT work) over the course of the morning. In short she had made no assumptions that leadership identity could be understood from studying this particular individual but thought this individual was as good as any to follow into the life of this organization and see what kind of leadership activity emerged once in the space. It is important to state from the outset that this researcher was theory-led in making such distinctions and was bringing theory as a sensitizing lens to assist in grappling with complexity unlike "the blank page" mindset of someone engaged in a more grounded theory exploration. A range of critical, process, and practice theories were helping this researcher hold leadership identity in a place of curiosity while suspending assumptions of what leadership or identity might look like and how those might be attached to individuals or groups. Although a number of interactions were observed, this chapter will only focus on one.

Locating leadership in observations of interactions is not an easy enterprise, to say the least (Kelly, 2008). It is certainly not straightforward to differentiate leadership from other social processes that happen in work environments such as management and technical expertise. One has the issue of deciding what is leadership and what is not. Researchers therefore tend to combine observations with interviews as a result to provide a point of calibration between how someone(s) attributes or talks to leadership as opposed to how they practice leadership. This can create its own issues where talk of leadership often contradicts practice of leadership. For instance Sveningsson and Larsson (2006) talked to a manager who affirmed his leadership as transformational and visionary but who was observed doing very mundane and routine managerial/administrative work. The researchers concluded that the subject of this study might be indicative of many knowledge-type workers thrust into managerial roles who create a fantasy leadership identity as opposed to any real leadership practice.

Clearly talking about leadership and doing leadership do not always equate to the same thing. Equally clearly, this phenomena we call identity would appear to sit on the more intangible and abstract end of the organizational construct scale. If I propose to investigate identity through predominantly observing leadership practice as opposed to interviewing subjects about their leadership practice then I have a considerable challenge on my hands. So why would I take this on? When academics discuss identity in a research-related piece of writing like this one, it can often sound esoteric, objectified, and somehow different from how most of us identify and are identified as "who we are" multiple times a day. Yet, identity is considered absolutely central to contemporary existence and is one of the big differentiators between our modern society and more traditional ones (Giddens, 1991). Given the practice context in this identity chapter, I seek to engage with identity as intimate, intuitive, and resolutely "common," albeit fluid and ambiguous in leadership moments and episodes, and seek to demonstrate how seeing and working in identity ways can shape and impact leadership practice.

This chapter will be built around an interaction that the author observed on a visit to a high tech, high growth, rapid pace, entrepreneurial, medium-sized business. Both the team leader and this interaction leader were chosen by the organization as exemplars of the kind of leadership that occurred in this context. This interaction then becomes a site to interrogate the identity emergence and dynamics of the leadership that did (or did not) shape the work of one of its teams. A layering of conceptual material from literatures that help recognize and work with identity will be introduced: practice, practice-oriented identity studies, and leadership identity. The overall intent is to explore how identity impacts leadership practice and whether it is possible to access identity work without predominantly relying on collecting "talk" of leadership practice. I propose that a practice orientation to both leadership and identity has the potential to offer unique insight into the mutual construction of leadership identity by both organization and subject, and holds some promise of not over-estimating either the subject or the context in such a process.

A stand-up meeting

Picture a very large, open plan room with approximately 100 people in. Those 100 people are sitting in front of computers in rows. Most of the rows are horizontal with pods of about 16 people facing each other. A number of long vertical rows bisect the room and seemingly construct boundaries that carve the room up into a number of areas or rectangular spaces. That all sounds very ordered and organized but the room doesn't feel that way at all. People are standing, chatting, and leaning over their stations, bags are on the floor, books (science fiction mostly) pile awkwardly on desks, lots of cartoons and reproduced visuals are pinned up behind computers and small toys, ornaments, figurines perch on computers and printers and in fact on any available technology. You wouldn't call it a loud room at all as people seem to talk fairly quietly between themselves but it's casual, relaxed, untidy, and personal. On the walls are a whole lot of work charts. Some of them are graphs showing work completed and many are tables of post-it notes on the move from the left-hand column to the right-hand as work is moved through "ready," "doing," "testing," and "completed" stages. By the quantity of graphs and tables on the walls, it is clear there are a number of teams in this room and they are pretty busy going by the sheer quantity of post-it notes at varying points of completion.

The team on which we are going to focus is in the far right of the room in the corner. When I get there they are all sitting at their desks and working on their computers. Like all the teams in this hall, they develop complex software and online infrastructure. I perch on an unoccupied chair watching them. Although some work alone, many work together in front of multiple screens. It's not silent and intent work like somehow I have pictured software construction to be. There's gentle talking between people, multiple screens flying up on computers, people looking at them and away and then back again, people walking round and on the move and swiveling chairs to join in to other conversations and swivel back again. Although it seems discontinuous work in the sense of people moving between different modes, it still seems like everyone has their own work on which they are focusing.

There's a team leader I've been shadowing for the morning. Let's call him Dan after one of the science fiction authors piled up on his desk. Dan would be in his early 30s and is wearing super casual jeans, brown T-shirt, sneakers, and a baseball cap—which doesn't make him stand out given combinations of those constitute a sort of uniform in this room. He has a team of about eight. His team of eight encompasses a number of young women and men who look fresh out of university (assuming they are out of university as the organization does have an internship scheme) and some older men (40s). One of the women smiles at me and strikes up a conversation about what she is doing. In the midst of that conversation she glances at Dan and says "I see the koosch ball. It's team time."

I look up and see Dan has got a koosch ball out of the drawer of his desk. It's an old, battered one that looks like it has got lots of use. He's still sitting at his chair, which is in a vertical row facing away from his team where some of the other team leaders sit, and he's lightly tossing it from hand to hand. That action is visible from where his team are sitting. No-one jumps up or flicks to attention but slowly over the next few minutes I start to notice them disentangling from their work. Some push their chairs back and swivel around looking around the area, some speed up their keyboard work as if they need to save or send quickly, while others begin what sounds to be a more casual conversation over greater distances with people further away. Dan himself starts to talk intently to one of his team members all the while bouncing the koosch ball. Somehow things feel in limbo as if people are transitioning into something else without a word being spoken. After a few minutes Dan gets up and walks towards the closest bank of post-it notes and starts to move some of them. People slowly join him when ready and there's spontaneous chat as people point to post-it notes. Things get quite animated with lots of laughter. The last few in the team come up to the board and without me quite noticing how they do so, they form a more formal circle and go quiet.

Dan is holding the koosch ball and he starts to talk. There's no formal opening up of the conversation and he seems to start as if this conversation is continuing on from one they have all had prior. He seems to be filling people in on where work is at and it sounds pretty frank to me. There's comments like "I'm not sure where we are heading on this ... " and "we thought we'd be done here but it's obvious we aren't ... ." The team members listen but don't join in. Then he stops, glances round the circle, and throws the koosch ball to someone; that someone simply recounts what they are working on individually. There isn't much eye contact and again the group listens. Dan listens too. When that person stops they look around for a moment and throw the koosch ball to someone else. And on it goes.

One of the older guys (let's call him Spike) has more energy than others. He hops from foot to foot, makes more eye contact than anyone else, and seems to be barely suppressing a desire to speak. That is unusual as no-one so far has openly pre-empted wanting it. On getting the koosch ball he launches into a very animated account of trying to solve a bug or glitch in the system without being able to successfully locate it. At this point spontaneous conversation breaks out and others join in and it's actually becoming a conversation where people are genuinely interacting. The conversation goes to and from Spike as more than half the group joins in. Dan stays fairly quiet at this point but shows he is engaged by nodding, making one-word-type comments ("yup," "true"). After 3 or 4 minutes he joins in. He says, "So there's two ways being suggested to move on this thing right?" He looks at Spike and Spike nods and leaps in again gesticulating wildly and adding other dimensions of this search for a bug or as he puts it "more than one." Again people look up and begin to nod and join in. Another few minutes pass and Spike eventually passes on the koosch ball but not until completing his spiel to the degree he wants to.

Everyone has had a go and the last person throws the ball back to Dan. Dan tosses the ball in his hand and says "we all good to go on?", but doesn't seem to expect an answer and no-one seems to expect to give him one. Dan glances at his watch and rushes off to his next meeting. Given I'm shadowing, I rush off too but I glance back to see Spike still standing with a couple of people who he had fired up in the stand-up meeting. Still gesticulating and still talking furiously between them.

Through the lens of practice, identity, and leadership

There's nothing about this story I imagine that would appear dramatic or unusual. Some readers would smile in recognition at the baseball cap, figurines on computers, and the series of post-it notes inviting movement on the walls. They would be those who know the feel of an IT space perhaps. Others could equally be shaking their head at a space that seems to run on such casual, quirky, non-urgent lines. They could be those whose own work space has a very different rhythm. Regardless of how familiar or alien this story is, it should be recognizable as a representation of work practice or of what really happens. Before we interrogate the identity and leadership in it, however, let's put words to what it means to take a practice perspective.

Practice

Attention to practice is driven by a sense of a gulf between researcher treatments of topics versus the lived experience of them and a sense that much of our research seems to "strip out most of what matters" (Weick, 2007, p. 18). Practice theory therefore begins by asking the question "what do practitioners experience 'out in the real world'" (Weick, 2003, p. 453) although, in contrast with how it might appear, that is anything but a straightforward question. In fact, answering that question means an entirely different kind of research attention and inquiry. Out in the "real world" practitioners do not tend to abstract and separate out processes and treat them as "stand-alone entities." In the "real world," practitioners encounter processes such as leadership "in a holistic manner" as "a meaningful, unfolding totality" (Sandberg & Tsoukas, 2011, p. 341). "What people actually do" (Carter, Clegg, & Kornberger, 2008, p. 88) is not easily captured by any research that works predominantly with practitioner's cognitive accounts of analyses of pre-set independent constructs such as leadership.

The premise we are offering here is that practice theory invites us closer to the lived reality of what people actually do. To do so it needs to grapple with a number of theoretical challenges. The first is the inherent situatedness, relationality, and interdependence of any self, other, artifacts, and contexts. That means any practice pursuit of identity and leadership engages with them amidst relationships, artifacts, and contexts. The second is the temporality of existence where action cannot be neatly sequenced as in a flowchart but is instead "entangled" in "anticipation, uncertainties, and urgency" (Nicolini, 2009, p. 123) meaning practitioners negotiate choice, decisions, and ambiguity at every step. This makes things like identity and leadership more of a practical accomplishment than the managed project that appears in many of our textbooks.

If we put together the relational and temporal principles of practice theory then we end up with a focus on what Dreyfus (1991, p. 69) has called "absorbed coping" where practitioners are immersed and embodied in a whole interconnected world. Much of the time this is routine, automatic and below the threshold of a cognitive, rational grasp but some of the time, when things become confused or unpredictable (something Dreyfus calls a temporary breakdown), we move to "involved thematic deliberation" (Dreyfus, 1991, pp. 72–73) or what Yanow and Tsoukas (2009) refer to as "analytic reflection" where we consciously pay attention to how and what we are engaging with. We would propose that identity and leadership through a practice lens are accomplished through both absorbed coping and involved thematic deliberation.

Our account of the standing meeting earlier in the chapter is thus an account of the "absorbed coping" of Dan and his team. At this stage of the chapter you should have a sense of this team amidst their world surrounded by the objects and people that constitute such a world. Any leadership achieved by anyone is done amidst rows of computer monitors, post-it notes, youth in jeans and sneakers, pyramids of science fiction books, cult series figurines, and reprinted cartoons. In most leadership literature, the everyday clutter and direct spatial context of leadership is usually absent or at best referred to only tangentially and minimally. However, it should be clear that any leadership that might happen in this space is constrained and enabled by this space and the objects and people in it. Given that no-one has single offices, conversations happen when people swivel their chairs close to others and begin talking where they are or as people walk through or from/to the large room. Something like a stand-up team conversation ritual makes total sense given that this workforce is never far from computer screens (even in meetings they bring and look at their laptops and tablets), and hence needs something or someone to call them into a different form of communication and connection with each other. A practice approach draws us into "a whole world" (given of course this "whole world" of a large team room sits in a further "whole world" of an organization and sector) where the doing of the constructs we academics like to study (in this case leadership and identity) are intimately intertwined with the routines that weave through real time, everyday space and work.

Identity

It is rare to study identity amidst the "whole world" in which practitioners live. The closest we would have to such an approach is ethnographic studies with their thick description of place, space, rituals, and norms, and the people who operate through such configurations. However, ethnographic studies of leadership are rare to say the least, with far more priority given to the direct verbal attribution or claiming of leadership through survey instrument or interview kinds of methodologies. The nearest to what we are trying to do here would be discourse approaches to leadership which seek for evidence of leadership in text (spoken or written forms of language such as in the form of a speech, email, prospectus), talk (within formal or informal conversation), and interaction (encounter between people that includes verbal and non-verbal engagement). Certainly discourse approaches would be congruent with a practice-type approach but there are other identity points of reference. We will seek to make these points visible in this section, while acknowledging the tensions in reading identity primarily through observation, as in the need to "refrain from objectifying identities as observable entities" (Ybema, Keenoy, Oswick, Beverungen, Ellis, & Sabelis, 2009, p. 304).

Identity is generally represented as a struggle between the expectations of self, others, and organization/community/society (Sveningsson & Alvesson, 2003). It is a struggle because in that intersection of expectations, individuals feel the need to represent themselves with coherence and distinctiveness while at the same time being aware of palpable contradictions, precariousness, fluidity, multiplicity, and fragmentation. Wrestling with such a struggle means that identity is an ongoing question or "project" (Giddens, 1991), which complicates choices of who to be and what to say and do in any moment. Identity researchers gravitate to discursive methods because that is where identity work (struggle) is most likely to be visible.

Observation is deemed a much more ambiguous identity research site given it is often identity coherence and distinctiveness that is most in view and not identity struggle. Nor can a researcher assume that a calm, confident, and assured identity performance does not involve significant precariousness and contradiction; or the reverse where evident identity difficulty and ambiguity belie a strong distinctiveness or coherence. On the other hand, scholars of interviewing in particular (Alvesson, 2003; Holstein & Gubrium, 2003) argue that the interviews that researchers predominantly use to probe into identity are not windows into identity work in real work/leadership contexts. Rather, they suggest, interviews are better seen as performances or constructions oriented at the research context, the perceived expectations or hopes of the researcher, and the nature of the interviewer/interviewee. Practice theory and approaches offer a bridge between what a researcher can see and feel on site alongside what they can hear and interpret prior or subsequent to the practice being explored.

In practice terms the starting place is with a "permanent dialectic between the self and social structure" with identity having "a potential mediating quality" (Ybema et al., 2009, p. 300). In the stand-up meeting story we see a whole host of mediating elements that construct the identities possible in this team. We see a team creating the culture of their organization just as that culture creates the identities in and of the team. Thus when Dan pulls on his jeans and dons his baseball cap, another team member puts another science fiction book on the teetering pile and different configurations of the team swivel their chair round to be immersed in a software discussion, they all sustain a way of being in this organization like others before them and doubtless others after them. However, they in turn are responding to the historical and cultural texture of an organization that distinctively blends the ability to look and behave casually with an extreme high performance pace and tolerance for uncertainty. In short their work identities are mediated through self and social structure mutually and simultaneously. This marks a significant departure from many identity studies in which identity appears to be often singular (something constructed by a self) and internal (constructed through self-stories and reflection).

From a practice perspective, identity thus is "complex, recursive and constantly under construction" (Ybema et al., 2009, p. 301). Given it is these things, "it implicates social maneuvering and power games" (Ybema et al., 2009, p. 306). So we see Dan as the possessor of the team koosch ball but unable or unwilling to verbally call the team to their stand-up meeting. He uses movement (walking away from his station), location (standing by the team process and results chart), and silence (waiting quietly for others to join him) to get this meeting started. Likewise his team does not rush to the meeting but keeps talking, finishes off their phase of work and swiveling their chairs amongst each other. We could read this sequence of actions as Dan "maneuvering" to gain the authority needed to start the meeting and his team illustrating their power to join him (or not) in a timely manner. The effect is of a form of minimalist authority where team leader and team act in interdependent ways to produce this event called a stand-up meeting. Individual and collective agencies are at play here as all "choose" to take part in this event and make their process of "choosing" quite visible.

Given we are not relying on anyone's reflection or discussion of leadership and identity to give insight into these, a new set of identity dimensions is required. This chapter is going to highlight three constitutive practice elements that traditionally have not been strong in identity research: physical space, routines and artifacts. I'm going to argue that these are particularly significant in giving insight into leadership identity.

Physical space

Physical space can be considered "inseparable" from the knowledge that is its very purpose (Lee & Amjadi, 2014, p. 723). Physical space is "intimately bound up with intentions, occupations and purposes," which makes it integral to the construction of identity (Dewey, 1938 [1991], p. 52, in Miettinen & Virkkunen, 2005, p. 443). Physical space provides an "emotional home for expert selves" (Knorr Cetina, 1997, p. 9). In the standing meeting account the physical space shapes a complex leadership space. Dan and the other team leaders sit facing away from their team but, apart from facing a different direction, they have identical desks, chairs, computers, and garb. We could interpret this in a number of ways: that team leaders are minimally differentiated from the members of their teams and share more similarity and proximity than difference; that distinction through position or title seems of little significance in this world; that team leaders sitting together suggest that the vertical relationships between team leaders are significant.

Team leaders sitting facing away from their teams is harder to interpret. From shadowing Dan more broadly I saw that much of what a team leader does was advocate, speak, and contribute on behalf of the work their team is charged with or represent the work of their team to other team leaders and beyond them to project, group, division, and executive leaders. Facing those other teams and the rest of the organization literally and symbolically then makes sense. Facing away from their own team similarly seems to have meaning. We could read it as a signal to the team that space is their own to lead, manage, fill, and shape, and from what the researcher could see while there, this is exactly what they were doing. As such facing away indicates that team leaders are not or should not be in micro-management, supervision, or surveillance over their teams. Their location on the periphery or boundary of team space, then, indicates a certain identity position for a team leader but a host of choices as well. Watching Dan move between being one of the team (wheeling his chair to join a conversation between members of his team), one of the team leaders (leaning back in his chair talking between them) and in terrain not connected with his team (leaning against a wall chatting to the overall project heads), shows Dan shaping a team leader modus operandi in relation with the overall spatial configuration in which he practices.

Routines

At the core of this observation is a routine (the stand-up meeting). It is rare to focus attention on routines when researching leadership, given that leadership is more often linked to exceptional moments and contexts more than mundane and recurrent ones. If we take a practice approach to leadership seriously though, the routines that make up the day-to-day series of activities that constitute the work of the organization are precisely where we need to look for the presence (or absence) of leadership. After all "organizational routines have been regarded as the primary means by which organizations accomplish much of what they do" (Feldman & Pentland, 2003, p. 94), and one could wonder how significant a contribution leadership is to what organizations do if it cannot be found in such "primary means."

Process and practice theories have created a renewed interest in routines. Routines in the past have been predominantly too quickly associated with stability, repetition, inflexibility, and even inertia, and considered of limited interest to scholars precisely because of these characteristics. However, increasingly scholars are seeing that routines are equally central to change processes and indeed are prime sites of variation, improvisation, and possibility (Feldman & Pentland, 2003). This more recent theorization on routine highlights its importance to constructs that are significant for leadership such as organizational or collective learning, conflict and power, interpersonal relationships, and meaning/interpretation. From a practice perspective, routines focus us particularly towards the "performance" of collectives and their choices or strategies that are always "enmeshed in far-reaching, complex, tangled webs of interdependence" (Feldman & Pentland, 2003, p. 104). If this is so then researching routines should shed light on distributed, relational, shared, and emergent configurations of leadership in which practice approaches are most interested.

In terms of this chapter we need to understand routines as integral to identity work. This should make intuitive sense given that we defined identity work previously as the tension between representing self in stable and coherent ways in the face of the ongoing struggle in "forming, repairing, maintaining, strengthening or revising" such representations or constructions (Sveningsson & Alvesson, 2003, p. 1165), which appears to parallel the precarious tension between stability and change in routines themselves. Consequently, there are two ways of analyzing routines with respect to identity: routines as either a resource or discipline for identity (Brown & Lewis, 2011).

Routines are a resource for identity where individuals creatively craft a construction of self within the possibilities, discourses, and relationships that are nested in such routines. Such a crafting is never unfettered and without constraint but nonetheless there are myriads of configurations, shapes, openings, contradictions, and spaces to claim for any sustained identity work in even the most established of routines. Equally we note that routines can be understood in disciplinary terms where usually hidden or disguised in the routine are dynamics of power and control that seek to manufacture certain identities above others. Precisely because such power and control are hidden and/or disguised then, while identities appear freely chosen, they are in fact a form of regulation co-opting and pre-selecting what identity representations are available. We are going to hold routines as both a resource and discipline for identity work and therefore in an ongoing tension.

The stand-up meeting routine demonstrates such a tension well. Clearly it is designed to pull people out of fairly autonomous and individual work trajectories and pull them together to pay attention to their existence as a team and the work that is located across and between them. Confining the speaking role to the possession of the koosch ball in theory gives anyone the capacity to claim and use a space of action (see the next section); however, a very tight script operates throughout this routine with only a few minutes available for each person. Like all routines this one has an ostensive dimension (the structure and "rules" which govern it) and a performative dimension (the improvisational and adaptive choices which people make momentarily any time the routine is activated) (Feldman & Pentland, 2003). In the version of the routine we see Dan is low key, serious, and rational whereas Spike is flamboyant, passionate, and energetic. That combination in this particular performance of the routine could be read in leadership terms as Dan holding the kind of structure and format that allows one of his team (such as Spike in this case) to seize the limelight, command the attention of the team, and redirect collective thinking in a particular direction that Dan could not have known about prior to beginning the routine. This surely is distributed leadership in action?

However, it is important to remember that Dan has the ultimate power over the koosch ball and the ability to mobilize and complete the routine when the koosch ball is in his hands. We note that such power over the koosch ball does not halt or stop the conversation between Spike and team members after the stand-up meeting has finished, suggesting that the koosch ball is a catalyst or intermediary of leadership action that can extend beyond and from the routine.

Artifacts

Identity is usually talked about as something one has (or more normally struggles with), rather than the proposition that who we are/want/need to be is intimately connected with artifacts. Nevertheless, it should be difficult to picture yourself or anyone else without a relationship to artifacts, be they computers, PowerPoint, books, power tools, or sports equipment. A practice approach argues that we have identity partly because of the artifacts with which we are associated. In the stand-up meeting story the key artifact is a koosch ball and we will use this koosch ball to explore the relationship between identity and artifact. I should note, however, that the choice of the koosch ball as a key artifact is a fairly arbitrary one. The process and results chart marking the location of the stand-up meeting could be considered equally important as could the swiveling, wheeled chairs that allow the team members to form and reform in different configurations at will. All artifacts, no matter how unexceptional they are, signify something about how work is produced between people.

However, artifacts have traditionally been overlooked in organizational studies, let alone leadership, because they have been seen as passive adjuncts to far more significant phenomena such as environments, structures, strategies, cultures, and technologies. Things people held or used or worked with from this research perspective could be understood as mere props for personalities, stories, and activities far more deserving of research attention. If we take up the challenge of studying processes like leadership "as they really happen"; however, then the simple truth is leadership happens as individuals and groups use, hold, and work with artifacts (see, e.g., Sergi, Chapter 6, this volume). The first challenge to doing so is to rethink the very nature of artifact, object, and tool. The tendency when we think of these at all is to view them as fixed, static, instrumental, and something to be merely used. The last of our terms "tool" would come the closest to such a definition; however, in leaving even tools in such a space, we neglect their role as intermediaries with the ability to broker realities such as power, status, control, and knowledge. Beyond tool, objects, and artifacts have an even more complex existence. If we could view them as historic, symbolic, textual, emotional, and social and not just "object-like," then we could see their capacity to facilitate identity, meaning, relationship, and purpose.

Stopping seeing artifacts in terms of "thingness" means beginning to see them as "non-fixed," active, agentic, and as epistemic or capable of embodying what is not known (Nicolini, Mengis, & Swan 2012, p. 613). Nicolini and his colleagues invite us to view artifacts as "triggers of contradictions and negotiation" that set up a "problem space" (Nicolini *et al.*, 2012, p. 621). It is the difference between seeing a koosch ball as a mere toy that is good to hold or throw versus seeing it as a signifying object with the capacity to constitute a leadership space. In the stand-up meeting account the very sight of it in Dan's hands signals a moving away from individual work stations into "team time" and a collective communication/workflow ritual. At the moment as the team catches sight of the koosch ball, we can begin to sense "the problem space" that the koosch ball creates. The team has choice in how they respond to the koosch ball after all. Dan's actions seemed to recognize this as he chose to juggle it in his hands for 3 to 4 minutes, walk casually up to the section of the wall with their posters full of post-it notes, immerse himself with the post-it notes, and in effect wait patiently for his team to pull themselves out of their work of the day and respond. That he never gave a verbal instruction or any sign of impatience could be read as an understanding of his team's "space of action" (Holmer-Nadesan, 1996) at this point.

However, artifacts are also symbols of authority that can be used to exercise or challenge power (Lee & Amjadi, 2014, p. 724), signify status, confirm dependence, independence or interdependence, and influence or shape individual and collective trajectories (Swan, Bresnen, Newell, & Robertson, 2007, p. 1814). Given that Dan is in possession of the koosch ball, he would have had some confidence that his team acquiesce in the ritual to follow. Certainly he seems comfortable in not giving any instructions or direction beyond the visibility of the koosch ball and his movement to the wall to make this ritual happen. Artifacts then "can be used to mobilize action" (Swan *et al.*, 2007, p. 1814). Dan presumably is a team leader even without the koosch ball in his hand but when he appears with the koosch ball and walks towards the spot by the wall he is mobilizing what someone in his team called "team time" and a different kind of connection and communication between his team.

Miettinen and Virkkunen (2005, p. 443) remind us that "norms of action and cognition are objectified into artifacts," hence the koosch ball opens up a certain kind of team time norm. We could see the stand-up meeting then as a breaking of the more technical/technology-oriented conversation/meeting norms of the rest of the day which the koosch ball enables. Both Dan and his team potentially become something different in the circle with the koosch ball. Indeed "the (re)constitution of objects is a central resource in the development of professional and organizational identities" (Engeström & Blackler, 2005, p. 312), and the koosch ball constitutes a different suite of identities. The identities on which we need to focus in this chapter are leadership ones so we'll bring leadership into this chapter directly and then turn to the question of leadership and identity.

Leadership

If you have read even a little of this book, you will be aware that tracking Dan for evidence of leadership is a forlorn endeavor for a practice-oriented approach. Hopefully it has become evident that while shadowing Dan was a point of entry into the organization, we have looked for leadership of which he is a part more than leadership which he "does." The introduction of this book states that a practice perspective would look for leadership "in immanent collective action emerging from mutual, discursive, sometimes recurring and sometimes evolving patterns in the moment and over time among those engaged in the practice" (Raelin, Chapter 1, this volume). If we read our interaction through the lens of this definition, we see the stand-up meeting as a routine or recurring pattern of activity in which this team engages. Leadership does not exist prior to the interaction but emerges (or not) from this meeting. That makes leadership a collective property or what this definition refers to as "mutual," where those who are part of the interaction play some role, whether they know it or not, in how leadership emerges. One way we can ask this of our interaction is to ask "what leadership configurations emerge when interactants share a newly formed leadership space?" (Chreim, 2015, p. 7).

We have already discussed that this space opens up when the team leader (Dan) picks up the koosch ball and moves to the designated part of the wall where this group tracks its progress. This is a routine that happens every day at approximately the same time but even though it is a routine it is not a pre-determined one. Both Dan and team have a myriad of choices about who to be in this recurring routine. Remember, our artifact, the koosch ball, constructs a "problem space" (Nicolini *et al.*, 2012, p. 621) that participants can mediate, negotiate, challenge, adapt, and subvert. Every time Dan picks up that artifact and throws it to someone else, he can never be entirely sure what will happen. Chreim (2015, p. 21) proposes "the more ambiguous the space the greater the room for actors to fill in" and that such "practices help structure the emergent leadership configuration."

On the day we see this stand-up meeting, it is Spike who is proactive about gesturing for the koosch ball, who creates real energy and conversational dynamics in the circle, and who creates some meaning that others seem to relate to both in the meeting and beyond. Dan alternatively listens, stays quiet, checks his understanding with Spike and the team, and waits for Spike to pass the koosch ball on. Dan maintains authority in this interaction as he paces the meeting and ensures the koosch ball passes to others but Spike gives the team something to be involved in and contribute to. Any leadership that we are prepared to recognize here happens within a configuration of Dan, Spike, and the team in relation to each other, their context and its norms, and the artifacts (post-it notes and koosch ball) that constitute the uncertainties and possibilities in and from this interaction. Given this interaction on this day played out in this manner, something new may be possible that was not there previously. Looking back at Spike and teammates still talking vigorously as both Dan and researcher leave, suggests the seeds of something possible. We might be prepared to call such emergent energy, connection, focus, and meaning evidence of leadership.

Leadership and identity

This chapter so far has interrogated "the absorbed coping" of one of the teams in this organization. However, having a researcher track Dan for a substantial part of the day probably did constitute a "temporary breakdown" of routine which did occasion some reflection and rationale from Dan as we walked to different parts of the building for different interactions. Thus, to this observational material we can add some of Dan's reflections about leadership. Dan thought the stand-up meeting went well but did not elaborate. In terms of his role, he likes being a team leader, admits that the technical leading aspect of his role is most comfortable and compelling and that he has to intentionally work at the relational "leading people" side of what he does. However, he made a distinction between *leader* and *leadership* that seems crucial here. In terms of *leadership* he admitted, that although he cannot exactly define leadership, he senses it is more than having an aggregation of leaders and feels the absence of something in this space. That absence is typified by him realizing he does not have something he needs like a contract or piece of information or some kind of larger leadership story that relies on some kind of cross-organizational collaboration and culture and that the largely technical environment directed by leaders does not enable that. This feeling of something missing, which he names as leadership, is something to him that seems to encompass something different from his team leader role.

Holmer-Nadesan, M. (1996). Organizational identity and space of action. *Organization Studies*, 17(1), 49–81.

Holstein, J. A., & Gubrium, J. F. (2003). *Inside interviewing: New lenses, new concerns.* Thousand Oaks, CA: Sage Publications.

Kelly, S. (2008). Leadership: A categorical mistake? *Human Relations*, 61(6), 763–782.

Knorr Cetina, K. (1997). Sociality with objects: Social relations in postsocial knowledge societies. *Theory, Culture & Society*, 14(4), 1–30.

Lee, C.-F., & Amjadi, M. (2014). The role of materiality: Knowing through objects in work practice. *European Management Journal*, 32(5), 723–734.

Miettinen, R., & Virkkunen, J. (2005). Epistemic objects, artefacts and organizational change. *Organization*, 12(3), 437–456.

Nicolini, D. (2009). Zooming in and zooming out: A package of method and theory to study work practices. In S. Ybema, D. Yanow, H. Wels & F. Kamsteeg (Eds.), *Organizational ethnography. Studying the complexities of everyday life* (pp. 120–138). London: Sage.

Nicolini, D., Mengis, J., & Swan, J. (2012). Understanding the role of objects in cross-disciplinary collaboration. *Organization Science*, 23(3), 612–629.

Sandberg, J., & Tsoukas, H. (2011). Grasping the logic of practice: Theorizing through practical rationality. *Academy of Management Review*, 36(2), 338–360.

Shortt, H. (2012). Identityscapes of a hair salon: Work identities and the value of visual methods. *Sociological Research Online*, 17(2), 22.

Sveningsson, S., & Alvesson, M. (2003). Managing managerial identities: Organizational fragmentation, discourse and identity struggle. *Human Relations*, 56(10), 1163–1193.

Sveningsson, S., & Larsson, M. (2006). Fantasies of leadership: Identity work. *Leadership*, 2(2), 203–224.

Swan, J., Bresnen, M., Newell, S., & Robertson, M. (2007). The object of knowledge: The role of objects in biomedical innovation. *Human Relations*, 60(12), 1809–1837.

Weick, K. E. (2003). Theory and practice in the real world. In H. Tsoukas & C. Knudsen (Eds.), *The Oxford handbook of organization theory* (pp. 453–475). Oxford and New York: Oxford University Press.

Weick, K. E. (2007). The generative properties of richness. *Academy of Management Journal*, 50(1), 14–19.

Yanow, D., & Tsoukas, H. (2009). What is reflection-in-action? A phenomenological account. *Journal of Management Studies*, 46(8), 1339–1364.

Ybema, S., Keenoy, T., Oswick, C., Beverungen, A., Ellis, N., & Sabelis, I. (2009). Articulating identities. *Human Relations*, 62(3), 299–322.

6

WHO'S LEADING THE WAY?

Investigating the contributions of materiality to leadership-as-practice[1]

Viviane Sergi

Introduction

What is leadership? This question has been puzzling thinkers and researchers alike for centuries. More prosaically, how can a phenomenon as elusive as leadership be studied and captured: "where" could leadership *be*? The answer to this question has most frequently been couched in terms of individuals—exceptional ones, ordinary ones, single persons, or teams. This key question has also led to the development of a variety of answers and approaches, typologies, and checklists—most of them pointing to the idea that leaders, as *individuals*, can develop, tweak, perfect, expand, and change their leadership. Leadership's effectiveness has thus received much attention over the years (Collinson, 2005). Consensus in this field remains rare, however (Collinson & Grint, 2005). In this chapter, I do not aim to add to this vast literature, nor will I develop an in-depth critique of it. Rather, I will explore what different researchers have been calling for recently: the inclusion of materiality in investigations—and in conceptualizations—of leadership (see Denis, Langley & Rouleau, 2010; Fairhurst & Connaughton, 2014; and Hawkins, 2015, among others). Instead of asking *who* might be leading, I start from a different question: what is leadership *made of*? This second question might sound like a convoluted variation of the first one, but, as I will discuss in this chapter, it opens the door to a different investigation of leadership in action. Echoing Hawkins (2015), my view is that including materiality in leadership study is not only possible and relevant in theoretical terms, but that it has value when it comes to understanding this phenomenon.

Being a researcher preoccupied with materiality, my reflection on leadership was sparked by this tendency towards a strict centering of leadership on individuals—be they singular (for an example of this criticism, see Fletcher, 2004) or plural (for an overview, see Denis *et al.*, 2012). By locating leadership *in* and *around* persons, and by using a language that directly or indirectly evokes leadership as something people *have*, we researchers have paid great attention to notions like traits, personality, charisma, and, more recently, interpersonal relationships. These concepts speak of leadership as a phenomenon concerned solely with persons: their characteristics (who they are), their competencies (the skills they have), or even their activities (what they do on a daily basis). There is no doubt in my mind that leadership is about persons and that they need to be at the heart of our inquiries into leadership. However, in these pages, I wish to explore the possibility of understanding and conceptualizing leadership differently: first, by adopting the practice perspective, and, second, by actively accounting for the contribution of materiality to leadership interactions. What can we understand about leadership if we start our inquiries from a different empirical and analytical point? This is exactly what the leadership-as-practice approach proposes by suggesting that we shift the locus of leadership from individuals to collective, material, and embodied practices enacted in context. The practice perspective, as applied to leadership, approaches this phenomenon as it is performed and allows us to consider a variety of elements that are woven into this performance. In doing so, it joins other constructionist and relational approaches that reconceptualize leadership through action, interactions, and relations (see for example Cunliffe & Eriksen, 2011 and Fairhurst & Grant, 2010).

Leadership studies have only recently adopted the practice perspective. Leadership-as-practice is still an emerging stream of research that promises to understand leadership from the starting point of its performance. These studies all ask a central question (albeit in different ways): How does leadership happen *in situ*? A central tenet of this stream of study is to move the focal point of inquiry from leaders to leadership itself (Crevani, Lindgren & Packendorff, 2010), which is then seen as something accomplished on a daily basis in organizational settings. The premise of these studies is that leadership emerges from interactions happening in context. This root is crucial to all studies of organizational phenomena influenced by the so-called "practice turn" (Schatzki, 2001), such as strategy-as-practice (e.g., Golsorkhi, Rouleau, Seidl & Vaara, 2010; Vaara & Whittington, 2012), project-as-practice (e.g., Blomquist, Hällgren, Nilsson & Söderholm, 2010; Hällgren & Wilson, 2008), practice studies of technology (e.g., Orlikowski, 2007), learning (e.g., Gherardi, 2005), and accounting (e.g., Fauré & Rouleau, 2011). All of these studies are grounded in the ideas that a better, more detailed understanding of these phenomena requires moving closer to action and considering what is routinely done by actors as they engage in these activities. In many instances, the practice perspective has been embraced by researchers in organization studies as a theoretical inspiration to enlarge the view of who, in organizational settings, contribute to action. For instance, this impulse has been at the core of the strategy-as-practice stream of research, in which many researchers have emphasized that strategy is not something an organization *has*, but rather something that people *do*—implying that, in this context, the definition of who is involved in such a "doing" of strategy must be expanded to include more "ordinary" actors than were usually presented in the more mainstream literature on strategy (for an overview of strategy-as-practice, see Vaara & Whittington, 2012).

Over the last fifteen years, we have seen practice studies of organizational phenomena multiply and reflections on what happens in practice deepen. We have seen a similar movement towards this practice in the vast field of leadership, which has opened a number of interesting lines of inquiry. These studies have offered us detailed accounts of how leadership is produced or experienced in various settings (e.g., Carroll, Levy & Richmond, 2008; Denis *et al.*, 2010) and how it creates context for action (e.g., Endrissat & von Arx, 2013), while showing us the variety of actors involved in this production (e.g., Raelin, 2011) or revealing how such a daily production unfolds (e.g., Vine, Holmes, Marra, Pfeifer & Jackson, 2008). These contributions all show that leadership is much more than the acts of "great men" presenting specific traits (Fletcher, 2004). Given that a number of studies belonging to the leadership-as-practice stream have firmly anchored their inquiry in opposition to the dominant leader-centric approach to leadership— aiming simultaneously at criticizing this conception and at renewing our understanding of it (see, for example, Crevani *et al.*, 2007, 2010)—it is not surprising to note that leadership-as-practice studies have mainly dealt with what is done by human actors in context, as they go about their tasks. When the leadership-as-practice agenda suggests moving our view of leadership closer to action, one of the key questions it investigates becomes, "Who contributes to action?", wherein "action" is specifically understood as "action that constitutes leadership."

Yet, as a number of researchers (including those in this volume) have underlined, there is much more at play than a simple focus on "what people do." Recent contributions to the practice perspective in organization studies have highlighted the various elements that are implied in practice and have tried to document them to develop a finer understanding of practice itself. Materiality is always involved when it comes to definitions of practice. Both Schatzki (2001) and Reckwitz (2002)—who offered two commonly used definitions of practice in organization studies—placed materiality at the heart of practice. More recently, Nicolini (2012) teased out various elements involved in the notion of practice and categorized them as five dimensions: work and effort, materiality, agency, knowledge, and power. Following the identification of these five fundamental dimensions of practice, and underlining the ubiquity of the concept of practice in many social theories, Nicolini proposed a "theoretical toolkit" approach to attend to them. These five dimensions underline the richness and inherent complexity of the concept of practice. They also highlight the challenge that studying practices poses to researchers, and it may be quite difficult to simultaneously address all of these dimensions in a single study. However, as it relates to my reflection, Nicolini's work on the concept of practice demonstrates that materiality is an integral part of the notion of practice.

that "things" can lead as humans can. Hybrid agency posits that agency is not located in actors—human or non-human—but rather emerges out of the associations between human and non-human actors as they happen in context. In this sense, action is always sociomaterial, echoing what has been said about the sociomateriality of practices (see for example Feldman & Orlikowski, 2011 and Orlikowski, 2007). There is a proximity between this relational conception of agency and what researchers who work on developing a relational understanding of leadership have suggested. The main difference lies in the space allocated to materiality. Second, the documented effects of materiality on collective action, like creating shared understanding, bridging actors and perspectives, or facilitating cooperation (see studies on boundary objects, like Bechky, 2003 and Yakura, 2002, for example), also can be seen as some of the commonly attributed effects of leadership. Other studies have shown that materiality can give a sense of direction and help in obtaining commitment and assigning tasks (see for example Callon, 2002; Sergi, 2013; and Winsor, 2006), effects that we can easily associate with leadership. When we think about leadership in terms of specific effects, the field of who and what can produce these effects suddenly widens. As studies that offer a more active role to materiality in organizational action often note, making such a move should not be interpreted as "removing" or "denying" agency to humans; it simply sheds a different light on organizational action. This widening has been nicely captured by Cooren's (2006) idea of organizations as "plenum of agencies," where the agencies can be human, non-human, textual, architectural, etc.

To summarize, from the practice perspective, materiality is one of the key dimensions identified in the definition of practice. Following this identification, the central issue becomes how to approach and address materiality. To do so, I have first suggested fully embracing a process ontology, because such a position allows researchers to get closer to action as it unfolds—in this case, a specific form of action we label "leadership." By getting close to leadership as action, we come to see it as more of a *product* of collective interactions, as a result—in other words, as an effect of collective action. In turn, this focus on what is happening *in situ* leads us to ask the following question: What contributes to action and what makes a difference in it (Cooren, 2004; Latour, 2005)? This question allows us to redefine the notion of agency, enlarging it to include materiality. Influenced by the Latourian idea of hybrid agency (amongst many other influences), the CCO perspective proposes to investigate how organizational phenomena, such as leadership, are constituted in communication—which implies considering both humans and non-humans as they are interacting, conversing, and involved in a variety of processes. Although embracing this line of inquiry in leadership studies has clear potential, as Tourish (2013, 2014) and Fairhurst and Connaughton (2014) have underlined, this potential remains to be explored. This chapter should be seen as a rejoinder to their calls to adopt this communicative lens in the study of leadership.

In line with these ideas, I have proposed two shifts in leadership study. The first one moves away from individual leaders and towards leadership, while the second one, rather than viewing leadership as a cause of action, sees it as a consequence of collective action, in which more than humans participate. Pushing these ideas further, I suggest conceptualizing leadership as one of the products of collective action, as the consequence of social practices accomplished through interactions involving various actants (to use Latour's concept), and as happening via processes constantly in movement. Moreover, to distinguish leadership from other products of ongoing flows of action, I propose considering products that not only propel and drive the continuation of action, but specifically those have directing, shaping, and/or ordering effects on the endeavors in which the actors are involved. I have chosen these three broad categories of results for empirically identifying leadership because they evoke the etymology of the word "leadership," which refers both to the action of *guiding* and to the notion of *shape* (Harper, 2015). My line of thinking also has been influenced by Crevani *et al.* (2010) and Lindgren, Packendorff and Tham. (2011), who have suggested that leadership should be viewed as interactions constructing direction, co-orientation, and action space.

Empirical illustration

One of the strengths of the CCO perspective comes from its detailed empirical applications. Indeed, given its strong methodological commitment to ethnographic work and description, Cooren (2006) has evoked the "radical empiricism" associated with the perspective. Moreover, such detailed descriptions have the power to offer vivid illustrations of the constitutive effects of communication. To illustrate the potential of the CCO perspective, I will use a vignette borrowed from a larger field study influenced by the ethnographic tradition (Czarniawska-Joerges, 1992; Van Maanen, 2001). This case study revolved around the Graph Project, a software development project taking place in a Montréal-based company named Soft-A.[2] The study's initial aims were to (1) develop a processual view of the way the project was organized over time, (2) identify the practices that made the project happen, over time, and (3) reveal how materiality contributed to these processes. The fieldwork consisted of observing meetings, conducting interviews, and collecting documents.[3] Given the nature of the work done in the project—in particular, writing code—documents were key to studying the project and seeing its management materialize. Work in software development teams at Soft-A entailed many individual tasks, and meetings were the main locus of collective work. I did not have permission to record the meetings; therefore I was unable to capture exactly what was said. Nevertheless, I noted all the interactions between team members, paying attention to the way activities and discussions developed, and who (or what) intervened during the conversations. My analysis led me to consider the results of these episodes of collective work through the unfolding of collective action. Although I could not conduct conversation analysis as is often done in CCO studies, I collected the necessary material to analyze the interactions and their effects on the team's actions. During my fieldwork, I also collected numerous documents such as plans, reports, and emails. In addition to the meetings, the production, circulation, and discussion of documents were central processes in the Graph Project. All meetings included long discussions of such previously circulated documents. It is through this combination of meetings, individual work, and documents that the Graph Project was structured, managed, and completed (see also Sergi, 2012).

With this study, I simultaneously looked at what the human actors did and also how non-human actors sustained action. I proposed and illustrated that all the processes and interactions in this project profited from the presence of various objects and tools, such as documents. They played a key role in constituting the project—but one that was different from the role of the human actors. Their presence shaped everyone's work and helped the project become tangible and hold on over time. They made a difference by facilitating, supporting, and advancing the project. It should be noted that what documents did—like making visible, articulating, and signaling various elements—is also linked to the properties of this class of objects. Textual objects are particularly apt at conveying a high degree of detail, moving through space and time without changing, and lasting, that is they are "immutable mobiles" (Latour, 1986). It is according to these properties that they were mobilized in the project, and it is also because of them that they had significant consequences for its realization. Overall, the actions they accomplished are among those that make any project happen: materializing the product, the work, and the collective; exposing and explaining what has been done, indicating the path to follow, initiating thought and discussion, organizing work, and warning and reminding team members of priorities and constraints (see Sergi, 2013, for more details about documents' contributions in projects).

In other words, understanding how the Graph Project moved from idea to completed product led me to discuss the various contributions made to this process by human and non-human actors, thus highlighting the project's socio-materiality. The material collected and analyzed during this case study offers many examples of leadership as being elaborated both by humans and non-humans during these team meetings. Following the ideas I discussed in the first section of this chapter, I identify leadership as what directed, shaped, and ordered the project's unfolding. The next section offers a detailed illustration of one such instance of leadership's hybrid production.

The chosen vignette corresponds to an episode taken from the beginning of the project, which revolved around a team meeting and a document mobilized during this moment of collective work. This is the team's fourth meeting and four team members are present: Sally, the project leader, Frank and Oliver, the main software programmers who will have the task of rewriting the code, and Matt, Sally's direct supervisor, whose presence is required to keep this project aligned with other projects happening simultaneously at the company.

A document—identified as "Document 7"—has been distributed by email before the meeting is held. Document 7 exposes for the first time the full approach that the team could follow to complete its work. It exposes how the work on part of the Graph application will be undertaken. Many screenshots accompany the code and illustrate how the Graph application will look once the code has been rewritten. The document explains what this work will entail and gives meticulous indications to the other developers; it informs the team members of all the modifications that need to be covered. The document also suggests ways to approach the work described within. But not everything pertaining to this approach has been covered before the meeting; passages in the document are written in capital letters so that the developers do not lose sight of them. Document 7 is also illustrated with other figures, including one that offers an overview of the application's elements, revealing which ones will be newly developed, and where they will be inserted in the code. This figure shows what will be concretized, provides reminders of all the details that must be adjusted, and highlights the continuity between past and future versions of Graph. Finally, Document 7 contains a section entitled "Limita- tions" that warns of the absence of an element that might have to be developed later on. The document ends with the next tasks to be completed and the number of days allotted to each of them, thus directing the developers' subsequent work.

After three previous meetings mainly dedicated to defining and specifying the nature and details of the Graph Project, the fourth meeting is more technical. Its main goal is to answer the questions of how to concretize decisions that have been made and agreed on, and how to conduct development. After the lengthy discussions that characterized earlier meetings and led to the definition of the Graph Project, the team members feel they know enough about the project's parameters to start considering its thorny technical issues. Deciding what the new Graph application will do and what it will look like is one thing, but figuring out how to achieve this is another, as it involves thinking about how each part of the code works and imagining how, once brought together, these changes will interact with each other. Envisioning the work to accomplish is difficult, espe- cially this early in the project; yet, it is necessary in order to plan, organize, and direct its development. This meeting is dedicated to laying the foundation for the actual realization of the work.

During the meeting, most of the discussions revolve around constraints, options, and choices. Two sources of constraints are evoked. The first stems from the project on which they agreed (what is expected of the new Graph applica- tion), and the other is associated with choices made when the previous version of Graph was written. The team's work is complicated by the fact that many directions could be taken in producing the new Graph application; each of them must be considered at this stage of the project, before altering the code. Also, because the team is developing a more detailed view of the project, aspects that could not be discussed before, such as technical elements, are now open to con- sideration. The exchanges cover every possibility the team members are con- sidering, weighing each one's strengths and weaknesses. These possibilities will not make a difference for the end users as they are not altering the Graph application's interface; however, the possibility they choose will impact their daily coding work. A series of interactions happen in these discussions and they all adopt a similar form: one of the developers makes a suggestion or asks a question, and the rest of the team, Sally included, discusses it. Sally closes the exchange by stating which decision has been taken, validates it with the developers, and then distributes the tasks to be accomplished.

The company's development methodology helps the team decide on the possibilities with which it is presented. Following a developer's comment about the "best moment" to start one of the many development tasks, the team members then ask themselves to which step of the methodology the particular task belongs. Given that technical elements do not always fit in pre-defined categories, the team members have to negotiate before agreeing on the best time to work on a task. This methodology also helps the team sort out what needs to be done sooner rather than later, and thus prioritize all the tasks that must be completed. Finally, all team members also conduct time estimations. When a task is mentioned, someone estimates the number of days needed to complete the task, which the other team members then evaluate based on their previous experiences.

Work organization and distribution is intertwined with the technical discussions. Altogether, these exchanges reveal that the team is thinking collectively; questions are asked, possibilities suggested, answers proposed and debated, and explanations given. Even though everyone participates in these discussions, distinctions between team members are visible in their interventions. The developers, Frank and Oliver, refer to technical points, and the project manager Sally translates them in management terms. Technical concerns are paramount this early in the project. For example, at some point, the team recognizes a delicate technical issue but is unable to decipher the mystery surrounding its discovery. The exchanges move from being about the technical issue, to trying to organize how to approach and deal with this unknown element. At a certain point, Matt tells Sally, "You'll have nice questions to answer … ," implying that this element will be difficult to solve. In the presence of this mystery, the team members search for the best expert to consult. Uncovering this element awakens not only a technical question, but also a managerial one. This puzzling element—and the consideration that comes with it—opens the door to a broader management discussion, one that touches on planning, sequencing of the tasks to start, and numbers of days to allot to each of these tasks. Most of these management decisions can only be made by referring to the technical dimensions of the project, but these have to be converted into managerial terms by Sally. She is particularly comfortable in this position as she has a strong technical background and much experience in leading projects. Towards the end of the meeting, she outlines her expectations for the next meeting, structuring the work to be completed, and identifying the targets to be reached. While presenting what has to be produced (in technical terms), she invokes project management issues: number of meetings to hold, allocation of tasks, and the time necessary to complete them.

In this ongoing and collective reflection, Document 7 plays an important and active role. First, the meeting is a direct consequence of its production. Without this document, the team members would not have been summoned to work on it, nor united at that specific moment in time. Document 7 can thus be seen as a temporary link, with the responsibility of assembling the otherwise dismantled team. Globally speaking, Document 7 encourages the team members to talk during the meeting, stimulating collective reflection. It also organizes the team's collective work: team members follow the order in which technical points are enumerated in the document. But Document 7 should not be seen as a simple list of points to cover; it is an intermediary object (Vinck, 2009) in itself, a part of the work that leads to the completion of the project. The team questions its content, but also refines it as lines of the document are singled out, scrutinized, and rewritten. All copies of Document 7 are covered with annotations by the end of the meeting.

At some point, the team members start considering a section of code exposed in Document 7. While they are reading, Frank, who prepared this code, explains his course of action and exposes the reasons for his proceeding in this way. Once he has finished, Oliver joins the discussion and explains how he is going to build on Frank's work. This section of Document 7 helps articulate what has already been accomplished and what remains to be done. The figure included in Document 7 supports and illustrates Oliver's explanations. In the course of this discussion, Sally and Matt question Frank about how he has articulated certain elements and about his reflection during this process. This second point is particularly important to share as it will help in guiding the other developers in their future work. They need to know what he has considered while preparing Document 7, what he has included and rejected, because this helps the team members create a unified approach to the work.

In the end, the team reaches a decision that, given its complexity, requires them to hold two more meetings during which they thoroughly cover the technical work sketched out during this meeting. This complexity was expected by the team, but they did not know when it would appear, nor which specific form it would take. This episode of collective work has not only allowed the team members to begin planning the work in a more detailed way, but also to slowly discover exactly what elements will be technically challenging. At this point, they are gradually including these challenges in their management of the project. As this snapshot of the Graph Project shows, this management is the fruit of a joint process, a consequence of interactions and collective work. After this meeting, the developments' foundations are laid and agreed on; the priorities for the next weeks are identified, described, and shared; and the planning and organization of the work are set. The project has gained in direction, shape, and order.

Leadership (understood, as presented, either as directing, shaping, or ordering effects stemming from interactions and collective action) is produced through the accumulation and articulation of many small elements: the answer to a question, a figure in a document, and the steps of the methodology. Seen in this light, leadership appears as a rather mundane *bricolage*, collectively elaborated as the interactions between team members unfold, the fruit of social practices aiming at making the project happen and helped by the various objects used by the team members. Of course, not everything that was resolved, negotiated, decided on, or established during this meeting should be interpreted as leadership. For example, discussing technical possibilities has more to do with the writing of the code than with leadership.

As previously discussed, taking materiality into account in studying leadership should lead to viewing how the assemblage of humans and non-humans contributes to creating leadership effects. It can be suggested that the intertwining of humans and non-humans (of which the most significant non-human is Document 7) generated direction, shape, and order during this moment in the project's life. It is also possible to identify which effects were created, at one point or another, by everyone and everything involved. By analyzing the vignette presented, we can recognize who or what produced some of the directing, shaping, and ordering effects that I associate with the collective production of leadership. This first requires listing all the effects that are created in interactions between human and non-human actors. They must then be sorted, as not all effects are related to leadership. Those linked to leadership can then be associated with the three broad categories of leadership effects. Table 6.1 summarizes the effects associated with this vignette I presented.

When comparing the state of the Graph Project before and after this meeting, it appears to have gained direction, shape, and order. Taken together, it is the combination of the people who met at that time, what they said, the choices they made, and what helped in producing a sense of direction that created leadership, temporarily, for the project. It is in this sense that leadership appears as a processual, collective, and mundane effect of unfolding action.

By choosing this approach, my intention was not to reduce the importance of human actors formally identified as "leaders." As my illustration has shown, Sally, the project leader, had a decisive influence on what happened during this specific episode by impacting the orientation of the meeting and having the power to impose decisions. In this sense, it is important to consider people in leadership positions, either formal or informal, and their specific mark and impact on the course of action. But if our inquiries question what leadership is by looking outside the individual leader's choices and behaviors, I believe it is fundamental that we open this phenomenon's definition to include other actors, so as to take into consideration anything that can have what I have labeled "leadership effects." I have defined such effects in terms of directing, shaping, or ordering, and used my illustration to reveal that these effects can be produced by a variety of elements: the project leader, the interactions and discussions between all team members at the meeting in question, Document 7 (via its presence and its content—lines of code, figures, list of tasks, etc.), and the development methodology.

TABLE 6.1 Producing leadership during the team meeting

Effects produced during the interactions	Category of leadership effects
• Negotiating what should be included and excluded from this project (Document 7, team members) • Defining targets to be reached before the next meeting (Sally, project leader) • Exposing the work to be done, suggesting ways to approach it (Document 7, team members) • Giving indications to developers (Sally, Document 7) • Warning of an element's absence, reminding of its importance for later on (Document 7)	Directing
• Laying the foundation of the development (Document 7) • Discussing constraints and options: debating possibilities, making choices (team members) • Showing what will be concretized through screenshots of the predicted final result (Document 7)	Shaping
• Sequencing and prioritizing the tasks to accomplish (Sally, development methodology) • Planning and estimating time (Document 7, team members) • Choosing the best expert to consult about a newly encountered technical mystery (team members) • Illustrating the relationships between various components (Document 7) • Identifying the next tasks to be accomplished and the time allocated to complete them (Document 7, team members)	Ordering

Documents make a difference in the production of leadership, as I have specifically shown in this vignette. This difference has led Cooren (2004) to talk of textual agency, which I also have explored (Sergi, 2013). If Document 7 makes a notable contribution to the process of elaborating leadership, its contribution goes beyond the specific instances where this production of leadership takes place. Generally speaking, because documents can be seen as immutable mobiles (Latour, 1986), exert a stabilizing power over the collective (Brown & Duguid, 2000; Geisler, 2001), and can make people act (Winsor, 2006), they not only help in solidifying the project and its numerous dimensions, but also expand, out of meetings and other instances of collective work, the directing, shaping, and ordering results produced *in situ*. Leadership, understood in these terms, is (at least partly) extended out of its site of collective elaboration. Document 7 will thus help stabilize what has been negotiated, in terms of direction, shape, and order, during the meeting. Because of their properties, texts grant greater stability to elements important to the continuation of action that would otherwise be more fragile and transient. After all, such a greater stability is obtained by mobilizing, or bringing into perspective, resources other than human actors (Latour, 2005; Strum & Latour, 1999). It is this general contribution of materiality that makes it especially relevant to the definition of leadership, and to its study.

Ultimately, this example also demonstrates that leadership, as collectively elaborated, can stabilize the project: it gives it shape (in the form of parameters to respect and tasks to complete), provides direction (where to go now, what to pursue, what to do next), and orders future action (by attributing work and deciding on the sequence of tasks to be accomplished). But such stabilization should not be confused with stability. As other scenes taken from the Graph Project would have shown, that which was produced via this specific assemblage provided leadership, but only for a certain time. From the work's progress, new technical surprises arose and time management difficulties were experienced. In turn, the leadership effects produced after this meeting became corroded by subsequent actions and unplanned circumstances, leading to a dismantling of this assemblage. The perspective explored here alludes to a provisional view of leadership, as effects that may last, or that may need to be re-produced over time.

Discussion and conclusion

To address the question of what leadership is, I have put forward three ideas in this chapter: first, that by rooting leadership in process ontology, we can see it as being processually elaborated while action is unfolding; second, leadership can be understood as a result, as an effect of action, and, more precisely, in terms of effects that produce directing, shaping, and ordering effects; and third, these effects stem from assemblages of human and non-human actors, simultaneously highlighting the materiality of leadership as well as its collective nature. Seen in this light, leadership appears as a provisional heterogeneous assemblage that changes, unexpected events, and the twists and turns of action can erode. As such, leadership is never fully stabilized, and reproducing leadership is always needed, as action evolves over time.

My reflection began with the practice perspective. As mentioned by various researchers (like Nicolini, 2012; Reckwitz, 2002; Reckwitz, 2001), the definition of the concept of practice already includes materiality, therefore making it intrinsically part of any practice. Viewing leadership as a practice thus implies acknowledging the place materiality holds in its daily production. However, until recently, materiality has rarely been included in leadership. To enrich our understanding of leadership, I have briefly presented in this chapter how such an inclusion could be achieved, both theoretically and empirically. The communicational nature of practices is rarely acknowledged in the practice perspective, while it is clear that interactions and practices happen through communication. As for leadership studies, communication has often been discussed, but very rarely in light of the CCO perspective. When we study practices, we observe people acting. In the context of leadership, we observe people interacting. Communication is already there, at the forefront. That is where leadership emerges; thus, it is not a stretch to give communication an important place in the production of leadership. It is an especially fruitful idea to define communication not as a vessel or as a resource, but as constituting phenomena. With its focus on processes and interactions and its hybrid conception of agency, CCO represents a promising and stimulating perspective for leadership studies.

My aim in presenting the selected vignette was two-fold. First, theoretically speaking, it served to briefly illustrate the potential of combining the previously described perspectives. I must underline, however, that this is only a partial illustration. Without the exact transcription of the conversations that took place during the meeting, some details regarding the local performance of leadership have been lost. The CCO-inspired approach can best be accessed when one can conduct conversation analysis, as, indicated by the variety of organization studies influenced by this stream of research, detailed accounts of what is happening in context and in interactions are the key empirical materials needed. This approach thus calls for a sensitivity to unfolding action and a broadening of that which is considered to be participating in this action, hence justifying why a process ontology and a hybrid view of agency are relevant bases for such an approach. Given this ontological anchoring, this approach could be applied to a number of organizational phenomena, and I have tried to showcase its potential for the study of leadership in the present chapter. Second, concerning method, this vignette gives an idea of how such studies are conducted and on what their analysis must focus. My approach can therefore be understood as a resolutely micro and empirical one that starts with—and stays close to—mundane action happening in organizational settings.

It is in this sense that I propose seeing leadership as a collective elaboration, always in action, being both socially and materially produced *in situ*. Moreover, it is by focusing not only on human actors but also on objects that I suggest conceiving leadership production as a co-construction. Fairhurst and Cooren (2009) have discussed how presence, this elusive quality of leaders, is both a hybrid construction and an attribute of individuals. My vignette should be seen as belonging to this same line of thinking, but with the difference being that I have looked at leadership, not leaders. However, just as they argued in their article, I view leadership as an assemblage, a combination of various contributions elaborated *in situ* that build on each other.

This perspective has a number of consequences. First of all, it implies that leadership must always be understood in context, and that it is fruitful to see it not as the cause of action, but as one of its consequences. Because it is a product of action, leadership is intimately tied to the social practices deployed, which points to the importance of seeing and understanding which actors are involved, what they are trying to achieve, and what they are struggling with when they are acting in organizational settings. Adopting a strong process ontology leads us to see leadership as being created, constructed, and made up, but also as transient and provisional. This indicates that leadership cannot be taken for granted, as it can become eroded by changes, unexpected events, and twists and turns. It also points towards the idea that leadership will (and might even have to) change form over time, depending on the circumstances. Directing, shaping, and ordering effects may be needed at all times in any organizational activity or endeavor, but the particular form they take will be closely connected to that which is happening at the moment.

Also, paying more attention to materiality when investigating leadership has benefits for our inquiries into this phenomenon. It leads to a finer understanding of how leadership is produced, as it becomes viewed as an emergent product of human and non-human actors (Fairhurst & Cooren, 2009; Hawkins, 2015; Mulcahy & Perillo, 2010). It can also lead us to identify the conditions and practices that help produce, or hamper, the leadership needed for the continuation of action. Finally, it also allows for considering how the design of material elements used and mobilized in organizational settings can influence their contribution to leadership in action and, more generally, to what is collectively achieved.

From a broader standpoint, one of the difficulties associated with the approach explored in this chapter pertains to the definition of leadership I have put forward. As is sometimes the case with studies adopting a strong process ontology, distinguishing the organizational phenomena from one another may prove to be complex. Are the effects I have identified in the brief analysis presented here really a question of leadership? Could they be linked to other phenomena, like organizing? My answer to this relevant question would be to simply follow one of the key methodological principles of the CCO perspective: start and work from the *terra firma* of interactions (Cooren, 2006). Seen in this light, there is no "essence" to leadership: there are only interactions constituting what can be interpreted by actors and researchers as leadership. Yet, the risk of diluting the concept of leadership (Denis *et al.*, 2012) remains and researchers should keep this in mind when conducting studies from this perspective.

Finally, this chapter has only touched on the vast topic of materiality, and the chosen vignette mobilized one specific category of materiality: documents. But materiality alludes to something much wider than simple objects. It would, therefore, be highly relevant for studies following the approach proposed in these pages to include the body in their empirical analysis, and also to better consider physical space. Bodies and embodiment have been studied in leadership (see for example Ropo, Sauer & Salovaara, 2013; Sinclair, 2005), and so has physical space (like in the case of Carroll, Chapter 5, this volume), but these topics have clear research potential, especially from the practice and CCO perspectives, as applied to leadership.

Notes

1 This chapter has benefited from presentations given on this topic at the ISLC conference in Lund, Sweden (2010), and at two symposiums at the Academy of

Management (2012 and 2014). Comments received during these presentations have contributed to developing and strengthening this chapter's ideas. I thank the various participants I met during these events for their valuable questions and remarks.
2 Details regarding the company and the persons interviewed have been modified to ensure confidentiality.
3 I observed 22 meetings, conducted 25 interviews, and collected 80 documents.

References

Alvesson, M., & Sveningsson, S. (2003). Managers doing leadership: The extra-ordinarization of the mundane. *Human Relations*, 56(12), 1435–1459.
Ashcraft, K. L., Kuhn, T. R., & Cooren, F. (2009). Constitutional amendments: "Materializing" organizational communication. *Academy of Management Annals*, 3(1), 1–64.
Bechky, B. A. (2003). Object lessons: Workplace artifacts as representations of occupational jurisdiction. *The American Journal of Sociology*, 109(3), 720–752.
Blomquist, T., Hällgren, M., Nilsson, A., & Söderholm, A. (2010). Project-as-practice: In search of project management research that matters. *Project Management Journal*, 41(1), 5–16.
Brown, J. S., & Duguid, P. (2000). *The social life of information*. Boston: Harvard Business School Press.
Brummans, B., Cooren, F., Robichaud, D., & Taylor, J. R. (2014). Approaches in research on the communicative constitution of organizations. In L. L. Putnam & D. Mumby (Eds.), *Sage handbook of organizational communication* (3rd edition) (pp. 173–194). London: Sage.
Callon, M. (2002). Writing and (re)writing devices as tools for managing complexity. In J. Law & A. Mol (Eds), *Complexities: Social studies of knowledge practices* (pp. 191–218). Durham, NC: Duke University Press.
Carroll, B., Levy, L., & Richmond, D. (2008). Leadership as practice: Challenging the competency paradigm. *Leadership*, 4(4), 363–379.
Chia, R. (1997). Essai: Thirty years on: From organizational structures to the organization of thought. *Organization Studies*, 18(4), 685–707.
Collinson, D. (2005). Dialectics of leadership. *Human Relations*, 58(11), 1419–1442.
Collinson, D., & Grint, K. (2005). Editorial: The leadership agenda. *Leadership*, 1(1), 5–9.
Cooren, F. (2004). Textual agency: How texts do things in organizational settings. *Organization*, 11(3), 373–393.
Cooren, F. (2006). The organizational world as a plenum of agencies. In F. Cooren, J. R. Taylor, & E. Van Every (Eds.), *Communication as organizing: Practical approaches to research into the dynamic of text and conversation* (pp. 81–100). Mahwah, NY: Lawrence Erlbaum Associates.
Cooren, F., Fairhurst, G. T., & Huët, R. (2012). Why matter always matters in (organizational) communication. In P. M. Leonardi, B. A. Nardi & J. Kallinikos (Eds.), *Materiality and organizing: Social interaction in a technological world* (pp. 296–314). Oxford: Oxford University Press.
Cooren, F., Kuhn, T. R., Cornelissen, J. P., & Clark, T. (2011). Communication, organizing and organization: An overview and introduction to the special issue. *Organization Studies*, 32(9), 1149–1170.
Crevani, L., Lindgren, M., & Packendorff, J. (2007). Shared leadership: A postheroic perspective on leadership as a collective construction. *International Journal of Leadership Studies*, 3(1), 40–67.
Crevani, L., Lindgren, M., & Packendorff, J. (2010). Leadership, not leaders: On the study of leadership as practices and interactions. *Scandinavian Journal of Management*, 26, 77–86.

Cunliffe, A. L., & Eriksen, M. (2011). Relational leadership. *Human Relations*, 64(11), 1425–1449.

Czarniawska-Joerges, B. (1992). *Exploring complex organizations: A cultural perspective*. Newbury Park, CA: Sage.

Denis, J.-L., Langley, A., & Rouleau, L. (2010). The practice of leadership in the messy world of organizations. *Leadership*, 6(1), 67–88.

Denis, J.-L., Langley, A., & Sergi, V. (2012). Leadership in the plural. *Academy of Management Annals*, 6(1), 211–283.

Endrissat, N., & von Arx, W. (2013). Leadership practices and context: Two sides of the same coin. *Leadership*, 9(2), 278–304.

Fairhurst, G. T., & Connaughton, S. L. (2014). Leadership: A communicative perspective. *Leadership*, 10(1), 7–35.

Fairhurst, G. T., & Cooren, F. (2009). Leadership as the hybrid production of presence(s). *Leadership*, 5(4), 469–490.

Fairhurst, G. T., & Grant, D. (2010). The social construction of leadership: A sailing guide. *Management Communication Quarterly*, 24(2), 171–210.

Fauré, B., & Rouleau, L. (2011). The strategic competence of accountants and middle managers in budget making. *Accounting, Organizations and Society*, 36(3), 167–182.

Feldman, M. S., & Orlikowski, W. J. (2011). Theorizing practice and practicing theory. *Organization Science*, 22(5), 1240–1253.

Fletcher, J. K. (2004). The paradox of postheroic leadership: An essay on gender, power, and transformational change. *Leadership Quarterly*, 15(5), 647–661.

Geisler, C. (2001). Textual objects: Accounting for the role of texts in the everyday life of complex organizations. *Written Communication*, 18(3), 296–325.

Gherardi, S. (2005). *Organizational knowledge: The texture of workplace learning*. Malden, MA: Blackwell Publications.

Golsorkhi, D., Rouleau, L., Seidl, D., & Vaara, E. (2010). *Cambridge handbook of strategy-as-practice*. Cambridge: Cambridge University Press.

Gronn, P. (2002). Distributed leadership as a unit of analysis. *Leadership Quarterly*, 13(4), 423–451.

Hällgren, M., & Wilson, T. L. (2008). The nature and management of crises in construction projects: Projects-as-practice observations. *International Journal of Project Management*, 26, 830–838.

Harper, D. (2015). Leadership. In *Online etymology dictionary*. Available at www.etymonline.com/index.php (accessed 29 May 2015).

Hawkins, B. (2015). Ship-shape: Materializing leadership in the British Royal Navy. *Human Relations*, 68(6), 951–971.

Helin, J., Hernes, T., Hjorth, D., & Holt, R. (2014). *The Oxford handbook of process philosophy and organization studies*. Oxford: Oxford University Press.

Hernes, T. (2008). *Understanding organization as process: Theory for a tangled world*. London: Routledge.

Hernes, T. (2014). *A process theory of organization*. Oxford: Oxford University Press.

Holmberg, I., & Tyrstrup, M. (2010). Well then—What now? An everyday approach to managerial leadership. *Leadership*, 6(4), 353–372.

Hosking, D. M. (1988). Organizing, leadership and skilful process. *Journal of Management Studies*, 25(2), 147–166

Larsson, M., & Lundholm, S. E. (2010). Leadership as work-embedded influence: A micro-discursive analysis of an everyday interaction in a bank. *Leadership*, 6(2), 159–184.

Larsson, M., & Lundholm, S. E. (2013). Talking work in a bank: A study of organizing properties of leadership in work interactions. *Human Relations*, 66(8), 1101–1129.

Latour, B. (1986). Visualisation and cognition: Thinking with eyes and hands. In H. Kuklick (Ed.), *Knowledge and society studies in the sociology of culture past and present*, Vol. 6 (pp. 1–40). Greenwich, CT: JAI Press.

Latour, B. (1993). *We have never been modern*. Cambridge, MA: Harvard University Press.

Latour, B. (1994). On technical mediation: Philosophy, sociology, genealogy. *Common Knowledge*, 3, 29–64.

Latour, B. (2005). *Reassembling the social: An introduction to actor-network-theory*. Oxford: Oxford University Press.

Lindgren, M., Packendorff, J., & Tham, H. (2011). Relational dysfunctionality: Leadership interactions in a Sarbanes-Oxley Act implementation project. *European Journal of International Management*, 5(1), 13–29.

Mailhot, C., Gagnon, S., Langley, A., & Binette, L. F. (in press). Distributing leadership across people and objects in a collaborative research project. *Leadership*. Online before print, doi: 10.1177/1742715014543578.

Mulcahy, D., & Perillo, S. (2010). Thinking management and leadership within colleges and schools somewhat differently: A practice-based, actor-network theory perspective. *Educational Management Administration & Leadership*, 39(1), 122–145.

Nicolini, D. (2012). *Practice theory, work, and organization: An introduction*. Oxford: Oxford University Press.

Oborn, E., Barrett, M., & Dawson, S. (2013). Distributed leadership in policy formulation: A sociomaterial perspective. *Organization Studies*, 34(2), 253–276.

Orlikowski, W. J. (2007). Sociomaterial practices: Exploring technology at work. *Organization Studies*, 28(9), 1435–1448.

Pearce, C. L., & Conger, J. A. (2003). *Shared leadership: Reframing the hows and whys of leadership*. Thousand Oaks, CA: Sage Publications.

Pentland, B. T., & Singh, H. (2012). Materiality: What are the consequences? In P. M. Leonardi et al. (Eds.), *Materiality and organizing: Social interaction in a technological world* (pp. 287–295). Oxford: Oxford University Press.

Pye, A. (2005). Leadership and organizing: Sensemaking in action. *Leadership*, 1(1), 31–49.

Raelin, J. A. (2011). From leadership-as-practice to leaderful practice. *Leadership*, 7(2), 195–211.

Reckwitz, A. (2002). Toward a theory of social practices: A development in culturalist theorizing. *European Journal of Social Theory*, 5(2), 243–263.

Rescher, N. (2012). Process philosophy. In *Stanford encyclopedia of philosophy*. Available at http://plato.stanford.edu/entries/process-philosophy/ (accessed 29 May 2015).

Ropo, A., Sauer, E., & Salovaara, P. (2013). Embodiment of leadership through material place. *Leadership*, 9(3), 378–395.

Schatzki, T. R. (2001). Introduction—practice theory. In T. R. Schatzki, K. Knorr-Cetina, & E. von Savigny (Eds.), *The practice turn in contemporary theory* (pp. 1–14). London: Routledge.

Sergi, V. (2012). Bounded becoming: Insights from understanding projects in situation. *International Journal of Managing Projects in Business*, 5(3), 345–363.

Sergi, V. (2013). Constituting the temporary organization: Documents in the context of projects. In D. Robichaud & F. Cooren (Eds.), *Organization and organizing: Materiality, agency, discourse* (pp. 190–206). New York: Routledge.

Sinclair, A. (2005). Body possibilities in leadership. *Leadership*, 1(4), 387–406.

Spillane, J. P., Halverson, R., & Diamond, J. B. (2001). Investigating school leadership practice: A distributed perspective. *Educational Researcher*, 30(3), 23–28.

Strum, S., & Latour, B. (1999). Redefining the social link: From baboons to humans. In D. Mackenzie, & J. Wajcman (Eds.), *The social shaping of technology* (2nd edition) (pp. 116–125). Buckingham: Open University Press.

Taylor, J. R., & Robichaud, D. (2004). Finding the organization in the communication: Discourse as action and sensemaking. *Organization*, 11(3), 395–413.

Tourish, D. (2013). *The dark side of transformational leadership: A critical perspective*. New York: Routledge.

Tourish, D. (2014). Leadership, more or less? A processual, communication perspective on the role of agency in leadership theory. *Leadership*, 10(1), 79–98.

Uhl-Bien, M. (2006). Relational leadership theory: Exploring the social processes of leadership and organizing. *Leadership Quarterly*, 17(6), 654–676.

Vaara, E., & Whittington, R. (2012). Strategy-as-practice: Taking social practices seriously. *Academy of Management Annals*, 6(1), 285–336.

Van Maanen, J. (2001). Afterword: Natives 'R' us: Some notes on the ethnography of organizations. In D. Gellner & Hirsch, E., (Eds.), *Inside organizations: Anthropologists at work* (pp. 231–262). Oxford: Berg.

Vinck, D. (2009). De l'objet intermédiaire à l'objet-frontière. *Revue d'anthropologie des connaissances*, 3(1), 51–72.

Vine, B., Holmes, J., Marra, M., Pfeifer, D., & Jackson, B. (2008). Exploring co-leadership talk through interactional sociolinguistics. *Leadership*, 4(3), 339–360.

Winsor, D. (2006). Using writing to structure agency: An examination of engineers' practice. *Technical Communication Quarterly*, 15(4), 411–430.

Wood, M. (2005). The fallacy of misplaced leadership. *Journal of Management Studies*, 42(6), 1101–1121.

Yakura, E. K. (2002). Charting time: Timelines as temporal boundary object. *Academy of Management Journal*, 45(5), 956–970.

7

TURNING LEADERSHIP INSIDE-OUT AND BACK-TO-FRONT

A dialogical-hermeneutical account

John Shotter

> What determines our judgment, our concepts and reactions, is not what *one* man is doing *now*, an individual action, but the whole hurly-burly of human actions, the background against which we see an action.
>
> *(Wittgenstein, 1981, no. 567)*

Introduction: philosophical "scene setting"

Raelin (2014) calls for "the reframing of leadership, as we know it" (p. 2), for us to no longer see it as residing simply in the traits or behaviors of single, special individuals, but to see it *as a practice*, as "the release of agency through its incarnation as a dialogic structure" (p. 2). By "agency," Raelin means a form of *collaborative agency* in which, rather than as individuals acting separately from each other, people acting in relation to each other become able to do things that they cannot do apart. As he sees it, something is created in people acting within two-way, back-and-forth, *dialogic relations* with each other that is impossible in one-way, *monological relations*.

Indeed, Raelin goes so far as to question whether the idea of leadership-as-practice can continue to be expressed in terms merely of "an influence relationship between leaders and followers." Instead, he suggests that we now need to "turn leadership on its head... [and to] consider whether a relationship of leadership may occur without *influence* in either direction" (p. 10)—for, in an influence relationship, people try to manipulate each other into carrying out ends that are *not mutually created*. When this is the case, power is exerted, and leadership is reduced simply to management, a movement toward new horizons is reduced to the efficient implementation either of already existing ends, or of ends *imposed on* a group of people by outside others. Whereas, as we shall see, when people in truly *dialogic relationships* meet, as Bakhtin (1986) puts it, "without rank" (p. 97), the creation of uniquely new ends, both unforeseen and unforeseeable, becomes a possibility.

But more than this is at issue: What is special about seeing *what we call leadership* as emerging in the course of an unfolding, *dialogically structured* process, occurring among all concerned within a social group, is that it is impossible to hold any of the individuals involved responsible for its emergence. I say "what we call leadership" because, as will become clear, as Raelin (2014) suggests, once we enter into two-way, *dialogical* (Bakhtin 1986; Gadamer, 2000) relations with the others in our surroundings, rather than one-way, *monological* ones, we find that, rather than discovering pre-existing things in our inquiries, we continually bring such "things" into existence. As a consequence, its "ownership" can be shared by all— it "belongs" to no-one in particular. Further, in such processes, everything that happens, everything that even single individuals do, happens in response to, as well as *in anticipation of*, how others in the group have *already acted*, and/or *will act* in the future. Thus in such circumstances as these, all involved can feel that they are working towards a *common good* (Sandel, 2012), towards ends of their own *critical creation*, in that as a *dialogically emerging* outcome, it cannot be arrived at by any merely "technical," "logical," or "calculational" means. For besides those directly addressed in such processes, at work in the background to any dialogue, as Bakhtin (1986) makes clear, is what he calls the *superaddressee*, a third party "whose absolutely *just responsive understanding* is presumed, either in some metaphysical distance or in distant historical time" (p. 126, emphasis added).

However, given our upbringing in western, Cartesian-Newtonian forms of thought, it is not at all easy to see leadership in this non-mechanistic and non-technocratic fashion. For, not only later in life as professional academics and intellectuals, but from birth, we are immersed in a *common sense* in which it is taken for granted that the world is made up of *separate, nameable things* in motion according to discoverable laws, rules, or principles—a common sense that, as we shall see, is very difficult to question and to move beyond. Thus, those of us who see scientific methods and modes of thought, along with theories couched in unambiguous technical concepts, as providing the *only pathway to reliably effective action*, will see little sense in the re-orientations I will propose below, especially to the extent to which I will extol the value of ill-defined and unfinished notions, open to yet further specification. How can clarity ever emerge from vagueness?

But as will become clear (I hope), if we are to take the fact that we owe our own very way-of-being-in-the-world—even as the self-contained Cartesian-Newtonian, rationalistic thinkers we currently take ourselves to be—as dependent on our living immersion in essential dialogically structured social worlds, then we need, not just to turn leadership on its head, but to turn it *inside-out*. We need to see leadership (along with many other major concepts in organization studies), not as something *within* particular people, but as something particular people *are always within*, and which is always open to being fashioned among them in *this, that*, or *some other* particular fashion in accord with the circumstances within which it is needed.

But even more than this, as well as turning it inside-out, we will also need to turn it *back-to-front*, in the sense of needing to *reverse* the direction of our inquiries, to explore the nature of what is occurring in a social group *before* "leadership-events" as such can occur. Thus, as Raelin (Chapter 1, this volume) makes clear in introducing the whole notion of leadership-as-practice, the purpose of this volume is to "extend its conceptualization through a number of critical themes that have not been sufficiently explored or, in some cases, not explored at all" (p. 1). And indeed, in introducing, primarily, the works of Wittgenstein (1953, 1969, 1980, 1981) and Bakhtin (1986), I will be exploring quite a number of other lines of thought not usually explored at all by afficionados only of social scientific modes of thought within the fields of organizational, leadership, and management studies. In fact my exploration will primarily be a *philosophical* one aimed, as Wittgenstein (1953) puts it, at bringing to light "what is possible *before* all new discoveries and inventions" (no. 126). For we need to be clear, not only about what is already at work within us enabling us to "come up with" metaphors, images, or theoretical formulations that we feel able to accept as "being like," or as "representing" a particular "state of affairs" of concern to us, but also about what kind of world we take it for granted that we are living in.

The nature of the common sense background to our lives

> What actually thinks within a person is not the individual himself but his social community. The source of his thinking is not within himself but is to be found in his social environment and in the very social atmosphere he 'breathes'. His mind is structured, and necessarily so, under the influence of this ever-present social environment and *he cannot think in any other way.*
>
> *(Fleck, 1979, p. 47)*

> Common sense is judgement without reflection, shared by an entire class, an entire people, an entire nation, or the entire human race.
>
> *(Vico, 1968, para. 142)*

How do we manage not to live in constant fear and uncertainty, but with a degree of confidence and trust that the others and othernesses in the world around us, will relate to us as we expect and anticipate them to do? Clearly, we do not in our daily lives live as research scientists, continually cudgeling our brains as to how to act for the best in each situation we encounter. Mostly, we just act, spontaneously, as the circumstances "call for us" to act. We act, we say, "intuitively," "instinctively," or "naturally" without the need, seemingly, for deliberate ratiocination (see Sadler-Smith, 2010). Clearly, this way of mentally relating ourselves to our surroundings spontaneously is quite different from our more deliberate, cognitive ways. Currently, in our more reflective, cognitive moments, we clearly still think of ourselves as living in a Cartesian-Newtonian world (see section below *Our Cartesian-Newtonian ontology and the kind of thinking it invites*).

But once we switch from thinking and talking of "things," and of human activities—from within that Cartesian-Newtonian, mechanistic world, in which everything exists in separation from everything else, to thinking of them from within an *organic* or *living* "world" of growing and developing "things," in which every "thing" is dynamically related to every "thing" else—then everything changes. We need a different, more fluid ontology to the "atomistic," Cartesian ontology basic to current, rationalistic forms of thought. Indeed, in viewing "things" in a living manner in our inquiries, we need to explore their relations to their surroundings, and to notice how they *show* those relations to their surroundings in the manner of their growth—for instance, we can "see" in the uneven shape and distribution of one tree's branches and foliage, how it has grown *in relation to* its close neighbors; or how, in the rings in its trunk, we can "see" the good summers and bad winters it has weathered. Consequently, in seeing everything, every "thing," as having its being *only* within its unfolding relations to its surroundings (Shotter, 2015a), many of our very basic assumptions need to be reversed.

Thus, instead of seeing life as simply residing *inside* this or that particular organism—and as drawing on the non-living resources in its surroundings for its sustenance—we need to see it as emerging and growing within a back-and-forth communication-like process occurring within the many currents of *intra*-mingling activities from within which it emerges. I use the prefix "intra-" here, rather than "inter-" because, following Barad, 2007, like the intricate system of currents in the earth's oceans, such currents all exist only *in relation to each other* (as well as, of course, in relation to the moon, the earth's axis, etc.)—and such streams of activity clearly do not exist in independence from each other, prior to their intermingling. Whereas, by contrast, in viewing something mechanistically, we ignore its surroundings and its efforts at *growing* in a particular manner in relation to them, and attempt to "see" *into* its inner workings, to discover the inner, hidden *causes* of its behavior. In other words, we will need to see the *livingness* of all things as being like the swirls or vortices, or many other *dynamic stabilities*, that emerge creatively from within initially, somewhat disorderly, fluid streams of activity. In short, do not ask what goes on *inside* such things, but what such things go on *inside of*.

Indeed, to be even more radical:

> Instead of starting our inquiries 'downstream' or 'after-the-fact', so to speak, with nameable, idealized, simply located, theoretical simplicities, and trying to build them up into complex entities, we must find the starting points for our inquiries further 'upstream' or 'before-the-fact', and begin *from within the midst of the complicated and diffuse flow of the many intra-twined activities occurring out in the local circumstances within which we are embedded.*
>
> (Shotter, 2015b)

At the root of all these changes is not only a change in our focus, in what we attend to, but also a change in our *ways* of looking, in *what* after each moment of fixation we *look for next*. In other words, a change in the sequencing of *what we expect to be connected to what*, as we survey the circumstances confronting us—a change in the embodied taken-for-granted *structures of anticipation* with which we go out to meet those around us, ready to respond to them in ways meaningful both to them and ourselves.

In short, a change in our *common sense*, as Vico notes above, is in the *judgments* we make spontaneously, without reflection, that result in the responsive feelings (movements) occurring within us in relation to what we see before us. As Fleck (1979) points out above, to repeat: "The source of [a person's] thinking is not within himself [or herself] but is to be found in his [or her] social environment and in the very social atmosphere he 'breathes'" (p. 47), and it is difficult for those of us "caught up in" such ways of thinking, to think in any other way. This is not at all a matter of Janis' (1972) "group think," in which individual members try to minimize conflict and reach a consensus decision without critical evaluation of alternative ideas or viewpoints, and by isolating themselves from outside influences. It is much deeper. As Wittgenstein (1953) puts it, we are held captive by a "picture," and we cannot easily "get outside it, for it [lies] in our language and language seemed to repeat it to us inexorably" (no. 115).

We need to distinguish between the kind of language-*influenced* thinking that we, as socially accountable adult thinkers, do deliberately and know of ourselves as being able to do deliberately, and the kind of language-*mediated* thinking that just happens, spontaneously within us. In this language-mediated thinking, we are unaware of its source, or of the degree to which it is in fact shaping and limiting in what it *makes available to us to think-with* (Shotter, 2010, that is the kinds of images and metaphors that we take *"naturally"* to *be like* crucial aspects of the circumstances we deal with in our daily lives. This distinction, as we shall see, is crucial, as unlike our deliberate thinking—which requires an *anxious effort* on our part to "get it right"—the thinking that just happens within us is of a kind that seems to occur effortlessly.

Although what I will call the *after-the-fact* properties of this kind of thinking have been extensively described in individuals (e.g., see Kahneman, 2011), we still lack a *before-the-fact* (explicated further in *Conclusions*) account of what is involved in our coming to as a member of a social group who all exhibit a version of this spontaneous, effortless way of thinking as the contextual background to their more deliberate forms of thought. In short, a theme that has not yet been sufficiently explored, is what is involved in a particular social group coming to share a particular *common sense*, such that each member—on finding themselves at any one moment with a particular experience in a particular circumstance of concern to the group—makes use of a *before-the-fact* set of *shared judgments* as to *how* they *should* respond. That is, their judgement *should be* expressed as being *like this* rather than *like that*, or as "calling for" *this* action rather than *that* (Shotter &

Tsoukas, 2014a,b)—for such a specific before-the-fact judgment *arouses a specific anticipation*.

This *before-the-fact* role of judgment—unlike its *after-the-fact* role, as to whether an event is good or bad for us—is concerned with *what kind of event* an otherwise indeterminate event is to *count as* for us. Indeed, as Wittgenstein (1953) noted: "If language is to be a means of communication there must be agreement not only in definitions but also (queer as this may sound) in judgments" (no. 242). Thus in possession of such a shared system of anticipation arousing judgments, as a member of a linguistic community, we judge that the various noises coming out of people's mouths are not just variations of breathy sounds, but that some sequences of verbal sounds are questions while others are answers, and similarly, that some bodily gestures are friendly and others aggressive, and so on and so on. Indeed, as Dewey (1929 [1958]) put it long ago, "to understand is to anticipate together, it is to make a cross-reference which, when acted upon, brings about a partaking in a common, inclusive, undertaking" (pp. 178–179). For the others around us can only coordinate their behavior with ours if we all share in a structure of anticipations, such that we can all, in our verbally articulated utterances, arouse anticipations in each other as to our possible next steps.

But as Wittgenstein (1969) went on to say later, to emphasize again the importance of the *shared nature* of such *before-the-fact* anticipation creating judgments: "I did not get my picture of the world by satisfying myself of its correctness; nor do I have it because I am satisfied of its correctness. No: it is the inherited background against which I distinguish between true and false" (no. 94). And without this "inheritance," our routine understanding of each other within a linguistic community would be impossible. A *common sense* is not only what a dialogue happens *in*, it also determines what it can occur in relation to.

However, although acknowledging it as "inherited" *situates* the process of a group coming to possess a common sense within the general, back-and-forth commerce of a group's everyday life activities, it does not clarify the nature of that process any further. For clearly, it is not inherited genetically like blue eyes, but is learnt informally after birth—very like learning our first language—in the course of people's everyday, spontaneous involvements with the particular others and othernesses around them. Thus, the learning process at work here is utterly different from classroom teaching, for what we learn is not facts or information, but, to repeat, what we call "shared judgments": that in *this* particular circumstance we *should* act *like this* and not *like that*. Learning to judge things as the others around us do, means that we must learn to *relate ourselves* to "events" or "things" occurring in our surroundings—dynamical things that can only be heard or seen in the unfolding temporal organization of our living, responsive relations to our circumstances—and *to talk of them in a distinctive manner*, to describe them being *like* Xs, rather than *like* Ys, while still being in fact *different from* Xs, and thus still amenable to other *likenings* as well. And to learn in this spontaneous way, without any explicit teaching, is something that our body *does for us*, so to speak, to a greater or lesser extent, according to the extent of our engaged involvements, the training we receive, and the degree of practice we exert. And indeed, working in terms of *likenesses* and *similarities* (and *differences*) rather than *correspondences*, that is identities, is also central, as we will see, to the Wittgensteinian approach I am taking here.

From problem-solving to the task of gaining "orientation"

Thus, as I see it, there are two major kinds of difficulty in our lives, not just one: there are 1) *cognitive difficulties* or *difficulties of the intellect*; and 2) *difficulties of orientation* or difficulties to do with *ways* of relating ourselves to our surroundings, what Wittgenstein calls *difficulties of the will*. Indeed, as he remarks:

> What [can make] a subject hard to understand—if it's something significant and important—is not that before you can understand it you need to be specially trained in abstruse matters, but the contrast between understanding the subject and what most people *want* to see ... What has to be overcome is a difficulty having to do with the will, rather than with the intellect
>
> *(Wittgenstein, 1980, p. 17)*

For often, our initial *impulse* is to pick out and name what we see as existing *in separation from all else around it*; it is that impulse that we need to "put on hold," so to speak, if we are to go *dialogical*.

1. We can formulate difficulties of the intellect as *problems* which, with the aid of clever theories, we can solve by the use of a "manipulational" form of reasoning, making use of inner mental representations that correspond to an outer reality in the sense set out long ago by Heinrich Hertz (1894 [1956]): "We form for ourselves images or symbols of external objects," he said, "and the form that we give them is such, that the necessary consequents of the images in thought are always the images of the necessary consequents in nature of the things pictured" (p. 1).
2. Difficulties of the will, however, are of a quite different kind, for they are to do with how we *orient* ourselves bodily towards events occurring around us, with how we *relate* ourselves to them, the *ways* in which we see them, hear them, experience them, and value them—for these are the *anticipatory ways of looking* that determine (in the sense of "giving shape to"), the lines of action we *resolve* on as appropriate within the essentially indeterminate situations which we find ourselves to be in.

For instance, with the well-known faces/vase ambiguous figure, if we first look with the overall schema of a face to guide us in our expectations, we could look first *from* what might possibly be a forehead *to* an expected eye region, and then *to* an expected nose region, and so on. Eventually, we are looking *from* all these details (if each of these expectations is to an extent fulfilled) *to* the overall perception of a face—in short, the figure can *satisfy* the expectations aroused by a face-way-of-looking. Similarly, with a vase-way-of-looking, we can look *from* a bowl region *to* a stem region *to* a base region, and find that *that* can be satisfied by the figure too. Where here, of course, I am making use of Polanyi's (1967, p. 10) well-known *from-to* structure of tacit knowing. If we were just to say that first we see faces and then we see a vase, that is describe our experience of the ambiguous figure in terms *only of our achievements*, we would lose that in so doing, we switched from first *trying* to see faces, and what that trying consisted in. Thus, the precise nature of our *before-the-fact* orientation is a crucial, determining factor in how we "go out to meet" and to "look over" what is arrayed before us in our surroundings.

Indeed, we can be so focally attentive to what we are expecting to see and anticipating what we will see next, that we can be utterly blind to other events occurring in our surroundings (e.g. see Simons, 2000). It is hence all too easy, given our everyday, Cartesian-Newtonian common-sense ontology, to ignore that, intrinsic to all living activities, is not only their *general* spontaneous responsiveness to events occurring in their surroundings, but their *particular* and *unique* nature.

Distinguishing between what we think we *want* and what our real *need* is, is crucial. For it is only too easy to say that what we *want* is leadership; while our real *need* is for us to feel oriented, to feel that we know "where" we are in relation to all the others around us, and the part we can contribute to all of us achieving a common goal. Thus, as Todes puts it, in each new situation we encounter, our first task in getting oriented is trying to make clear to ourselves, *what* it is in that situation that we lack; as he puts it:

> the whole sense of our exploration and discovery of the world is prompted by the sense of having been initially lost in the world ... It was not that we *had* lost something, but that we *were* lost ... Our whole quest of discovery is thus initially prompted by need rather than desire. It is initially 'directed' not to get what we want but to discover what we want to get ... The meeting of a need first makes the need recognizable for what it is.
>
> *(Todes, 2001, p. 177)*

Our *wanting* "leadership" does not at all make clear *what* in the particular situation we happen to be, is actually *needed*—after the particular need has been met, of course, we will then say: "Ah last, some leadership has been exhibited."

Indeed, to return to the point I made above—about not asking what goes on *inside* people, but what people go on *inside of*—we can now note that, as Wittgenstein (1981) put it above, it is within the context of "the whole hurly-burly of human actions" (no. 567) that we can see *the meaning* of a particular activity; even if that meaning is a *need* for something sensed as lacking (Todes, 2001). This is brought home very nicely in the case of Dan, a team leader in an IT company, that Carroll (Chapter 5, this volume) is "shadowing" for a morning. Although he admits that, she says, "he doesn't really know what leadership is ... he feels the absence of it often and that absence is typified by him realizing he doesn't have something he needs like a contact or piece of information or some kind of larger direction and that the largely technical environment and work doesn't enable that. This feeling of something missing, which he names as leadership, is something to him that seems to encompass something different from his team leader role" (p. 104).

Yet, as Carroll makes clear in her account of his intra-activities within his team, he aims to have a *work space* that is "their own to lead, manage, fill, and shape," (p. 99), without him having to tell them in any specific detail what to do within it. In this sense, we can agree with Barker (1997), "... it is not the leader who creates leadership, it is leadership that creates the leader" (p. 354)—if, that is, we can see the use of the word "leadership" in a *before-the-fact*, rather than an *after-the-fact* manner.

Our Cartesian-Newtonian ontology and the kind of thinking it invites

> I resolved ... to speak only of what would happen in a new world, if God were to create, somewhere in imaginary space, enough matter to compose it, and if he were to agitate diversely and confusedly the different parts of this matter.... and afterwards did no more than to lend his usual preserving action to nature, and to let her act according to his established laws.
>
> *(Descartes, 1968, p. 62)*

This image of our world as made up of separate entities in lawful motion is pervasive in almost all our everyday thinking, and still rife in much of our professional forms of talk in business and organizational studies. Thus, for instance, we talk of *leadership, management, decision making,* of *strategies,* of *marketing,* of *branding,* of *workplace organization,* of the *seven factors* comprising the McKinsey 7S model, as if all these nameable features of the business and organizational world can be identified and studied as self-contained entities in a scientific manner, and as if research in relation to each topic is research on "the same thing."

Indeed, under the influence of the Cartesian-Newtonian ontology implicit in our current, taken-for-granted idea of what it is to be rational, there is a tendency to orient towards all the circumstances we find bewildering or disorienting (along with those that are strange and new to us), as if they pose a *problem* for us, a problem that we can solve by a process of *reasoning* involving a number of well-known steps: 1) *analyze* the newness or strangeness as a problem to be solved into a set of already well-known, nameable elements; 2) find a *pattern* or *order* among them; 3) *hypothesize an agency* responsible for the order (call it, say, "leadership," or some other such entity); 4) find further evidence for the agency being at work in the world; 5) enshrine the agency in a theory or theoretical system; 6) *manipulate* the strangeness (now known in terms of the theory) to produce an advantageous outcome; 7) call this "*the solution*" to the problem; 8) turn "*to apply*" the theory elsewhere.

Motivating the idea that this is a "sure fire" way of arriving at an effective way of coming to a "correct" way of acting in what initially was a puzzling situation, is Descartes' (1968) idea that: "[The] long chains of reasoning, quite simple and easy, which geometers use to teach their most difficult demonstrations, had given me cause to suppose that everything ... is linked in the same way ... [so that] there can be nothing so distant that one does not reach it eventually, or so hidden that one cannot discover it" (p. 41); and this, so to speak, "sets the scene" for us as to what counts as "thinking rationally."

As I want to contrast this "geometric" or "calculational" form of thought with a more dialogical-hermeneutical form, it is useful to consider the nature of this process in terms of both its *properties*, and its *effects on the self* of investigators:

1. The *properties* of the process:

    It is a search for regularities;
    It establishes a single order of connectedness among certain perceived aspects of one's circumstances;
    Occasionally, "the solution" can occur "in a flash of insight";
    It works wholly within the realm of the already known to elaborate it internally.

2. Effects *on the self* of the investigator:

    The self of the investigator remains unchanged in the process;
    We remain outside the other or otherness, we are "set over against" it;
    We are not engaged or involved with it;
    We do not get to know it "from within" its functioning within its own context of existence;
    We acquire extra *knowledge* about it in the form of facts or information;
    We gain a *mastery* over it.

But it may very well be that our ability to sustain a scientific discourse in relation to a situation puzzling us may owe more to the sameness of the words we use in talking *about* it, than the sameness of the phenomena in relation to which we are talking (and writing). There is a "categorizing" tendency at work in language that can easily mislead us into thinking that the meaning of words is an inherent property of the words themselves; and to forget that their meaning is dependent on their *use* within a particular context. Thus, the words used within a particular context have a meaning that is no longer quite the same when these words are reproduced out of context. Thus, to repeat, do not ask what goes on "in" our expressive actions, what their *content* is, but what our actions go on *within*, what they are *contained in*—for this is what is involved in moving from the urge to relate to the others and othernesses around us *objectively*, to relating to them in a *dialogical-hermeneutical* manner. It is their *singular, situated meaning*, not their fixed, pre-established *form* or *shape*, that matters to us.

Entering into dialogical-hermeneutical relationships with others; beginnings and beginnings, but no endings

There is an altogether different way of relating ourselves to the others and othernesses around us: we can "enter into" a dialogically structured relationship to them, and, as we "dwell on, or with" them for a while, we can gradually arrive at an orientation toward them as their "inner nature" becomes familiar to us. This is similar to how we get to know our "way around" inside a city which is at first unfamiliar to us by exploring its highways and byways according to the different projects we try to pursue within it.

In becoming familiar with "things' in our surroundings in this way, we can come to know, not just their inert, objective nature, but to know them in terms of a whole realm of possible responsive, living relations that we might have to them. We can come to orient toward them in terms of their yet-to-be-achieved *values*, the "calls" they might exert on us to "go on" with them in one way rather than another—where the development of sensitivities to such calls is, of course, not at all a part of the problem-solving process.

The sequence of steps involved, and their nature, is quite different from those of the problem-solving process outlined above:

1. We need to begin by treating the other or otherness as still radically unknown to us;
2. We must then "enter into" dialogically structured relations with it, that is become involved or engaged with it;
3. To do this, we must "open" ourselves to being spontaneously "moved by it," we must relate to it responsively and responsibly—this is crucial: we always know when a person is "with" us or not, whether at a party they are responsively "following" us, or whether they are looking over our shoulder to find others they want to be with;
4. This sense of contiguity, of contingency, of the other's responses to us being contingent on our own, is very basic—present even in new-born children;
5. To "enter into" dialogically structured relations with another requires "tact," "courtesy";
6. We must not only "follow" the other, but also provide opportunities for them to "follow" us;
7. The other "calls on" us—comes both to be "with" us, as well as to "call out" responses from us;

8.   The other can affect us, move us—their meaning for us in the responsive movements they "call out" from us;

9.   We are "answerable" (partially) to their calls as they are (partially) to ours—we do not reply to every aspect of their influence upon us.

The descriptions of the character of the above nine steps, all have to do with the nature of our living relations to the others and othernesses around us; the following five steps are to do with the nature of the consequences of our *meetings* with those others in that manner:

1.   An "it" appears between us: produced neither solely by "me" or by "you" (see the mention above of Bakhtin's (1986) notion of the *superaddressee*, who calls upon all participants to "do justice" in their responses to the expressions of those around them);

2.   The "it" is *our* it: there is *poiesis* at work between us—the sensed creation of an overall *tension* or *tendency* requiring satisfaction;

3.   The tendency has a shaped and vectored sense to it;

4.   Central to our giving shape to our actions is our *sensitivity* or *sensibility*, not only to the particular details of the other's responsive activities, but also to this "it";

5.   As we "dwell on, with, or within" the detailed nature of our current situation, there is a gradually growth of familiarity with its "inner nature";

6.   Once in focus, we can have a sense of the *value* of its yet-to-be-achieved aspects, its horizon, the prospects it offers us for "going on" within it;

7.   We can gain a sense of "at homeness," an orientation within it, we can come to know our "way about" in relation to it, to find our "footing" within it.

In contrast to processes occurring within a Cartesian-Newtonian ontology, in terms of both its *properties*, and its *effects on the self* of investigators, *dialogical-hermeneutical* processes could not be more different:

1.   The *properties* of the process: "once-occurrent events of Being" (Bakhtin, 1993, p. 2) or *singularities* are crucial—what matters are single, unique events that make a difference. Rather than collecting data, we need to talk in terms of "noticings," of what we are "struck by." In so doing, we can establish a multiply ordered *sense of connectedness* among all the perceived aspects of the others and othernesses around us, but our familiarity with it grows only gradually and is never finished; it exists on the edge between the radically unknown and the realm of the known, and is continually at work expanding its boundaries.

2.   The *effects on the selves* of those involved: people's selves are changed in such encounters. We become involved with, immersed in, the "inner life" of the

other or otherness around us; everything we do is partly shaped by those others, in being a response to what they are doing or might do. At first wholly "bewitched" by the "authoritative voice" of our predecessors, as our familiarity with it grows, that voice becomes one voice among the many other voices within us. Rather than mere *knowledge* of its nature, we gain *orientation* towards it, that is we grasp how to "go on" within a changed relation to it; but we never gain mastery over it, or any other voices—others can always surprise us, no matter how familiar to us they have become.

Indeed, to go a step further, central to the whole *dialogical* approach to language use, as outlined by Bakhtin (1981), is the claim that:

> The word in living conversation is directly, blatantly, oriented toward a future answer-word; it provokes an answer, anticipates it and structures itself in the answer's direction. Forming itself in an atmosphere of the already spoken, the word is at the same time determined by *that which has not yet been said but which is needed and in fact anticipated by the answering word*. Such is the situation of any living dialogue.
>
> *(Bakhtin, 1981, p. 280, my emphasis)*

But more than this, as Bakhtin also makes clear:

> An utterance is never just a reflection or an expression of something already existing and outside it that is given and final. It always creates something that never existed before, something absolutely new and unrepeatable … [The] something created is always created out of something given (language, an observed phenomenon of reality, an experienced feeling, the speaking subject himself, something finalized in his world view, and so forth). What is given is completely transformed in what is created.
>
> *(Bakhtin, 1986, pp. 119–120)*

And what is created *belongs to all* the participants within the dialogue.

The use of "general concepts" in relation to "particular hermeneutical unities"

> The leadership process is like a river. Contained by its bed (the culture), it can be said to be flowing in one direction, yet, upon close examination, parts of it flow sideways, in circles, or even backwards relative to the overall direction. It is constantly changing in speed and strength, and even reshapes its own container. Under certain conditions, it is very unified in direction and very powerful; under other conditions it may be weak or may flow in many directions at once.
>
> *(Barker, 1997, p. 352)*

In fact, even more than just a flowing river, we can imagine the whole process of leadership-as-practice as beginning with drops of rain (intimations of new possibilities) falling here and there but nowhere in particular. At first gathering in rivulets, which then run into streams, which then intra-mingle into rivers, which after much wandering and meandering (as Barker suggests), run into estuaries, and finally into the sea, *with gravity giving a "direction" to the whole, flowing process.* Where the placement of each drop is not at all decisive, as the final result is determined by the overall direction of gravity—where this image is taken from Fleck (1979), who is concerned to understand how, in scientific research, "a 'true' finding can arise from false assumptions, from vague first experiments, and from many errors and detours ... " (p. 78).

I have outlined this image in some detail as I think the kind of dialogically structured activity that we conduct in coming to our *prima facie* understandings of each new situation we encounter—before formulating a more organized *plan* of activity of how to act within it—has a similar sequential, *developmental trajectory*. We have to "wander" around in each new circumstance, "wondering" as to the meaning of each new feature we encounter, testing possible ways in which *to express its nature in words*, while sensing how it "talks back" to us as to whether our words are fitting or not, and as we do so, gradually coming to a grasp of its nature as an intra-connected whole. With each feature, each "part" of the whole, coming to draw its nature from its *placement*, and thus its *unique relations* or *the unique part it comes to play*, within the unfolding dynamics within the developmental growth of the whole. And in picking up a fragment here, and another there, we seem to arrive gradually, *in a kind of dialogical, back-and-forth process*, at a unique *sense of*, or *feeling for*, a particular situation, prior to our going on to use our words in describing that situation in a "fitting," that is socially acceptable, *representational* fashion. Thus another image that I would like to suggest here, is that the *particular* unities of meaning we come to construct in our "wanderings" and "wonderings" are similar to those we construct as we read a text.

Indeed, the *hermeneutical* process involved—that of coming to a *uniquely new*, not previously experienced understanding—is quite different from the *general* kinds of understanding we seek in scientific forms of inquiry. Clearly, we do not begin our reading with a pre-established "framework" or set of abstract concepts *representing* features of the reality portrayed in the text, in terms of which the *meaning* of the first words we encounter need to be "interpreted" and "understood" as particular instances of something more general, with all their uniqueness lost. Nor is it the case, as we pick up a significant fragment here and another there, that we are aiming at finding a single, finalized meaning for all time, an *objective understanding* that can be *represented* by a purely spatial (pictorial) *form*.

Instead, we begin by being prepared to immerse ourselves within an at-first indeterminate whole in its full individuality (as the unique, distinctive whole it *is*), known to us at first only globally, as situated within a particular genre (as a novel, textbook, instruction manual, etc). We then proceed to conduct a step-by-step movement, from part-to-whole and back again as we read each word, gradually specifying or internally articulating their meaning in relation to a gradually developing *living order* adapted to the undistorted accommodation of all the particular, discernible details we encounter in our explorations within the original global whole. And what is special about this process, is that it is something that our bodies seem to do for us, unconsciously and spontaneously, without our having to carry it out deliberately.

Further, in connecting disparate and diverse things, such *particular hermeneutical unities* are quite unlike *abstract concepts* formulated in terms of a set of features or properties that are, in *general*, common to a whole set of different circumstances. As we shall see, rather than working merely to collect a set of disparate things into a category, solely in terms of their shared similarities, they can be used in *connecting* such things into an inexhaustible network, not of features common to *all*, but of similarities and differences, and of many different kinds of relationships. Indeed, they are each particular unities formed from a collection of unmerged particularities, within which the particularities are inter-linked without losing their particularity. Indeed, it is important to emphasize that they are not *mixtures*, or *amalgams*, or *blendings*, or an *averaging*, but outcomes of a very basic human power. A power that, as Vico (1988) puts it, "fashions the images of things … at the same time that it originates and produces new forms … it is this that differentiates the forms of things, sometimes separating them, at other times mixing them together" (pp. 42–43). While focusing on one facet of such a whole, we also seem able to move forward or back to become aware of others, or even sideways, to see its "placement" as a unity within a larger landscape of other such unities.

Further, to the extent that they consist in people's expressions, within a particular circumstance, they are organized into *a unique structure of particular anticipations* which can guide us in our uttering of meaningful talk in relation to that circumstance. They work to couple us into a forward-hearing immersion within the unfolding flow of whatever social activity we are involved—an anticipatory sensing that I would like to compare with what we can all sense as at work within us, as we make the effort to sequence our words in our own everyday speakings.

In the natural sciences, it is perfectly alright to begin our inquiries by *reflecting on* the world around us and to guide our further inquiries by the expectations aroused in us by "our conceptualizations." I put the phrase "our conceptualizations" in quotes because, in natural science-based, theory-first approaches, we assume that to solve the problems we face, we must discover the *actual entities* hidden behind appearances that are *causing* our difficulties. We assume we can begin to do this by the empirical testing of deliberately formulated *representations* of those entities, while ignoring the already socially shared anticipations influencing the structure of our everyday responses to the words used in such formulations. But there is something wrong in trying in our everyday lives to make use of our concepts in this way. As William James (1909/1996) points out: "When we conceptualize, we cut out and fix, and exclude everything but what we have fixed. A concept means a *that-and-no-other* ... whereas in the real concrete sensible flux of life experiences co-penetrate each other so that it is not easy to know just what is excluded and what not" (pp. 253–254).

What we cut out and fix in our everyday lives is a region from the flowing reality within which we all are immersed, in which intramingling strands of activity have created a *dynamic stability* (Shotter, 2013) that we all can notice, a *confluent aspect*, a region that exists as such only *in relation to* everything else around it, which cannot exist in separation from it. Yet we have an over-riding urge to treat such noticeable regions that we can point out to others, as a self-contained nameable "things" *that can be taken as separate* from all other such things. Yet, if we were to divorce them from their dynamic embedding in their flowing sur-roundings, as the *relational things* they are, they would cease to exist (Shotter, 2015a). Yet, we have, need, and still make perfectly good use of our concepts in our daily lives, in the face of their somewhat limited nature. How is this possible?

Clearly, we need to distinguish between what we can call *formal, representa-tional,* or *Cartesian* forms of thought, and *poetic, responsive,* or *Wittgensteinian* forms. That is, between 1) ways of thinking in which people commit themselves to using a "framework," "perspective," "theory," or "model," that they take as *cor-responding* with reality, and *through* which they perceive and act on the world around them—which elsewhere (Shotter, 2010) I have called *aboutness*-thinking; and 2) forms of thought in which people make use of *particular understandings*—what Wittgenstein (1953) called "*objects of comparison,*" that are meant, he says, "to throw light on the facts of our language by way not only of similarities, but also of dissimilarities" (no. 130). In this kind of (essentially dialogical) thinking—which elsewhere I have called *withness*-thinking (Shotter, 2010)—people may feel free to use a whole set of such "poetic comparative devices" in looking at and acting within their surroundings world without feeling wholly committed to any of them. At least initially, a task in our everyday lives is to begin explorations in relation to the (intuitive?) sense of *unique possibilities* open to us in our current circumstances, not in relation to established *general facts,* and then to proceed further to articulate our particular circumstances in more inner detail.

In the past, of course, such talk of *feelings* and *sensings* and *intuitions* has been thought of as being utterly unscientific, as clearly lacking in *objectivity*—that is, as not only failing to be "true" to "reality" but also as lacking in public shareability. Thus investigations into such experiences have been dismissed as merely idiosyn-cratic and introspective, as leading to a focus on events that, in Cartesian terms, we would quite unsuitably call, "merely subjective."

Such remarks, clearly, are misplaced. We only have to attend to what we all in one sense of "know" in coming to be a speaker/listener of our native language, to appreciate that such a form of embodied knowing can be (like a common sense), for almost all practical purposes, shared among a group of people. Indeed, that we can all perceive *meanings* in the stream of a noises issuing from the mouths of our fellows is nothing short of amazing.

Yet about that stream, as William James remarked:

> The truth is that large tracts of human speech are nothing but *signs of direction* in thought, of which direction we nevertheless have an acutely discriminative sense, though no definite sensorial image plays any part in it whatsoever ... Their function is to lead from one set of images to another ... Now what I contend for, and accumulate examples to show, is that 'tendencies' are not only descriptions from without, but that they are among the *objects* of the stream, which is thus aware of them from within, and must be described as in very large measure constituted of *feelings of tendency*, often so vague that we are unable to name them at all.
>
> *(James, 1890, pp. 253–254)*

It is our sharing in those *feelings of tendency*, of which we have an *acutely discriminative sense*, that allows us all (mostly) to be able to coordinate our own unique individual utterances and actions in with those of the others around us.

Indeed, as Rorty (1999) comments: We cannot regard truth as a goal of inquiry. The purpose of inquiry is to achieve agreement among human beings about what to do, to bring consensus on the end to be achieved and the means to be used to achieve those ends. Inquiry that does not achieve coordination of behaviour is not inquiry but simply wordplay (p. xxv).

From "after-the-fact" to "before-the-fact" accounts of leadership

How, then, does all this relate to how we think about and talk about leadership? Evidently, as we have seen, what we call our *conceptualizations* can be used in two very different ways: 1) one is in an *after-the-fact representational* fashion, as stating a claim about the *factual nature* of the hidden reality thought to be responsible for observed events, that is "as a preconceived idea to which reality must correspond" (Wittgenstein, 1953, no. 131). In other words, after having collected some data (observations) from our circumstances, we apply our concepts in a *retrospective, explanatory* fashion, *as aids in our thinking*, in our attempts at *solving* "the problems" we assume we are facing. In this use, as we will be making precise claims as to the nature of the reality we are occupying, they will need to be formulated in a clear and unambiguous manner; and our aim in listening to what a person has to say will be to "get the picture," and our critical task will be to assess whether it is a "picture" we can agree with or not. This use, clearly, is in line with what Raelin (2014) calls "the individualistic paradigm" (p. 2), in which a single person tries to exert a one-way, monologic *influence* on those around them.

In the other, 2) we listen for how a speaker's sequence of words *in their speaking* can "move us," how they can work in us as a *before-the-fact aid to our perception* to direct our attention, not only to *this aspect* of what is happening in our current circumstances rather than *that*, but also, as Bakhtin (1981) points out, to arouse particular *feelings of anticipation* (tendency) within us as to what, *possibly*, might happen next. It is this switch to looking at leadership, prospectively, in the course of its occurrence, to see the many different ways in which it can be displayed, rather than retrospectively, after its happening, in an attempt to explain it, that makes all the difference. For a start, instead of seeing *leaders* as already existing beings possessing special but very *general* capacities and faculties, less well developed in those designated to be their *followers*, we need to see leadership, as such, as gradually emerging within a social group, and as taking on one or another specific form in accordance with the *needs* (Todes, 2001) of the circumstances in question.

Our *after-the-fact* models of leadership have, for the most part, as Barker (1997) points out, been "defined ostensively" (p. 347), by referring to people *already occupying* leadership positions. But as he makes clear, this approach—in which named *outcomes* of a productive process are posited as the *ideal forms* that guide the process towards their own productive realization—leaves us ignorant of the actual process of leadership itself, especially in those situations in which "the goals (of leadership) are not specific, or when the imposition of order does not solve the problem" (p. 350). Indeed, a logical circularity is involved here which, if we were doing logic rather than conducting a practical inquiry, would be called *petitio principii*—the fallacy of assuming as a premise a statement that has the same meaning as the conclusion. "The fallacy that arises," said Dewey (1896), "is virtually the psychological or historical fallacy ... A state of things characterizing an outcome is regarded as a true description of the events which led up to this outcome; when, as a matter of fact, if this outcome had already been in existence, there would have been no necessity for the process" (p. 368). That is, we could have gone straight to the outcome rather than having to perform a complicated sequence of movements in reaching it.

In an attempt to move away from the heroic model, from what Barker calls the "dyadic supervisor/subordinate relationship" (p. 350), he suggests that leadership be conceptualized as "a *dynamic* process of interaction that creates change," and that if it is, "then the leadership roles may not be, perhaps should not be, clearly defined" (p. 351). Indeed, he goes further to suggest that leadership is a *developmental* process in which those being trained to work in a company come to develop an "understanding of themselves and a conventional base from which to explore experiences: in other words, they learn to 'manage' themselves" (p. 359).

It is just this process, in which those in a company come to "manage" themselves, that Storch and I (Storch & Shotter, 2013) explored in the consultancy company, of which Storch himself had been a founding partner. A little like Dan in Carroll's account, but more deliberately, Storch had set out to create a company (Attractor) in which the "leader" was not in any sense an authoritarian, heroic leader—an *ideal form* leader—but an "imperfect" or "good enough" leader. This terminology was suggested by Anne Marie (an employee, not her real name) who, in describing her sense of the leadership in Attractor, said:

> it is not by the book ... it has no manual ... so one has to find one's own direction and way into it, and it then becomes the way that one really believes in. It may sound a bit silly to talk about 'imperfect' leadership, but there is also something really down to earth about it, something very human. It doesn't become a distant leader out of reach—it offers you an opportunity to feel yourself instead of just following the pretty roads laid out for you.

Another, similar comment was offered by Brandt (a senior manager):

> Being employed in Attractor is not about being good enough theoretically but about daring to let go of perfection and to be present. I practice this in relation to all new employees. I give people a kind of a paradoxical message: You can become much better, but at the same time you are good enough—otherwise you would not be here!
>
> *(quoted in Storch & Shotter, 2013)*

If, as Barker suggests above, leadership involves a developing, dynamic process of intra-activity, then leadership roles cannot be (and, perhaps, should not be) clearly defined. There are no *ideal forms* of it. Thus, just as Winnicott (1988) suggested the term "good-enough mothering," both "to convey an *unidealized* view of the maternal function," while still holding in mind the "absolute dependence" of the baby on its environment, while it is "always travelling towards (but never reaching) independence" (p. 90), so we (Storch & Shotter, 2013) suggested the notion of "good-enough leadership" for similar reasons. In other words, we saw a leadership process at work in Attractor that began much as mothering begins, with a sensitivity and a responsiveness to what she senses as our *needs* (Todes, 2001)—the unsatisfied tensions she can perceive us as feeling in the incipient, that is not-yet-wholly-clear intentions she can see us as *trying* to execute—as she feeds, comforts, plays, and otherwise actively intra-acts with us.

And what such a mother does for us, in our learning to become an autonomous, self-controlling member of our own society and culture, is not to sit us in a classroom and to embark on teaching us in accord with a pre-planned curriculum, but to *circumstance* or to *occasion* (Adato, 1980) situations in which we can, not only satisfy (some) of our incipient intentions, but also learn from her their social value, their meaning. Thus, at this early stage in our development, it is our "tryings" (and "failings") that are important to her, not our achievements. Storch, in approaching the employees in Attractor in a similar manner (as they themselves described it), seemed to have created a company of consultant-practitioners able to develop (and sustain) their own autonomous ways of working, while at the same time, still displaying and sustaining a certain "house style." As I see it, Dan is depicted as just such a "good-enough" leader in Carroll's account (Chapter 5, this volume).

Also, as Simpson (Chapter 8, this volume) illustrates, whereas inter-actions, as we call them, start with independently defined actors, and lead us into investigations of what happens *between* them, *trans*-actions—or *intra*-actions, as I have called them—lead us into conducting our inquiries in a very different fashion, into observing and inter-relating a whole range of detailed activities within the organization in question. As she points out:

> If organizational practice is understood as the unceasing flow of actions by means of which work is accomplished, then leadership surely resides in those emergent turning points, or leadership moments, that re-orient the flow of practice towards new, or at least different, directions. Without leadership, the flow of practice would continue unchanged, but even with leadership (understood in terms of trans-actional agency) there is still no guarantee of success in terms of instrumental outcomes. Agency simply produces movement; there is no presumption that change is necessarily for the better, although a lack of change is unlikely to be sustainable over the long term.
>
> *(Simpson, Chapter 8, this volume, pp. 169–70, my itals)*

In other words, although it may seem that *heroic* leaders can achieve pre-ordained outcomes by the sheer strength of their characters, the opposite would seem to be the case. Simpson's account of how the New Zealand rugby team, the All Blacks, has maintained an average win rate of 75% over their entire 110 years of history, illustrates the impossibility of explaining this record of success in terms of any individual leader-practitioners who might be identified with this sports team. As she argues, correctly I think, we can find at work distributed throughout all the team's activities, on and off the field, an aspect of every way of thinking about leadership that we have ever proposed as important (Simpson, Chapter 8, this volume).

I have already mentioned Carroll's account (Chapter 5, this volume) of how Dan *occasions* (Adato, 1980) his *situated leadership* at crucial moments, when he has a sense of a *need* for his team to come together, a sense of lack, the need to regain a *shared orientation*. Thus the stand-up koosch ball meeting begins with him stating, as Carroll notes, with some "pretty frank" comments: "'I'm not sure where we are heading on this …' and 'we thought we'd be done here but it's obvious we aren't …' The team members listen but don't join in" (Carroll, Chapter 5, this volume, p. 94). Dan then throws the koosch ball at someone, who simply recounts what they are working on; and then Spike launches into a very animated account of a bug or glitch in the system that he cannot locate, and an animated conversation breaks out among the group. After 3 or 4 minutes, when everyone in the group has had a say, Dan after remarking that there seem "two ways to move on," draws the stand-up meeting to a close with: "we all good to go on?"—a shared orientation seems to have been regained, at least for the moment. And Dan rushes off to another meeting, to leave his team again, each to their own devices.

Conclusions: leadership-as-practice

> What makes agency collaborative, given that agency requires a social interaction to begin with, is that it be a fair dialogical exchange among those committed to a practice; in particular, that the parties display an interest in listening to one another, in reflecting upon perspectives different from their own, and in entertaining the prospect of being changed by what they learn.
>
> *(Raelin, 2014, p.7).*

Thus, as we move from an *after-the-fact* use of the concept of leadership to its very many *before-the-fact* uses, as a consequence of another person's words "calling out" responses from us that we might not have exhibited ourselves, we can find—as Raelin (2014) suggests in the quote above—that there is the prospect of our being changed. This change occurs not merely by gaining a new item of factual knowledge, but in our very being-in-the-world by how we can be affected by other people's words. Indeed, as Carroll notes:

> In the stand-up meeting story we see a whole host of mediating elements that construct the identities possible in this team. We see a team creating the culture of their organization just as that culture creates the identities in and of the team ... they in turn are responding to the historical and cultural texture of an organization that distinctively blends the ability to look and behave casually with an extreme high performance pace and tolerance for uncertainty.
>
> *(Chapter 5, this volume, p. 98)*

This describes a specific form of situated leadership, similar to that exhibited in the All Blacks and in Attractor, a form of leadership that affects everyone in their identity, in who they "are" both to themselves and to the others around them.

Thus what is so special about such situated leaders is that instead of "the leader" imposing aims of his or her own *desiring*, they can *occasion* dialogically structured circumstances within which the *needs* of each team or company member can come to expression, and in such circumstances, they can each experience themselves as coming to live in a *new world* in which "things," previously rationally invisible to them can come "into view."

Thus, it is in this second, dialogic use of our many different concepts of leadership—using them in a *prospective, descriptive* manner with the aim, not at all of solving problems (at least, not immediately), but of acquiring an *orientation*, a *way* of relating ourselves to events in our surroundings—that they can be of great practical use to us. Each particular concept can, in terms of the *structure of anticipations* that it can arouse in us, as we *look over* or *survey* the situation before us, allow us to "see," not only *what* the situation *is*, but to see how *this aspect* within it is connected *that aspect* and so on. It is this comparison between these two different uses of our concepts—in terms of their orientation towards giving us *science-like* accounts and *philosophical* accounts of *cognitive* and of *perceptual* help to us—that I see as crucial to clarifying *the meaning* of Raelin's (2014, and Chapter 1, this volume) account of leadership-as-practice for our inquiries into the nature of what we call leaders, and leadership.

If it is the case, as Raelin (Chapter 1, this volume) has outlined, that leadership needs to be studied, not in terms of the traits or behaviors of special individuals, but as a dialogical, community process, then there is need, not for yet more *scientific* explorations driven by the urge to arrive at a final, correct, general account of what leadership *is*, but for more particular, situated, *philosophically* structured inquiries into how, what we call leadership can emerge in many different ways in *this*, or *that*, or some other *particular* situation (see O'Connor, 1995; Shotter, 2015b). It is with this, perhaps less ambitious aim in mind, that I have provided the dialogical-hermeneutical account I have begun to articulate above. It is less ambitious because it is, of course, tantamount to proposing that we relinquish the still unfulfilled—and, as I see it, *forever unfulfillable*—dream of seeking the very general concept of leadership we desire. Also, it is being content with the limited, partial, and situated results we *can in fact obtain*—which, in the end, will, I believe, perhaps surprisingly, turn out to be of far greater practical use and value to us.

References

Adato, A. (1980). "Occasionality" as a constituent feature of the known-in-common character of topics. *Human Studies*, 3, 47–64.

Bakhtin, M. M. (1981). *The dialogical imagination* (C. Emerson and M. Holquist trans. and M. Holquist Ed.) Austin, TX: University of Texas Press.

Bakhtin, M. M. (1986). *Speech genres and other late essays*. (V. W. McGee trans.). Austin, TX: University of Texas Press.

Bakhtin, M. M. (1993). *Toward a philosophy of the act*, with translation and notes by V. Lianpov, edited by M. Holquist. Austin, TX: University of Texas Press.

Barad, K. (2007). *Meeting the universe halfway: Quantum physics and the entanglement of matter and meaning*. Durham, NC and London: Duke University Press.

Barker, R. A. (1997). How can we train leaders if we do not know what leadership is? *Human Relations*, 50(4), 343–362.

Descartes, R. (1968). *Discourse on method and other writings*. Trans. with introduction by F. E. Sutcliffe. Harmondsworth: Penguin Books.

Dewey, J. (1896). The concept of the reflex arc in psychology. *Psychological Review*, 3, 13–32. Reprinted in W. Dennis (Ed.), *Readings in the history of psychology*. New York: Appleton-Century-Crofts, 1944.

Dewey, J. (1929 [1958]) *Experience and nature*. New York: Dover.

Fleck, Ludwik (1979). *Genesis and the development of a scientific fact*. Chicago, IL: University of Chicago Press (originally publishede 1935).

Gadamer, H.-G. (2000). *Truth and method* (2nd revised edition) (J. Weinsheimer and D. G. Marshall trans.). New York: Continum.

Hertz, H. H. (1956). *The principles of mechanics*. New York: Dover (orig. German published 1894).

James, W. (1890 [1950]) *Principles of psychology*, Vols. 1 & 2. New York: Dover.

James, W. (1996). *A pluralistic universe: Hibbert lectures at Manchester College on the present situation in philosophy*. Lincoln and London: University of Nebraska Press (originally published 1909.

Janis, I. L. (1972). *Groupthink: Psychological studies of policy decisions and fiascoes*. Boston: Houghton Mifflin.

Kahneman, D. (2011). *Thinking, fast and slow*. London: Penguin Books Ltd.

O'Connor, E. (1995). Undisciplining organizational studies: A conversation across domains, methods, and beliefs. *Journal of Management Inquiry*, 4(2), 119–136.

Polanyi, M. (1967). *The tacit dimension*. London: Routledge and Kegan Paul.

Raelin, J. (2014). Imagine there are no leaders: Reframing leadership as collaborative agency. *Leadership*, Online First, 25 November.

Rorty, R. (1999). *Philosophy and social hope*. New York: Penguin.

Sadler-Smith, E. (2010). *The intuitive mind: Profiting from the power of your sixth sense*. Chichester: John Wiley.

Sandel, M. (2012). *What money can't buy: The moral limits of markets*. London: Penguin Books.

Shotter, J. (2010). *Social constructionism on the edge: 'Withness'-thinking and embodiment*. Chagrin Falls, OH: Taos Institute Press.

Shotter, J. (2013). Reflections on sociomateriality and dialogicality in organization studies: From 'inter-' to 'intra-thinking'… in performing practices. In P. R. Carlile, D. Nicolini, A. Langley & H. Tsoukas (Eds.), *How matter matters: Objects, artifacts, and materiality in organization studies* (pp. 32–57). Oxford and New York: Oxford University Press.

Shotter, J. (2015a) On "relational things": A new realm of inquiry—Pre-understandings and performative understandings of people's meanings. In R. Garud, B. Simpson, A. Langley, & H. Tsoukas. *The emergence of novelty in organizations* (pp. 56–79). Oxford: Oxford University Press.

Shotter, J. (2015b) Undisciplining social science: Wittgenstein and the art of creating situated practices of social inquiry. *Journal for the Theory of Social Behaviour*, Article first published online: 22 January, doi: 10.1111/jtsb.12080.

Shotter, J., & Tsoukas, H. (2014a) Performing phronesis: On the way to engaged judgment. *Management Learning*, 45(4), 377–396.

Shotter, J., & Tsoukas, H. (2014b) In search of phronesis: Leadership and the art of judgment. *Academy of Management Learning & Education*, 13(2), 224–243.

Simons, D. J. (2000). Current approaches to change blindness. *Visual Cognition*, 7 (1/2/3), 1–15.

Storch, J., & Shotter, J. (2013) 'Good enough', 'imperfect', or situated leadership: Developing and sustaining poised resourcefulness within an organization of practitioner-consultants. *International Journal of Collaborative Practice*, 4(1), 1–19.

Todes, S. (2001). *Body and world*, with introductions by H. L. Dreyfus & P. Hoffman. Cambridge, MA: MIT Press.

Vico, G. (1968). *The new science of Giambattista Vico* (T. G. Bergin & M. H. Fisch Eds. and trans.). Ithaca, NY: Cornell University Press.

Vico, G. (1988). *On the most ancient wisdom of the Italians* (L. Palmer trans.). Ithaca, NY: Cornell University Press.

Winnicott, D. (1988). *Babies and their mothers*. London: Free Association Books.

Wittgenstein, L. (1953). *Philosophical investigations* (G. E. M. Anscombe trans.). Oxford: Blackwell.

Wittgenstein, L. (1969). *On certainty* (G. E. M. Anscombe & G. H. von Wright Eds. and D. Paul & G. E. M. Anscombe trans.). Oxford: Blackwell.

Wittgenstein, L. (1980). *Wittgenstein's lectures: Cambridge, 1930–32* (D. Lee Ed.). Oxford: Blackwell.

Wittgenstein, L. (1981). *Zettel* (2nd edition) (G. E. M. Anscombe & G. H. V. Wright Eds.). Oxford: Blackwell.

PART III

Social interactions

8

WHERE'S THE AGENCY IN LEADERSHIP-AS-PRACTICE?

Barbara Simpson

Leadership-as-practice is one of a number of emergent threads in the leadership literature that seek to de-center the individual "leader," turning the analytical gaze instead towards more contextualized, participatory, engaged, and relational understandings of leadership. Such a radical re-theorization necessarily entails a close examination of all the adjacent constructs that are implicated in conventional leader-centric thinking. Concepts such as traits, capabilities, and behaviors, which are explicitly aligned with individual "leaders," clearly have limited relevance to this new conceptualization of leadership. However, there are other important concepts that cannot be so readily expunged from the new leadership lexicon. For instance, the classical sociological categories of "agency" and "power" seem integral to any understanding of leadership as a way of moving and acting in the world (Raelin, 2014). Re-examining such key categories is, therefore, an essential prerequisite to the emergence of new ways of understanding leadership.

In this chapter, I set about the task of unraveling "practice" to reveal what agency might mean in the context of leadership-as-practice. To facilitate this analysis, I invoke a framework proposed by the Pragmatist writers John Dewey and Arthur Bentley (1949 [1960]) in their book *Knowing and the Known*, which reports the collaborative inquiry that unfolded between them over more than fifteen years of correspondence (Ratner & Altman, 1964). Their project was to develop a new vocabulary that would restore the epistemological wholeness of human experience without having to reduce it to either the experienc*ing* of idealism, or the experienc*ed* of realism. In their analysis, they sought to highlight the assumptive and empirical implications of different modes of inquiry by identifying three distinct categories of action: self-action, inter-action, and trans-action.[1] Dewey and Bentley described self-action as a "[p]re-scientific presentation in terms of presumptively independent 'actors,' 'souls,' 'minds,' 'selves,' 'powers,' or 'forces,' taken as activating events" (Dewey & Bentley, 1949 [1960], p. 72). In their view, this self-actional orientation remains dominant in contemporary social science thinking, and indeed it is precisely this dominance in the field of leadership that has prompted the call for new approaches such as that promised by leadership-as-practice.

The second category, inter-action, is in Dewey and Bentley's view a product of the scientific thinking that characterizes the modern world. They define inter-action as a dyadic way of acting in a world that comprises "particles or other objects organized as operating upon one another" (Dewey & Bentley, 1949 [1960], p. 73). This type of thinking underpins much of the recent literature that casts leadership as shared, pooled, or spread ((Denis, Langley, & Sergi, 2012). The final category, trans-action, departs from the other two modes of action at an ontological level. Whereas self-action and inter-action share an ontological commitment to a reality comprising identifiably discrete entities, trans-action invokes a processual ontology that attends to emergent becoming rather than substantive being (Tsoukas & Chia, 2002). Reflecting this ontological difference, Dewey and Bentley defined the trans-actional as "see[ing] together, extensionally and durationally, much that is talked about conventionally as if it were composed of irreconcilable separates" (1949 [1960], p. 69). This trans-actional view resonates with at least some of the literature that Denis *et al.* (2012) classify as "producing leadership."

In what follows, I will explore each of these modes of action in turn, elaborating on their definitions, and then exploring their implications for the notion of agency. In each case, I also consider what leadership might mean in relation to these different expressions of agency.

Leadership as self-action

Dewey and Bentley critiqued self-action as a primitive treatment of knowledge that pre-dates scientific thinking. They dismissed it as an archaic, or antique approach, but one that nevertheless deserves attention as a comparator with the more sophisticated modes of inter-action and trans-action. The central assumption of self-action is that things, or entities, act under their own powers (1949 [1960], p. 108), reflecting vitalist assumptions that attempt to account for unexplained events in terms of invisible forces, or an *élan vital* that somehow, mysteriously animates lived experience. As a philosophical movement, vitalism was largely discredited in the natural sciences during the nineteenth century as scientists increasingly sought explanations for empirical experience in terms of underlying mechanisms. Arguably, however, vitalism continues today as a strong influence in the social sciences where the complexities of lived/living experience resist reduction to mechanistic logics that draw overly simplistic connections between discrete phenomena.

This debate between vitalism and realism is to some extent reflected in another well-worn debate—that between free will and determinism, or agency and structure. The self-actional freedom to act according to one's own will is here contrasted with a realist world view in which actions are determined by social norms and structures. On one hand, agency implies the self-actional expression of rationality, autonomy, and expertise, while on the other, structure reflects the normalizing and deterministic influences of social contexts (Caldwell, 2005). However, as has been well recognized by, for instance, Giddens (1984) and Bourdieu (1990), this dualistic separation between agency and structure causes problems for those who seek a more wholistic appreciation of practice. Over the past half century or so, social theorists have become increasingly skeptical of overly rationalized models of agency, dismissing them as excessively psychological in their analytical focus, and too committed to the assumption that individuals can shape their own worlds. In the words of Emirbayer and Mische (1998, p. 962) "[t]he concept of agency has become a source of increasing strain and confusion in social thought ... maintain[ing] an elusive, albeit resonant, vagueness."

Questions about agency, and in particular about the nature and effects of self-action are nowhere more evident than in the leadership literature. There is a vast body of work (for a comprehensive review, see for instance Bolden, Hawkins, Gosling, & Taylor, 2011) that focuses on the self-action of individual "heroic" leaders, who are regarded as circumscribed entities possessing an inherent, though somewhat mysterious "power to" take action. Agency is expressed in practice by those leader-practitioners who are recognized as having this power to act. Thus leadership and agency are inextricably and tautologically inter-related. Research in this domain tends to follow the principles of methodological individualism, attending to the unique qualities of these leader-practitioners, which although perhaps correlated with perceived success, offer no insight into how particular qualities actually produce leadership. It is this failure of explanation that led Alvesson and Sveningsson (2003) to accuse leadership of mysteriously disappearing whenever analysis seeks to go beyond the superficial. In a similar vein, Fletcher (2004) argued that the puzzling resilience of patently inadequate notions like "charismatic leadership" may be accounted for by hidden, and consequently under-explored phenomena such as gender dynamics. This in turn suggests an urgent need for more subtle approaches to research that can penetrate beneath the surface of leadership. The lack of explanatory power of the self-actional view also has knock-on effects for leadership development, which often seeks to improve the skills and competencies of individuals, but without adequate theoretical or empirical justification for this focus.

Leader-centerism, and its associated centering of agency, results in the public glorification and vilification of individual "leaders" as their stars are seen to wax and wane. In the celebrity culture that increasingly dominates Western consciousness, this privileging of the actions of individuals results in dysfunctional understandings that fail to inquire into the more systemic and social dimensions of agency and change. For instance, the post-match press conference that follows most elite sports fixtures draws attention to specific individuals such as the team captain and the coach/manager, attributing the team's successes and failures to these individuals and their extraordinary talents. For most of the fans, this press conference is as close as they'll ever get to their team, so it is inevitable that they will focus their adulation on these imputed leader-practitioners. However, this focus is unsupportable for a team like the All Blacks, New Zealand's national rugby team, which has maintained an average win rate of 75% over its entire 110 years of history, making it "possibly the most successful sports team, in any code, ever" (Kerr, 2013, p. vii). It is simply not possible to explain this record of success in terms of the individual leader-practitioners who have been associated with this team over these many years.

Leadership as inter-action

For Dewey and Bentley, the notion of inter-action owes much to the modernist epistemology of Sir Isaac Newton, for whom the world is an extended mechanism comprising material entities acted on by simple forces to produce instrumental outcomes, but where the entities themselves remained unaltered in this process. Inter-actions were classically assumed to occur independently of context. That is "[s]pace and time were treated as the absolute, fixed, or formal framework within which the mechanics proceeded—in other words, they were omitted from the process itself" (Dewey & Bentley, 1949 [1960], p. 111). It is this assumption that underpins the whole of experimental science, which supposes that reality may be understood by holding some variables constant while others are manipulated to explore the consequences of their specific inter-actions. Although this decontextualization of lived experience has been vigorously critiqued over many years now, inter-actional models in the social sciences nevertheless often retain a sense of rational and autonomous inter-actors that are independent of each other, and of their spatial and temporal contexts.

A popular metaphor for this inter-actional view is that of a game of billiards, where balls act on each other bringing about changes in speed and direction of movement, but remaining unchanged in themselves. Billiard balls inter-act with each other in a controlled environment, a billiard table, where the interplay of forces between them may be reasonably anticipated. Obviously, however, billiard balls on the forest floor, or on a ski slope, or in a speeding train might not inter-act in the same predictable ways. Furthermore, it is highly improbable that billiard balls remain unchanged over prolonged periods of play. Inter-action, however, offers no adequate means of engaging with entities if the nature of their being is constantly changing.

Inter-acting entities may be understood as things, essences, actions, states of being, discourses, practices, institutions, or indeed any circumscribed, substantialist unit of inquiry. Understanding movement and interplay between inter-actors must begin from a pre-formed sense of what these entities are. Emirbayer (1997) pointed out that this preference for "things first" is deeply ingrained in language, especially the English language, which first structures experience with nouns, and only then uses verbs to express the movements of these "things". For Dewey and Bentley, inter-action is necessarily dualistic in opposing, or balancing one "thing" against another "in causal interconnection" (1949 [1960], p. 108). Thus the inter-actional context is one of dialectical struggle as inter-actors jostle for position and influence. Out of this struggle, emergent entities are further defined, or re-defined, in between the inter-actors. The focus of research in the inter-actional domain then, is centered on entities. Researchers in this domain often employ variance techniques (Langley, 1999), which although they may demonstrate cor-relations between emergents and inter-actors, nevertheless leave unanswered questions about how change actually comes about.

From this inter-actionist stance, agency takes on a quite different meaning from the self-actional "power to" exercise one's own will. Rather, it is re-defined in dyadic terms as "power over," or between (inter-) entities. It is the capacity to influence other inter-actors, which implies deliberate intentionality in its appli-cation, but as is also the case for self-action, agency continues to be centered on the acting entities. The difference is that it need not be confined to certain indi-viduals as it can shift around, residing temporarily in a variety of entities. Fur-thermore, scholars in the science and technology studies tradition (e.g. Callon, 1986; Latour, 1987; Pickering, 1995) argue for a non-human form of material agency that is irreducible to conventional expressions of human agency; in other words, inter-actors may be human or non-human. Agency then, is not simply an inherent quality of the self-actor, but rather it is directed towards other entities through practices, or routinized sequences of activities, around which inter-actions are coordinated and organized. These practices are the cultural contexts that circumscribe inter-active agency, defining "communities of practice" within which agency may be disciplined and routinized in the form of standard operating procedures. Pickering (1995, p. 16) suggested that practices are to human agents as machines are to non-human agents: "they are both repetitive and machinelike and they collaborate in performances." He proposed therefore, that the study of practices belongs within the domain of cultural studies, where context is recognized as an important determinant of inter-action.

Leadership scholars have enthusiastically embraced inter-action as potentially more fruitful than self-action as an underpinning orientation. Arguably it is inter-actions between leaders and followers that dominate the majority of recent developments in the leadership literature (Drath, McCauley, Palus, van Velsor, O'Connor, & McGuire, 2008; and also the extensive literature on Leader-Member Exchange (LMX) theory, e.g. Graen & Uhl-Bien, 1995). Those seeking a more plural, less indi-vidualized expression of leadership have explored the possibilities of leadership that is collective, collaborative, participative, or distributed (Denis *et al.*, 2012), where agency still resides in individuals, but perhaps only temporarily or in ways that are delimited by other inter-actors. Inter-action also admits the possibilities of leadership through non-human, discursive, and more systemic forms of agency by recognizing the potential for action to emerge between competing inter-actors and from disparate practices.

The common ground in all inter-actional approaches to leadership is that entities come first, and the connections or networks that animate these entities are secondary (Emirbayer, 1997). For example returning to the All Blacks, their former coach, Graham Henry, attributed their success, at least in part, to what he calls "dual leadership". That is, a shared leadership that allows any team member to "step up" at any time and take responsibility for finding a way to win. Thus the players are all potential leaders who are expected to actively contribute to each other's leadership. The metaphor that Henry uses to describe this form of leadership is "pass the ball," which means "enabling and empowering the individual by entrusting them with responsibility for the success of the team" (Kerr, 2013, p. 47). In this manner, leadership is continuously passed among the players and their managers, directly challenging more conventional notions of centralized, top-down management. The ball-in-motion is the connection, or the interplay, between players, but it is the players themselves who are the developmental focus of the "pass the ball" metaphor as they each step into leadership.

A brief philosophical diversion

In passing from the self-actional and inter-actional to the next section, where I discuss the trans-actional, we cross what Steyaert (2007, p. 465) referred to as an "invisible line" between the conventional discourses of research, and new and radically different ways of thinking about, and engaging with processes of inquiry. This line separates what I will characterize as representationalist and performative approaches, a distinction that is already well-established in social science debates (e.g. Anderson & Harrison, 2010), but is far less evident in the contemporary organization studies literature.

According to Barad (2007), representationalism is a by-product of the Cartesian separation of objects from subjects, and of things from other things. It assumes that the stuff of the world can be accurately represented by words, signs, and concepts, and that language can be treated as "a transparent medium that transmits a homologous picture of reality to the knowing mind" (Barad, 2007, p. 97). However, in the desire to represent the world faithfully, as it really is, the significance of practices gets bracketed out, especially the practices that produce representations. Critical scrutiny of representationalism first began when the physical sciences started to inquire into the actual processes of producing scientific knowledge. Dewey also was very critical of what he called the spectator theory of knowledge, which privileges the knowledge claims of those who are located outside the experiences they describe. In his view, this account of knowledge production is linked to the impossible quest for epistemological certainty (Dewey, 1929). To be clear about these critiques though, the challenge to representationalism does not prohibit the use of representations. Indeed, how else can we talk about, and account to others (and ourselves) for our experience? "The issue at hand is what role representations play and how referentiality is conceived" (Barad, 2007, p. 410, endnote 15).

Critics of representationalism have called for more non-representational theories (Thrift, 2008), or at least a move to more-than-representational modes of inquiry (Lorimer, 2005). This in turn has led to increasing interest in performativity as an alternative account that seeks to understand how subjects are called into being. Here, thinking, observing, and theorizing are material-discursive processes that engage with, and are part of the experienced world (Barad, 2007). Whereas representationalism assumes determinate objects that may be apperceived by knowing subjects, performative accounts understand subjects and objects as co-emergent in their entangled engagements. The performative idiom contests that most basic, and largely unexamined assumption of representationalism that language can determine what is real, shifting instead to a process ontology that focuses on a world of practice, movement, and doing. As Donna Haraway (1992, p. 313) remarked, "the world is precisely what gets lost in doctrines of representation and scientific objectivity." Performativity seeks to transcend substantialist Cartesianism, but in doing so, it demands a radical rethinking of how practice becomes, and how we can engage with questions of this becoming through our own practice of research. Thus the invisible line between representationalism and performativity marks a fundamental ontological distinction that has profound implications for how we engage with, and frame research questions.

Leadership as trans-action

In dramatic contrast with the representationalist, substantialist ontology common to Dewey and Bentley's definitions of self-action and inter-action, trans-action puts process first. Its starting point is a world that is active and in continuous flow, a world filled with agency (Pickering, 1995) where "things" are provisional and evanescent (Shotter, 2015), serving only to punctuate the flow and make it sensible. This processual ontology invites a radically different way of thinking and talking about our world, one that rejects representationalist assumptions. The challenge here is to develop a genuinely performative language that is distinct from the more familiar idiom of representationalism. This new language must contest the dualistic assumptions that carve our worlds up into discrete and opposing entities, turning attention instead towards movement, flux, flow, emergence, passage, continuity, confluence, diffluence, turbulence, and smoothness. This is precisely what Karl Weick was getting at when he exhorted us to "become stingy in [our] use of nouns, generous in [our] use of verbs, and extravagant in [our] use of gerunds" (Weick, 1979, p. 44).

Many scholars in pursuit of more performative language have taken to inventing or redefining words in ways that better reflect the ongoing processes of engagement with, rather than objective separation from, the worlds in which we live. Indeed, Dewey and Bentley have themselves inserted hyphens in the labels for their three categories of action precisely because they wanted to distinguish their language from more conventional usage. Similar emphases have been sought, for instance, by Heidegger (2010, p. 53) in his "being-in-the-world," which encompasses the existence of the self in relation to the whole, by Barad's (2007, p. 33) use of "intra-action" to express the emergent and mutual constitution of meanings through material-discursive engagement, and by the distinction that Shotter (2006, p. 585) makes between "withness-thinking" and "aboutness-thinking," which highlights the differences between performative and representationalist idioms, respectively. Other writers, such as Bruno Latour (2005), have invented entirely new terms (e.g. "immutable mobiles") and radically redefined common terms (e.g. "translation") to access new ways of thinking and speaking about the wholeness of lived/living experience. Effective navigation through this terminological minefield requires an in-depth understanding of the ontological and epistemological assumptions underpinning these various terms in their usage.

Put simply, trans-action "is to be understood as unfractured observation—just as it stands, at this era of the world's history, with respect to the observer, the observing, and the observed" (Dewey & Bentley, 1949 [1960], p. 104). Rather than entitavizing life and splitting it up into fragmented representations, Dewey and Bentley were seeking a wholistic and temporal way of accounting for our lived/living experience. Trans-action "regards extension in time to be as indispensable as is extension in space (if observation is to be properly made), so that 'thing' is in action, and 'action' is observable as thing, while all the distinctions between things and actions are taken as marking provisional stages of subjectmatter to be established through further inquiry" (Dewey & Bentley, 1949 [1960], p. 123). The constituent "parts" of trans-action can never be understood by extracting them from the whole; simple causality is undone by the mutual emergence of all the constituting elements, which thus act as both context and outcome in the ongoing flow.

Given Dewey and Bentley's earlier references to the linkage between the scientific thinking of classical mechanics and the modernist assumptions of interaction, it is perhaps unsurprising that they continued to draw on developments in science to map the more post-modern orientation of trans-action. In particular, they referred to the shift in focus from material substances to fields of energy, marked for instance by Maxwell and Einstein, as evidence for an ontological shift in science that is paralleled in the move from inter-action to trans-action. They were careful though, not to claim superiority of the latter mode of inquiry. In the same way that scientists find it more or less useful to conceive light as particles or waves depending on the question they are seeking to answer, so also the choice between inter-actional or trans-actional modes of action will depend on the questions being asked. Dewey and Bentley did, however, suggest that trans-action offers the potential for fresh insights into the questions that are of central interest to researchers today.

Whereas inter-action starts with independently defined inter-actors and then investigates what happens between them, trans-actors are implicated as the ongoing, relationally relevant meanings that emerge from trans-actions (Simpson, 2009). Trans-actors, whether they be human or non-human, micro or macro, are defined within, rather than prior to, the dynamic unfoldings of trans-actional "becoming." The performative idiom resists the reduction of dynamic movements to constituent elements that may be afforded any concreteness beyond the trans-actional situation. Such elements are regarded as transitory abstractions that necessarily dissolve, or are at least questioned, as particular situations evolve. Thus this approach seeks to liberate us from the rigidities of dualistic, substantialist thinking. Dewey and Bentley (1949 [1960], p. 133) illustrated how this works with the example of a hunter who shoots a rabbit. This situation may be functionally accounted for "in an interactional form in which rabbit and hunter and gun enter as separates and come together by way of cause and effect." However, if we are to explain this event in the broader societal context of what it means to hunt "[n]o one would be able successfully to speak of the hunter and the hunted as isolated with respect to hunting." It is in the constitutive entwining and continuous refiguration of hunter, hunted, and hunting that an unfractured observation of the situation may be realized.

Another distinguishing feature of the trans-actional view is its commitment to emergence, understood as the unanticipated generation and development of novelty, which is integral to any understanding of performativity. Trans-actional engagements transform trans-actors as they enact new and unfolding meanings in ongoing trans-actions, whereas inter-actors and self-actors remain unchanged through their actions. The notion of emergence (at least in the West) has a long history, reaching back more than 2500 years to Heraclitus, but it is only in the past 150 years that it has once again become a matter for serious consideration by scholars. Over this period, emergence has been variously interpreted through spatial, relational, and temporal lenses, as, respectively, a self-organizing phenomenon, a network phenomenon, or a processual phenomenon (Garud, Simpson, Langley, & Tsoukas, 2015). Whereas the first two of these lenses focus self-actionally and inter-actionally on what novelty emerges, the third is more concerned with how the process of emergence unfolds trans-actionally. Writers who contributed most to early developments of a trans-actional understanding of emergence include Henri Bergson, Alfred North Whitehead, Karl Marx, and the American Pragmatists, especially Charles Sanders Peirce, William James, John Dewey, and George Herbert Mead. This view is also evident in contemporary organization studies, especially in the sensemaking and organizational learning literatures (see for example Weick, 1995), and also in the dynamic notion of "becoming" (Tsoukas & Chia, 2002). For all of these writers, emergence is understood as a process that is immanent in the spatial and temporal unfolding of performative experience.

The performative idiom invites a processual view of practice as the ongoing, trans-actional accomplishment of work. Pickering (1995, p. 4) made a critical distinction between "practice" as the work that extends and transforms meanings over time, and "practices," which he described as specific sequences of activities, or routines, that may be invoked repeatedly to simplify day-to-day experience. Whereas practice is continuously emergent, practices are valued for their routineness. If it is practices that characterize the sphere of inter-actions, then it is the continuously evolving spatial and temporal entanglements of practice that uniquely define the trans-actional perspective. Practice is concerned with the perpetually unfolding dynamics of living, which Bakhtin (1984, p. 293) framed in terms of dialogue: "Life by its very nature is dialogic. To live means to participate in dialogue: to ask questions, to heed, to respond, to agree, and so forth." It is a process of meaning-making that continuously generates something new. Just as Heraclitus famously claimed that it is not possible to step into the same river twice, Bakhtin recognized that the same words cannot convey precisely the same meaning when spoken in a different context.

Mead (1934, pp. 253–260) developed this notion of dialogue in terms of a conversation of gestures. Rather than an instrumental inter-actional transmit/receive model of communication, his conversation of gestures is concerned with the dynamics of social coordination and cooperation, which he argued are dependent on being able to stand in the shoes of others, taking on their roles and attitudes. So for instance, when I offer a communicative gesture it is moderated by the response that I can anticipate by trying to put myself in the position of the other. Both I and my respondents are thus integral to, and inseparable from, the conversational process in which we are engaged, and through which we each acquire a self-critical awareness of our emerging social situation.

> Hence social control, so far from tending to crush out the human individual or to obliterate his self-conscious individuality, is, on the contrary, actually constitutive of and inextricably associated with that individuality; for the individual is what he is, as a conscious and individual personality, just as in as far as he is a member of society, involved in the social process of experience and activity, and thereby socially controlled in his conduct.
>
> *(Mead, 1934, p. 255)*

It is conversation then, conceived broadly in terms of both words and actions, that provides the vehicle for the performative becoming of practice.

If we accept this trans-actional view of practice as the ongoing dialogical accomplishment of meaning, how then should we understand the notion of agency? In an inter-actional sense, agency is defined in opposition to structure, as the source of change in an otherwise stable world. However, it is precisely this type of dualistic thinking that is challenged by the trans-actional approach, which starts from the experience of living in a field of continuity and flow, rather than a world that has already been sliced up into discrete entities. What is needed is a conceptualization of agency that builds on "doings" over time rather than the isolated "doers" of action. Both Giddens (1984) and Bourdieu (1990) have recognized the limitations that dualistic (entitative) thinking imposes on our understandings of practice, but in seeking solutions, neither has engaged a fully performative idiom with its underlying anti-dualistic and processual assumptions.

My own thinking in this respect has been significantly influenced by Mead's less well-known work *The philosophy of the present* (Mead, 1932), in which he explored the temporality of emergence in social trans-actions (Simpson, 2014). For him, the present moment is the continuously emerging locus of conscious action. It draws simultaneously on pasts and futures as epistemic resources that inform present actions, and which are also continuously re-forming as we endeavor to stand in each other's shoes. New presents emerge "betwixt and between the old system [past] and the new [future]" (Mead, 1932, p. 73) as turning points that redirect the flow of practice. Without these turning points, Mead argued, there cannot be any experience of temporality or movement; we are effectively suspended in time and space until the next turning point arises. Agency then, is manifest in the movements and directional shifts associated with turning points. "[I]t is an enactment, not something that someone or something has" (Barad, 2007, p. 178). This definition makes no recourse to either human or non-human agents that "cause" change, seeing agency instead in the continuously unfolding movements of social engagement. Here it is practice, rather than actors or agents, that is prior to agency.

Consistent with the principles of Pragmatism shared by Dewey and Mead, this trans-actional account is profoundly democratic. As such, it has been criticized for naivety in failing to address issues of power. This criticism, however, is founded on an entitative understanding of power as some "thing" to be acquired, possessed, and exercised over others by self-actors or inter-actors. To the extent that trans-actions generate movement and change, they are arguably saturated in power and influence, but in a way that shapes movement rather than as a property of discrete entities. Follett (1996), another Pragmatist thinker, contrasted the "power over" of inter-actionism against "power with," which she described as jointly developed, coactive power. Whereas the inter-actional view distributes agency and power among multiple entities, I suggest that it is only by stepping away entirely from entitative thinking, as the trans-actional approach does, that we can come to a truly decentered and performative perspective on agency. Then

> [o]ur task is not to learn where to place power; it is how to develop power ... Genuine power can only be grown, it will slip from every arbitrary hand that grasps it; for genuine power is not coercive control, but coactive control. Coercive power is the curse of the universe; coactive power, the enrichment and advancement of every human soul
>
> *(Follett, 1996, p. 119)*

This close connection between agency and movement has particular appeal when it comes to thinking about leadership. If organizational practice is understood as the unceasing flow of actions by means of which work is accomplished, then leadership surely resides in those emergent turning points, or leadership moments, that re-orient the flow of practice towards new, or at least different, directions. Without leadership, the flow of practice would continue unchanged, but even with leadership (understood in terms of trans-actional agency) there is still no guarantee of success in terms of instrumental outcomes. Agency simply produces movement; there is no presumption that change is necessarily for the better, although a lack of change is unlikely to be sustainable over the long term. This view of leadership usefully informs inquiries that seek to unravel the complexities of how leadership arises and how it is sustained in organizational practice. Empirical studies that take this stance are still few and far between, possibly because although decentering leadership is an intellectually appealing idea, it is still difficult to operationalize in practice. Examples include the study by Crevani, Lindgren, and Packendorff (2010), who traced the real-time development of performative actions in meetings to show how leadership moments emerge as re-directions and re-orientations. They were particularly concerned to emphasize "the potential of leadership in every situation" (2010, p. 84). Carroll and Simpson (2012) took a different approach based on conversational trans-actions posted on an online forum. They identified leadership moments in the sociality that emerges when one trans-actor is able to stand in the shoes of another, producing new meanings for all of the participants. In addition, there are a few examples of scholars who are theorizing from a trans-actional perspective (see for example Hosking, 2011; Shotter, 2006), providing exemplars that could usefully be brought in to the leadership literature.

Returning once again to rugby, the spirit of the All Blacks is a work-in-progress, continuously weaving a sense of purpose that not only has meaning for every current player, but is also linked to All Blacks of the past and All Blacks not yet born. This strong sense of history and the responsibility to leave a legacy for future players is a reflection of the Maori idea of *whakapapa*, which refers to the genealogical lineage of ancestors, stories, myths, and symbols that brings each of us to the present moment, and extends from us into the unending future. The abiding symbol of the All Blacks' *whakapapa* is the black jersey, which each player wears on the field of play with a strong sense of responsibility to "leave the jersey in a better place" (Kerr, 2013, p. 14) for the future of the game.

> When a player makes the All Blacks, they're given a book. It's a small black book, bound in fine leather, and beautiful to hold. The first page shows a jersey—that of the 1905 Originals, the team that began this long *whakapapa*. On the next page is another jersey, that of the 1924 Invincibles, and on the page after, another jersey, and another, and so on until the present day. It is a visual *whakapapa*, layered with meaning, a legacy to step into. The next few pages of this All Black handbook remind you of the principles, the heroes, the values, the standards, the code of honour, the ethos, the character of the team. The rest of the pages are blank. Waiting to be filled
>
> *(Kerr, 2013, p. 183)*

This *whakapapa* is, in effect, the meaning of leadership that has emerged trans-actionally, and continues to evolve as the story of the team. It reminds players of their time and place in history, and invites an ongoing collective conversation about the team's future. By placing leadership at the heart of what they do, the All Blacks manifest a genuinely performative and processual practice.

Discussion

My argument in this chapter draws on Pragmatist writers such as John Dewey, George Herbert Mead, and Mary Parker Follett, for whom "practice" was a key preoccupation as they sought to advance an understanding of practical action that is both relevant to, and informed by the lived/living processes of concrete human experience (Bernstein, 1972; Simpson, 2009). There is rich potential for fresh insight to be drawn from their comprehensive articulation of a philosophy of practice, suggesting useful ways of extending the notion of leadership-as-practice. I am conscious that the explicitly scientific basis of Dewey and Bentley's three categories of action may be alienating for readers who do not have a disciplinary background in science. However, science has been probing the trans-actional domain for at least the past 100 years, so there is a lot to be gained by reaching across the entitavizing boundaries of disciplinary thinking to explore the wider domain of postmodern inquiry.

Drawing on Dewey and Bentley's (1949 [1960]) three categories of action (self-action, inter-action, and trans-action), I have teased out three contrasting expressions of agency, which in turn relate to three different process perspectives of leadership-as-practice: "The Leader-Practitioner," "Leadership as a set of practices," and "Leadership in the flow of practice." Each of these is grounded in its own unique set of philosophical assumptions and distinguishing characteristics (summarized in Table 8.1). Firstly, the Leader-Practitioner is the most familiar model in the contemporary leadership literature. Here, agency is a matter of an objectively distinct, individual agent's expression of free will exercised through the presumed inherent power of the agent to take action. It is understood purely in terms of the attributes of the agent with neither physical nor social contexts having any bearing on events. This practitioner-centric view of leadership resonates with Dewey and Bentley's "self-action," but it is widely critiqued for its lack of explanatory power and its tendency to resort to mysterious or invisible forces to account for actions. The underpinning ontology associated with this perspective assumes an objective reality populated by discrete entities that exist independently of any observer, and which can be universally represented in words and images.

Secondly, leadership may be understood as a set of practices. Here I draw on the distinction made by Pickering (1995) between practices and practice, where the former comprise the routines and standard operating procedures that are learned and sustained through inter-actions in organizations and other social contexts. Although these practices are socially constructed, they readily take on entitative qualities that may resist change. This orientation towards practices assumes circumscribed entities inter-acting in a relatively stable environment to construct relatively persistent practices, all of which may be described in sub-stantialist representationalist terms. The site where agency plays out is in the spaces between entities as they endeavor to influence each other by exerting "power-over." The outcomes of inter-actions are contingent on their context, but the context itself functions as a stable crucible within which inter-actions occur. The nature of inter-actions is defined by the inter-actors, which may be human or non-human, thing or discourse, but are always associated with each other through dyadic or network linkages. Consistent with the modernist underpinnings of the inter-actional model, time is regarded as an independent variable that marks the orderly passage of events. Whether it is measured by the ticking of a clock or the dawning of a new era, time provides a chronological context that sits outside, rather than within inter-actions.

Thirdly, leadership may be understood from within the flow of practice, where here practice refers to the wholistic and continuous nature of the collective effort that transforms the meanings of situations (Pickering, 1995). This orientation towards flow and ongoing accomplishment invites a performative idiom, by which I do not mean to imply a diametric opposition to representationalism, but rather a very different way of engaging in inquiry. Performativity does not deny the representational importance of words and images in our conversational trans-actions, but it does afford greater priority to flow and process. In this idiom, the origins of presents cannot be explained by chronologically distant pasts, but rather, are constantly in-the-making through trans-actional improvisation. These presents are continuously enacted by trans-actors whose trans-actional engage-ments not only transform their contexts, but also their selves. Agency here is no longer dependent on individual agents to carry the action; rather it is manifest in the movements and changing directions that emerge as trans-actors seek to coordinate their work together. These trans-actions are saturated in power that arises as a collectively developed, co-active "power with," and they are also threaded through with relationality and temporality as the generation of meanings unfolds through the conversational dynamics of mutual engagement. The funda-mentally processual and performative dimensions of this trans-actional view of leadership demand vigilance to avoid falling back into the familiar territory (and language) of representationalism in research.

These three practice perspectives of leadership are roughly aligned with the typology comprising "practitioner," "practice," and "praxis" that was originally proposed by Whittington (2006) in relation to strategy-as-practice, and has sub-sequently been introduced into the leadership domain by Carroll, Levy, and Richmond (2008). I have endeavored to deepen understanding of this typology by delving into underlying philosophical assumptions and their implications for related sociological constructs such as agency and power. My analysis reveals a fundamental cleavage between representationalist and performative approaches to

TABLE 8.1 Comparison of three different practice perspectives of leadership

	The Leader-Practitioner	Leadership as a Set of Practices	Leadership in the Flow of Practice
Category of action	Self-action	Inter-action	Trans-action
Agency	Exercise of free will	Influencing others	Ongoing coordinated accomplishment of work
Power	Power to ...	Power over ...	Power with ...
Context	Irrelevant	Structure as a fixed container within which action takes place	Context and trans-actors are mutually engaged in an emergent whole
Relationality	Irrelevant	Dyadic and network inter-linkages	Mutually constituting temporally unfolding relationships
Temporality	Irrelevant	Time as an independent variable	Temporal experience is enfolded in and emergent with trans-actions
Ontological assumption	Substantialist, Representationalist	Substantialist, Representationalist	Processual, Performative

leadership research, a duality that is already evident elsewhere in the organization studies literature. For instance, Latour (1986) differentiated between ostensive and performative approaches to power, and adopting this same duality, Feldman (2000; Feldman & Pentland, 2003) has elaborated an extensive theory of routines. Similarly, in the area of organizational cognition and learning, Thompson (2011) distinguished between the entitative notion of "communities of practice," and the related process of "legitimate peripheral participation." It is in the nature of dualities that, unlike dualisms, they cannot be resolved or reconciled (Dewey, 1917); they offer two different, and fundamentally incommensurable approaches to understanding phenomena such as power, agency, learning, and leadership. Thompson (2011) quite rightly pointed to the problems that arise when ontologically distinct constructs are allowed to drift together, generating confusion and challenging the authority of any claims to new knowledge.

By way of example, "relational leadership" has been used to describe both inter-actional (Uhl-Bien, 2006) and trans-actional approaches (Hosking & Shamir, 2012), which I have differentiated in terms of the representationalist/ performative duality. This apparent blurring of paradigms occurs because the underlying distinction between "entity" and "constructionist" positions used by Ospina and Uhl-Bien (2012) is confounded by the double meaning of constructionism: it may refer to either entitative or processual approaches depending on whether the researcher focuses on what has been constructed, or how constructing is going on. It is the former entitative approach that appears to inform Ospina and Uhl-Bien's continuum of leadership stances, which spreads along the objective/ subjective dimension of ontology (2012, p. xxxiii, figure I-1). Both ends of this spectrum draw on an inter-actional understanding of entities as either objects or subjects; however, neither engages with the trans-actional dynamics of practice. To avert confusion, and following Emirbayer (1997) and Hosking and Shamir (2012), my preference is to reserve the term "relational leadership" for trans-actional practice, in which trans-actors are both within and emergent from the flow of process.

Recognizing the problems of paradigm incommensurability in the leadership literature, Ospina and Uhl-Bien (2012) have argued for an accommodation of the plurality of approaches seen in the interplay between paradigms. I also see this as a productive way forward for the emergent field of leadership-as-practice. Para-phrasing Deleuze and Guattari (2004, p. 428), representational science stabilizes and solidifies the vagueness and transience of performative science, which in turn continually seeks to liberate representationalism from its bounding constraints. Although the "Leader-Practitioner" and "Leadership as a set of Practices" orien-tations are already well established in the literature, neither is able to shuck off the "epistemological straightjacket of modernism" (Carroll et al., 2008, p. 372). Both of these approaches remain constrained by a representationalist idiom that focuses inquiry first on entities, and only then on the actions of these entities. The third orientation, "Leadership in the flow of Practice," is a radical departure from substantialist and representationalist approaches that is explicitly processual and performative in its theoretical and philosophical positioning. I argue that this orientation has much to offer to both the re-theorization of leadership, and the practical understanding of leadership as an ordinary everyday process that bubbles up naturally in any organizational setting. However, for this contribution to be realized, it is imperative to challenge the dominant discourses that are deeply embedded in our modern Western ways of thinking and acting. My hope is that the leadership-as-practice community will pay particular attention to developing a language that goes some way towards breaking down the uncritical blending of potentially incommensurable modes of inquiry.

In conclusion, I am proposing that all three practice perspectives of leadership, each with its own unique expression of agency and power, have legitimate offerings to make in both the theory and practice domains, but there is analytical value in teasing them apart to gain deeper understandings of leadership-as-practice. It is clear, for instance, that the All Blacks engage all three orientations in their weekly practice of training and development:

1.   Immediately after the Saturday game, a press conference engages with the heroes (Leader-Practitioners) of the day. This is often the only image of leadership accessible to fans and other external observers, so they inevitably acquire a somewhat distorted view of how leadership works within the team.

2. The following day, the team meets to analyze (inter-actionally) the game and to set in place the practice routines to be followed in the coming days. This meeting is facilitated by the coaches, who also draw in experience and insight from the on-field leadership (a shared leadership model).

3. The remainder of the week sees a gradual transfer of responsibility and ownership to the players themselves, allowing them to become sensitized to the trans-actional possibilities of turning points generated in the flow of the game. "By the time they play on Saturday the players have taken over the asylum" (Kerr, 2013, p. 49).

Each perspective offers different insights into the nature of the All Blacks' leadership, and the absence of any one would inevitably result in an impoverished analysis. However, given the very different assumptions underpinning each orientation, I would be wary of any attempt to produce a grand unified theory of leadership. There is much more subtlety to be had from treating each as a distinct lens for analysis.

Note

1   Here I follow Dewey and Bentley in hyphenating these three words to emphasize their different implications for practice, "enabl[ing] us to stress the inner confusions in the names as currently used" (Dewey & Bentley, 1949 [1960], p. 108).

References

Alvesson, M., & Sveningsson, S. (2003). The great disappearance act: Difficulties in doing 'leadership'. *Leadership Quarterly*, 14, 359–381.

Anderson, B., & Harrison, P. (Eds.) (2010). *Taking place: Non-representational theories and geography*. Burlington, VT: Ashgate.

Bakhtin, M. (1984). *Problems of Dostoevsky's poetics* (C. Emerson trans. and Ed.). Minneapolis: University of Minnesota Press.

Barad, K. (2007). *Meeting the universe halfway: Quantum physics and the entanglement of matter and meaning*. Durham, NC and London: Duke University Press.

Bernstein, R. J. (1972). *Praxis and action*. London: Duckworth.

Bolden, R., Hawkins, B., Gosling, J., & Taylor, S. (Eds.). (2011). *Exploring leadership: Individual, organizational & societal perspectives*. Oxford: Oxford University Press.

Bourdieu, P. (1990). *The logic of practice* (R. Nice, trans.). Stanford, CA: Stanford University Press.

Caldwell, R. (2005). Things fall apart? Discourses on agency and change in organizations. *Human Relations, 58*(1), 83–114.

Callon, M. (1986). Some elements of a sociology of translation: Domestication of the scallops and the fishermen of St. Brieuc Bay. In J. Law (Ed.), *Power, action and belief*. London: Routledge.

Carroll, B., Levy, L., & Richmond, D. (2008). Leadership as practice: Challenging the competency paradigm. *Leadership, 4*(4), 363–379.

Carroll, B., & Simpson, B. (2012). Capturing sociality in the movement between frames: An illustration from leadership development. *Human Relations*, 65(10), 1283–1309.

Crevani, L., Lindgren, M., & Packendorff, J. (2010). Leadership, not leaders: On the study of leadership as practices and interactions. *Scandinavian Journal of Management*, 26(1), 77–86.

Deleuze, G., & Guattari, F. (2004). *A thousand plateaus* (B. Massumi, trans.). London: Bloomsbury Academic.

Denis, J.-L., Langley, A., & Sergi, V. (2012). Leadership in the plural. *Academy of Management Annals*, 6(1), 211–283.

Dewey, J. (1917). Duality and dualism. *Journal of Philosophy, Psychology and Scientific Methods*, 14, 491–493.

Dewey, J. (1929). *The quest for certainty*. New York: Milton, Balch, & Co.

Dewey, J., & Bentley, A. F. (1949 [1960]). *Knowing and the known*. Westport, CT: Greenwood Press.

Drath, W. H., McCauley, C. D., Palus, C. J., van Velsor, E., O'Connor, P. M. G., & McGuire, J. B. (2008). Direction, alignment, commitment: Toward a more integrative ontology of leadership. *Leadership Quarterly*, 19, 635–653.

Emirbayer, M. (1997). Manifesto for a relational sociology. *American Journal of Sociology*, 103, 281–317.

Emirbayer, M., & Mische, A. (1998). What is agency? *American Journal of Sociology*, 103(4), 962–1023.

Feldman, M. (2000). Organizational routines as a source of continuous change. *Organization Science*, 11, 611–629.

Feldman, M., & Pentland, B. (2003). Reconceptualizing organizational routines as a source of flexibility and change. *Administrative Science Quarterly*, 48, 94–118.

Fletcher, J. K. (2004). The paradox of postheroic leadership: An essay on gender, power, and transformational change. *Leadership Quarterly*, 14, 647–661.

Follett, M. P. (1996). *Mary Parker Follett Prophet of Management: A celebration of writings from the 1920s*. Boston: Harvard Business School Press.

Garud, R., Simpson, B., Langley, A., & Tsoukas, H. (2015). Introduction: How does novelty emerge? In R. Garud, B. Simpson, A. Langley, & H. Tsoukas (Eds.), *Process research in organization studies: The emergence of novelty in organizations*. Oxford: Oxford University Press.

Giddens, A. (1984). *The constitution of society: Outline of a theory of structuration*. Berkeley and Los Angeles, CA: University of California Press.

Graen, G. B., & Uhl-Bien, M. (1995). Relations-based approach to leadership: Development of leader-member exchange (LMX) theory of leadership over 25 years: Applying a multi-level multi-domain perspective. *Leadership Quarterly*, 6(2), 219–247.

Haraway, D. (1992). The promises of monsters: A regenerative politics for inappropriate/d others. In L. Grossberg, C. Nelson, & P. Treichler (Eds.), *Cultural studies*. New York: Routledge.

Heidegger, M. (2010). *Being and time* (J. Stambaugh trans., D. J. Schmidt, Ed.). Albany, NY: State University of New York Press.

Hosking, D. M. (2011). Telling tales of relations: Appreciating relational constructionism. *Organization Studies*, 32(1), 47–65.

Hosking, D. M., & Shamir, B. (2012). Dialogue: A dialogue on entitative and relational discourses. In M. Uhl-Bien & S. Ospina (Eds.), *Advancing relational leadership research: A dialogue among perspectives* (pp. 463–476). Charlotte, NC: Information Age Publishing.

Kerr, J. (2013). *Legacy: 15 lessons in leadership*. London: Constable.

Langley, A. (1999). Strategies for theorizing from process data. *Academy of Management Review*, 24(4), 691–710.

Latour, B. (1986). The powers of association. In J. Law (Ed.), *Power, action and belief.* London: Routledge.

Latour, B. (1987). *Science in action: How to follow scientists and engineers through society.* Cambridge, MA: Harvard University Press.

Latour, B. (2005). *Reassembling the social: An introduction to Actor-Network-Theory.* Oxford: Oxford University Press.

Lorimer, H. (2005). Cultural geography: The busyness of being 'more-than-representational'. *Progress in human geography,* 29(1), 83–94.

Mead, G. H. (1932). *The philosophy of the present.* La Salle, IL: Open Court.

Mead, G. H. (1934). *Mind, self and society.* Chicago, IL: University of Chicago Press.

Ospina, S., & Uhl-Bien, M. (2012). Introduction—Mapping the terrain: Convergence and divergence around relational leadership. In M. Uhl-Bien & S. Ospina (Eds.), *Advancing relational leadership research: A dialogue among perspectives* (pp. xix–xlvii). Charlotte, NC: Information Age Publishing.

Pickering, A. (1995). *The mangle of practice: Time, agency and science.* Chicago, IL and London: University of Chicago Press.

Raelin, J. (2014). Imagine there are no leaders: Reframing leadership as collaborative agency. *Leadership.*

Ratner, S., & Altman, J. (Eds.). (1964). *John Dewey and Arthur F. Bentley. A philosophical correspondence, 1932–1951.* New Brunswick, NJ: Rutgers University Press.

Shotter, J. (2006). Understanding process from within: An argument for 'withness'-thinking. *Organization Studies,* 27(4), 585–604.

Shotter, J. (2015). On "Relational Things": A new realm of inquiry—Pre-understandings and performative understandings of people's meanings. In R. Garud, B. Simpson, A. Langley, & H. Tsoukas (Eds.), *Process research in organization studies: The emergence of novelty in organizations.* Oxford: Oxford University Press.

Simpson, B. (2009). Pragmatism, Mead, and the practice turn. *Organization Studies,* 30(12), 1329–1347.

Simpson, B. (2014). George Herbert Mead. In J. Helin, T. Hernes, D. Hjorth, & R. Holt (Eds.), *Oxford handbook of process philosophy and organization studies.* Oxford: Oxford University Press.

Steyaert, C. (2007). 'Entrepreneuring' as a conceptual attractor? A review of process theories in 20 years of entrepreneurship studies. *Entrepreneurship and Regional Development,* 19(6), 453–477.

Thompson, M. (2011). Ontological shift or ontological drift? Reality claims, epistemological frameworks, and theory generation in organization studies. *Academy of Management Review,* 36(4), 754–773.

Thrift, N. (2008). *Non-representational theory: Space, politics, affect.* London: Routledge.

Tsoukas, H., & Chia, R. (2002). On organizational becoming: Rethinking organizational change. *Organization Science,* 13(5), 567–582.

Uhl-Bien, M. (2006). Relational leadership theory: Exploring the social processes of leadership and organizing. *Leadership Quarterly,* 17, 654–676.

Weick, K. E. (1979). *The social psychology of organizing.* Reading, MA: Addison-Wesley Publishing Company.

Weick, K. E. (1995). *Sensemaking in organizations.* Thousand Oaks, CA: Sage.

Whittington, R. (2006). Completing the practice turn in strategy research. *Organization Studies,* 27(5), 613–634.

9

DEVELOPING LEADERSHIP AS DIALOGIC PRACTICE

Kenneth J. Gergen and Lone Hersted

The movement toward understanding leadership as an emergent outcome of interlocking practices represents a profound shift in leadership scholarship. This is so in several significant ways. In contrast with much traditional inquiry, the focus shifts from independent entities to interdependent or co-constituting amalgams. Thus, there are no leaders independent of the relationships of which they are a part. Leadership is thus an emergent outcome. Further, the relational amalgams of interest include not only human beings, but the physical world of which they are a part. Thus, reconceptualized is the concept of "social" in the *social* science tradition. The present movement also departs from tradition in its emphasis on process as opposed to fixed attributes or structures. For example, rather than assessing the traits of good leaders or the structure of the organization, the focus shifts to the possibilities of ever changing patterns. Finally, the focus on leadership-as-practice favors a replacement of structuralist explanations of human action with a post-structuralist orientation. Muted are explanations of leadership that rely on processes or structures lying *behind* a pattern of action—psychological on the one hand and macro-structural on the other. Rather, the explanatory emphasis is centered on the ongoing patterns of relationship. For example, to explain the function of a given utterance, we might look to the pattern of ongoing exchange in which it is embedded—including bodily actions, the physical surrounds, and the traditions from which it draws.

At the same time, it is important to realize that this movement in leadership scholarship is also synchronous with developments elsewhere in organizational studies, and indeed within the intellectual and professional world more generally. The shift of focus from independent entities to relational amalgams has captured the interest not only of organizational scholars (see, e.g., Gergen, 2009; Hosking, Dachler, & Gergen, 1995; Uhl-Bien, 2006), but scholars across the sciences (see, for example, Donati, 2011; Mitchell, 1988; Pickering, 1995). Similarly, organizational theorists have joined ecologists and post-humanists, among others, in attempting to undermine the human/non-human binary (Braidotti, 2012; Law & Hassard, 1999). Possibly reflecting the rapid transformation in global conditions, the shift from structure to process has been pivotal in both organizational scholarship (Helin, Hernes, Hjorth & Holt, 2014; Hernes, 2013; Hernes & Maitlis, 2010) and elsewhere in the intellectual world (Gergen, 2015). More radically, this focus on process subtly undermines major assumptions of the positivist orientation to social science. Because entities disappear into co-constitution, and stabilities give way to process, the traditional scientific commitment to illuminating a systematic, and predictable world of cause and effect falls moribund (Deleuze, 1994; Ingold, 2011; Keller, 2006). And, it is possibly the twentieth-century shift in literary theory—from structuralism to post-structuralism—that paved the way for contemporary explanations that focus on relations among actions themselves, as opposed to off-stage abstractions.

These are enormously stimulating developments in theory, metatheory, and metaphysics. As the present volume attests, they have also given rise to new forms of organizational analytics and approaches to research. But what is to be said about the contribution of these ideas to ongoing practices in contemporary organizations? At what point do these innovative developments in theory and inquiry begin to make a difference to our common forms of leading, organizing, and daily living? There is no falling back on the early empiricist view that our theories and research are somehow laying up treasures in the storehouse of Truth. Rather, as academics we too are engaged in an array of practices. The question is whether our academic practices remain lodged within our own circles of participation, or can be used for the enrichment of cultural life. It is to such ends that we address ourselves in the present offering.

Both authors have a longstanding interest in relational leading, and most relevant, to the function of dialogue in leadership practice (Hersted & Gergen, 2013). Whether an organization prospers or perishes, in our view, depends importantly on the relationships among its participants. These relationships are primarily dialogic in character. Thus, the important question is whether our dialogic practices can bring diverse people or groups into productive coordination, ease or eradicate conflict, motivate and inspire people, and handle the emotional dynamics that bring people together or push them apart. We also believe that dialogic processes are optimally conceptualized in terms of practice, as that term is employed in the present volume. However, for us, the major challenge is one typically described as *knowledge transfer*. If dialogue is conceptualized as a form of relational practice, how are those skills acquired that will contribute to effective organizational functioning? It is this question we address in what follows. First, we outline our approach to "dialogue-as-practice." This will be useful in placing the study of dialogue firmly within the leadership-as-practice (L-A-P) framework. However, in many learning contexts—seminars, workshops, publications, and training programs—we also find it useful to sketch out some of these assumptions as pre-lude to practical engagement. With these assumptions in place, we will then describe two pedagogical practices focused on leadership development. As we shall see, these will also link L-A-P to the educational process itself. We thus explore the synchronous relationship between leadership, dialogue, and education-as-practice.

Dialogue as coordinated action

As a scholarly endeavor, disquisitions on dialogue are impoverished. There is an enormous body of literature centered on the individual person. Psychological explanations of human behavior move across the full spectrum of the social sciences. Although less voluminous, there is ample inquiry into the nature of social groups or structures—families, organizations, nation states, etc. In effect, if we presume that the world is made of up independent entities, our interest will center on the nature of the entities. And if we primarily understand the world in these terms, rela-tionships between and among the entities become difficult to theorize. Typically, we resort to billiard-ball, cause-and-effect explanations. Historically, the study of dialogue—inherently a relational phenomenon—is thus a late-comer to the academic world, and finds no home in any traditional field of study.

Furthermore, in cases in which dialogue has taken center stage, most accounts are highly prescriptive. Most theorists celebrate dialogue as a cherished form of exchange. Difficulties result from the reasons for cherishing dialogue being many and varied. In Buber's seminal work (Buber, 1923), dialogue is a special way of orienting to the other, in which boundaries are broken, and one ultimately approaches a state of spiritual unity. David Bohm's (1996) popular book, *On Dialogue*, defines dialogue as a form of communication from which something new emerges; participants must evidence a "relaxed, non-judgmental curiosity" (p. ix). Grudin's *On dialogue* champions the "reciprocal exchange of meaning ... " (Grudin, 1996, p. 11). In contrast, Putnam and Fairhurst (2001) see dialogue as a route to the convergence of views. Eisenberg and Goodall (1993) are concerned chiefly with enhancing the voices of minorities. Isaacs (1993) defines dialogue as "a sustained collective inquiry into the processes, assumptions, and certainties that compose everyday experience" (p. 25). And for Maranhao (1990), dialogue should generate the kind of skepticism that invites continuous inquiry.

Rather than equating "dialogue" with any particular vision of ideal inter-change, we find it useful to return to the simple, traditional, and more neutral definition of dialogue as conversation. Of course, this definition is also ambiguous and conceptually thin. Moreover, most existing accounts of dialogue derive from the individualist tradition. Each participant serves as an independent entity, and their utterances are viewed as outward expressions of private mental states—intentions or meanings. On this account, dialogue is a form of inter-subjective connection or synchrony. Public actions are expressions of private meanings. We will not describe here the profound and intractable shortcomings of this dualist, or mind-world, account of communication (see, e.g., Gergen 1994). Rather, in keeping with the L-A-P orientation, we bracket the realm of mind (the structuralist orientation), and focus on discursive actions themselves. We focus on the function of utterances within ongoing conversation. We draw here especially from Wittgenstein's (1963) metaphor of the language game, Garfinkel's (1965) explorations of ethnomethodology, Austin's (1962) illumination of the performatory character of speech, Shotter's (1984) concept of joint-action, and the writings of the Bakhtin circle (Bakhtin, 1981) on dialogism.

Given dialogue as a public practice, how can we theorize the process as relational, or co-constituted? Here it is useful to begin with the utterance as a simple, vocal sound. At what point, we might ask, does a vocal sound become a word, that is, a meaningful component in a system of language? In a recent film, *Mr. Turner*, Timothy Spall portrays the famous painter J.M.W. Turner as a man little given to articulate expression. Rather, in this portrayal Turner frequently responds to his consociates with a series of grunting sounds, or utterances. Yet, the sounds are neither random nor biologically necessitated. Rather, they serve as meaningful integers within the conversational flow. What grants them the status of words is essentially the manner in which they function within the ongoing conversation. For example, if someone is speaking to Turner, he grunts periodically at the close of the speaker's sentence. The speaker would then proceed to the next sentence. One might say that the utterances indicated that Turner was paying attention, and whether he agreed with the speaker or not, affirmed that the speaker was understood. Or, to put it otherwise, the grunts came to be language as they were integrated into a pattern of *coordinated action* (or co-action).

To press further, the particular meaning of an utterance is not contained in itself, but acquires its meaning largely by the way it is taken up by one's consociates. If one tells a story, and no-one pays attention, the story is no more meaningful than random grunts. However, if others respond in laughter, the story becomes humorous; if they respond in anger, the story has been an irritant. The story is neither humorous nor irritating in itself, but becomes so in the process of co-action. In this context, Wittgenstein's (1963) metaphor of the language game is also useful. The metaphor calls attention specifically to the coordinated or rule-relevant activities of the participants in generating meaning. The words, "strike" and "home run" acquire their meaning by virtue of the way they function in talk of baseball. Words invented by a single individual (a "private language" in Wittgenstein's terms) would not in themselves constitute meaningful entries into dialogue. In this sense, the traditional binary separating monologue and dialogue is misleading. The term monologue cannot refer to the utterances of one person alone, for such utterances would fail to communicate. It would not constitute language. The meaning of any utterance depends on its functioning within a relational matrix. Monologue is better understood as an extended (or dominating) entry of a single voice into a dialogue; in this sense monologue is dialogue with uneven participation.

The process of co-action is not simply an exchange of words alone. Again to draw from Wittgenstein (1963), the language games in which we participate are embedded within broader *forms of life*. This is first to draw attention to the embodied character of dialogue. Clearly the efficacy of spoken words is fastened to the simultaneous movements of the speakers' bodies, tone of voice, and physical proximity. The efficacy of one's words may depend importantly, for example, on whether one is clutching a shovel, a dagger, or a bouquet of flowers. Further, dialogic efficacy cannot ultimately be separated from the material context. Thus, the meaning of "strike" and "home run" do not only depend on the rules of baseball talk, but on their function within a form of life that includes balls, bats, bases, fields, players, umpires, hotdogs, and so on. Broadly speaking, the ways in which we walk, talk, laugh, cry, worship, engage in warfare, and virtually everything else we do, become sensible—or not—by virtue of collaborative action. In Bakhtin's terms, "to live means to participate in dialogue." And by implication, we gain insight into leadership-as-practice by viewing it through the lens of dialogue as practice.

In what follows, we offer two applications in the domain of leadership development that take dialogue as the linking vehicle to effective leadership practice. In the scenarios depicted, readers will note that the unit of analysis is the relational process, not the actions of individuals. As a leadership practice, the outcomes of the process may be a transformation of the very pattern that encouraged the first word or gesture. In this way dialogue can potentially overturn the historical trajectories in which we live.

Dialogic scenarios: Generative and degenerative

With the concept of co-action in place, we may explore its potential both for patterning and emergence. Every conversation is at once familiar and unique. It is familiar because we always borrow from past traditions of co-action. Indeed, if we did not draw from a common tradition it would be difficult to communicate at all. At the same time, every conversation is unique, as history and context are always changing. The same words spoken a second time will not have the same significance as the first time, simply because they are a repetition. Consider warnings, reprimands, or funny stories. The polysemic process is without terminus. Yet, it is useful to focus first on that which is familiar, as it provides the background against which we can treat the challenge of emergence.

Drawing from pragmatic linguistics, the concept of the *adjacency pair* is helpful, directing our attention as it does to the linking of two utterances, first from a speaker and then from a responder. What is most interesting about such pairs is their conventionality. If you have been exposed to the first, you will typically be conscious of what can or cannot follow. Among the simple cases: *question/answer; compliment/appreciation; greeting/greeting; request/comply*. We also find in these pairs an illustration of the principle of co-action as just described. A question becomes a question by virtue of its being answered; an answer is an answer by virtue of its following a question; nor can compliments and greetings stand as such until there are compliances and reciprocal greetings. Daily life proceeds as smoothly as it does primarily because we simply repeat the familiar sequences. However, our conversations are seldom limited to a single pair. Conversation unfolds over time, and can take many different directions. We can term these broader patterns *dialogic scenarios*. Dialogic scenarios are common patterns of conversation. Three of them are especially important in terms of skillful engagement in dialogue: *sustaining, generative*, and *degenerative* scenarios. Sustaining scenarios are embodied in the common, day-to-day conversations or chit-chat that has no specific goal. Although such conversation may seem a waste of time in the organizational setting, it is in just such conversation that participants are assured of their good standing, forge friendships, create trust, and otherwise contribute to a positive morale. In generative scenarios, however, there are often goals—either implicit or explicit. Here the participants build on each other's contributions, as one might say, the conversation "goes somewhere." There is learning, creativity, and possibly a sense of delight. Many of the dialogues suggested by the literature on creativity by design (Gaynor, 2002) or which take place in the "design" phase of an Appreciative Inquiry (Cooperrider, Sorensen, Whitney & Yaeger 2000) would be illustrative. In both cases, participants are positioned in such a way that they add significance and dimension to each others' offerings.

In contrast, degenerative scenarios move toward silence, animosity, or the breaking of a relationship altogether. They may begin subtly: one offers a proposal, and the reply is a critique; one gives an order, and there is sullen resistance; one blames the other, and the reply is counter-blame. All these adjacency pairs can invite subsequent degeneration. Arguments can often take the form of degenerative scenarios. Argumentation as a scenario is particularly interesting in terms of co-action. Each interlocutor attempts to present a strong position. However, the antagonist will typically locate ways of discounting the position—through inattention, changing the subject, or demonstrating the weakness of the position. In effect, what the speaker takes to be a strong argument does not register in the dialogue as a strong argument. Likewise the offering of the antagonist. Professionals concerned with conflict reduction are often resistant, then, to Habermas' (1981) view that the honest exchange of good reasons will produce accord. The good, objectively supported reasons of one are subverted by the good and objectively supported reasons of the other. Practices of bargaining, mediation, and collaborative peace building offer more promise.

Conversational choice-points

As proposed, dialogue borrows from longstanding traditions or scenarios. With sufficient repetition, the moves become naturalized. They have been practiced so often that they sometimes seem biological in origin. We are told, for example, that responding to an attack with aggression is a genetic propensity. This naturalization of our conventions is especially important in the case of degenerative scenarios, for it is just such scenarios that can bring tension, antagonism, and disruption to an organization. It is here that the concept of conversational choice-points is important. In principal, *whatever is said makes no requirements on what follows.* An utterance only comes into meaning through the co-active response. An utterance only becomes blame or criticism, for example, by virtue of how it is supplemented in the utterance that follows. In this sense, every turn in an ongoing dialogue offers a choice-point. Whatever has been said, the next speaker has options to create its significance. Thus, in every utterance, one has the potential to move the conversation in a generative or degenerative direction. This is only a "potential," and not a determinant, as one's interlocutor now stands at a choice-point, and the significance of one's utterance can be reshaped.

At times it is difficult to realize the availability of these potentials. One becomes "lost in the argument," or "moved by righteous indignation." Yet, as we have seen, every utterance also bears traces of myriad contexts of usage; every utterance is polysemic in potential. What might conventionally seem to be "a funny story," for example, may also be seen as "an ingratiating tactic," "narcissistic," "a wasting of time," "an avoidance of intimacy," and so on. In a Bakhtinian sense, participants bring with them heteroglossial repositories—vast and largely unused potentials for shifting the direction of dialogue. The challenge of leadership is that of accessing the repository, or indeed, forging new amalgams. For example, the scenario of mutual blame—in which Person A blames Person B for a failure, and B replies by blaming A—is ubiquitous. The direction is degenerative. Yet, history does supply a range of less obvious moves in the game, including apology, accepting partial blame, making light of the situation, abandoning the scenario either through silence or commentary on the scenario itself. The important point is that mutual blame is not a fixed scenario; participants always have a choice of whether and how to play.

Understanding as a relational achievement

We finally turn to the issue of understanding. It has long been held that dialogic process can play a key role in producing mutual understanding. Whether such understanding is a matter of moving from chaos to order, or resolving conflicts within the organization, dialogue is the major means to this end. How is it, then, that we come to understand each other, and why is misunderstanding so common? What is it to "understand" for which dialogue serves as the vehicle? These are important questions, but we rapidly realize that the traditional concept of understanding is unserviceable. Our common view of understanding draws from the dualist tradition touched on above. As we say, to understand someone is to "know what's on his mind," "what's in her heart," "what she is thinking," and the like. That is, we rely on a structuralist view that meaning lies somewhere "inside the head" and words, gestures, and facial expressions are only the vehicles through which meaning is conveyed to others. What can a post-structural approach offer as an alternative? Here it is first useful to touch on the problematics of the traditional view. The problem of interpreting other minds has challenged some of the West's most learned scholars for several centuries. In philosophy the challenge is often characterized as the "problem of other minds" (see, e.g., Avramides, 2001; Ryle, 1949); for Biblical scholars it is the problem of hermeneutics, or how to properly interpret text. How is one to understand God's intentions from the words of the Bible, the Prophet's wishes from the verses of the Koran, or an author's intentions from a poem or complex text? For some 300 years, hermeneutic scholars have been devoted to working out a plausible rationale for justifying interpretations of texts. Yet, there is no commonly accepted solution. The problem is particularly difficult to solve, because there is no principled relationship between "a thought" and an utterance; no utterance is a necessary indicator of any particular thought. If a colleague says to an office mate, "I am not happy with your work," is this an indication of a minor frustration, a major irritation, or simply a casual comment? Or, perhaps it is not any form of unhappiness, but simply the individual's style of talking, a power maneuver, or a signal of pathology. Or, perhaps it is none of these … or all of them simultaneously! Yet, any attempt to clarify the meaning of the utterance will yield but another utterance (or bodily signal). Because this signal too has no principled connection with an intention, its meaning remains equally ambiguous. The interpreter can never exit the *hermeneutic circle*, a self-referring process in which no interpretation can be justified save through reference to yet another interpretation.

It is here that the post-structural view becomes a major asset. On this account, we abandon the mind/action dualism, and turn attention to the process of co-action. In this frame we can trace the production of mutuality not to minds, but to collaborative action. This view, in turn, gives us new purchase in the problem of what it means to understand. Mutual understanding may essentially be viewed as a form of scenario, or in Austin's (1962) terms, a mutually felicitous pattern of coordinated actions. It may be, for example, to tell a story of grief to which the other replies with sympathy, to tell of a troubled situation to which the reply is quiet advice, or to voice a strong opinion to which the other assents. Reducing conflict in an organization is thus to move within dialogue in such a way that a degenerative scenario is subverted, and replaced with a sustaining or generative scenario. Mutual understanding, then, is akin to dancing smoothly or paddling a canoe together.

Leadership and the development of dialogic skill

We shift now to a more direct concern with enriching dialogic practices in the context of organizational leadership. In developing leadership-as-practice, what learning processes can best impart "dialogic knowledge?" Here we immediately confront a significant challenge. We traditionally view knowledge as inhering in a set of propositions. Thus, books and journal articles are means of disseminating knowledge, and the library is viewed as a storehouse of knowledge. The learning process is essentially about mastering and applying propositions, and the central pedagogies are didactic in form. We might thus conclude that the mastery of the above account of dialogue would enhance skillful participation in dialogue. There is some wisdom in this view, but it is limited. A manager might well be sensitized by this account to the relational nature of dialogue and the many ways in which his or her words may be misunderstood; he or she might begin to search for new "ways to talk" and begin to understand how much his or her status as manager depends on relating well to those about. But, ultimately, this account is a form of "propositional knowledge"; these are propositions "about the world" but removed from specific locations of applicability. This practice in "knowing that" gives us little purchase in the market place of "knowing how" to participate in the practice of dialogue. One cannot learn to be a skilled tennis player entirely through reading a book on tennis. How, then, to move theory into action? In what follows we share two approaches in which we have been engaged. The first relies on dialogic rehearsal and reflection, and the second on role-play.

As scholars, we first turned naturally to our major means of imparting what we take to be knowledge: the written word. But in this format how could we move from propositional knowledge to knowledge in practice. The difficulty is compounded by the fact that one cannot be dialogically skilled as an independent individual. Leadership is created in co-action, and no participant can control the meaning of his or her own utterances. Any proposition dictating "how to do it" would not only be misleading, but continue to support the tradition of the individual leader. We thus set out to write a form of textbook, *Relational leading: Practices for dialogically based collaboration*. In each chapter we first included accounts of various aspects of dialogic process, reflecting many of the ideas discussed above. In effect, the reader was introduced to a practice orientation to leading. The intent here was not to dictate practice, but to sensitize the reader to dimensions of his or her subsequent practice. Second, we created a set of dialogic scenarios— written scenes from everyday organizational life. Our aim was to engage our readers in a *vicarious rehearsal*, that is to draw them into the drama in such a way that they might imaginatively pretend they were participating. In this way we were making use of a common cultural process in which we listen to stories as if we are the protagonist. Importantly, we listen to stories by commonly asking ourselves, "what would I do under the circumstances?" In this way we subtly prepare ourselves for future contingencies.

Yet, because of its inherently unpredictable character, we felt that sensitization and vicarious rehearsal of dialogue were insufficient. We thus added a third and reflective component to the pedagogical process. Rather than didactically explaining to readers why we thought certain conversational moves were superior to others, we attempted to energize their own reflection. If there are fundamentally no "right" or "wrong" moves in a conversation, to what should one be sensitized? For what should one be readied? An analogy to learning skills in chess is relevant. A teacher can develop on paper an array of possible board configurations, and ask the learner what move he or she would make in each of these cases. The two of them could then discuss the advantages and disadvantages of each. One thus gains increased sensitivity to the pros and cons of possible moves.

We drew from a repository of scenarios common to organizational life, including for example, scenarios related to team development, guided organizational change, interpersonal conflict, organizational innovation, and coaching. Perhaps the greatest challenges to leadership originate in contexts of conflict—disagreements, jealousies, injustices, competitions for power, and so on. As we have also seen, conflict can commence with any adjacency pair, and the slide into degenerative scenario can be rapid. This means that those in leadership positions can easily be swept into such scenarios. Here we share one such conflict into which we invited our readers (from Hersted & Gergen, 2013):

> We're in a development department of new products in the computer games industry. Claudia is the manager of the department with 30 employees, and Kevin is the head of one of her project groups.

> KEVIN: Look Claudia. I need to talk to you. Do you have a moment?
> CLAUDIA: Of course. What's up?
> KEVIN: It's about the decision you made yesterday at the staff meeting about closing down the new project.
> CLAUDIA: Yes. So, what's the problem?
> KEVIN: I was very surprised that you decided to close down the new project without talking to me about it first.
> CLAUDIA: Well, I knew that you would just fight against closing the project, so why should I discuss this issue with you?
> KEVIN (RAISING HIS VOICE): Well, I'm the coordinator of that project. You appointed me to be responsible for it, and I've been working hard on it. I really put a lot of effort into it. So don't you think you owe me some respect? You should have talked to me about it before announcing the closure?
> CLAUDIA: Don't be so emotional, Kevin. This project had become a waste of money. You knew that, and just kept working on it without monitoring what was going on. It wasn't paying off, and I tried to tell you that in a dozen ways. It was an interesting and expensive experiment, but it's now time to just let it go.
> KEVIN: This isn't fair! The project was under development, and we just started it four months ago. We're in the middle of a process, and we've been involving a lot of people and stakeholders. How can you just close it down without discussing it with me? I could have shown you the

strategy for the project ... and you might have understood the logic ... actually we were on a good track ... .

CLAUDIA: Actually I gave you a chance, Kevin, but you and your people didn't create any results, and you didn't listen. Look, the competition in our business is hard, and we can't waste our resources on projects that don't pay off. I have to make the decisions here, and they aren't easy. But this one was clear.

KEVIN: Well I'm fully aware of how we spend our resources. I just think that you should have talked to me first. The way you did it was disrespectful to me and to the people who've been working hard on this project.

CLAUDIA (RAISING HER VOICE): Oh... Kevin, your arrogance is the problem here. I dropped the project because you weren't capable of realizing what a failure it was! Anyway, you should respect my decisions without questioning. I am the boss, after all, and I need to work with people who trust my decisions; so don't fight against me. The issue is closed.

(Kevin walks out of Claudia's office, slamming the door. The next day he delivers his resignation.)

At the close of the scenario we invited the readers into reflection. We posed several questions that created connections between the actions in the case and the conceptual framework outlined earlier. Consciousness of the scenario-like quality of such interchanges, the possibility for multiple constructions, and the origins of meaning in co-action were all paramount. We thus asked, for example, "How would you characterize the scenario in this conversation?" with the intent of sharpening the reader's consciousness of the way in which the co-active moves escalated the hostility. We then asked, "Can you trace the responsibility for the outcome?" with the aim of drawing attention to the co-active creation of the scenario. To highlight the socially constructed nature of the realities each brought to bear, we asked, "Did either Claudia or Kevin have the better argument? Was either right?"

Crucially, we also directed attention to the conversational choice-points. We asked where in the dialogue could either Kevin or Claudia have made a different move, one that could possibly invite the other into a less antagonistic reply. We encouraged readers to dip into their own conversational repositories to locate more satisfactory alternatives. Could they avoid the degenerative slide? In sum, our attempt was to develop a new form of "textbook" in leadership, one that was congenial with the conception of leadership, dialogue, and learning as practice.

Developing dialogic skills in action

If the aim of leadership development is to enhance skill in practice, the limits of a text-based pedagogy are clear. There must be immersion in the actual practices, an enlargement in "knowing how," such that leaders become "creative way-farers" in dialogic relationships. In this light, one of the authors (LH) developed a leadership development practice that situated potential leaders in the context of ongoing action. The pedagogical practice here made major use of role-playing, combined with creative reflection. The main idea was to develop a skill-enhancing pedagogical method drawing from the rich traditions of the dramatic arts and group coaching. In the case of the dramatic arts, playing the role of another person—for instance a young boy, a colleague, a mother—the "actor" begins to move and speak as the other. During the role-playing the "actor" becomes bodily involved and begins to experience the world from the perspective of the other; hereby acquiring the skill to "identify with the other." In this process the "actor" begins to grasp and understand the logic of the other person and the context from which he or she re-acts in various situations. The ability to change perspective and identify with others can be an important step in enhancing leadership skills in connecting to and relating sensitively to others. The role-playing directs attention to different embodied ways of responding (see also Shotter 2012), which means an expansion in communicative resources. This learning through *mimesis* is fundamental to role-playing.

At the same time, as in the preceding practice, the idea was to add a reflective dimension to the role-playing. In addition to enriching one's skills for dialogue and action, it seemed essential to expand consciousness of the skill. Through reflection, one can generalize across diverse contexts, deliberate on shortcomings, and actively consider new alternatives. In part, this concern with reflection was realized as participants both enacted roles and commented on the process. Often, they were encouraged, on the basis of their comments, to create and enact alternative scenarios. In this way they became active "spect-actors" (Boal, 1979). To intensify reflection and create a collaborative learning space, we made use of a reflecting team consisting of individuals who looked at the episodes from multiple perspectives without judging the "actors." By working with the reflective team, the participants began to reflect on the episodes and possibilities for improvement through alternative actions. Through the dialogue the participants began to practice *reflection-on-action* with the hope of enhancing their subsequent capacities for *reflection-in-action* (Schön, 1987). Essentially, then, through a process of engaged role-playing combined with polyphonic reflection, the hope was that participants would acquire both dialogic skill and an expanded relational awareness in their daily organizational practice.

The dialogue training involved some 60 participants over an 18-month period, and included those in managerial positions and employees in an institution that provided care for neglected adolescents. In the project the participants worked with episodes from their own organizational context—episodes selected and presented by the participants themselves. These episodes dealt with challenges concerning communication and relationships, and reflected tensions that often had led to polarization, alienation, and conflict within the organization and in relation to the surroundings. These tensions and conflicts not only involved managers, employees, and external working partners, but the young people living at the institution, their parents, and other important actors. Episodes touched on the use of force, sexual abuse, prostitution, alcohol and drug abuse, deviation from the institutional rules, tensions among managers and employees, conflicts in the group, along with ethnic and cultural conflicts within the organization.

The chosen episodes often contained what Mezirow calls *disorienting dilemmas* (Mezirow, 1994). According to Mezirow, working with disorienting dilemmas can lead to important and possibly *transformative learning*. Drawing from these dilemmas, the participants physically played out and experimented with different scenarios, employing what we might call *embodied imagination*. While working with these challenging episodes or disorienting dilemmas, we questioned the actual practice (in gentle ways) and tried to look at the episodes from new perspectives and to reflect on and experiment with different options for communication and action. The idea was to move from degenerative to generative scenarios by focusing on conversational choice-points. In this way, the project worked with the notion of learning-from-within a social situation and reflecting on it. Learning is here understood as being embedded within relational action, experience, and experimentation. The efficacy of these experiences was further enhanced through the following components.

Learning goals

Working from within a constructionist premise and drawing on inspiration from action research, it was important to initiate the dialogue training process by inviting the participants into a dialogue about the desired learning outcomes. While talking about learning goals and listening to each other, the participants clearly inspired each other and several of them started building on each others' ideas by adding dimensions to their own learning goals. Among the learning goals, the participants mentioned their wish to explore how they could talk together more openly, become better at listening and communicating, gain clarity on their roles and tasks in the institution, and be more appreciative. The participants wrote their learning goals in personal notebooks and after a little dialogue in plenary, they presented these on a poster hanging on the wall. During the process of dialogue training we often returned to these learning goals, and some were modified and refined by the participants themselves. For instance, one of the leaders declared in the first phase "I wish to be clear in my communication" as his personal learning goal, and then later on in the process, he modified it to "I wish to be clear and appreciative in my communication." This kind of development suggested that the group was engaged in a transformative learning process.

Rules for play

The dialogue training was extremely serious on the one hand, and on the other, it also contained many playful aspects. The latter were important to loosen up and build confidence among the participants as well as to enhance motivation. According to earlier research, rules, play, risk-taking, and creativity can be considered closely connected and interwoven (Chemi, Jensen & Hersted 2015). According to Huizinga (2002) play is a "free activity" that is more or less structured by its own rules and unfolds in accordance with its own boundaries of time and space. Play is "standing quite consciously outside 'ordinary life' as being 'not serious,' but at the same time absorbing the player intensely and utterly" (p. 2). Therefore, to create a frame for the work, we agreed on rules for being present, focused, non-judgmental, and respectful.

Facilitation

LH served as the facilitator throughout the process. The first task was a matter of ensuring a nurturing and trusting frame for the role-play experiences. Furthermore, it was important to ask reflective questions to facilitate dialogue. In these processes it is essential that the facilitator takes a humble or *not-knowing-position*, while simultaneously organizing and guiding the process. The facilitator must encourage the participants to imagine alternative scenarios in appreciative and respectful ways. It is a question of being and moving *with* the participants, but at the same time carefully challenging their taken-for-granted assumptions. The facilitator can never be fully neutral (impossible from a constructionist perspective), but should attempt to be an attentive observer and an inspiring co-creator.

The polyphonic reflecting team

As a central feature of the learning, in each role-playing session selected participants served as a reflecting team. Participants were told that they were not obliged to do the role-playing, and that it was fully legitimate to participate as observing and reflecting team members. The selected members were positioned as active observers of the episodes enacted by their colleagues. Before the *mise-en-scène* began, each of the reflecting team members was given tasks by the facilitator consisting of observing and listening from specific perspectives, for instance the perspective of an adolescent, a teacher, a social worker, a team leader, the director of the local municipality, a representative from the union, a mother, a father, etc. The team was encouraged by the facilitator not to express judgments but instead to show *curiosity* and *wonder* in humble ways based on their observations. The reflecting team members spoke directly with the role-players by invitation from the facilitator, and they were also encouraged to talk together publicly as a team about what they had observed during the role-play. Sometimes a member from the reflecting team was inspired to join in and replace one of the role players to experiment with alternative ways of moving in the dialogue.

General learning outcomes

Was this form of learning-as-practice effective in strengthening skills in leading through dialogue? "Efficacy" is always a problematic word, as there are important questions of power and multiple perspectives in terms of what counts as effective, for whom, and with what consequences. However, it was important to acquire a sense of how this form of pedagogy was experienced by the participants, and if there were ways in which it could be improved. To this end three semi-structured focus group interviews were conducted, each of one hour's length, with three representatives from different categories of participants in each focus group (e.g. designated leaders, pedagogues, social workers, school teachers, kitchen workers, and people employed in the administration). The feedback from the participants suggested that the process yielded positive learning outcomes. In the following we offer a few of the comments from these focus group interviews concerning embodiment, plurality in perspective, and improvisational readiness.

Body consciousness

Something that makes this approach different from more traditional leadership training methods is its dimension of embodiment. One learns in and through action. We are dealing here with embodied knowledge, or in Shotter's (2012) terms, a *knowing-from-within* or *an understanding of a relational-responsive kind* (p. 107). However, from a pedagogical standpoint the important question is whether participants emerge with an enriched sense of the ways in which bodily expressions contribute to dialogic outcomes. There are positive indications. As one of the participants expressed:

> It is important to consider if it is appropriate to assume a relaxed and loose body posture depending on the person you are having a conversation with. It is also essential to think about how open and inviting your appearance is, and just all in all to think about if the position you are sitting in is suitable for the social environment. Often I am sitting with my arms crossed like this, and this position I mostly try to avoid at work also depending on who I am talking to.

Another added:

> The awareness of one's own bodily expression is really important, and I have definitely felt this awareness, which is a good thing. Also if I know that I am going to have a certain conversation with someone, I am now able to run

the event through in my head before the meeting starts and use some of the things we have learned. I am able to imagine which scenarios will possibly take place in the forthcoming conversation … and I also use this when dealing with other colleagues but in a different way.

This latter remark was particularly interesting, as it expanded the pedagogical aims of the project. It suggests that role-playing invites the imaginative rehearsal of possible scenarios as a kind of *private theatre* where inner dialogues take place. One may then enter dialogue with greater preparedness and a larger conversational repertoire.

Plurality in perspective

As reasoned earlier, role-playing the lives of others should be useful in expanding perspectives. One learns in an embodied way how to identify with the other. A number of participants affirmed that indeed the practice did succeed in enriching perspectives. As one of the managers expressed:

When circumstances ask for it, you remember some of the things you have learned and are much more aware of what kind of position and approach you should choose. Because of that, I find the exercises rather useful. When I'm going to engage in a conversation with someone, I think about the different techniques I can choose from, and sometimes I take the perspective of a student and place myself in his/her position. That would possibly work when trying to get a social worker to take a different approach and ask the right questions like: how would you think about it if you were in the students' position? […] I have made use of that method, also in relation to the teachers. In specific situations I have asked the teachers to identify with the students, and feel what it is like to be in their situation.

Another participant expanded on the issue of perspective:

Well, I think it is very useful to experiment with different perspectives. If you are dealing with a person it is unquestionably a good idea to try and see things from the other person's perspective. And, the ability to do that is something you can work on for the rest of your life, because it is actually very difficult to see things from a different perspective than your own. Sometimes specific situations cause particular reactions, and … well, in that way I find the things we have learned very useful.

It is interesting to see that the participants realized the emergent character of dialogue, the significance of context, and the utility of reflection in preparing for improvisation.

Readiness for improvisation

Given the enormous variations in the content of any scenario, and the fact that every turn offers a choice-point for multiple alternatives to follow, the key to successful participation is improvisation. One of the aims was that participants would come away with an enhanced flexibility and a readiness to adapt and create as the situation allowed. The preceding remark suggested that many did benefit in this way. As one of the participants also pointed out:

> During the role-playing exercises I have learned a lot and received a different and new view of certain conflicts and aspects, and I know that my group members had the same experience. After the exercises I often heard people talking: "why didn't we do it like that, why didn't we say this instead of that ... ?" In that way it definitely seems like we all learned a lot.

It appeared that the training challenged taken-for-granted assumptions. By reflecting from different perspectives and trying out alternative solutions the participants appeared to expand their repertoire of communicative acts. We emphasized the point that there are always multiple ways of responding and one always has a choice. One of the managers added:

> It's the real challenge, I think, when trying to use all these things looking forward. Acknowledgement is the necessary and important thing here. For instance when X is saying: "Maybe we should try to replay the thing you just did before?" I find it a great idea. It is useful to think about what you can change and do better ... and, also trying to learn from each other.

These comments and others from the focus group interviews suggest that role-playing, combined with a polyphonic reflecting team, can be a useful tool for facilitating leadership development. Instead of illuminating fixed, linear strategies for action, emphasis was put on improvisation or "wayfinding" (Chia & Holt 2008) in a continuous and largely uncharted interchange. The majority of the managers and employees said that they learned a lot about communicating with their colleagues, other working partners, the adolescents living at the institution, and the parents of the adolescents. They also noticed the beginning of positive change in their organizational culture. In general, it appeared that the educational practice contributed to the participants' communicative skills in constituting reality, building up generative and sustainable relationships, constituting identities, and the creation of new opportunities and new practices in the organization.

Conclusion

Our aims in this chapter have been several. First, we have attempted to link the account of L-A-P with an account of dialogic process. By unpacking a theory of dialogue-as-practice, we can see more clearly some of the implications for action in the organizational context. The actions of people take place, by and large, within dialogic relationships. Further, we have attempted to link these twin concerns with the challenge of leadership development. How can the theoretical orientation of L-A-P be cashed out in terms of developing dialogic skills? This led us, in turn, to conceptualize the pedagogical process of leadership development as a practice (essentially, pedagogy-as-practice). In this context we reported on two attempts to enhance leadership skills in dialogue, the first text-based, and the second, action-based. Although these accounts are necessarily limited, and leave many important questions unanswered, there are several implications that deserve special attention. At the outset is the more general question of how to link the highly general and abstract array of concepts included in the practice orientation to leading to actual activity. In part this is the question of the pragmatic utility of practice theory. As we see it, the focus on dialogue is ideally situated as a linking vehicle. While it is difficult to know how to formulate such concepts as relationality, process, and emergence in terms of ongoing action, the practice of dialogue is experience near. Thus, to articulate a theory of dialogue in terms that are congenial with the general orientation, lends itself to actionable consequences.

To extend this discussion, it is an interesting question as to whether the conceptual components of a theory of dialogue may be effectively extended to the full range of activities comprising organizational life. For example, a theory of dialogue is primarily focused on discursive exchange. At the same time, the practice of dialogue is a fully embodied performance. But in what degree can the concepts congenial to this context (e.g. co-action, scenarios, choice-points) be extended to non-discursive actions (e.g. relations with technology, food, nature, physical structures)? Herein lies a topic for rich discussion.

A second issue emerges from the particular practices of leadership development outlined above. A practice orientation to leadership is unique in its removing leadership from the minds and actions of individuals, and placing it within co-constituting relationships. While intellectually bracing, such a view is difficult to assimilate into leadership development programs composed of participating individuals. In effect, one works with individuals as a means of enhancing a relational process. And for the individual, there is no skilled action until another's actions affirm it as a skill. Is such a pedagogy not misconceived? As suggested in the second project described above, it is fruitful to work with multiple participants at different levels in the same organization. Enhanced coordination within such groups should contribute to the organization's collective intelligence and capability for action.

Yet, we should not underestimate the potential of individual-centered development for relational enrichment. We have laid out a theory of dialogue that points to the potential for an individual, at any choice-point, to perform in such a way that the ensuing dialogue may move in either a generative or degenerative direction. And, while the performance does not demand or require the interlocutor's subsequent response, there is what Pearce and Cronen (1982) call a *logical force* that will favor one response over another. If greeted by a friend, it is highly conventional to return the greeting (as opposed, for example, to singing a song or staring at one's shoes). Failing to respond with a greeting is to risk alienation. Thus, the greater the one's resources for performance, the more likely one may enlist the cooperation of the other. In the project described above, trainees were essentially increasing their resources for action at the choice-point. Like seasoned basketball players, they were learning how to move effectively within the ongoing flow of complex relational patterns. In this sense, action and reflection may indeed contribute to one's capacity to invite less conflictual, and more productive relationships within the organization and without.

References

Austin, J. L. (1962). *How to do things with words*. New York: Oxford University Press.
Avramides, A. (2001). *Other minds*. London: Routledge.
Bakhtin, M. M. (1981). *The dialogic imagination: Four essays by M.M. Bakhtin*. C. Emerson & M. Holquist (Eds.) Austin: University of Texas Press.
Boal, A. (1979). *Theatre of the oppressed*. New York: Theatre Communications Group.
Bohm, D. (1996). *On dialogue* (L. Nichol, Ed.). New York: Routledge.
Braidotti, R. (2012). *The posthuman*. London: Polity.
Buber, M. (1923). *I and thou*. New York: Scribner.
Chasin, R., Herzig, M., Roth, S., Chasin, L., Becker, C., & Stains, R. (1996). From diatribe to dialogue on divisive public issues: Approaches drawn from family therapy. *Median Quarterly*, Summer Issue 13(4).
Chemi, T., Jensen, J. B., & Hersted, L. (2015). *Behind the scenes of artistic creativity: Processes of learning, creating and organizing*. Frankfurt: Peter Lang.
Chia, R., & Holt, R. (2008). Strategy as wayfinding. Paper for the 24th EGOS Colloquium. Amsterdam.
Cooperrider, D. L., Sorensen, P. F., Whitney, D., & Yaeger, T. F. (2000). *Appreciative inquiry: Rethinking human organization toward a positive theory of change*. Champagne, IL: Stipes.
Deleuze, G. (1994). *Difference and repetition* (P. Patton, trans.). New York: Columbia University Press. (Original work published 1968).
Derrida, J. (1976). *Of grammatology* (G. C. Spivak, trans.). Baltimore, MD: Johns Hopkins University Press. (Original work published 1967).
Donati, P. (2011). *Relational sociology: A new paradigm for the social sciences*. London: Routledge.
Garfinkel, H. (1965). *Studies in ethnomethodology*. Englewood Cliffs, NJ: Prentice-Hall.
Gaynor, H. (2002). *Innovation by design*. New York: AMACOM.
Gergen, K. J. (1994). *Realities and relationships: Soundings in social construction*. Cambridge, MA: Harvard University Press.
Gergen, K. J. (2009). *Relational being: Beyond self and community*. New York: Oxford University Press
Gergen, K. J. (2015). From mirroring to world-making: Research as future forming. *Journal for the Theory of Social Behaviour*, 45, 287–310.
Grudin, R. (1996). *On dialogue: An essay in free thought*. New York and Boston: Houghton Mifflin.
Habermas, J. (1981). *Theory of communicative action V.1*. Boston: Beacon Press.

Helin, J., Hernes, T., Hjorth, D., & Holt, R. (2014). *The Oxford handbook of process philosophy & organization studies*. Oxford: Oxford University Press.

Hernes, T., & Maitlis, S. (Eds.) (2010). *Process, sensemaking, and organizing*. Oxford: Oxford University Press.

Hersted, L. & Gergen, K. J. (2013). *Relational leading: Practices for dialogically based collaboration*. Chagrin Falls, OH: TAOS Institute Publications.

Hosking, D., Dachler, H. P. & Gergen, K. J. (Eds.) (1995). *Management and organization: Relational alternatives to individualism*. Aldershot: Avebury. Reprinted on WorldShare Books: www.worldsharebooks.net, 2012.

Huizinga, J. (1955). *Homo Luden: A study of the play element in culture*. Boston: Beacon Press.

Ingold, T. (2011). *The perception of the environment: Essays on livelihood, dwelling and skill*. London: Routledge.

Isaacs, W. N. (1999). *Dialogue and the art of thinking together. A pioneering approach to communicating in business and in life*. New York: Doubleday.

Keller, C. (2008). *On the mystery: Discerning divinity in process*. Minneapolis, MN: Fortress Press.

Law, J., & Hassard, J. (1999). *Actor network theory and after*. London: Wiley.

Maranhao, T. (Ed.) (1990). *The interpretation of dialogue*. Chicago, IL: University of Chicago Press.

McNamee, S. and Gergen, K. J. (2001). *Relational responsibility*. Thousand Oaks, CA: Sage.

Mezirow (1994). Understanding transformation theory. *Adult Education Quarterly*, 44, 222–232.

Mitchell, S. (1988). *Relational concepts in psychoanalysis: An integration*. Cambridge, MA: Harvard University Press.

Pearce, B., & Cronen, V. (1980). *Communication, action, and meaning: The creation of social realities*. New York: Praeger.

Pickering, A. (1995). *The mangle of practice: Time, agency, and science*. Chicago, IL: University of Chicago Press.

Rahim, S. A. (1994). Participatory development communication as a dialogical process. In S. White, K. Sadanandan Nair & J. Ascroft (Eds.), *Participatory communication, working for change and development*. New Delhi: Sage.

Rodriguez, A. (2001). *Diversity as liberation (II): Introducing a new understanding of diversity*. Cresskill, NJ: Hampton Press.

Ryle, G. (1949). *The concept of mind*. London: Hutchinson.

Shotter, J. (2012). *Social construction on the edge: 'Withness'-thinking and embodiment*. Chagrin Falls, OH: TAOS Institute Publications.

Taylor, J. R., & Van Every, E. J. (2000). *The emergent organization: Communication as its site and surface*. Mahwah, NJ: L. Erlbaum.

Thatchenkery, T. J. & Upadhyaya, P. (1996). Organizations as a play of multiple and dynamic discourses: An example from a global social change organization. In D. J. Boje, R. P. Gephart & T. J. Thatchenkery (Eds.). *Postmodern management and organization theory* (pp. 308–330). Thousand Oaks, CA: Sage.

Uhl-Bien, M. (2006). Relational leadership theory: Exploring the social processes of leadership and organizing. *Leadership Quarterly* 17, 654–676.

Weick, K. E. (1995). *Sensemaking in organizations*. Thousand Oaks, CA: Sage.

Wells, G. (1999). *Dialogic inquiry: Towards a socio-cultural practice and theory of education*. Cambridge: Cambridge University Press.

Wittgenstein, L. (1963). *Philosophical investigations* (G. E. M. Anscombe trans.). London: Blackwell.

Yankelovich, D. (1999). *The magic of dialogue: Transforming conflict into cooperation*. New York: Simon & Schuster.

10

CONVERSATIONAL TRAVEL AND THE IDENTIFICATION OF LEADERSHIP PHENOMENA

Caroline Ramsey

Introduction

Amidst all the leader-celebratory treatments of leadership (Hosking, 2011), there has been over the last 15 years or so, an emerging exploration of leadership that is distributed, shared (Denis, Langley & Sergi, 2012; Thorpe, Gold & Lawler, 2011), or understood in terms of relationships (Uhl-Bien, 2006) or as a practice (Crevani Lindgren & Packendorff, 2010; Raelin, 2011). Undoubtedly, these relational and practice approaches have provided new insights into leadership, and an emerging array of empirical work has started to explore the relational practices involved. Several authors (e.g. Denis *et al.*, 2012; Shamir, 2012) have, however, challenged relational leadership writers to define what actually constitutes leadership from their relational perspective and how it can be distinguished from other organizational processes. For only then, it has been argued, can leadership be researched as a distinct phenomenon. In a sense, the leadership-as-practice movement is able to respond to this challenge by pointing to activities (see, e.g., Crevani and Endrissat, Chapter 2, this volume; Raelin, Chapter 1, this volume). In this chapter I set out to offer an optic for examining leadership created relationally in the practice of moment-by-moment interplay. My focus will be on conversation, which I will treat primarily as an invitational, ontological practice. I shall argue that conversations "travel" as participants improvise on the contributions of others, moving conversations in emergent trajectories, along topic lines towards conclusions or differences, and via a variety of modes, for example argument, questioning, or affirmation. It is, I shall argue, the way that conversations travel that provides us with access to the relational practices that create and distinguish organizational phenomena such as leadership.

This argument will be built in four stages. First, I will provide a brief resume of relational approaches to leadership that have emerged strongly in the last ten to fifteen years. Next, I will discuss how we can build vocabularies for discussing moment-by-moment talk and leadership in organizations and, in so doing, can identify moments of leadership. Third, I will introduce some extracts of talk from a meeting by way of an illustration of how conversational travel can be used and the insights that can be gained through such an optic. Finally, I will use this illustrative empirical material to engage different discursive practices of inquiry in dialogue with conversational travel considering where they may contribute to each other in developing a richer, empirical study of relational leadership.

Relational treatments of leadership

The exploration of leadership as a particular type of relationship rather than as a status, task, or capacity has picked up pace over the first decade of the new century. Mary Uhl-Bien (2006) has drawn on Hosking and Morley's (1991) distinction of entitative and relational treatments of relating, to distinguish between two different ways that researchers have centered relationships in their study of leadership. Entitative approaches see relationships as taking place *between* entities such as leaders and followers, be they organizations, teams, or individuals. Our understanding of those relationships would be based, therefore, on the attributes, attitudes, and intentions of those entities. So, in focusing on leadership relationships, researchers have attended to the properties and behaviors of individuals. Uhl-Bien identifies several streams of research within this entitative (she uses the term entity) approach to leadership-within-relationships. Most focus on leader-follower relationships, albeit within different contexts or focuses for study. So, Uhl-Bien has used leader-member exchange (Graen & Uhl-Bien, 1995) to explore leader follower dyads, and Hollander (1995) attended to the cognitive and perceptual processes of identifying leaders. Elsewhere, charismatic (Howell & Shamir, 2005), network (Balkundi & Kilduff, 2005), and post-industrial (Rost, 1995) contexts have been studied to examine differences in leadership relations.

In contrast, a relational approach (Uhl-Bien, 2006) theorizes leadership as emerging amidst relational processes, rather than through an individual's actions within relationships. Uhl-Bien (2006) draws heavily on the relational constructionism of Dian Hosking and her colleagues (Dachler, 1991; Dachler & Hosking, 1995; Hosking, 1988, 2007, 2011; Brown & Hosking, 1986; Hosking & Fineman, 1990; Hosking & Morley, 1991) to build a picture of research attending to the relational activities of participants within emergent leadership relating. More recently other approaches, for example, practice-based (Raelin, 2011; Crevani et al., 2010), process (Wood, 2005), or performative (Denis et al., 2012), also foreground social relating as generative of leadership.

Uhl-Bien (2006) articulates a relational research agenda as asking:

... how the processes of leadership and management in organizations emerge—e.g., how realities of leadership are interpreted within the network of relations; how organizations are designed, directed, controlled and developed on the bases of collectively generated knowledge about organizational realities; and how decisions and actions are embedded in collective sense-making and attribution processes from which structures of social interdependence emerge and in turn reframe the collectively generated organizational realities.

(Uhl-Bien, 2006, p. 662)

This is social constructionism with a strong cognitive emphasis: "realities of leadership are interpreted," organizational management is based on "collectively generated knowledge," and actions are "embedded in collective sense-making." In more recent work, Fairhurst and Uhl-Bien have contrasted two models of communication; a transmission model and a meaning-centered approach. Although there are significant differences in this approach, I would suggest that they both continue to have a cognitive, sensemaking emphasis. Transmission models understand communication as a "conduit" (Fairhurst & Connaughton, 2014), while a meaning-centered view of communication asserts that " ... the processes by which *meanings* get created, contested, and negotiated are fundamental to understanding leadership" (Fairhurst & Uhl-Bien, 2012, p. 1046, emphasis added). One of the authors that Fairhurst and Connaughton identify as taking a meaning-centered view is John Shotter. I want to suggest that we can engage helpfully with Shotter and his colleagues (Shotter, 1996, 2008, Chapter 7, this volume; Shotter & Katz, 1996; Cunliffe, 2002) in a somewhat different manner. I would suggest that they offer us an ontological (in contrast with an epistemological or meaningful) treatment of communication. Talk, argued Shotter, gestures, strikes, and moves are emergent realities created in a "temporal unfolding" flow (Shotter, 2006, p. 588). It is this third, generative model of communication that I want to work with for the remainder of this chapter.

This alternative strand of relational constructionist argument foregrounds a world, or history-making dynamic to social relating (e.g. Hosking, 2000; Hosking & McNamee, 2006; Shotter, 1996, 2008; Ramsey, 2014; Simpson, 2009; Carroll & Simpson, 2012). Here attention is focused on the action performed rather than sensemaking; leadership *activity* is understood as socially created. Such a shift in our attention will become significant as I attempt to build a method and frame for inquiry within relationally created leadership.

Developments required in relational treatments of leadership

Both Uhl-Bien (2006) and Denis and his colleagues (2012) have written of a need to develop (a) a richer empirical base for a relational perspective and (b) a clearer articulation of what constitutes a phenomenon that might be called leadership.

To a considerable extent Uhl-Bien's (2006) call for empirical work has been met (e.g., Carroll & Simpson, 2012; Crevani *et al.*, 2010; Cunliffe & Eriksen, 2011; Fairhurst, 2007; Fairhurst & Connaughton, 2014; Larsson & Lundholm, 2010; Fairhurst & Uhl-Bien, 2012; Wodak, Kwon & Clarke, 2011). However, it is worth pointing out that, with the exception of Carroll and Simpson's research, in all the other specific studies there is a pre-identified leader relating with other or others. There is a problem here, as once a researcher identifies a leader it then becomes possible to locate their relational actions within the intentions, attitudes, or discursive strategies of the leader and followers. This will, consequently, blind us to the agency of relational processes that writers such as Hosking (2007, 2011; Dachler and Hosking, 1995) point toward.

The issue of what actually constitutes leadership; what, in Drath and his colleagues' (Drath *et al.*, 2008) words, is its ontology is left somewhat uncertain. Indeed, Alvesson and Svengingsson (2003) have argued persuasively from their empirical research that leadership as a distinguishable concept disappears when organizers are asked to account for their organizing. Kelly (2014) made a similar point when he argued that leadership is an "empty signifier ... that does not signify anything specific or fixed" (p. 905). In a way, this uncertainty (Denis *et al.*, 2012) is part of what drives researchers back to predefined leaders, for the relational activity of an identified leader is most certainly of interest. This, however, returns us to the work of the entitative researchers that Uhl-Bien (2006) identified and reduces our ability to attend to the relational practices that create leadership. So what is it that constitutes leadership? How can we identify it in its occurrence within relatings rather than in its personnel and identities? To be able to explore this question, I need to develop vocabularies for considering conversations and thus the leadership created in them.

Building a vocabulary and repertoire of conversational travel

In many ways it is too restrictive to limit relational practices to talk. Looks, tone of voice, gestures, and actions, for example, all convey meanings and relational invitations. However, given that my intent in this chapter is to explicate and discuss the way in which conversations' travel offers an optic for examining relational leadership, I will centre my discussion on talk in conversation. Even so, when we reach the illustrative analysis of a conversation, tone of voice and speed of conversational turns are noted as being significant.

Although many authors have now started to point to the importance of relational processes in constituting organizational phenomena, the methods by which we may inquire into the nature of these processes, such as conversation, are still complicated and partial. Within the organizational field (good reviews can be found in Fairhurst, 2007; Fairhurst & Uhl-Bien, 2012; Fairhurst & Connaughton, 2014; Nicolini, 2013), the methods that have been commonly used generally work on the basis of seeking to split conversation into its constituent parts. So conversation analysis might draw our attention to turn taking and sequential turns, whereas those using big "D" discourse analytic methods (Alvesson & Kär-reman, 2000; Burr, 2003) would look for how systems of wording from wider communities are used, and still others might look for how frames, humor, or particular word forms are used. The logic of these methods is that if we can only find the "bricks" from which conversations are built, then we might be able to "see" how they are put together and understand the relational processes of a phenomenon, such as leadership, better. There are, however, problems with this overall project to explore the building of conversation from its constituent parts. In particular, writers such as Searle (1995), Shotter (1995), and Barad (2003) have argued that conversations are "primitive realities," and that splitting them down will obfuscate as much as clarify. A question that might be helpful to explore is, therefore; how can we study conversations as "wholes?"

Three shifts in our analysis will facilitate our exploration of conversations. First, we can treat talk as invitational rather than meaningful. Such a move allows us to draw on the performative approach to talk in Speech Act theory. Second, we can draw on Gergen's (1994, 1995) articulation of the act + supplement relating within the social construction of power. This then leads to a third shift, which is to make use of offers with acceptances or blocks from improvised theatre (Johnstone, 1999). I will explore each shift more carefully.

Talk as invitational

In suggesting that we can treat talk as invitational, I am not arguing that talk has no meaning. I am, rather, suggesting that we can examine talk as a relational activity that contributes to succeeding action. Our talk not only expresses mean-ing, it also invites response. Bakhtin (1981) suggested that every utterance antici-pates the next utterance and our utterances are, in a sense, called forth by prior utterances. Shotter and his colleagues (Shotter, 1996; Shotter & Katz, 1996; Cunliffe 2002) proposed an understanding of talk as being a social poetics where our talk is relationally responsive to a flow of conversation. The talk not only conveys content, but also moves, strikes, gestures. Its effect is as much visceral as cognitive. In this way, talk not only invites, it also contributes. That I talk to you about tennis, rather than the topic of leadership at a conference, might contribute to you questioning who might win the next major championship. However, it will not determine that you do so as you draw our conversation back to the leadership topic discussed in the previous session. This point that our talk invites and contributes to the direction of our conversation rather than determines it, will become important in later sections.

My argument makes sense within a performative understanding of talk. Talk does things. Austin (1962) and later Searle (1969) developed speech act theory, where talk was understood in terms of locution (the words used), illocution (the intent of the words used), and perlocution (the effect of the words used). Much of Searle's development of Austin's earlier work focused on the illocutionary force of an utterance. However, this is to see only one element of the whole of conversation. Later, Searle (1995), in arguing that conversation is a primitive reality, drew our attention to the perlocutionary force in conversation, suggesting that a conversation was created within a collective or shared intentionality. Barad (2003) makes a similar point as she suggests that our utterances are *intra*-actions within a phenomenon. The shift that we are being asked to make here is to see conversation as the generative player, rather than the individual. A participant's utterance is now seen not so much as an expression of his or her thought or intention, but as an intra-action only gaining agency within that particular conversation at a particular moment to a particular effect.

Sequential talk as a process of act + supplement

Following this logic, talk takes an ontological form of invitation to relate and contribute to how that relating might go on. The next question is to explore how intra-actions within a conversation create action. In seeking a relational appreciation of power, Gergen (1994, 1995) argued that the meaning (and we could add intention) of any act is always equivocal until supplemented. So, my advice (an act) might be received by you as wise counsel (a supplement), in which case our relationship will develop accordingly. On the other hand, should you take my words as an unwelcome intrusion, then our relationship will develop on a different trajectory altogether. Of course, the meaning and intention will not be finalized in one supplement, for each utterance will supplement any prior response. In my example, it might be that noticing your irritation at my intrusion, I apologize and explain myself in a manner that is more acceptable to you. Our conversation is therefore travelling along a trajectory created by the intra-actions of our acts and supplements, always capable of taking twists and turns, accelerating or tarrying at different moments.

Supplements: accepting or blocking offers

Improvised jazz has had a significant impact on organization studies. Surprisingly, improvised theatre, with its use of talk and verbal coordination has prompted fewer articles and where it has been discussed (e.g. Dusya & Crossan, 2005) it has been in terms of encouraging creativity. Improv theatre does, however, have the potential to provide us with a helpful perspective on the moment-by-moment manner in which we organize. When an actor initiates a scene by movement or speech, (s)he is said to have made an offer (Johnstone, 1999), which other performers can either accept or block. Accepting does not imply agreement, but rather works with the scene or narrative proposed by the initial movement or speech; an acceptance may fit entirely with the initial act or develop it somewhat. A block refuses to work with the initial act and shifts the scene or plot in some way. Acceptance or block is not a simple either/or choice but will involve many shades of either accepting or blocking. Interestingly, Johnstone (1999) has an entire chapter on the ways that improv performers might block an offer, but very little on how (s)he might accept it.

Conversation travel and moments of leadership

We have now laid out a vocabulary of language tools with which we can construct a relational, or performative, approach to conversation. As conversational participants talk together, they supplement prior contributions and so a conversation develops, perhaps by changing topic, pausing to consider important points or hurrying to a conclusion. The language of improvised theatre allows us to hear how certain lines of conversation are blocked or accepted and so the conversation travels, constructed through a shared intentionality that need not be broken down into constituent parts. Once seen in this light, conversations travel in a trajectory: along topic lines, towards agreement or conflict or, perhaps, towards the performance of phenomena such as winning, losing, concluding, or leading. Conversations might also be said to travel by different modes, say argument, inquiry, or affirmation.

I want to suggest and, I hope, illustrate, that as we watch or hear a conversation travel, so we will be able to notice times when the trajectory or the mode of a conversation changes. I call these moments of leadership. At such moments we can explore the social interplay that creates them. This perspective on leadership, as moments within social relationship, re-imagines leadership not as a particular, distinct type of organizational behavior but as a possible quality of any organizational relating where a difference is made. Consequently, it treats Denis and his colleagues' (Denis et al., 2012) question about how leadership might be differentiated from other forms of organizational behavior by encouraging us to look for moments of leadership within all forms of organizational relating. More needs to be said.

Building a vocabulary and repertoire of leadership

Shamir (2012) made two criticisms of what he termed a radical social constructionist approach to leadership. First, he argued, that the "multiple realities" premise of social constructionism does not support a study of the regularities and patterns involved in leadership processes. Second, by arguing that leadership will be different in every situation, a social constructionist approach fails to create a usable, and useful, distinction between leadership and other social relations. For reasons that I explain below, I am not certain that I need to identify a distinct and consistent definition of leadership that would satisfy Shamir's challenge. However, even if I would seek to hold any characterization I make of leadership lightly, it still makes sense for me to explore and outline a vocabulary of leadership that I think will render a relational perspective useful to discursive leadership researchers.

As Alvesson and Spicer (2012) point out, finding a clear definition of leadership is very difficult, with two-thirds of articles not offering any definition, the final third providing no common view with new developments in distributed leadership, for example, adding further complications. I am persuaded by Wood's (2005), Alvesson and Svengingsson's (2003), and Kelly's (2014) arguments that the phenomenon is very difficult to find clearly in empirical study of human practice. As people recount events, they might explain what happened through the language of leadership. And, I suspect that all of us (readers and writer) would have positive and negative stories of our own organizational life that make immediate sense if recounted in the language of leadership. For example we might recount a period where we were finding work difficult and tell of someone who helped us through to a resolution of our difficulties. Of course, many language tools are available to us. Maybe this person counseled us, taught us, inspired us, encouraged us, and so on, but which of these language tools belong in the language of leadership? Or maybe we'd speak of a friend, a confidante, a teacher, or cleric? This, it seems to me is the strength of Kelly's (2014) argument that leadership is a second order construct that makes sense, post hoc, of phenomena that made a difference.

So, before I identify my current, and possibly transitory, position in relation to a meaning-use of leadership, I would want to challenge an assumption that is to be found in Shamir (2012) and Denis *et al.* (2012) and that raised concerns for Fairhurst and Uhl-Bien (2012). The assumption is that in defining leadership in some manner, I will also be *distinguishing* it from other social processes. One possible argument is that leadership is distinct from, say, social influence. In different ways, Eisler (1988) and Gilligan (1982) argued that there were two models of talk for handling difference; to look for differences and distinctions or to look for linkages and relatedness. Eisler called the first method a dominator model (Gilligan wrote of a masculine voice), for the construction of differences and distinctions inevitably leads to a scope for ranking and, ultimately, the ability for one voice to dominate another. Eisler argued that a practice of linking and relating differences can be expressed within a partnership model of relating (Gilligan's term was a feminine voice). Rather than look for what distinguishes and marks out leadership as a distinct organizational phenomenon, I want to leave open the possibility in my research that I may notice what connects and relates leadership as a process with other processes that shape our organizations. I want to leave open the possibility that leadership and other social or organizational practices might, in Bakhtin's (1984) term, interplay because, like Dostoevsky's characters, these practices are unfinalizable; they are always in the process of becoming something more, or less.

Kelly's (2014) argument that leadership has an "ideological function" rather than an ontological being is helpful here. Both Wood (2005) and Kelly (2008) argued that our research seeking after leadership produces a category mistake, which precludes us from being able to see the very object of our study. Indeed, Alvesson and Svengingsson (2003) suggest that once you explore leadership empirically, it disappears entirely as a distinct phenomenon, lost in a variety of diverse and often contradictory descriptions of actions and relations. Like Ryle's (1949) tourist in Oxford still looking for "the university" as they are shown colleges, laboratories, and senate buildings, so leadership researchers continue to search for leadership when a whole array of actions and relations relevant to an account of leadership are available. As Shotter (2006) has pointed out, Wittgenstein would ask us not to look for new, significant-but-hidden dynamics but rather to look at the very obvious things that are happening, which we so often do not notice. The importance that Kelly attaches to the ideological function of leadership fits nicely with Barad's (2003) post-humanist articulation of agency. For Barad, an idea—such as leadership—is real and has an agency as it makes a difference. Kelly argues this very point saying "leadership … *makes a difference*" (Kelly, 2014, p. 912, emphasis in the original). It should probably be noted that "a difference" is not necessarily restricted to change.

Still, it would make sense for me to articulate what kind of idea of leadership I have in mind, so to speak, as I write this chapter. I have argued above for a shift in our attention on conversation away from illocutionary matters of intention and locutionary matters of what is said (the sequential, but discreet contributions to a conversation from participants) towards a perlocutionary emphasis on how a conversation travels. In the light of this position, Drath and his colleagues' (Drath et al., 2008) articulation of leadership being identifiable in its outcomes of direction, alignment, and commitment, is attractive. However, from a practice perspective, Crevani and her colleagues (Crevani et al., 2010) suggested that this focus on entities called outcomes is inadequate for creating a process ontology for leadership in the making. Consequently, one way of identifying leadership contexts might be to look for times when conversations navigate, align, or commit. For an analyst, working after the fact with text, audio, or video recordings, it will be straightforward to see these processes as emergent but may be less easy to do for participants within the moment of organizing (Shotter, 2006). In the same way, that Shamir (2012) suggested that there will always be an element of asymmetric power within leadership relations, so I would expect that there will always be a degree of intentionality; that leadership will involve an element of intentional construction of direction, alignment, and commitment. Intentionality is tricky and, as argued above from Searle and Shotter, is best understood as a collective or shared process. However, within the moment-by-moment unfolding of action and interplay, participants' actions will also invite and contribute intentionality to the social performance and co-participants will be able to supplement any intention that they notice.

I do, however, want to hold this definition lightly for two reasons. First, I am not a little concerned that this definition might, in Barad's terms, have an agency over my writing and drag me, unintentionally, towards a "concretizing" category error (Kelly, 2008; Wood, 2005). Second, I am proposing that we look "at" leadership-as-practice through a new optic: conversational travel. In making such a suggestion, I want to leave myself open to noticing new and surprising things "about" leadership.

An illustrative example

To illustrate the kind of leadership-as-practice research that I think can become possible, given a use of conversational travel as an optic, I will use extracts from a video-recorded meeting. The extracts below are taken from an extended array of video material, recorded during a six-month investigation conducted by a consultant who is present in the conversations I extract. In an early journal-type segment, he explains his interest as being about how useful his extensive experience within private industry might be to managers and clinicians working in the British National Health Service. There are over a hundred hours of professionally recorded video material from this inquiry.[1] I can make no claim that the particular meeting that I have chosen is representative of other meetings during the inquiry; indeed, in some regards this meeting is quite different from other formal and informal conversations. However, my intent at this moment is merely to illustrate a possible inquiry practice rather than provide an authoritative account of conversation that justifies my theorizing on the nature of meetings or conversations in general.

Essentially, the four extracts below construct two matched pairs that illustrate processes of offering, blocking, or accepting. They are taken from a conversation between four participants (the consultant, a CEO, a general manager, and a surgeon) evaluating past and proposing future actions in a project to cut waiting lists at a general hospital in England. The video was transcribed and then watched repeatedly to identify moments when the conversational travel appeared to change. Once identified, those moments were extracted by taking about 20 lines before and after for closer analysis. For this chapter I chose two such moments of leadership and provide below a pair of extracts for each moment; in each case one extract shows a period of conversation in which little seems to happen in terms of generating a conversational trajectory that all participants buy into. In the second extract of each case, a change in conversational mode or trajectory occurs.

An overview of the conversation

The meeting lasted just over an hour and a constant refrain was the consultant's bewilderment about the way the department had approached reducing waiting lists. As the story emerges, it appears that the department had tried a range of actions and initiatives to enable faster or more productive working practices. Finally, it seems that an answer was found in the apparently simple expedient of working two extra surgery sessions per week. The consultant on twelve separate occasions expresses surprise at the length of time it took the department to work through difficult options while ignoring an apparently obvious and easy one.

CONSULTANT: That's actually what we're talking about. I have to say, I don't understand how we've gone round so many other [options] … You know, if that's [two extra sessions] the answer, why didn't we start with that? Why?

He uses somewhat different words each time, but this is the gist of what might be called a conversational gambit (surprise gambit), positioning himself one down, as a questioner, so as to invite other participants to be surprised, seeing their current organizing practices as strange and so worthy of discussion and improvement. Later in the meeting, these "surprise gambits" are reinforced by questions about communications, expertise. and wasted effort.

The hospital team never picks up on the consultant's "surprise" theme. In improvisational terms they block this offer whenever it is made. Instead they celebrate the learning they've done, the way the team has worked enthusiastically together and discovered options that won't work. On two occasions, however, this riff of "surprise" offer and block is broken, and it is these two occasions that I want to explore more closely so as to highlight the potential contribution of conversational travel to leadership inquiry.

Of locums and substantive posts

Extract 1 comes shortly after one of the consultant's (Con) "surprise gambits." The surgeon (Surg) counters his surprise by arguing that the UK's national health service is not like the private sector, with management able to do what it likes such as sacking people or building what it likes, etc. The conversation continues:

Extract 1

CON: I understand the complications but actually the solution here is very simple, isn't it? You know, if you buy the argument that you want to do is to get down to a nil waiting list, and you don't want it to be any net extra cost, just getting two sessions going—to my surprise, I mean, I hadn't thought it was as simple as that, but apparently it is—solves the problem. It's not talking about firing anybody or, you know … we're actually talking about maybe adding to what we do. It's not a negative thing this. It's a positive thing. It's not having to face up to a load of redundancies. There aren't those issues involved in this. It's actually quite straightforward.

SURG: It basically comes to the physical space. We as ophthalmology, we have to work in a dedicated ophthalmic theatre. Other people, they can share it. There's an empty theatre maybe you can …

CON: We have the space.

SURG: Where's the space?

CON: As I understand it there's another session available on a Monday morning and there's another session ...

SURG: We are using that.

CON: Another session available on a Monday morning, as I understand it. There's a free session available on a Monday morning in the same theatre.

What we see here might be called a "contest" conversation. The surgeon blocks the consultant's offer that this move is not threatening by moving the topic to space for surgery. Lines 9–18 see the conversation bouncing back and forth in short contributions at speed; each countering the other's point. This extract is not untypical of much of the meeting's talk. However, a few moments later the surgeon picks up on the consultant mentioning surgery space on Friday afternoon and the conversation goes on:

Extract 2

SURG: But once I think, which is coming to August next year or even before that, once we've established and changed with the modernization of the Medical Career Center, we know what we are doing, and I think we have a meeting on 20th October, Brian, to discuss that particular issue, to change titles maybe of some of our staff. Then they can do it on their own.

CON: How do you change title? Is there a process you have to go through?

SURG: Because we will lose them otherwise. They are well-trained people and they are already at their end stage, and at the moment their title is trainees. They cannot operate on their own physically. You have to be there with them.

CEO: Even if they are ...

SURG: Even if they are capable.

CEO: Even if ... even if the case ...

CON: What swings them from that status to being able to operate on their own?

CEO: Well, them not being a trainee. They need to get a substantive appointment, basically, where they're not a trainee.

SURG: Then they will be a surgeon.

CEO: Then it's, to some extent, it's up to the organization then to sign them off.

SURG: Sign them off. Yes.

CEO: Suitable for performing ...

CON: And when can you do that?

SURG: We'll do that once ... when they finish their training period officially.

CON: And they finish officially.

Here we can see quite a significant change in the conversation, and the audible change is also significant, for the surgeon's offer creates a shift to talking about careers, training, and regulations about when a trainee surgeon can operate without supervision. From line 6 onwards the tone of the consultant's contributions changes. He is seeking information about a topic in which he does not have the necessary information. He is, in effect, accepting a "one down" position, but this time, I would suggest, it is no gambit. He genuinely needs information before being able to contribute helpfully. The surgeon and CEO explain the process by which trainee surgeons qualify and then move to substantive roles where they can operate without supervision, therefore making use of the extra theatre sessions that the consultant has been discussing.

I want to suggest that there is a significant change in the mode of conversational travel here, moving from what I have called a contest conversation to one that is more exploratory. We could call this second extract a moment of leading, but what is interesting is that once you get in amidst the moment-by-moment relational processes of leadership, it is not easy to identify a leader. Three participants, the consultant (l. 6), surgeon (ll. 7–9), and CEO (ll. 14–15) all contribute to the turn in conversational travel; the leadership moment consists of both the offer *and* acceptance. Both are active and creative. Each utterance invites a response and contributes to how that response can sensibly be made. Each provides and constrains the space for the continuation and emergence of a mode of conversational travel.

Markets and growth

Sometime later the conversation has travelled on. There have been times when it seems that the consultant's constant refrain of the "surprise gambit" has created defensiveness among the hospital team. During one such period, the surgeon and general manager, perhaps fearing that they were being positioned as resisting change, asserted their enthusiasm for initiating improvement processes so that waiting lists could be reduced. In the next extract, the consultant uses this theme of enthusiasm to emphasize how the ophthamology department wasted time and effort in several initiatives, which someone should have spotted immediately. He says:

Extract 3

CON: ... And somewhere in this there's a lesson to be learned, and it's about having an evaluation much more quickly that stops wasting your enthusiasm, your enthusiasm and, to a certain extent, yours because you've been removed from it, on things that aren't going to work ... I don't doubt your enthusiasm and I, you know, it's not the end of the world, and it's pretty damn clear to me that we ... where we go now is very obvious.

SURG: We are very focused.

CON: We are where we are, and we know where we go. We know what the answers are. All that makes sense to me. There's no point in now trying to have some other magical solutions.

CEO: We know what won't ... We know now what won't work.

CON: Yes, you do.

CEO: And to some extent that is important.

CON: That's something. That's something.

CEO: Because, actually at any one time, one of those things may have worked. At any one time we may have had a breakthrough, you know.

CON: Do you think ... ?

At this moment, the conversation seems to be in some kind of holding trajectory. The consultant's challenging offer that time and enthusiasm have been wasted in forlorn ventures is blocked by the surgeon's comment about being "very focused." Then, there's the CEO's suggestion that at least they now know what won't work and so even these forlorn ventures had been worth trying. The conversation continues in a similar manner for another four minutes or so discussing the problems of doing building work with operating theatres. The conversation then drifts into a discussion of demand for the surgeon's work, and the CEO makes the following remark:

Extract 4

CEO: But we're back, really, to the sense that, one way, because even if we were to take up this spare capacity we've got, we would consume that, and we'd now then need to look at what next.

SURG: Exactly.

CEO: Because if we're efficient and effective, the demand will increase.

CON: Will probably increase.

CEO: And we'll be back to the same problem. We've run out of space again.

SURG: What do we do next?

CEO: And the issue we'll come back to, we'd probably need a twin theatre of some kind.

SURG: Yes.

CEO: But perhaps then we're working to a different timetable, time scale, and we're possibly looking at a different business case in terms of income being generated through that would pay it off more quickly.

CON: Are you starting to see people coming from outside the area?

CEO: Yes, we are.

SURG: We already have.

GM: We have.

SURG: We already have.

CON: In a significant … ? That's more than it used to be?

SURG: More than it used to be. We have because now all GPs in the area, they get a leaflet by the health authority which is a laminated thing. They stick it near their computer, and it will tell them, well, this hospital, oh, this is only two months and this hospital's four months. Do you like to go there? It's only ten miles. And I think we… it started working this, and I've got certainly a few patients from Sheffield recently.

CEO: I've got some figures on this.

CON: It's such an important …

CEO: It's gone up by something like 25% in terms of people from outside.

CON: Has it?

SURG: From outside

Now the trajectory of the conversation changes as they move from discussing theatre design and build to discussing market demand and growth. As with Extract 2, it is tricky to see the leadership coming from one person. The CEO raises the topic as a problem of capacity (l. 7), the consultant asks the question that continues the shift of the conversation (l. 14) and the GM (l. 17) and surgeon (ll. 16 & 18) both accept the invitation to discuss patient demand growth. The different participants contribute to the leadership change, but none of them design or direct it.

Conversational travel within discourse analytic inquiry: A conversation

The brief analysis above is inadequate to building any substantive theory, but that was never its intent. Rather, I have sought to illustrate how conversational travel might be used within a micro-discourse analysis. In doing so, I have sought to set up an opportunity for conversations with those who work with a variety of discourse analytic methods. In this section, I consider how conversational travel might converse with three different methods for analyzing small "d" discourse. First, I consider Wodak and her colleagues' critical discourse analytic work that examined conversations where consensus was built more or less successfully (Kwon, Clarke & Wodak, 2014; Wodak et al., 2011). Second, I will discuss Larsson and Lundholm's (2010) use of conversation analytic (CA) devices to account for influence within mundane managerial contexts and, finally, I link to Carroll and Simpson's (2012) use of "framing movements" that created "turning points" in an online forum conversation.

I noted above that the leadership enacted in Extracts 2 and 4 was ephemeral. In an hour-long meeting that was marked more often by blocks than by acceptances, an exploration of why consensus was so hard to find would be interesting. Wodak and her colleagues contrasted two meetings, with the same participants involved. In the first meeting any consensus gained appeared to be short-lived (Kwon *et al.*, 2014), whereas they concluded that consensus building was more successful in a second meeting. The difference between the meetings was in the number of topics discussed and the length of time given to them. In the meeting that failed to reach sustainable consensus they noticed that a "plethora of topics" were only "superficially addressed," whereas the meeting that reached a sustainable consensus involved a "recursive cycling through topics" (Wodak *et al.*, 2011, p. 611).

It could be suggested, following Wodak and her colleagues' argument, that the consultant in the hospital meeting also kept returning to a similar topic. He kept attempting to return the conversation's focus to the length of time spent exploring hopeless initiatives while missing the obvious one. From Wodak's perspective he was unsuccessful in building a sustained consent or even holding to his preferred topic. How can we understand what was going on? It is interesting to note that Wodak and her colleagues centered their attention on the discursive strategies of leaders, while use of the optic of conversational travel attends more to the per-locutionary creation of conversation by giving equal attention to the act, in this case, of the consultant and the supplements of others in the meeting. A failure to sustain the two particular lines of changed conversation trajectory or mode is also visible in subsequent act + supplement relations.

Larsson and Lundholm (2010) also focus on a relationship and the moment-by-moment relating of an identified leader (Ronald) and subordinate (Ken). It is significant that in the extract they analyze, the leader's agenda dominates the conversation. They take care to note that the subordinate cannot be seen as a following dope in the conversation because they show how he too is active in his use of member-ship categorization and contribution to the sequential flow of their conversation. Larsson and Lundholm's work is an important contribution to our understanding of the conversational working of organizational management. How managers and their subordinates talk in the reconciling of agendas for action is surely important.

Looking back on the extracts above, it would make an interesting analysis to examine the meeting looking, for example, at membership categorization actions. For example is the consultant categorized as an outsider who does not understand the values and practices of the NHS? Do his repeated surprise gambits break into a sequential flow of conversation in an unhelpful manner? A conversational ana-lytic inquiry into the meeting I considered above would certainly yield insights. However, conversation analysis works with identified, and in Bakhtin's term, finalized participants acting, more or less strategically out of and within their locally endorsed interactional practices. In contrast with Bakhtin (1984), this is investigation of interaction, not interplay, and valuable though it may be, CA drags Larsson and Lundholm into an entitative analysis of individual's actions; missing key elements of the relational creation of a phenomenon. So, member-ship categories are *used* rather than seen as being in construction. Furthermore, the situation in the hospital meeting room was quite ambiguous as to who was the "leader" at that particular moment. The CEO, consultant, and surgeon all could, and perhaps did, make bids for primacy in terms of authority, but the perlocutionary impact of the conversation is uncertain in terms of the identity of a leader. Does it not make sense to take an alternative, but not exclusive, shift of attention to the perlocutionary conversation and see in key moments socially performed, act + supplement processes of leadership?

Carroll and Simpson's (2012) examination of an online leadership development course is more congenial with the use of conversational travel as an optic in two ways. Even more than in the meeting I looked into above, any claim to positional authority-leadership in the group they studied was impossible. So, here was an investigation not of how leaders might act-talk, but of the relational processes that emerged into perlocutionary leadership. Second, and perhaps most interesting in their articulation of framing in conversation is what potential help the three discursive movements that Carroll and Simpson identified—kindling, stretching, and spanning—might have offered the consultant in framing his conversation in a way that he appeared to fail to do.

Each of these methods of inquiry would contribute insight to my study of the consultant's meeting with hospital management above. However, I have also noted where they bring constraints to what a researcher can notice. Additionally, I would want to propose that use of conversational travel as an optic can contribute to these micro-discursive methods of leadership research in three ways. First, attending to conversational travel can help relational leadership researchers select where to look. By offering a device by which moments of leadership can be picked out from the background of conversations, conversational travel can enable discursive researchers to explore the relational processes that are affecting a shift in or a re-invigoration of practice. So, it might be that exploring ongoing relations through the conversational travel optic might have drawn Larsson and Lundholm's attention to different moments in Ronald and Ken's conversations, not typified by dominance of the manager's agenda. Perhaps there might have been other conversations where Ken articulated a "vision" for this particular client that shifted Ronald's view? The conversation Larsson and Lundholm studied will have been nested in other conversations. This is only speculation, of course, but my point is that conversational travel can pick out significant moments that might be missed by other discourse analytic devices. It does also suggest that we should seek to add a longitudinal element to our current, mostly episodic research into micro-discursive processes. In the case of our hospital meeting, there are additional episodes that a fuller investigation into the relationally performed leadership could draw on to understand better the offers and blocks within this meeting.

This point directs our attention to the second contribution that conversational travel can make, for it turns our attention away from the people with their strategies and sensemaking to the conversations of which they are a part. In doing so, it foregrounds processes of relational construction and interplay as generative processes rather than interactions that are the consequence of people's actions. So, in the case of Wodak and her colleagues' study of the two meetings, fore-grounding the mode and trajectory of conversational travel might have drawn their attention to the impact of discursive strategies of others in those meetings rather than the emphasis on the senior executives' discursive strategies, which leads us to the third contribution that attention to conversational travel might make to leadership-as-practice research. For one of the intriguing things that comes out of my brief study of one short meeting is that, at the moments of leadership, it was not one person that led but several utterances that contributed to the change in conversational trajectory and/or mode through improvisational act (offer) and supplement (acceptance or block). Using conversational travel as an optic resources inquiry gives equal weight to all intra-actions (Barad, 2003), exhibiting them as a potential agency to make a difference in conversation.

Implications for the study of leadership

I have conceded that the above study is illustrative of conversational travel as an optic of inquiry and is inadequate to the task of reaching conclusions about lea-dership in conversation. Rather it is a gesture, a noticing or a pointing toward possible inquiry. My interest in this chapter has been to explicate and illustrate the potential of conversational travel to the study and practice of leadership. Still, however, I want to argue that this short study raises some interesting points that merit further investigation by L-A-P researchers.

The study of leadership as a social practice: Gestures towards future research

For academics engaging with the phenomena of leadership, there are four impli-cations of this study that merit further investigation. First, with all the limitations that I acknowledge above, this study does seem to highlight a social practice of leadership that does not require a prior accreditation of leader and follower roles. In both Extracts 2 and 4, by looking at the conversational travel and its constituent processes of act + supplement (offer-block/acceptance), we can watch as several people shape (lead) changes in the mode or trajectory of a conversation's travel. A significant point to note here is that an improvisational "acceptance" is not necessarily a passive compliance with another character setting the agenda. Rather, the improv acceptance can also act generatively as an accelerant, adding emphasis and significance to a topic or mode of conversation. The extracts above provide us with evidence that an overly clear distinction between action and response, leader or follower will tend to obstruct our view of the co-created, moment-by-moment agency of sequential utterances. This is a creative interplay of emerging phenomena, rather than an interaction of finalized actors. Attending to conversational travel helps the analyst notice and explore the agency of the conversation rather than the actors.

Second, I would want to note the ephemerality of the leadership we see. Following Bakhtin's (1984) lead, by understanding the participants in our conversational extracts as unfinalized characters, we do not see one participant adopting the role of leader within a particular social process and then maintaining it. Instead we see several participants' contributions leading the conversational travel at different moments. For example, less than ten minutes after the change away from the consultant's "surprise gambit" in Extract 4, he returns to this gambit again. Just as leadership appears to be built in the moment-by-moment act + supplements of several participants, so those participants appear to both initiate or respond, offer or block/accept on different occasions.

This ephemerality is tricky. The question that it poses is whether leadership that has no sustained effect is any kind of leadership at all. What conversational travel, by its focus on moment-by-moment, jointly performed conversations, brings to our attention are episodes of ephemeral and sustained moments of leadership. Shamir (2012) in arguing that leadership will always involve some element of asymmetric power acknowledges that this is problematic, but that this very problem raises the need for further research. In the same way, I want to suggest that identifying moments of leadership in relating that might be ephemeral or sustained is interesting and worthy of more research. These extracts, when analyzed through the optic of conversational travel, point to an ebb and flow in leadership relations that would not be so visible if looking at the relating activities of established leaders and followers.

Third, attending to leadership within conversational travel, seems to offer researchers a significant shift of attention away from the illocutionary activities (Austin, 1962) of intentions, plans, and strategic use of discursive practices. Instead, conversational travel draws our gaze to a perlocutionary (Austin, 1962) process of social interplay. This is methodologically interesting because it does not require researchers to hypothesize about what is going on inside the heads, so to speak, of the participants or interpret meanings from their actions and words. Instead we have laid before us a perlocutionary performance. Of course, there will then be an interpretive process of sense making, but this can be done through an explicit dialogue between data and theoretical or conceptual frames.

Finally, looking at leadership through the optic of conversational travel points to a modified identity of leadership; rather than being a distinct form of organization it appears as a possible quality of any organizational relating. An emphasis on the perlocutionary force in moments of leadership turns our attention away from the people who lead, their skills, intentions and strategies, and actions towards the relational moments that stimulate change or reinforce stability, the moments that make a difference (Kelly, 2014). Leadership is therefore seen as an emergent, ephemeral, and socially performed moment that makes a difference in organizing. Furthermore, this quality of leadership may well be noticed in a wide range of organizational phenomena; as judgments are made or conclusions reached, as persistent ways of working (organizational culture?) become sedimented or changed, or as workers are motivated, trained, or alienated. Of course, one line of inquiry might be into how some individuals seem to be regularly visible in such moments of leadership, so much so that they become labeled as leaders. I think, however, that there are many more interesting questions to ask about leadership, and the conversational construction of that manner of relating, before looking at particular individuals again. These brief extracts appear to engage with Alvesson and Svengingsson's (2003) suggestion that, when examined empirically, leadership disappears. However, I would suggest that as we see the different participants interplay, there is a suggestion that it is not leadership that disappears, but leaders.

Note

1   I was not involved in this original inquiry or recording, but was provided access to these extracts as a member of staff at the Open University, UK. I would like to acknowledge that institution's generosity in allowing me to continue working with these recordings.

References

Alvesson, M., & Kärreman, D. (2000). Taking the linguistic turn in organizational research: Challenges, responses, consequences. *The Journal of Applied Behavioral Science*, 36(2), 136–158.

Alvesson, M., & Spicer, A. (2012). Critical leadership studies: The case for critical performativity. *Human Relations*, 65(3), 367–390.

Alvesson, M., & Svengingsson, S. (2003). The great disappearing act: Difficulties in doing "leadership". *Leadership Quarterly*, 14, 259–381.

Austin, J. L. (1962). *How to do things with words*. Oxford: Oxford University Press.

Bakhtin, M. (1981). *The dialogic imagination*. Austin: The University of Texas Press.

Bakhtin, M. (1984). *Problems of Dostoevsky's poetics*. Minneapolis: University of Minnesota Press.

Balkundi, P., & Kilduff, M. (2005). The ties that lead: A social network approach to leadership. *Leadership Quarterly*, 16(6), 941–961.

Barad, K. (2003). Posthumanist performativity: Toward an understanding of how matter comes to matter. *Journal of Women in Culture and Society*, 28(3), 801–831.

Brown, H., & Hosking, D. M. (1986). Distributed leadership and skilled performance as successful organization in social movements. *Human Relations*, 39(1), 65–79.

Burr, V. (2003). *Social constructionism*. London: Routledge.

Carroll, B., & Simpson, B. (2012). Capturing sociality in the movement between frames: An illustration from leadership development. *Human Relations*, 65(10), 1283–1309.

Crevani, L., Lindgren, M., & Packendorff, J. (2010). Leadership, not leaders: On the study of leadership as practices and interactions. *Scandinavian Journal of Management*, 26(1), 77–86.

Cunliffe, A. L. (2002). Social poetics as management inquiry: A dialogical approach. *Journal of Management Inquiry*, 11, 128–146.

Cunliffe, A. L., & Eriksen, M. (2011). Relational leadership. *Human Relations*, 64(11), 1425–1449.

Dachler, H. P. (1991). Management and leadership as relational phenomena. In M. V. Cranach, W. Doise & G. Mugny (Eds.), *Social representations and the social bases of knowledge* (pp. 169–178). Bern: Hogrefe & Huber.

Dachler, H. P., & Hosking, D. M. (1995). The primacy of relations in socially constructing organizational realities. In D. M. Hosking, H. P. Dachler, & K. J. Gergen (Eds.), *Management and organization: Relational alternatives to individualism* (pp. 1−28). Aldershot: Avebury.

Denis, J.-L., Langley, A., & Sergi, V. (2012). Leadership in the plural. *Academy of Management Annals*, 6(1), 211−283.

Drath, W. H., McCauley, C. D., Palus, C. J., Van Velsor, E., O'Connor, P. M. G., & McGuire, J. B. (2008). Direction, alignment, commitment: Toward a more integrative ontology of leadership. *Leadership Quarterly*, 19, 635−653.

Dusya, V., & Crossan, M. (2005). Improvisation and innovative performance in teams. *Organization Science*, 16(3), 203−224.

Eisler, R. (1988). *The chalice and the blade*. London: Unwin

Fairhurst, G.T. (2007). *Discursive leadership: In conversation with leadership psychology*. Los Angeles, CA: Sage Publications.

Fairhurst, G. T., & Connaughton, S. T. (2014). Leadership: A communicative perspective. *Leadership*, 10(1), 7−35.

Fairhurst, G. T., & Uhl-Bien, M. (2012). Organizational discourse analysis (ODA): Examining leadership as a relational process. *Leadership Quarterly*, 2, 1043−1062.

Gergen, K. J. (1994). *Realities and relationships*. Cambridge, MA: Harvard University Press.

Gergen, K. J. (1995). Relational theory and the discourses of power. In D. M. Hosking, H. P. Dachler, & K. J. Gergen (Eds.), *Management and organization: Relational alternatives to individualism*. Aldershot: Avebury.

Gilligan, C. (1982). *In a different voice: Psychological theory and women's development*. Cambridge, MA: Harvard University Press.

Graen, G. & Uhl-Bien, M., (1995). Relationship-based approach to leadership: Development of leaders-member exchange (LMX) theory of leadership over 25 years: Applying a multi-level multi-domain perspective. *Leadership Quarterly*, 6(2), 219−247.

Hollander, E. P. (1995). Ethical challenges in the leader-follower relationship. *Business Ethics Quarterly*, 5(1), 55−65.

Hosking, D. M. (1988). Organizing, leadership and skilful process. *Journal of Management Studies*, 25(2), 147−166.

Hosking, D. M. (2000). Ecology in mind, mindful practices. *European Journal for Work and Organizational Psychology*, 9(2), 147−158.

Hosking, D. M. (2007). Not leaders, not followers: A post-modern discourse of leadership processes. In J. R. Meindl & B. Shamir (Eds.), *Follower-centered perspectives on leadership: A tribute to the memory of James R. Meindl* (pp. 243−263). Greenwich, CT: IAP.

Hosking, D. M. (2011). Moving relationality: Meditations on a relational approach to leadership. In A. Bryman, D. Collinson, K. Grint, B. Jackson & M. Uhl-Bien (Eds.), *Sage handbook of leadership*. London: Sage Publications Ltd.

Hosking, D., & Fineman, S. (1990). Organizing processes. *Journal of Management Studies*, 27(6), 583−604.

Hosking, D. M., & McNamee, S. (Eds.) (2006). *The social construction of organization*. Malmo: Liber AB.

Hosking, D. M., & Morley, I. E. (1991). *A social psychology of organising*. Chichester: Harvester Wheatsheaf.

Howell, J. M., & Shamir, B. (2005). The role of followers in the charismatic leadership process: Relationships and their consequences. *Academy of Management Review*, 30(1), 96−112.

Johnstone, K. (1999). *Impro for storytellers*. London: Faber and Faber Ltd.

Kelly, S. (2008). Leadership: A categorical mistake? *Human Relations* 61(6), 763−782.

Kelly, S. (2014). Towards a negative ontology of leadership. *Human Relations*, 67(8), 905–922.

Kwon, W., Clarke, I., & Wodak, R. (2014). Micro-level discursive strategies for constructing shared views around strategic issues in team meetings. *Journal of Management Studies*, 51(2), 265–290.

Larsson, M., & Lundholm, S. E. (2010). Leadership as work-embedded influence: A micro-discursive analysis of an everyday interaction in a bank. *Leadership*, 6(2), 159–184.

Nicolini, D. (2013). *Practice theory, work and organization*. Oxford: Oxford University Press.

Raelin, J. (2011). From leadership-as-practice to leaderful practice. *Leadership*, 7(2), 195–211.

Ramsey, C. M. (2014). Management learning: A scholarship of practice centred on attention? *Management Learning*, 45(1), 6–20.

Rost, J. C. (1995). Leadership: A discussion about ethics. *Business Ethic Quarterly*, 5(1), 129–142.

Ryle, G. (1949). *The concept of mind*. London: Hutchinson.

Searle, J. R. (1969). *Speech acts: An essay in the philosophy of language*. Cambridge: Cambridge University Press.

Searle, J. R. (1995). Collective intentions and actions. In P. Cohen, J. Morgan & M. E. Pollack (Eds.) *Intentions in communication*. Cambridge, MA: Bradford Books, MIT Press.

Shamir, B. (2012). Leadership research or post-leadership research? Advancing leadership theory versus throwing the baby out with the bath water. In M. Uhl-Bien & S. M. Ospina (Eds.), *Advancing relational leadership research*. Charlotte, NC: Information Age Publishing Inc.

Shotter, J. (1995). In conversation: Joint action, shared intentionality and ethics. *Theory and Psychology*, 5(1), 49–73.

Shotter, J. (1996). Social construction as social poetics: Oliver Sacks and the case of Dr P. In B. Bayer & J. Shotter (Eds.), *Reconstructing the psychological subject*. London: Sage.

Shotter, J. (2006). Understanding process from within: An argument for 'withness'-thinking. *Organization Studies*, 27(4), 585–604.

Shotter, J. (2008). *Conversational realities revisited*. Taos, NM: The Taos Institute.

Shotter, J., & Katz, A. (1996). Articulating a practice from within the practice itself: Establishing formative dialogues by the use of a 'social poetics'. *Concepts and Transformations*, 1, 213–217.

Simpson, B. (2009). Pragmatism, Mead, and the practice turn. *Organization Studies*, 30(12), 1329–1347.

Thorpe, R., Gold, J., & Lawler, J. (2011). Locating distributed leadership. *International Journal of Management Reviews*, 13(3), 239–250

Uhl-Bien, M. (2006). Relational leadership theory: Exploring the social processes of leadership and organizing. *Leadership Quarterly*, 17(6), 654–676.

Wodak, R., Kwon, W., & Clarke, I. (2011). Getting people on board: Discursive leadership for consensus building in team meetings. *Discourse and Society*, 22(5), 592–644.

Wood, M. (2005). The fallacy of misplaced leadership. *Journal of Management Studies*, 42(6), 1101–1121.

PART IV
Application

11

GENDERED RELATIONSHIPS AND THE PROBLEM OF DIVERSITY IN LEADERSHIP-AS-PRACTICE

Jackie Ford

Introduction

Conceptions of leadership as a practice are concerned with how leadership emerges *as a practice* rather than residing in the traits, character, or behaviors of individuals—in which traditional approaches to the study of leadership place emphasis. This practice "unfolds through day-to-day experience. The social and material-discursive contingencies impacting the leadership constellation ... do not reside outside of leadership but are very much embedded within it" (Raelin, Chapter 1, this volume, p. 3). Its focus is very much on a purposive nature to the practice in which the participants' efforts seek a distinctive outcome.

What is apparent from the emerging discussions within the nascent but developing leadership-as-practice (L-A-P) literature is that it still dwells within the historical context of the organization and its teams of people. Owing to this tendency to be historically developed, the practice view of leadership may run the risk of reinforcing many traditional or perhaps taken for granted assumptions about organizational life, including assumptions of gender neutrality, as well as presumed neutrality in relation to other multiple-layered social identities such as race/ethnicity, social class, age, sexuality, etc. It may also ignore power differentials and continue to privilege long-established patterns and institutionalized norms, as explored later.

The practice view of leadership, on the other hand, rejects notions of individual influence and control, and a linear and monolithic approach in favor of collective engagement, divergence, intersubjectivity, and ambiguity. Of further significance in L-A-P debates is the crucial importance of interrogating the taken for granted assumptions and meanings that "bear the imprint of social domination" (Raelin, 2008). Given the relational and material nature of the L-A-P approach, there is value in adopting a critical, post-structural lens to explore the situated and embodied aspects of leadership as a way of drawing attention to the issues of diversity and inclusion that still pertain within organizational life.

The practice view offers those of us who study leadership the opportunity to explore many levels of interaction among individuals. Their material worlds, language, and embodied experiences are also as meaningful as the artifacts, technologies, and physical arrangements, as well as the interpersonal and intercultural relationships. However, there is perhaps a danger that the power asymmetries and embodied and material representations may be marginalized in such research, and this chapter makes a strong plea for researchers (and practitioners) to keep these issues very much to the fore of their thinking. Recognizing the intersubjective dynamics and their complexity, ambiguity, and tensions are important, especially in their challenges to the individualistic and controlling aspects of more traditional ways of viewing leadership. Thus, engagement with qualitative, intersubjective and discursive (narrative) forms of inquiry and ethnographic approaches will usefully generate co-constructed knowledge. However, it still may not surface the underlying power, gendered (and other) differences that impact on such relationships. These are at the heart of explorations that this chapter seeks to offer.

Current writings on leadership, such as from recent Critical Leadership Studies (CLS) literature, suggest a need to explore these hidden aspects of difference and the process of concealment within the practice of leadership. In L-A-P, we would wish to learn about the full scope of dynamic exchange that constitutes leadership, in other words, not only what is said but also what is not spoken. Who is included in such dynamic exchanges and who is not party to the collaborative interactions in the workplace?

My own career journey and experiences to date, combined with my research over the last twenty years lead me to argue for a more critical and reflexive account of what is happening in the organizational world under the guise of leadership. I am interested particularly in the relationships between people in organizations and am critical of the theories that reduce them to homogeneous beings, trapped in the prevailing way of thinking or talking. There is more than a stirring of interest in research into critical leadership studies that focus on heterogeneity rather than homogeneity, on difference rather than conformity, and the L-A-P agenda provides us with an opportunity to understand and experience leadership from within a much richer, contextual lens.

Raelin (2011, p. 195) suggests that the L-A-P approaches seek out leadership "in its music and activity rather than in the traits and heroics of individual actors." This raises important observations through a critical lens on leadership studies—in which the embodied and the material are manifest—which are the focus of this chapter.

Scope and purpose of the chapter

1. To provide a background for a more critical approach to the study of leadership;

2.   To use ideas informed by CLS and especially feminist post-structural theories to explore the taken for granted assumptions and power asymmetries that belie traditional theorizing in this area; and

3.   To explore L-A-P theorizing that goes beyond mainstream notions of leadership and looks in-depth at power, knowledge, language, and (inter)subjectivity as inter-related strands through which to examine and revise our understandings of leadership.

Critical approaches to the study of leadership

As we know from earlier chapters and from our wider readings within leadership studies, heroic and individualistic forms of leadership still dominate the literature in which much energy is invested in elaborate claims that the appointment of an effective leader will lead to the transformation of an organization, its people, and structures, moving it to a higher level of achievement through an almost supernatural process. This affords a central and heroic status to the leader as corporate savior, or as an organizational redeemer. The model is one of organizational idol, endowing leaders (usually at the pinnacle of the company) with a high-status leadership role in transforming the organization. The connotations with biblical imagery and prophet-like behaviors are not lost on critiques of this cult industry (Tourish, 2013). Much of this literature focuses almost exclusively on the nature, the types, and the need for leadership and this has led to the valorization of masculine characteristics and behaviors as the norm—while at the same time pretending and/or assuming gender blindness.

Major criticisms of this masculine, heroic discourse are that individual difference is denied, context ignored, and little or no consideration is given to the influence of diverse settings as well as diverse subjectivities and power relationships within which people in organizations operate. Furthermore, there is a broad tendency both in leadership research and among practitioners to focus exclusively on the top director or executive roles, to portray the leader as a superior being, uni-directionally interacting with subordinates. Such studies fail to recognize both the ubiquity of leadership in organizations (its presence at all levels of the hierarchy) together with an understanding in more recent literature that we occupy multiple subject positions (both at work as well as within wider identities) that require us—at various times—to move between and within our various roles as leaders, followers, teamworkers, peers, parents, partners, friends, etc. (Ford, 2006; Ford, Harding & Learmonth, 2008; Fournier & Grey, 2000; Raelin 2008, 2014; Watson, 2001). Until the last decade or so, there has been an almost total absence of theorizing on leadership that goes beyond positivist approaches. We are now beginning to see a turn to critical studies of leadership that opens opportunities to redress this imbalance and to generate research and theorizing that draws from other disciplines and perspectives. This recognizes that there is a need for leadership studies that tell us something about the subjective, the personal, and the interpersonal, and about how people talk and dream about leadership. Although there is evidence of change, this is nevertheless a slow process (Tourish, 2011).

More of a momentum is gathering pace through an emerging body of writing on what is being referred to as "Critical Leadership Studies" (CLS) (Ford, 2010; Collinson, 2011; Harding, Lee, Ford & Learmonth, 2011). CLS is defined as "the broad, diverse and heterogeneous perspectives that share a concern to critique the power relations and identity constructions through which leadership dynamics are often produced, frequently rationalised, sometimes resisted and occasionally transformed" (Collinson, 2011, p. 181). CLS scholars frequently draw from the more established field of Critical Management Studies (CMS), which has long sought to provide a critique and challenge to the taken-for-granted assumptions in mainstream management theorizing; to expose asymmetrical power dynamics; and to open up new ways of thinking and alternative forms of organizing and managing. As Collinson (2014, p. 37) argues, "CLS builds on CMS to highlight the numerous inter-related ways in which power, identity and context are embedded in leadership dynamics."

The collective term, CLS, does not offer a unifying theory (as that would undermine its intentions to include more pluralistic and multitudinous ways of understanding leaders and leadership), but it seeks to problematize mainstream perspectives that overshadow writing and thinking on leadership. These conventional approaches have tended to undervalue the complexity and diversity of leadership dynamics and have accepted without question the notion that leaders are in charge and that followers will carry out their orders. Drawing on more exploratory, interpretive and in-depth questioning of the research and practices of management and organization studies, such critical research provides opportunities to reconsider the dominant discourses of leadership and to explore a plurality of interests and voices that shed fresh light on the research field. It enables a challenge to basic assumptions in use in mainstream leadership research, especially in relation to appreciating the complexity of workplace dynamics, developing alternative ways of researching, conceptualizing, and practicing leadership (Collinson, 2014; Ford et al., 2008; Ford, 2015; Tourish, 2013).

These critical approaches also require the researcher to move from a positivist stance of the objective pursuit of the truth, and towards a more active and reflexive role "constructing the very reality s/he is attempting to investigate" (Chia, 1996, p. 42). As academics in our research, we construct leaders and create leadership as much as we study them. That is, we make visible something called leadership and we develop subject positions (characteristics and identities of leaders) into which those who are designated organizational leaders will step. However, we cannot assume a straightforward translation of theory into the constitution of subject positions or identities. We need to look at the social, material, and cultural contexts into which we assume theories are inserted.

So, why do we need such studies? Critical leadership scholars (as well as L-A-P scholars), recognize that so much of the writing on leadership is constructed through a leader-follower pairing, with the followers being the (subordinated or inferior) other to the leader's (dominant or superior) position. A more critical and reflexive approach to the study of leadership is needed, which pays attention to situations, events, institutions, ideas, social practices, and processes that may be seen as exercising undue influence of those involved as leaders. More specifically, a post-structural approach offers a theoretical basis for analyzing the subjectivities (the very identities) of men and women in relation to language as well as other cultural practices and material conditions. This approach allows us to look with fresh lenses on leadership theories. The whole sense of leadership itself is both historical and subject to change, and thus universal theories on leadership are open to challenge and debate (Ford, 2015). Post-structural thinking throws a challenge to the subject in the Western philosophical tradition of the dis-embodied abstract individual governed by conscious and rational thought. Instead, it seeks to problematize the still pervasive assumptions of whole and coherent subjects with a unified sense of who we are (our identity or sub-jectivity). Post-structuralism thus calls attention to the way the considerable industry of leadership has shaped our ideas and resulted in reductionist views of what it means to be a leader.

As I've hinted above, leadership can be perceived as a performative process, in which the use of the very word "leader" brings into being socially constructed positions whereby some individuals must aspire to a complex identity, which others follow (Butler, 1993). To define and describe leadership is to recognize its slippery nature, its meaning shaped by both the individuals' own experiences, personal background, and reflexive thoughts, as well as by other people involved within the local context (Alvesson, 2002; Ford et al., 2008; Smircich & Morgan, 1982). Nevertheless, a recognition of the social context and the socially con-structed nature of leadership may still overlook a fundamental dimension in the study of organizational life, notably that this performative process of leadership is achieved through a range of exclusionary practices that aim to offer a standar-dized, one-dimensional definition of what a leader in an organization is expected to be. One such exclusionary practice is the failure to consider the androcentric nature of organizational life and the lack of recognition of this concept in many organizational research studies. The adoption of a critical feminist post-structural stance enables consideration of such shortcomings and may offer useful reflections for those who embrace L-A-P approaches.

Gender, diversity, and embodiment: A critical feminist study of leadership

Organization theory has traditionally and right up to the 1970s neglected gender aspects. Employees have been viewed either from a supposedly gender neutral (male) perspective, or from the point of view that considers only the male part of the organizations as interesting. Even those texts that purport to discuss the people-related issues in organizations fail to take account of concerns such as gender, women, men, femininity, and masculinity (Legge, 1995). Despite the development of extensive scholarship on gender and organizations, mainstream accounts continue to ignore the relationship between organizational arrangements and gender. Hatch (2010, cited in Jeanes, Knights & Yancey Martin, 2011) maintains that nearly all theories of organizations and management ignore gender, and Jeanes *et al.* (2011) argue that the resounding silence on explorations of gender implicitly conveys that gender considerations are just not an issue. Feminist organizational analyses and the study of men and masculinities, on the other hand, have problematized the depiction of gender in organizations, and a range of theoretical perspectives have been adopted in the pursuit of exposing such neglect. These studies have included consideration of essentialist and constructed accounts of gender; boundaries between families and work organizations; between processes of production and reproduction; the domination of gender power and gender class and race; and the powers and paradox of sexuality. Thus not only have gendered considerations been absent from study, but so have other multiple layered social identities such as race/ethnicity, age, social class, disability, and sexuality.

Recent years have witnessed some progress in studies of gender and organizations, and this has served the purpose of calling into question the assumed gender-neutral and gender-absent nature of organizational theory that mainstream writing perpetuates (Acker, 1998). In many ways, mainstream organizational theory continues to be constructed as non-gendered, although there remains ample evidence that it is written from the perspective, culture, and discourse of a male with its "espoused theories of empiricism, rationality, hierarchy, leadership, management and other masculinised concepts" (Hearn & Parkin 1993, p. 149). Whereas men are portrayed as fitting organizational behavior, women are associated with the "feminine" characteristics of caring, nurturing, and sharing that are deemed to be more appropriate for the domestic sphere and the reproduction of the home and the family. So, the cultural construction of femininity around body and emotions, and of masculinity around disembodiment and rationality, has made men the "natural" inhabitants of organizational life, while positioning women as out of place in organizations (Gherardi, 1995). Furthermore, Gherardi argues that the presence of women in organizations calls for "remedial" work that seeks to address the ambiguity that their position as "female occupants in a male world" creates. Remedial work refers to individual and collective strategies that may be used by both women and men to restore the (gender) order when such order has been disturbed by women stepping out of their feminine position. Fournier and Keleman (2001) identify many studies that show the effort that women have to invest in presenting what Judy Marshall (cited in Fournier & Keleman) calls "viable public images," images that make them acceptable in the organizational world (see also Gherardi, 1995; Brewis, 1999). For example, women may make themselves acceptable in employment by being discrete and invisible; by requesting permission to speak in meetings or other behaviors demonstrating a lack of assertiveness, so as to repair the damage done by "infringement of the symbolic order of gender" (Gherardi, 1995, p. 141).

Writers on leadership have also largely ignored gender theories. This absence is rather peculiar given a widespread recognition that organizations contribute actively to the ways in which gendered (and other) identities are constructed (Ford *et al.*, 2008). The gendered identity permissible among managers is limited to that of heroic masculinity. Connotations of leadership in the literature frequently take the form of the masculine competitive, aggressive, controlling, and self-reliant individualist, and thus the question as to whether leadership is indispensable in our organizations may hinge on whether we perceive a need to continue to support notions of forceful, manipulative, logical masculine practices. This serves to reinforce the dominant ways in which the practice of leadership involves strong elements of masculinity that act to strengthen male identities and thereby reproduce asymmetrical gender relations (and other multiple-layered social identities) in organizational life. The whole notion of leadership has been historically constructed through a dyadic leader-follower pairing (Raelin, 2014), with the followers being the (subordinated) other to the leader's (dominant) position (Ford *et al.*, 2008).

Understandings of leadership and heroic masculinity have been so closely interwoven as to be both invisible and indivisible. Leadership theories have "pretended gender neutrality or displayed gender blindness but have inevitably imported male values and characteristics as the norm, and have been *phallocentric*—viewing the world implicitly from a masculine point of view" (Hopfl and Matilal, cited in Fulop & Linstead, 2009, p. 522). This privileging of men and masculinity is apparent and yet remains frequently unreported within management texts and practices, and appears especially to be the case when leadership behavior is examined within organizational settings. Feminist critics point out how the existing body of organization and management theory assumes implicitly that managers and workers are male, with male stereotypic powers, attitudes, and obligations. The delineation of organizational structures, alleged forms of organizational cultures and everyday workplace practices have all been depicted as constituting the "ideal employee" and especially the ideal manager as a disembodied and rational figure, one which fits more closely to the cultural images of masculinity rather than femininity. Femininity, on the other hand, has tended to be associated with embodiment, emotions, and sexuality; as such, it is constituted as subordinate to "male" rationality and possibly out of place in rational organizations (Acker, 1990, 1998; Calas & Smircich, 1992; Ford, 2006; Fournier & Keleman, 2001). Leadership practices can thus be seen as a mechanism for masculine domination and not the neutral, objective, and unproblematic approaches that mainstream literature, or possibly practice perspectives may suggest (Calas & Smircich, 1991; Collinson & Hearn, 1994; Fletcher, 2004; Fondas, 1997; Sinclair, 2011).

A more critical and reflexive approach to the study of leadership is needed. More specifically, a post-structural feminist approach offers a theoretical basis for analyzing the subjectivities of men and women in relation to language, other cultural practices, and the material and embodied conditions of their lives. In relation to my own research interests, such an approach allows fresh light to be shed on leadership theories. My research study of leadership within a major local authority in England provides such an illustration. I interviewed 18 managers drawn from senior, middle, and junior managerial roles, using in-depth life history narrative methods both for data gathering and analysis (Ford, 2006). In depictions of leadership, my analysis shows how managers adopt the language and rhetoric of one approach to leadership, while at the same time as practicing a totally contradictory approach. Trudie was one of the four female directors employed within the council in a front-line service directorate. What is of notable interest in her account is the extent to which she described how she drew on the co-existence of macho-management and post-heroic discourses of leadership. Trudie was passionate, articulate, and explicit about what to her represented effective and ineffective leadership in local government organizations. In common with many of the other managers interviewed, Trudie's narrative presents a deliberate shift in more recent years away from adopting a more stereotypically feminine approach to her work and managerial relationships, and towards performing a masculine subject position, presenting a more competitive macho approach. Her account provided numerous examples of the extent of her adoption of what she construed as masculine behaviors and acquiring the skill to "think like a man" and this is illustrated in her discussion of how she chose to stay at work rather than take a family holiday so that she could ensure that her directorate benefitted financially from informal corridor deals on budgetary negotiations:

> I would love to get away February half-term break and I've got my diary clear. Daren't book it, 'cos that might be the week [...] that corridor deals are done on the political budget-making and, you know, the same was true [last year] and I had a week clear and I didn't go and that week, a conversation in the corridor made a million pound's difference and if I hadn't been there, we wouldn't have had a million pounds in the budget. So the nature of the job is such that some things have to take precedence.

It was evident from Trudie and other respondents that the prevailing organizational culture highly valued those managers who achieved targets and delivered efficiency savings, reinforcing competitive masculine practices of striving to maintain the largest share of the scarce resources across directorates and perpetuating the "old boys' network" in which key decisions are made outside of the formal organizational arrangements, in corridors or other ad hoc settings. This adoption of masculine norms of behavior is consistent with wider findings in the literature in which female (and male) managers construct themselves as powerful forces in a competitive and challenging environment.

Similar discourses of macho management cultures were observable from the transcripts of both middle-level managers (service heads) and front-line (principal and senior) officers. Timothy has been working as a Service Head for the last ten years. He depicted his approach to leadership as one that recognized the need to support and encourage staff and yet reflected that this was something to which he had not paid much attention in recent years. He recognized that there was a danger of becoming so embroiled in dealing with the day-to-day pressures and demands of the job that there was a risk of neglecting the personal and inter-personal relationships. He argued that "you get so entrenched in where you have to be that you tend to forget about everything else."

The accounts of these managers highlight how the dominant leadership discourse within the organization reproduces a traditional macho-management identity and practice. While the male directors sought to distance themselves from this dominant discourse, at the same time their accounts also reveal who they are as managers in the organization, but also how different leadership and organizational discourses compete with one another (Ford, 2006).

Gendered accounts of leadership can add considerable value as a challenge to universal theories of leadership. Furthermore, recent debates from diversity and inclusion scholars are opening up new ways to explore organizational practices that include leadership (Ford & Harding, 2007; Ford, 2010; Romani & Holgersson, 2015).

L-A-P scholars are advised to pay heed to gendered accounts of leadership and to recognize the importance of *inclusivity, polyvocality*, and *diversity* in leadership studies. By being inclusive, barriers for all organizational participants are removed such that they are freely able to contribute to the collaborative endeavors of leadership. Polyvocality embraces the presence of multiple voices rather than the privileging of the one voice (the putative leader), and diversity in leadership studies encompasses heterogeneity across organizations rather than the valorizing of just one particular hegemonic approach.

Understanding leadership calls for the consideration of social processes, a culturally sensitive and locally based interpretive approach that is mindful of individual's experiences, identities, power relations, and inter-subjectivities. It also embraces the presence of a range of masculine and feminine workplace behaviors. Greater awareness of the various discourses and positions that constitute subjectivities allows elucidation of oppressive discourses and subject positions.

Looking at leadership through a gendered perspective also exposes the many assumptions relating to gender neutrality and makes possible an exploration of why people at work operate in the ways that they do and why organizations are organized and policies enacted in the ways that they are (Ely. Foldy & Scully, 2003). Feminist theories, across the different traditions, provide challenge to our understandings of our social life and knowledge, and one of the most significant contributions of feminist theories has been both the exposure and problematizing of gender relations (Flax, 1993) as explored below.

The value of feminist theory

Feminist theory affords several intellectual and practical values. First, it sustains social criticism by revealing subordination and the moral and political implications of that subordination. Making intellectual sense of the subordination of women has turned out to be a more encompassing project than political analyses of it may suggest, as it has exposed much of the white, male, able-bodied, and heterosexual bias of the history of ideas and of society. It has enabled feminist scholars to reveal several distinct errors, notably sexism (i.e. taking men to be of greater value than women) and androcentrism (taking maleness or masculinity to be the norm for human-ness or humanity). Second, feminist theories provided lenses through which ideas and social practices can be analyzed. These theories have shown that much of what we do, and how we conceptualize what we do, is affected by gender. Third, such theorizing offers visions of liberation, of what life, people, and society would be like without the subordination of women, or of black and other minorities or on the grounds of class or able-bodiedness or sexuality.

Feminist post-structuralism and CLS

Feminist post-structural perspectives call into question the gender categories, which earlier approaches (such as liberal and structural) regard as given and unproblematic. Feminist post-structural accounts provide a challenge to such studies for treating men and women as unified groups and undifferentiated categories. They recognize the uncertain, shifting, and unequivocal meanings of such terms as men and women, male and female.

Arslenian-Engoren (2002) suggests that the philosophical underpinnings of the feminist post-structural framework can be found in the adoption of the post-structural philosophy of Foucault, which enables us to analyze and challenge notions of meaning, a unified subjectivity and relationships of power in modern society. Weedon (1997, p. 40) defines feminist post-structuralism as "a mode of knowledge production which uses post-structuralist theories of language, subjectivity, social processes and institutions to understand existing power relations and to identify areas and strategies for change." These concepts of language, subjectivity, and power are core features of post-structural thinking.

So, feminist post-structural analyses result when gender issues are incorporated into a post-structural framework. It offers a means to understand and alter hierarchical social networks that use power to silence and marginalize discourses related to gender. Feminist post-structural writers seek to transform gender dimensions, to develop new ways of understanding sexual differences and to uncover androcentric biases within socially, politically, and culturally established institutions. It is recognized that there are many forms of post-structural thought, rather than any unifying concept, but what these various forms share are fundamental assumptions about *knowledge and power, language and discourse,* and *subjectivity*, and these are explored briefly in the next section. The focus of my research interest in post-structural theories is the extent to which they can be appropriated so as to offer a gendered understanding of organizational life.

Feminist post-structural theories replace unitary notions of woman and feminine gender identity with plural and multifaceted constructions of social identity, treating gender as one relevant strand, but also considering other strands such as class, race, ethnicity, and age (Calas & Smircich, 1996, p. 237)

In sum, feminist post-structuralism enables fresh light to be shed on leadership theories. The whole notion of leadership itself is both historical and subject to change. Feminist post-structural perspectives have sought to deconstruct existing metanarratives and develop new theoretical approaches, which insist on historical and geographical specificity and no longer claim universal status. Thus, universal truths around leaders and leadership are open to challenge and debate.

Power, knowledge, language, and subjectivity

Attention to subjectivities and social identities also surfaces many questions about the role of power and knowledge in leadership practices and the context within which leadership is enacted. As has been noted elsewhere, leadership and power are inextricably intertwined (Burns, 1978; Ospina & Foldy, 2009; Carroll, Ford & Taylor, 2015; Ford, 2015). By exploring questions of diversity in leadership studies we can consider not only the Foucauldian interpretations of the productive resource of power and agency, but also seek to make sense of the "web of institutionalized inequities that systematically, and at the expense of others, provides privilege to some communities and some perspectives" (Ospina & Foldy, 2009, p. 877). Furthermore, explorations of leadership and power allow us to consider questions of agency and ways in which individuals and groups resist or transform such injustices in ways that generate opportunities for neglected voices to be heard.

Reflecting on my research study of managers within the local authority, functionalist perspectives of leadership effectively ignore the impact of broader social relations in their consideration of the complexity of interpretations of leadership. What is increasingly important is the need to consider the multiplicity of meanings attached to the concept of leadership, and the way that the role of subjectivity and agency is underplayed (Bresnen, 1995).

What emerged from this study is that there are two dominant accounts of leadership, but these are asymmetrical. Macho discourses are clearly in the ascendancy, and there is little evidence of post-heroic approaches occurring in practice. This suggests that power and control is also relevant as well as social identities. What these managers depicted is the co-existence of competing and contradictory discourses of leadership (in symbolic senses) to the extent that considerable anxiety, fear, and insecurity is experienced (in material senses).

Rather than the dominant leadership discourses forming the managers' subjectivities, these vied as sources of power among many others, including life outside work, gendered differences and approaches and differing career patterns that warrant further research and analysis (Ford, 2006; Ford & Collinson, 2011). It is therefore important to explore in depth the diverse effects of different social experiences and contexts that influence how leadership is conceptualized and practiced. This also leads me to call for more reflexive understandings of our role as academic educators and developers. Nancy Harding and I expressed concern about the dangers inherent in leadership development programs in their production of formulaic, prescriptive, and competency-based outcomes that serve to limit the ways in which managers as putative leaders can practice the craft of leadership that such programs seek to foster (see Ford & Harding, 2007). Our ambition was to introduce managers to more reflexive, critical, collaborative, and dialogical approaches to practicing leadership that draw more on their experiences and relationships in the workplace, and that encourage those involved in leadership practices to become more aware of how they (co-)constitute, maintain, and retain control over their shared realities and multiple leadership identities.

Through exploring a power lens on L-A-P we can better acknowledge the significance of social inequalities and potential injustices in the workplace. As L-A-P decenters the individual while recognizing the role of evolving practices, the practices themselves, including their inequities, need to be revealed and decentered. The role of agency is clearly central to such issues and a focus on social identities (including race, gender, class, age, sexuality, etc.) more readily accentuates structural and cultural issues in the workplace, which in turn reinforce the significance of considering both micro and macro dynamics of power that inevitably influence the experiences of leadership in the workplace (Ospina & Foldy, 2009). Structural concerns include recognizing that social relations at work are part of a deep-seated, broader system of relations between unequal social groups based on gender and/or class and/or race. Of central concern here is the creation by dominant groups of structures that serve the interests of these groups and seek to maintain this group's dominance. In relation to gender for instance, differences are identified as an underlying social division in which women are systematically oppressed to service the interests of other more powerful social groups, particularly men but also whites and ruling classes (Halford & Leonard, 2001).

Post-structural theory rejects the notion of absolute truth and objectivity in favor of the plurality of meaning. As feminists have observed, dominant conceptions of "reality" and "truth" in patriarchal Western society have tended to be male constructs, which reflect and perpetuate male power interests (Flax, 1993; Gavey, 1997). As suggested in the previous section, feminist explorations have exposed different truths and realities and these have cast doubt on the notion of one reality and one truth. Similarly, from a post-structural perspective, knowledge is socially constructed through "a specific kind of production with definite relations to the social and material world" (Venn, 1984, cited in Gavey, 1997, p. 52). Thus knowledge is ephemeral and inherently unstable; it is not neutral and is closely associated with power, with power generating knowledge and knowledge initiating power. So, those who are deemed to have the power to regulate what counts as truth (e.g. the position as leaders in organizations) are able to maintain their access to material advantages and power. Feminist post-structural goals of scholarship include developing understandings or theories that are historically, socially, and culturally specific and that are explicitly related to changing oppressive gender relations. Thus, rather than the realist endeavor to discover reality, reveal the truth, or uncover the facts, the feminist post-structural project is concerned with disrupting and displacing oppressive knowledge and meaning.

Thus, goals of scholarship within post-structural feminist theory include developing understandings that are historically, socially, and culturally specific, and that are explicitly related to changing oppressive gender relations. Rather than "discovering" reality, "revealing" truth or "uncovering" the facts, feminist post-structural writers would instead, be concerned with disrupting and displacing dominant (oppressive) knowledge (Gavey, 1997). Feminist post-structural writers recognize the diverse, fragmented, and contradictory lives of men and women in organization. Attention is focused on gendered subjectivities (and other multiple, layered social identities) and their plurality, ambiguity, and fragmented nature within asymmetrical power relations.

Turning to language, the liberal humanist view of language is seen as transparent and expressive, merely reflecting and describing pre-existing subjectivity and human experience. Feminist post-structuralism is predicated on the understanding that language and discourse *constitutes* subjectivity. Meaning is actively created through language and is therefore neither fixed nor essential. In terms of discourse, Weedon's feminist post-structural account is influenced by the Foucauldian notion that language is always located in discourse, which is defined by Hollway (1989, p. 231) as "a system of statements which cohere around common meanings and values that are a product of social factors, of powers and practices, rather than an individual's set of ideas." So, this reflects particular ways of constructing meaning, based specifically on particular groups, cultures, and historical periods. Feminist post-structuralists seek to emphasize the material bases of power, notably social, economic, and cultural arrangements and the need for change at this level of discourse. These discourses are multiple, offering numerous conflicting ways of giving meaning to the world. They offer "subject positions" (Hollway, 1984) for individuals to take up, and these various positions (identities, behaviors, ways of seeing the world) vary in terms of the power they offer individuals.

Constituted through language and discourse, subjectivity refers to the "conscious and unconscious thoughts and emotions of the individual, her sense of self and her ways of understanding her relation to the world" (Weedon, 1997, p. 32). Positivist research usually locates an essential, coherent and unique nature and subjectivity in the individual, whereas post-structuralism seeks to "decenter the subject." Rather than the humanist assumptions of a unified, rational self, feminist post-structuralism proposes a subject that is fragmentary, inconsistent, and contradictory. It denies the existence of an essential female or male nature and seeks to problematize the hegemonic assumptions that we are whole and coherent subjects with a unified sense of identity, and drawing on Kristeva's psychoanalytic understanding of subjectivity and language, witnesses instead a subject in process. Thus a post-structural position on subjectivity relativizes the individual's sense of self by making it in effect a discourse that is always in the process of becoming (Chia, 1996) and is open to continuous redefinition. However, this is not to deny the importance of particular forms of individual subjective investment, which can have a powerful impact on our identities. Nor is it to deny the significant role of material structures such as work, family, education, and so on, all of which constitute and discipline our sense of self.

Flax (1993) challenges unitarist approaches to subjectivity and promotes the importance of exposing the historically constituted character of all ideas about human nature. She argues that feminist concepts of gender have many implications for our thinking about subjectivity. She suggests (p. 97):

> feminists argue that our thinking about and practices of gender are historical artefacts, that gender is an effect of complex, historically variable sets of social relations in and through which heterogeneous persons are socially organized as members of one and only one of an exclusionary and (so far) unequal pair—man and woman.

In this way, masculine and feminine identities are not determined by a pre-given, unchangeable biological substratum but are created by and reflect structures of power, language, and social practices, and our struggles with and against these structures.

Applying these notions to our endeavors to define leadership can be seen as a means of exerting control or seeking to regulate individuals' identities within organizations. Such approaches provide putative leaders with a means of self-regulation and self-monitoring in which they are "cultivated" to become "autonomous, self-regulating, proactive individuals" (du Gay, 1996, p. 60, see also Rose, 1999). Managers' very identities and senses of self are thus crafted by their experiences in workplace settings. Through defining the leadership practices and behaviors expected of their workers, organizations may unwittingly provide a vocabulary and way of behaving that constrains managers qua leaders into how their very identity is constructed. The powerful voices of the organizational "leaders" seek to persuade the rest of the workforce to conform to organizational norms and behaviors (Alvesson & Willmott, 2002; Knights & Willmott, 1992).

In response, managers and other professionals within these organizational settings may (or may not) collaborate in this discursive production of themselves by adopting the very behaviors and skills that are being promulgated. Once having taken up a particular position as one's own, a person inevitably sees the world from the vantage point of that position and in terms of the particular images and beliefs that this perspective offers. Management consultants and indeed academics, trainers, and educators seek to define and fix the concept of leadership on the organization's behalf and thereby collude in the presentation of a core identity for identified leaders within organizations (Ford & Harding, 2007). This view presumes a unitary identity, a coherent view of the self against which it is possible to gauge whether an individual's actions are true or false, genuine or spurious, good or bad. Furthermore, it embeds an assumed homogeneity of approach to leadership.

Through researching and theorizing on gender, it is possible to expose the mythical character of self-determining, individualistic and autonomous ideas of subjectivity. Gender is one of the conditions of possibility of modern subjectivity. Gendering "is an integral part of the process of becoming and being an individual subject. One becomes a boy or a girl, not a person" (Flax, 1993, p. 97). Our language and sets of social practices exist through which (gendered) subjectivity is constituted and by which individuals make sense of it to themselves and others. As gendering is such a complex and over-determined process, it is not possible to be conscious of all its determinants, effects, and consequences. In the very nature of going about our daily lives, of working and having relationships, our gendered selves are made to fit with and be intelligible to others. In this way, we are "inserted into pre-existing, gendered social locations and practices" (Flax, 1993, p. 97). So, questions of gender and other multiple layered social identities are too important to ignore in writings on leadership, management, and organization.

Summary and implications for leadership-as-practice

A subjectivist, post-structural perspective shows how depictions of leadership are thoroughly embedded in relationships and experiences, in local context—and thus, in practices. This encourages the development of more relational, inter-subjective approaches and disrupts the complacency that is present in many contemporary accounts of leadership. Developing subjective approaches opens up the possibility for reflection, for questioning assumptions and for surfacing different meanings and so creating, through the acts of dialogue, new meanings and understandings. Allowing a subjective perspective or inter-subjective exchange, can lead to wider possibilities for development. In many respects this might be seen as anathema to traditional views as it presents the opposite of the universal or immediately generalizable experience, which competence-based approaches to leadership, for example, dictate. These traditional approaches still underpin much research and practitioner debate in the study of leadership that more recent L-A-P and CLS-inspired accounts seek to challenge.

Such relational and inter-subjective approaches provide greater opportunities to encourage deeper insights by examining interpersonal dynamics, which open up unconscious motivations. They challenge the fixing and coding of "leaders" that more conventional approaches to leadership appear to encourage. The intention is to build on joint conversations between the managers and their staff, peers, boss, and others in the employment relationship while taking account of the particular institutional contexts in which these relationships take place. This encourages us to recognize the importance not only of difference (by gender, race, class, age, sexuality, etc.), but also to embrace and value such diversity and strategies for inclusion in our workplaces.

Injecting a critical voice that can inform more reflexive and collaborative practices may be one way of encouraging a leadership-as-practice approach that turns away from the demands of coordination and control towards relational and inter-subjective practices. The encouragement of self-reflexivity and critical questioning of taken-for-granted aspects of the experiences of managers may facilitate a determined critique among managers that can lead to resistance to organizational control. This may be achieved through active interpretation of storied accounts of peoples' experiences and reflexive dialogical critique in which many interpretations can be surfaced and in which we can make sense of peoples' experiences in numerous ways.

Some of the implications of such thinking for L-A-P require much closer interrogation of what has perhaps been overlooked in the search for more colla-borative forms of engagement. This raises a number of questions that L-A-P scholars and others interested in more critical perspectives on leadership studies should explore. So, for example, is L-A-P and its underlying ideology, such as one proposed by Philip Woods (Chapter 4, this volume) as that of "co-development," truly emancipatory or does it run the risk of continuing—even if inadvertently— to require workers to engage in a rational dialogue that may marginalize or even ignore issues of sexism, racism, and other exploitations that maintain the pre-dominant phallocentric social order? Some of the early L-A-P accounts seem to present a degree of value neutrality but we know that any exploration of the social and material practices and discourses of leadership will need to contend with issues of gender and other multiple social identities such as race, age, social class, sexuality. Similarly, as I explore above, such identities will be replete with ambiguities and contradictions.

Second, what is the stance of L-A-P in relation to diversity and inclusion? How can the collective potential of L-A-P be achieved to ensure that the voices of other than white males are heard in more collaborative forms of leadership? There is a risk that control of work processes and conversations may still be regulated by power elites who can manipulate the organizational discourse by advancing "best practices" and other structural and cultural norms and expecta-tions that are still embedded within historical traditions. Can participants identi-fied as part of any leadership constellation join together to resist oppression from such elites and democratically control their own fate? Otherwise, might L-A-P discourse merely re-institute existing identities that give a false sense of harmony between workers and managers?

Finally, is there access to sources of knowledge production so that any corre-spondence between knowledge and power is exposed and made contestable? The development of new knowledge would need to take account of the social, political, historical, and cultural processes that have led to existing practices.

Towards more critical thinking on leadership

This is a really stimulating time to be researching and studying leadership—never mind the challenges of actually practicing it. We note from debates within this book—as well as discussions within CLS more broadly—that traditional approaches to studying leadership continue to privilege the leader within hierarchical structural representations. Organization charts list leaders as those most senior (and therefore most important) in these companies. There appears to be much consensus in the leadership literature that leaders and leadership are important in today's organizations. It is taken for granted that leadership exists within organizations and that it can be improved and that its main purpose is to maximize the effectiveness and efficiency of organizations. The roles that leaders need to undertake now include the model of a leader such that the very self (the subjectivity) of the leader is consumed in this leader identity. In effect, we become the leader and all that this entails as an identity. But we do not believe that this is the whole picture. Such uncritical ways of seeing leadership are thus disciplinary, exclusionary, and highly conservative.

Emerging and more critical theories of leadership recognize the more dispersed, flexible, fluid and decentralized forms of organizations that encourage a shared, distributive, and relational leadership dynamic that has informed the work of L-A-P scholarship (Carroll, Levy & Richmond, 2008; Crevani, Lindgren & Packendorff, 2010; Raelin, 2011, 2014). There is more than a stirring of interest in more critical leadership studies that focus on plurality, ambiguity, complexity, and heterogeneity rather than homogeneous and uni-dimensional forms, presenting us with new opportunities to understand and experience leadership from within much richer, contextual empirical studies. So, this analysis does not just stop at the pursuit of critique and theorizing about what scholars are writing. It also offers some emancipatory potential: of new ways of thinking about, researching, and practicing leadership in organizations.

References

Acker, J. (1990). Hierarchies, bodies and jobs: A gendered theory of organizations. *Gender and Society*, 4(2), 139–158.

Acker, J. (1998). The future of gender and organizations. *Gender, Work and Organization*, 5(4), 195–206.

Alvesson, M. (2002). *Understanding organizational culture*. London: Sage.

Alvesson, M., & Willmott, H. (2002). Identity regulation as organisational control: Producing the appropriate individual. *Journal of Management Studies*, 39(5), 619–644.

Arslenian-Engoren, C. (2002). Feminist poststructuralism: A methodological paradigm for examining clinical decision-making. *Journal of Advanced Nursing*, 37(6), 512–517.

Bresnen, M. (1995). All things to all people? Perceptions, attributions and constructions of leadership. *Leadership Quarterly*, 6(4), 495–513.

Brewis, J. (1999). How does it feel? Women managers, embodiment and changing public sector cultures. In S. Whitehead & R. Moodley (Eds.), *Transforming managers: Gendering change in the public sector*. London: UCL Press.

Burns, J. M. (1978). *Leadership*. New York: Harper and Row.

Butler, J. (1993). *Bodies that matter*. New York: Routledge.

Calas, M., & Smircich, L. (1991). Voicing seduction to silence leadership. *Organization Studies*, 12(4), 567–602.

Calas, M., & Smircich, L. (1992). Using the F word: Feminist theories and the social consequences of organizational research. In A. J. Mills & P. Tancred (Eds.), *Gendering organizational analysis*. New Park, CA: Sage.

Calas, M., & Smircich, L. (1996). From the woman's point of view: Feminist approaches to organizational studies. In S. Clegg, C. Hardy & W. Nord (Eds.), *Handbook of organization studies*. London: Sage.

Carroll, B., Ford, J., & Taylor, S. (Eds.) (2015). *Leadership: Contemporary critical perspectives*. London: Sage.

Carroll, B., Levy, L., & Richmond, D. (2008). Leadership as practice: Challenging the competency paradigm. *Leadership*, 4(4), 363–379.

Chia, R. (1996). The problem of reflexivity in organizational research: Towards a postmodern science of organization. *Organization*, 3(1), 31–59.

Collinson, D. (2011). Critical leadership studies. In A. Bryman, D. Collinson, K. Grint, B. Jackson & M. Uhl-Bien (Eds.), *The Sage handbook of leadership* (pp. 179–192). London: Sage

Collinson, D. (2014). Dichotomies, dialectics and dilemmas: New directions for critical leadership studies? *Leadership*, 10(1), 36–55.

Collinson, D. & Hearn, J. (1994). Naming men as men: Implications for work, organisation and management. *Gender, Work and Organisation*, 1(1), 2–22.

Crevani, L., Lindgren, M., & Packendorff, J. (2010). Leadership, not leaders: On the study of leadership as practices and interactions. *Scandinavian Journal of Management*, 26(1), 77–86.

Ely, R., Foldy, E. & Scully, M. (Eds.) (2003). *Reader in gender, work and organization*. Oxford: Blackwell.

Flax, J. (1993). *Disputed subjects: Essays on psychoanalysis, politics and philosophy*. London: Routledge.

Fletcher, J. K. (2004). The paradox of postheroic leadership: An essay on gender, power and transformational change. *Leadership Quarterly*, 14, 647–661.

Fondas, N. (1997). Feminization unveiled: Management qualities in contemporary writings. *The Academy of Management Review*, 22(1), 257–282.

Ford, J. (2006). Discourses of leadership: Gender, identity and contradiction in a UK public sector organization. *Leadership*, 2(1), 77–99.

Ford, J. (2010). Studying leadership critically: A psychosocial lens on leadership identities. *Leadership*, 6(1), 1–19.

Ford, J. (2015). Leadership, post-structuralism and the performative turn. In B. Carroll, J. Ford & S. Taylor (Eds.), *Leadership: Contemporary critical perspectives* (pp. 233-254). London: Sage.

Ford, J., & Harding, N. (2007). Move over management we are all leaders now. *Management Learning*, 38(5), 475–493.

Ford, J., & Collinson, D. (2011). In search of the perfect manager? Work-life balance and managerial work. *Work, Employment and Society*, 25(2), 257–273.

Ford, J., Harding, N., & Learmonth, M. (2008). *Leadership as identity: Constructions and deconstructions*. Basingstoke: Palgrave Macmillan.

Fournier, V., & Grey, C. (2000). At the critical moment: Conditions and prospects for critical management studies. *Human Relations*, 53(1), 7-32.

Fournier, V., & Keleman, M. (2001). The crafting of community: Recoupling discourses of management and womanhood, *Gender, Work and Organization*, 8(3), 267–290.

Fulop, L., & Linstead, S. (2009). Leadership and leading. In S. Linstead, L. Fulop & S. Lilley (Eds.), *Management and organization: A critical text* (2nd edition) (pp. 473–538). London: Palgrave Macmillan.

Gavey, N. (1997). Feminist poststructuralism and discourse analysis. In M. Gergen & S. Davis, *Toward a new psychology of gender: A reader* (pp. 49–54). London: Routledge.

du Gay, P.(1996). *Consumption and identity at work*. London: Sage.

Gherardi, S. (1995). *Gender, symbolism and organizational cultures*. London: Sage.

Halford, S., & Leonard, P. (2001). *Gender, power and organizations*. Basingstoke: Palgrave.

Harding, N., Lee, H., Ford, J., & Learmonth, M. (2011). Leadership and charisma: A desire that cannot speak its name? *Human Relations*, 64(7), 927–950.

Hearn, J., & Parkin, W. (1993). Organizations, multiple oppressions and postmodernism. In J. Hassard & M. Parker (Eds.), *Postmodernism and organizations* (pp. 148–162). London: Sage.

Hollway, W. (1989). *Subjectivity and method in psychology: Gender, meaning and science*. London: Sage.

Jeanes, E., Knights, D., & Yancey Martin, P. (Eds.) (2011). *Handbook of gender, work and organization*. Chichester: Wiley.

Knights, D., & Willmott, H. (1992). Conceptualising leadership processes: A study of senior managers in a financial services company. *Journal of Management Studies*, 29(6), 761–782.

Legge, K. (1995). *Human resource management: Rhetoric and realities*. Basingstoke: Macmillan.

Ospina, S., & Foldy, E. (2009). A critical review of race and ethnicity in the leadership literature: Surfacing context, power and the collective dimensions of leadership. *Leadership Quarterly*, 20(6), 876–896.

Raelin, J. A. (2008). Emancipatory discourse and liberation. *Management Learning*, 39(5), 519–540.

Raelin, J. A. (2011). From leadership-as-practice to leaderful practice. *Leadership*, 7, 195–211.

Raelin, J. A. (2014). Imagine there are no leaders: Reframing leadership as collaborative agency. *Leadership*, Online First, 1–28.

Rose, N. (1999). *Governing the soul: The shaping of the private self*. London: Routledge.

Romani, L., & Holgersson, C. (2015). Inclusive leadership for sustainable work practices. In L. Zander (Eds.), *Research handbook of global leadership: Making a difference*. Cheltenham: Edward Elgar.

Sinclair, A. (2011). Leading with the body. In E. Jeanes, D. Knights & P. Yancey Martin (Eds.), *Handbook of gender, work and organization* (pp. 117–130). Chichester: Wiley.

Smircich, L. & Morgan, G. (1982). Leadership: The management of meaning. *Journal of Applied Behavioural Studies*, 18(3), 257–273.

Tourish, D. (2011). Leading questions: Journal rankings, academic freedom and performativity: What is, or should be, the future of Leadership? *Leadership*, 7(3), 367–381.

Tourish, D. (2013). *The dark side of transformational leadership: A critical perspective*. London: Routledge.

Watson, T. (2001). *In search of management: Culture, chaos and control in managerial work* (revised edition). London: Thompson Learning.

Weedon, C. (1997). *Feminist practice and poststructuralist theory* (2nd edition). Oxford: Blackwell.

12

METHODOLOGIES TO DISCOVER AND CHALLENGE LEADERSHIP-AS-PRACTICE

Stephen Kempster, Ken Parry and Brad Jackson

In search of leadership-as-practice

The preceding chapters outline the nature of the phenomenon of leadership-as-practice. They speak to a variety of aspects impacting its emergence, recursivity, and ongoing construction. Research to provide insight, theorization, and contribution to a phenomenon that is continually becoming will not be straightforward and will necessitate careful consideration in design. To address such complexity, this chapter outlines the view that approaches to researching leadership-as-practice require three foci: first, attention to the ontology of what is being researched—for example being clear on the unit of analysis; second, related to the difficulties of researching L-A-P, the pursuit of a holistic methodological practice such as using multiple techniques to help illumination and triangulation; and, third, a focus on generating theory, especially process theorizing.

As outlined in particular by Carroll (Chapter 5, this volume) and Sergi (Chapter 6, this volume), the assumed ontology of leadership-as-practice focuses on activity that occurs between people and materiality situated within particular contexts. Such situated activity has a rich history, and such activity is in continual emergence shaped by antecedents and recursive interactions. These aspects place some striking challenges to researching leadership-as-practice. Notions of undertaking experiments, issuing questionnaires, and engaging in interviews are problematic. For example, who do we issue the questionnaire to or invite for interviews if practice occurs between people? Can we create an experiment to measure activity if it is a phenomenon that is inextricably linked to a history, and a place? How can we measure this activity through these instruments and procedures? In essence it seems highly unlikely that this is possible. In this sense we problematize the applicability of nomothetic approaches typical of the natural sciences that focus on objective phenomena with epistemic goals of generalization and the search for truths. However, this does not mean that theorizing is impossible in L-A-P research that is mostly based on the ideographic method typical of the humanities which strives to understand the meaning of contingent, unique, and often subjective phenomena. We assert the opposite to be the case. Theorizing should be the primary outcome.

Ontological clarity

We suggest that researchers engaging in exploring leadership practice need to start with a clarity of ontological thinking and imaginatively craft techniques that *serve* as relevant and rigorous approaches to illuminate, describe, and explain leadership practice. That is, we adopt Bhaskar's (1978) axiom of the need for epistemology to be the handmaiden to ontology. To this end, we encourage L-A-P researchers to design and apply a range of techniques that can be focused on the continual sense of grasping historic antecedent influence, phenomena emergence, becoming, and recursivity. We anticipate that such a range of techniques can be applied within specific studies to enable emerging themes to be triangulated to render greater confidence in accurately discerning and describing the phenomenon under examination and greater confidence in the plausibility of explaining why such practices have become manifest and how these practices are recursive. Although such descriptions and explanations are situated, we suggest that it is desirable that researchers seek to compare sites of investigation to discern commonalties of explanations.

Not that any two practices would be the same. How could this be? How could two or more sets of leadership practices have the same histories, have the same actors, have the same materialities, or the same sense of meanings associated with being, doing, and knowing within a specific context. What we suggest instead is comparative research which would seek to identify common or generative influences on practice emergence and recursivity and would describe and explain the variation: in a sense a process theorization of leadership-as-practice.

Theory-testing is relevant but far from exhaustive. It has a role to play but its role needs to be considered carefully. We have a phenomenon that has a history, is contextual and embedded in relational knowing, being, and doing, and that is continually emergent. These dynamic properties of emergence and recursivity that malleably interact with socio-materiality require an acceptance that, at best, theory-testing would lay out as limitations associated with levels of analysis. We suggest an emphasis on theorizing in which contribution would be placed on plausibility and practical adequacy rather than inferential generalization. Yin's (1994) notion of analytic generalizability drawn from case comparison has value but caution is needed when developing theory in the form of testable propositions or through searching for facts with a nomothetic theory output. This is because we are seeking to understand a phenomenon and not a population. In this way an expectation would lean towards ideographic qualitative rather than predominantly quantitative methods, with opportunities for mixed methods.

There are general research issues that also must be incorporated. One issue might be the notions of criticality and critical realism, which lend themselves to ideographic methodologies. Another issue which also lends itself to ideographic methodologies is the role of agency, ideology and "historical" abduction. A third issue is that data which reflect dialogue, activity, relational-ness, and artifacts/symbols/language could just as feasibly be used in ideographic as nomothetic methods. In essence we suggest the importance of building a holistic methodology.

Holistic methodology

The holistic methodology opens up particular lines of investigation to examine the commonalities among various L-A-P cases. For example, how does leadership get accomplished between people? Is there a tendency for particular influences shaping practice emergence to be prevalent? Do these become manifest in similar ways and similar combinations? Although the holistic approach gives priority and necessity to examine context, we should not rule out "traditional" or mainstream leadership methods that require quantitative data and analyses. However, in the spirit of leadership-as-practice, and being true to the methodological validity that comes with data triangulation, we see quantitative research as data—data that are analyzed qualitatively along with observations, interviews, discourse, documents, and the full range of information available.

The contextual contingencies of leadership must be understood and their impact tested. Also, we can test qualitatively for the emergence of themes and categories that explain how context impacts leadership practice(s). However, we suggest that research needs to give emphasis to levels of analysis and adopt approaches that can make this highly visible. For example, we recognize Pawson and Tilley's (1997) notion of realist research, which seeks to identify outcomes (emergent and recursive leadership-as-practice) shaped by particular mechanisms embedded in a specific contextual frame (team, organization, profession, sector, nation, global). Similarly, discourse analysis of practices can be examined specifically and also compared/critiqued across micro, meso, grand, and mega levels (Alvesson & Karreman, 2000).

Process thinking

The processual nature of leadership practice must be understood if we wish to generate knowledge about how it emerges and unfolds. Processual phenomena lend themselves to fully qualitative methodologies. Ethnographies and grounded theory are examples that are relevant here and we shall illustrate how such approaches along with others can be utilized.

We expect that leadership-as-practice research mostly will be informed through ideographic research, particularly in the early stages of theorizing. Building out from firm foundations, we fundamentally need to know the rich detail of experiences to first describe what appears to be site-specific leadership-as-practice. Yet such research should not necessarily feel constrained from going further to explain and compare (even test) these explanations. For example, how might a theory offered from one site be present in other sites, what processes shape practice manifestations, and are they present in other situations? If they are, do they operate in similar ways? Or are some processes present but not having the same effect (perhaps because of the dominance of site-specific processes); or are they not present and the manifestation of L-A-P is a consequence of a very different configuration of influences? Through such comparative examination, theory development of L-A-P may emerge. This would always be contingent and therefore not inferentially generalizable. This is not the goal. Rather we see process theorization as able to illustrate plausible explanations for the manifestation of L-A-P at higher levels of abstraction, and that this resonates with practitioners. If it resonates, then the theory is getting close to the reality of practitioners and has relevance to everyday leadership practice, in other words, the theory is becoming practically adequate (Kempster & Parry, 2011).

Chapter structure

The chapter is structured to provide an illustration of this epistemological approach. We have written the chapter from the position of a researcher wishing to commence the journey of revealing, describing, and explaining leadership-as-practice. We have not sought to address methodological issues relevant to each chapter of this book in turn. This would result in a form of encyclopedia of methods. Rather we seek to outline how research could be undertaken with the primary goal to develop theorization on L-A-P. The outline of our chapter is as follows. We first examine methodological debates from the related area of strategy-as-practice. This is most illuminating and indicates a series of avenues as well as cul-de-sacs that fellow researchers have traveled. We draw on this learning to give us a heads-up on expected challenges and some steps to take and those to avoid. Building on this we travel our own methodological journey. We suggest that the journey should commence with having a commitment to theorizing upfront and throughout. We give emphasis to process theorizing of leadership-as-practice as suitable to the ontology of L-A-P with its historic, emergent, and recursive nature. We outline a holistic and integrated methodology linked to such theorizing. We suggest that process theorizing can connect description, explanation, and measurement orientations thereby building up from the ground a theoretical understanding of leadership-as-practice. Considerations of units of analysis, sampling, and triangulation are explored along with aspects of data access and ethics. Subsequently, we consider a series of approaches to both data collection and data analysis that can be utilized in the holistic methodological approach. We conclude the chapter with an outline of Cultural Historic Activity Theory (CHAT) and the opportunity it holds for L-A-P research as an integrating method to align the preceding approaches.

Learning from others: Strategy-as-practice

We are, of course, never alone in our quest. Studying practice has been explored by many before us (perhaps the earliest Bourdieu 1977; Giddens, 1984; and subsequently Schatzki, Knorr Cetina & Von Savigny, 2001; Reckwitz, 2002). So what can we learn from others before we plough on with approaches for research? A most useful field to draw from is that of the strategy-as-practice (S-A-P) field. There have been debates and commentaries that shed much light on cul-de-sacs to be avoided and fruitful avenues to be explored.

Prominent in the debates regarding the exploration of S-A-P research is the notion of modes or orientations of research. Orlikowski (2010, pp. 23–28) has helpfully summarized this into three modes:

- The first—an empirical mode—is practice as a phenomenon which sees researchers having a "commitment to understanding what practitioners do in practice" (2010, p. 24). Approaches reflect a desire to be grounded in the empirical world with a degree of scepticism of theorizing as this cannot capture the complex detail of what actually happens in practice. The essence of the mode is to "bridge the gap" between theorizing and lived experience through "illuminating the empirical details of organisational life on the ground" (2010, p. 24). The consequence to research is a commitment to deep engagement, observing, or working with practitioners. Issues of open access, managing large quantities of qualitative data, and ethical responsibilities require careful consideration.

- The second—a theoretical mode—is practice as a perspective which focuses on everyday activity to point to the "structural consequences that are produced, reinforced or changed through time" (Orlikowski, 2010, p. 24). In this way practice as a perspective seeks to develop practice theories that subsequently are used to study organizational activity. It is a sense of seeing practice as a lens through which to examine social reality. Any research orientation towards theorizing lends itself to approaches that seek to build and apply theories, such as grounded theory and ethnography. Tensions exist though in such theory development in embracing the emergent sense of practice and what aspects to bracket out or draw boundaries around.

- The third—a meta-theoretical mode—is practice as a philosophy that gives ontological primacy to practice as constituting social reality. Schatzki, for example, asserts that social life is constituted as "nexuses of practices and material arrangements" (Schatzki, 2005, p. 471). This view clearly has much resonance to arguments in this book (see, e.g., Crevani & Endrissat, Chapter 2, this volume; Sergi, Chapter 6, this volume). It suggests first and foremost a challenge to traditional social research that draws on a representational epistemology. In its place the practice as a philosophy assumes a performative epistemology in which "knowing comes from a direct material engagement in the world" (Schatzki, 2005, p. 30). The result is a malleable interaction shaping the emergence of social reality.

The approach we draw on to structure the remainder of the chapter is the second mode—that of *practice as a theoretical perspective*. This is the realm in which the field of leadership studies has been most predominantly situated. It is the realm, therefore, in which the L-A-P perspective can most readily demonstrate its relative worth compared with other more established methodologies. We will describe approaches that seek theory development to help explicate the phenomena of leadership-as-practice. Prior to engaging in this discussion we need to look again at the lessons learned from S-A-P research that reflect mode two.

Approaches to undertaking practice as perspective in S-A-P

Drawing on the work of Langley and Abdullah (2011), S-A-P research can broadly be seen to adopt an empirical focus on activity that has been informed by two earlier methods prevalent in strategy research (see, e.g., Eisenhardt, 1989; Gioia, 2004). Both are usefully instructive for L-A-P seen through the practice as perspective theorization mode.

Langley and Abdullah (2011, p. 205) suggest that both are directed by distinct epistemological tenets. The Eisenhardt (E) case method is post-positivist with the aim of developing theory in the form of testable propositions, through searching for facts with a nomothetic theory output. The Gioia (G) case method is interpretive. It seeks to model informant meanings drawn from an understanding of events with an output of a process model (that could be novel). Both seek to theorize/model processes beyond the context of the data. The "E" method seeks multiple cases with a sharp focus on one key dimension while seeking to be similar on other dimensions; the data are gathered through interviews with a broad range of interviewees, with data analysis seeking to measure the impact of this dimension across multiple sites against performance. The "G" method gives attention to a single case selected for what it can reveal while relying on interviews complemented by observations, with the data analysis building a process model from informant perspectives akin to grounded theory.

We are sympathetic to the aims and objectives of both methods. Both seek to provide different insight offerings. "G" can be used to address a gap and build a theory/model by obtaining an in-depth understanding of a phenomenon within a single context. Subsequent "G" research will elaborate on the phenomenon, in some instances confirming its presence but also offering an explanation for any difference. "E" allows this theory/model to be tested in multiple contexts to provide a greater confidence of the theory more broadly, in a sense enhancing the plausibility of the theory. For example, Langley and Abdullah (2011, p. 220) draw on the work of Johnson, Prashantham, Floyd and Bourque, (2010) to illustrate the use of multiple case studies, building from an early in-depth case, to focus on a particular dimension of success and failure in strategy workshops using ritual theory. In contrast, Balogun and Johnson (2004) used a single case and applied it as an interpretive lens to examine diaries to analyze middle-manager sensemaking.

The practice turn has offered up several methods that might be useful for L-A-P analysis. S-A-P researchers sought to understand strategy practitioners, like we wish to understand those involved in leadership, and the emerging recursive patterns of socio-materiality within activity (Langley & Abdullah, 2011, p. 219). The methods that have been utilized to reveal implicit knowledge and socio-materiality in practice have been ethnographic (see, e.g., Rouleau, 2005). Recursivity has been illuminated through in-depth longitudinal studies (Kaplan, 2011). Narratives and vignettes have been used to reveal underlying socio-political dynamics (Rouleau, 2005, 2010).

An emerging insight from the S-A-P community is that a commitment to theories of social practice provides a strong grounding for the research. Langley and Abdullah (2011) suggest that the lack of unified theory and an eclectic breadth of vocabulary make it difficult to integrate S-A-P contributions. However, they helpfully suggest three common elements to practice theorizing: first, knowledge is embedded in practical activity and it is tacit, thereby limiting the utility of interviews; second, material objects are deeply entwined in everyday practices "mediating how and what is accomplished" (2011, p. 221), hence the given assumption of socio-materiality. The implications for research give salience to methods that enable fine-grained attention to how material elements interact with agents to recursively shape practice. Kaplan's work on the impact of Powerpoint slides speaks loudly to the method of "cartography" to guide data interpretation of the practices within presentations (Kaplan, 2011, p. 21). Third, building on the preceding two elements, is the fundamental notion that practices are recursive. This necessitates a long timeframe to see the unfolding and emergent nature of recursivity in practices making longitudinal research a necessity to illustrate this process (see Jarzabkowski, 2008).

The publication of S-A-P work is also illustrative and informing. The voluminous data that emerges from practice-oriented research have been problematic to fit journal expectations about such aspects as credibility, validity, and contribution. Emerging hints and tips suggest that the metaphor of the microscope may be helpful (Rouleau, 2005), such as in examining "the whole through its tiny parts." Rouleau's use of vignettes is highly regarded to give a strong credible examination of an "underlying phenomena whose workings are finely traced out developing a cumulative understanding" (Langley & Abdullah, 2011, p. 223). Another well-regarded approach to illustrate recursive manifestation of practices is the use of a sawtooth representation where action and institutional structures are portrayed as parallel lines that interact (see, e.g., Barley & Tolbert, 1997, and its application in S-A-P in Jarzabkowski, 2008; or in critical realist studies such as in Harrison & Easton, 2004).

Our overall assessment of the S-A-P research effort to date has been the limited coherence of its empirical research towards theory building as well as its limited connection with practitioners, which is somewhat ironic given its name and its intent. The S-A-P community appears to suffer from the lack of epistemological recognition of the "practice turn" (Chia & MacKay, 2007). The effect is to suggest that S-A-P is a "community of people interested in similar empirical phenomena and drawing on a loose collection of theoretical lenses that have something to do with practice" (Langley & Abdullah, 2011, p. 224). This rather prophetic comment should hold some powerful cautionary resonance with L-A-P researchers who are keen to enter the fray. At the time of this writing, it is understood that S-A-P colleagues report that leading "American" journals have been rejecting practice-based research for its lack of broad theorizing and replication. The inability of the S-A-P community to connect their work with practitioners is a critical challenge for L-A-P researchers not to repeat. Keeping relevance and rigor in a close-coupled relationship from the outset would, therefore, seem to be highly desirable for researchers, practitioners, and for any leadership development activity to keep well in mind.

What can be known about L-A-P?

The primacy of theory development

The question of this section orients discussion to design approaches that address how a scholarly contribution can be framed. We outlined at the beginning of the chapter the necessity of researchers being explicitly clear on the ontology being addressed. The emergent and recursive nature of L-A-P requires a holistic research strategy that seeks to contribute through the development of theory. As a fledging development in the field of leadership studies, L-A-P has a wonderful opportunity to guide the development of theorizing from the ground up. This process would begin by setting out a broad canvass of the phenomena that constitute L-A-P (as outlined in the preceding chapters), and then seek to frame/ guide research to move from exploration, through description and explanation ultimately onto measurement. In such a framing we suggest researchers should embrace the notion of community contributions such as through linking to others' work, filling in gaps, revealing new areas as well as challenging contributions; and all the while being clear on their contribution to L-A-P theory development. In this way we are challenging leadership scholars to practice and model the type of distributed leadership that many propose as the highest form of leadership.

With regard to theory development, the fledgling nature of L-A-P suits the encouragement to embrace broad notions of grounded theory focused on social processes. It need not follow strict protocols and procedures from different epistemological camps, such as: post-positivism (e.g., Corbin & Strauss, 1990), constructionism (Charmaz, 2006), and critical realism (Kempster & Parry, 2011). Rather, it sees the necessity of developing process theories of what is occurring within specific contexts. These explicit contexts are called the substantive context, from which a substantive theory will emerge. Some of the context-based benefits of process theories allow for:

- embracing the recursive and emergent dynamics within L-A-P;
- giving attention to the idiosyncratic nature of contextual practices;
- pointing to antecedent influences; and
- addressing the temporal nature of practices.

Importantly, although process theories can be compared in different contexts, the principle of grounded theory seeks to illuminate social processes in a particular context related to a specific phenomenon. Parry (2002) and Parry and Meindl (2002) have operationalized several grounded theory research projects into questionnaire research and surveyed nationally for the manifestation of these processes across the country. The result is the Social Processes of Leadership (SPL) scale. With questions like "people in my team facilitate the flow of information within the work unit" and "people in my team rely on each other for support," it resonates clearly with the practice notion of leadership. This theory of the social process occurring is offered up for comparison with other contexts. The approach can embrace either or both of the "E" or the "G" approaches to the case method described above. In this way both nomothetic and ideographic approaches can be combined, although sequencing is likely to prove useful in theory development. We illustrate this in Table 12.1.

In essence Table 12.1 seeks to show how an integrated approach focusing on process theorization that builds from the ground up can enable mixed methods to be applied to researching L-A-P. In the spirit of multi-method research, L-A-P studies can and should combine ideographic and nomothetic methods. By way of

TABLE 12.1 An integrated approach to process theorization

Stage	Context	Grounded theory: Level of analysis	Approach
Description	Single	Process of single context	Ideographic
Explanation	Single and multiple	Process common across contexts	Ideographic and nomothetic
Measurement	Multiple	Process common across contexts	Nomothetic

example, Kan and Parry (2004) triangulated data that were holistically analyzed qualitatively by the Grounded Theory method. The data that were analyzed consisted of conventional qualitative interview and focus group data, but were also complemented by survey data using the MLQ. The variation across data provided for a rich explanation of the phenomenon. This research was the subject of Kempster and Parry's (2011) promotion of critical realist grounded theory. As with most social process research, the basic social processes that came from this research resonated with the "practice" notion of leadership. Grounded theory research emphasized the social processes at stake, and importantly, it examined leadership within a substantive context. In light of the experiences and lessons learned from the S-A-P research, the integration of both stages of research, methods and levels of analysis leading to theory generation are most important if L-A-P is to gain broader credibility and make a lasting contribution to leadership studies. Connected with credibility is the need to build out from single cases. Following Bryman's (2006) call, we suggest a holistic approach to research that either adopts multiple methods within an ideographic frame or mixed methods across both nomothetic and ideographic frames in the form of both qualitative and quantitative studies.

Developing a holistic research approach

Why do we need a holistic approach? Fundamentally, this addresses the concern identified in S-A-P research of the very real difficulty of revealing the tacit and subterranean nature of practice. In our introduction we asserted that relatively traditional instruments applied to cross-sectional research, such as interviews and questionnaires, cannot illuminate what's occurring in sufficient depth to get traction on the socio-materiality of situated leadership practices. In-depth approaches such as observation are necessary. However, we suggest that single techniques alone may both reveal and obscure what is occurring. Multiple methods designed to capture aspects in a holistic manner are, therefore, encouraged. In this way, the benefits of triangulation can be demonstrated. Triangulation within a single context is most important to gain the credibility of the proffered process theory.

How do we show that a single case is valuable? At the early stages of developing L-A-P, there is the necessity to take a deep plunge into a specific context to reveal the underlying practices, occurring in the leadership constellation (see, e.g., Raelin, Chapter 1, this volume). Relating back to Table 12.1, detailed descriptions of single cases need to be made. Subsequent research can begin to test emerging theories to see if they are applicable in other contexts and highlight why they may require refinement, but initially depth is all important. For example, without depth how can the antecedents of the socio-materiality be drawn out? Without in-depth multi-methods, how can we know how the socio-materiality has changed through time? Furthermore, longitudinal research is essential to capture the unfolding nature of recursive practices and their effects. Such recursivity may take various forms, and different techniques may illuminate different aspects. Triangulation of in-depth multi-methods provides credibility to the emerging process theorization. As researchers, we should be able to justify the necessity of single case research through ideographic research, *and* get published in the mainstream journals should we so desire! More importantly, we will have obtained a richer grasp of what is transpiring so that both theorists and practitioners can gain in insight.

However, in the process of going deep, it is clearly important to carefully delineate the unit of analysis. In a commentary on undertaking S-A-P research, Johnson, Langley, Melin and Whittington, (2007) guided researchers to consider the importance of choosing and defining the unit of analysis being examined. Johnson *et al.* (2010) highlighted the need to attend to micro details of practice, yet also pointed to the vexed issue of how micro? For example, how would studying what people wore at a particular planning retreat provide support to process theorization? In this case the micro unit would probably need to be extended to a planning retreat and draw on: past episodes of retreats, activities leading up to the retreat, the context of the organization, the purpose of the retreat, histories shaping the relationships, the physical setting for the retreat, organizational political pressures, and, finally, the clothes people wear.

Issues of access and ethical considerations

The nature of the unit of analysis and the depth of research relate to aspects of access and research ethics. The ability to undertake in-depth research through observation of meetings, or even attending a planning retreat, is problematic. Aspects of confidentiality and perceived disruption to organizational activity are understandable concerns. Creating the time available for undertaking research that involves being in an organization for extended periods is difficult for both the researcher and the host organization to manage. Such problematic issues are magnified in longitudinal research. As a validity question, researchers being present in everyday practices impacts the practices observed. So when we speak of multi-methods, there is a pragmatic perspective that needs to be grasped; namely, what is doable? In some respects problematic aspects of obtaining and sustaining access can lead to innovations for data collection, such as video-taping meetings, asking people in a specific leadership relationship to keep blogs, keeping diaries, or capturing critical incidents. Alongside these multi-methods, time-bound observations and informal interviews can be undertaken. Nomothetic research can side-step many of the access issues through the use of questionnaires and structured interviews, but the temptation must be resisted, otherwise the tacit subterranean dimensions of socio-materiality will be overlooked. The issue of multi-methods has already been addressed. Rather than duplicating the research, which is often a problem with multi-methods, the answer might lie in triangulation. Kan and Parry (2004) have already opened up the possibility of using triangulated data. Triangulated data give us a holistic view on practice without the worry of duplicating the research. An example of such an approach is the Social Processes of Leadership (SPL) scale (Parry, 2002), which, ironically, is the nomothetic operationalization of multiple ideographic research projects into social processes of leadership.

Some approaches to reveal L-A-P: Mostly ideographic

The key word here is to "reveal" L-A-P. At this point, we are not proposing to test for L-A-P or to test for links between L-A-P variables. We are looking for what might emerge from a more holistic examination of the phenomenon of L-A-P. With criteria like "emergent" and "holistic," such research will tend to more readily lend itself toward ideographic rather than nomothetic methods. We will examine the following suggested methodologies by way of provocation.

Narrative and conversational analysis

Parry and Hansen (2007) argued that people follow the story as much as they follow the "leader" or even what the titular leaders say. Hence, the narrative becomes important to understanding how people interact in a practice sense in organizational settings. There is no one "narrative analysis," although some people study the narratives that occur in organizations. Very little leadership research has examined the narratives of organizations, let alone the narratives of leadership. Usually, it is done within the context of charismatic or inspirational leadership, and even then, invariably as a vehicle of senior business or political leaders. Consequently, narrative becomes a skill of the leader, rather than a practice that is shared or distributed across the population of a leadership practice. However, the narrative, or the story in the abstract that people follow becomes important, especially within L-A-P.

Parry and Kempster (2014) used aesthetic narrative positivism to study the identities and narratives, indeed the narrative identities, of charismatic leadership. The data for this research came from the lived experience of executives. The implicit theories and the lived experiences of managers were translated into identities and movie genres that seemed to reflect the images that people had in their minds about charismatic leaders whom they had experienced. In so doing, data were both nomothetic and ideographic. The analysis was both qualitative and quantitative. This research can be replicated within the substantive contexts of leadership practices in a range of environments. Narrative and conversational analysis lends itself to a dramaturgical mode of research. Burke's dramaturgical analysis has already been used by Sinha and Jackson (2007) to research leadership practices and processes. There is much scope for this in future L-A-P research.

The Critical Incident Technique (CIT)

The Critical Incident Technique was developed by Flanagan as "a procedure for gathering certain important facts concerning behavior in defined situations" (Flanagan, 1954, p. 335). The epistemological foundations of CIT are "rooted in the phenomenological research tradition," where the purpose is "to enter another's frame of reference so that the person's structures of understanding and interpretive filters can be experienced" (Brookfield, 1990, p. 179–180). It encourages respondents to discuss their own experiences through recalling of incidents, rather than commenting on a specific interview question (Collis & Hussey 2003, p. 165). CIT allows respondents to tell their incidents in a way that could be described as stories or narratives (Bryman & Bell, 2003). Snell sees the value of CIT as stemming from "being grounded in the complexities of actual practice in the field setting, rather than being based on mere espousals and generalisations by respondents" (Snell, 1999, p. 511). As such, it provides a most useful approach to explore leadership practice with its attention on situated activities. It has a sense of a forensic focus "to go straight to the heart of an issue and collect information about what is really being sought" (Easterby-Smith, Thorpe & Jackson, 2008, p. 150). It asks of respondents to recall what happened, how it happened and why? Chell suggests that CIT allows "development of case-based theory grounded in actual critical events" (Chell, 1998, p. 71), reflecting much of the Gioia approach we described earlier. Chell goes on to assert that CIT is a technique of data collection that "enables one to understand the context of action, the tactics, strategies and coping mechanisms adopted and the outcomes, results or consequences of people's actions and the new situation with which they are faced" (1998, p. 62). The CIT has been used successfully in a number of research studies in such areas as health and nursing (Norman, Redfern, Tomalin & Oliver, 1992); education (Brookfield, 1990; Woods, 1993; Preskill, 1996); and extensively in small businesses (Tjosvold & Weicker, 1993; Chell, 1998; Chell & Pittaway, 1998; Cope & Watts, 2000; Kaulio, 2003). Save for the recent work of Gregory (2010), there is limited use of CIT in the field of leadership. We suggest it holds much promise to support grounded process theorizing on L-A-P.

Ethnography and autoethnography

Ethnography is a long-established method for researching sociological and anthropological phenomena in organizational settings. A study of culture is the essence of anthropological research. We appreciate by now that understanding the culture of the leadership setting is central to an understanding of L-A-P. We need to understand "what is going on," to quote a well-worn and oft-repeated mantra. The culture of the leadership context can be researched using Bass and Avolio's (1994) Organizational Description Questionnaire (ODQ). This instrument tests the transformational and transactional characteristics of organizational culture. Now that we can understand the utility of triangulation, if not of multi-method research, we can see that data sourced via the ODQ can complement more traditional ethnographic data sourced ideographically and give a fantastic insight to L-A-P processes and phenomena.

However, there are many types of organizational ethnographies, and many ways of "doing" ethnography. One such method is organizational autoethnography. There is no one clear definition of what autoethnography is. Essentially however, it is a hyper-reflexive modification of ethnography. In one sense, the researcher interviews her or his self. Therefore, autoethnography offers a great potential contribution to organizational research. As explained by Boyle and Parry (2007), the intensely reflexive nature of autoethnography as an autobiographical form of research, allows the organizational researcher to connect intimately the personal to the cultural through a "peeling back" of multiple layers of consciousness, thoughts, feelings, and beliefs. Consequently, autoethnography provides some of the richest and most original data available to organizational researchers, and to L-A-P researchers in particular. We have the chance to delve deeply into the emotional impact of leadership practice on other members as well as on those who provide the leadership.

However, Kempster and Stewart (2010) and Kempster and Iszatt-White (2013) have taken the argument one step forward. They have argued for, and researched and published the method called co-constructed or co-produced auto-ethnography. Rather than expecting one person to be both researcher and sub-ject, this method allows the key person still to be the subject of this powerful hyper-reflexive method, but to have a researcher "looking over their shoulder" and coaxing along the insights and the interpretations. In this way, the embedded knowledge is both generated and conveyed to the reader while being placed within the context of an extant body of knowledge. The researcher is part-mentor and part-coach as the subject interrogates their own experience of L-A-P. Possibly more than any other method, co-constructed autoethnography might provide the richest form of insight into leadership-as-practice.

Activity theory: A method for integrating approaches to researching L-A-P?

The preceding discussion has given emphasis to ideographic approaches that are encouraged to be drawn together into a holistic methodology to obtain the benefits of triangulation. We conclude the chapter by exploring the application of a social theory to L-A-P research, that of cultural historic activity theory (CHAT). This is because the theory holds out much promise for L-A-P as it reflects the key tenets of practice-based theorizing; namely, socio-material emer-gence and recursivity, focus on collective and structured meaning, and activity informed through history and developed through interaction.

We considered a complementary alternative, that of Actor-Network-Theory (ANT). ANT has been considered to be a process-oriented sociology (Law, 1992) that provides an array of concepts, techniques, and principles with which to examine the construction of relationships. Callon (1986) argues that ANT attempts to offer a perspective, complete with its own language, for analyzing the co-evolution of society, technological artifacts, and knowledge of nature. A key tenet in ANT is that the "stuff of the social isn't simply human"(Law, 1992, p. 381), giving equal weight to the agency of human and "non-human" actors. We suggest that ANT could be reinterpreted as a method for exploring L-A-P because of its focus on materiality, relationships, and various actors, and how these elements shape activity and ongoing transformation. However, we have settled on CHAT for the following reasons: first our familiarity with it; second, and importantly, for its attending to the relationship of history and emergent situated practices malleably interacting with materiality to shape orientation to activity; and third, for the overt purpose of process theorizing.

Activity theory as a community of leadership practice

Cultural-historical activity theory (CHAT) has already presented itself as a useful tool for research in organizational studies (Blackler, 1993, 2009), strategic practices (Jarzabkowski, 2003), human resource management practices (Ardichvili, 2003), and organizational and individual learning (Schulz & Geithner, 2010).

Activity theory draws from the work of Vygotsky (1978) who drew on a Marxist assumption of human nature continuously changing through productive activity (Blackler, 1993; Engeström, 2001). Engeström suggested that "the individual [should] no longer be understood without his or her cultural means, and society [should] not be understood without the agency of individuals who use and produce artifacts" (Engeström, 1987, p. 5). Drawing on Takoever and Kempster's (2014) interpretation of CHAT in the context of leadership as practice, activity theory is depicted as system of activity where the triangle of action (object—subject—artifacts) is situated within the context of existing and pre-established rules, community, and division of labor (see Figure 12.1).

Engeström (2001, pp. 136–137) suggests four principles of the activity system that have much resonance to leadership-as-practice:

1. The prime unit of analysis is a "collective, artifact-mediated and object-oriented" activity system.
2. The multi-voiced nature of an activity system where individuals bring their lived experience, values, interests and opinion is such that the activity system "carries multiple layers and strands of history engraved in its artifacts, rules and conventions" (2001, p. 136).
3. The activity systems emerge, develop, and are recursive and transformational over long periods of time, and their evolution needs to be understood through their history of evolving activity, discourses, and materialities.

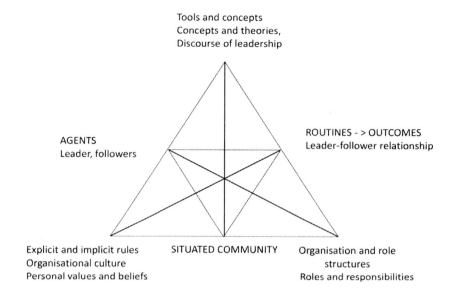

Tools and concepts
Concepts and theories,
Discourse of leadership

AGENTS
Leader, followers

ROUTINES - > OUTCOMES
Leader-follower relationship

Explicit and implicit rules
Organisational culture
Personal values and beliefs

SITUATED COMMUNITY

Organisation and role
structures
Roles and responsibilities

FIGURE 12.1 The activity system of a community of leadership practice

4.   As activities are open systems, every time a new element is adopted (e.g., a new idea, or tool, new structure, new people) it will collide with the old elements and lead to emergence.

We suggest that CHAT can be used as a structure to look holistically at L-A-P. It offers up a framework to guide methodological thinking as well as a research design and data analysis. It can help delineate a unit of analysis. Taking the example of what to wear to an away-day, activity theory would be able to frame the examination. The wearing of clothes to work is a routine set within expectations and assumptions of the community, the leadership relationships, and the nature of the work being undertaken. The change of clothes can be seen as an artifactual change and the resulting impact on the away-day being the object of activity. CHAT asks researchers to look at the changing nature of the object of activity and the various elements impacting the activity and see how they have changed through time. Focusing on the different nature of clothes worn at previous away-days can be explored in-depth as well as other activities and expectations, such as personnel changes from previous years, evolving norms, different expectations and discourses, and so forth. In this way CHAT looks back to explain and provides rich descriptions. It can enable process theorizing of the changes and the recursive patterns related to a particular unit of analysis, but situated in a broader understanding of practice. In this way it can allow for rich theorizing drawn from a unit of analysis. Finally, it is a framework that can helpfully examine both formal and informal aspects of practice and connect both together. For example, how does the small talk in the corridor (Larsson & Lundholm, 2010; Sjostrand, Sandberg & Tyrstrup, 2001) play out in the boardroom?

Conclusion

It is telling but not that unusual for a new research field called L-A-P, about which most of the chapters in this collection speak enthusiastically and persuasively, to offer promise of L-A-P as a "new dawn" for leadership studies. Similarly L-A-P proffers its relative merits compared with the more established mainstream approaches that have predominated during the "long night" of the subject. This chapter has gently and politely suggested that we need to get over the expansive "critique, potential and promise" phase of a new research approach and settle down to the "real" and considerably less exciting but critical task of working out how we are actually going to conduct empirical research that will be robust, insightful, compelling, and influential beyond our own immediate community of research practice.

It is to this somewhat daunting, at times onerous, but necessary task that we have dedicated our attention in this chapter. In this task we have been guided by both the salutary and cautionary track record of the "advanced" guard that the considerably larger and better resourced S-A-P research community has conveniently presented us. After all, shouldn't strategy always prefigure leadership? In light of our smaller yet typically more enthusiastic numbers and our comparatively limited resources, it is imperative that we consider the possibility of practicing the kind of distributed and systemic leadership that we so often actively proselytize yet rarely, with the notable exception of the editing of this currently volume, actually practice.

This quality of leadership should not only extend to members of our immediate research community but to other leadership scholars located in different but related research traditions, as well as the leadership practitioners that we aim to better understand, educate, and transform. Related to this, we wish to close by making a plea for a stronger commitment to conducting empirical work despite its time-consuming, expensive, and uncertain nature rather than yet more conceptual critiques and polemic propositions. By way of incentive, we humbly submit that it will be the cleverly designed and exceptionally well-executed empirical studies that will ultimately win the day for L-A-P research. We hope that those who are sufficiently committed to the L-A-P worldview will be specifically assisted by this chapter and the volume in general. Go forth and practice to your heart's content!

References

Alvesson, M., & Karreman, D. (2000). Varieties of discourse: On the study of organizations through discourse analysis. *Human Relations*, 53(9), 1125–1149.

Ardichvili, A. (2003). Constructing socially situated learning experiences in human resource development: An activity theory perspective. *Human Resource Development International*, 6(5), 310–325.

Balogun, J., & Johnson, G. (2004). Organizational restructuring and middle manager sensemaking. *Academy of Management*, 47(4), 523–549.

Barley, S. R., & Tolbert, P. S. (1997). Institutionalization and structuration: Evidence from observations of CT scanners and the social order of radiology departments. *Administrative Science Quarterly*, 31, 78–108.

Bass, B. M., & Avolio, B. J. (1994). Transformational leadership and organizational culture. *International Journal of Public Administration*, 17(3/4), 541–555.

Bhaskar, R. (1978). *A realist theory of science*. New York: Harvester Press.

Blackler, F. (1993). Knowledge and the theory of organizations: Organizations as activity systems and the reframing of management. *Journal of Management Studies*, 30, 863–884.

Blackler, F. (2009). Cultural-historical activity theory and organization studies. In A. L. Sannino, H. Daniels & K. D. Gutierrez (Eds.), *Learning and expanding with activity theory* (pp. 19–39). New York: Cambridge University Press.

Bourdieu, P. (1977). *Outline of a theory of practice*. Cambridge: Cambridge University Press.

Boyle, M., & Parry, K. W. (2007). Telling the whole story: The case for organizational autoethnography. *Culture & Organization*, 13(3), 185–190.

Brookfield, S. (1990). Using critical incidents to explore learners' assumptions. In J. Mezirow (Ed.), *Fostering critical reflection in adulthood: A guide to transformative and emancipatory learning* (pp. 177–193). San Francisco: Jossey-Bass.

Bryman, A. (2006). Integrating quantitative and qualitative research: How is it done? *Qualitative Research*, 6, 97–113.

Bryman, A., & Bell, E. (2003). *Business research methods*. Oxford: Oxford University Press.

Callon, M. (1986). Some elements of a sociology of translation: Domestication of the scallops and the fisherman of St. Brieuc Bay. In J. Law (Ed.), *Power, action and belief: A new sociology of knowledge?* London: Routledge.

Charmaz, K. (2006). *Constructing grounded theory: A practical guide through qualitative analysis*. London: Sage.

Chell, E. (1998). Critical incident technique. In G. Symon & C. Cassell (Eds.), *Qualitative methods and analysis in organisational research: A practical guide* (2nd edition) (pp. 51–72). London: Sage Publications.

Chell, E., & Pittaway, L. (1998). A study of entrepreneurship in the restaurant and café industry: Exploratory work using the critical incident technique as a methodology. *Hospitality Management*, 17, 23–32.

Chia, R., & MacKay, B. (2007). Post-processual challenges for the emerging strategy as practice perspective: Discovering strategy in the logic of practice. *Human Relations*, 60(1), 217–242.

Collis, J., & Hussey, R. (2003). *Business research: A practical guide for undergraduate and postgraduate students* (2nd edition). Basingstoke: Palgrave Macmillan.

Cope, J., & Watts, G. (2000). Learning by doing: An exploration of experience, critical incidents and reflection in entrepreneurial learning. *International Journal of Entrepreneurial Behaviour and Research*, 6(3), 104–124.

Corbin, J., & Strauss, A. (1990). Grounded theory research: Procedures, canons and evaluative criteria. *Qualitative Sociology*, 13: 3–21.

Easterby-Smith, M., Thorpe, R., & Jackson, P. R. (2008). *Management research* (3rd edition). London: Sage Publications.

Eisenhardt, K. M. (1989). Building theories from case study research. *Academy of Management Review*, 14(4), 532–550.

Engeström, Y. (1987). *Learning by expanding: An activity–theoretical approach to developmental research*. Helsinki: Orienta Konsultit Oy.

Engeström, Y. (2001). Expansive learning at work: Toward an activity theoretical reconceptualization. *Journal of Education and Work*, 14(1), 133–156.

Flanagan, J. C. (1954). The critical incident technique. *Psychological Bulletin*, 51(4), 327–358.

Giddens, A. (1984). *The constitution of society*. Berkeley, CA: University of California Press.

Gioia, D. A. (2004). A renaissance self: Prompting personal and professional revitalisation. In R. E. Stablien & P. J. Frost (Eds.), *Renewing research practice* (pp. 97–114). Stanford, CA: Stanford University

Gregory, S. (2010). *'Purchasing prostitutes in Paris': An exploration of the influence of ethics on the decisions of managers*. PhD Thesis, Lancaster University.

Harrison, D., & Easton, G. (2004). Temporally embedded case comparison in industrial marketing research. In S. Fleetwood & S. Ackroyd (Eds.), *Realism in action in management and organisation studies* (pp. 194–210). London: Routledge.

Jarzabkowski, P. (2003). Strategic practices: An activity theory perspective on continuity and change. *Journal of Management Studies*, 40, 23–55.

Jarzabkowski, P. (2008). Shaping strategy as a structuration process. *Academy of Management Journal*, 51(4), 621–650.

Johnson, G., Langley, A., Melin, L., & Whittington, R. (2007). Introducing the strategy as practice perspective. In G. Johnson, A. Langley, L. Melin & R. Whittington (Eds.), *Strategy as practice: Research directions and resources*. Cambridge: Cambridge University Press.

Johnson, G., Prashantham, S., Floyd, S., & Bourque, N. (2010). The ritualization strategy workshops. *Organization Studies*, 31(12), 1589–1618.

Kan, M., & Parry, K. W. (2004). Identifying paradox: A grounded theory of leadership in overcoming resistance to change. *Leadership Quarterly*, 15(4), 467–491.

Kaplan, S. (2011). Strategy and PowerPoint. An inquiry into the epistemic culture and machinery of strategy making. *Organization Studies*, 22(2), 320–346.

Kaulio, M. A. (2003). Initial conditions or process of development? Critical incidents in the early stages of new ventures. *R&D Management*, 33(2), 165–175.

Kempster, S., & Iszatt-White, M. (2013). Towards co-constructed coaching: Exploring the integration of coaching and co-constructed autoethnography in leadership development. *Management Learning*, 44(4), 319–336.

Kempster, S., & Parry, K. W. (2011). Grounded theory and leadership research: A critical realist perspective. *Leadership Quarterly*, 22(1), 106–120.

Kempster, S., & Stewart, J. (2010). Becoming a leader: A co-produced autoethnographic exploration of situated learning of leadership practice. *Management Learning*, 41(2), 205–219.

Langley, A., & Abdullah, C. (2011). Templates and turns in qualitative studies of strategy and management. *Research Methodology in Strategy and Management*, 6, 201–235.

Larsson, M., & Lundholm, S. E. (2010). Leadership as work-embedded influence: A micro-discursive analysis of an everyday interaction in a bank. *Leadership*, 6(2), 159–182.

Law, J. (1992). Notes on the theory of the actor-network: Ordering, strategy and heterogeneity. *Systems Practice and Action Research*, 5(4), 379–393.

Norman, I. J., Redfern, S. J., Tomalin, D. A., & Oliver, S. (1992). Developing Flanagan's critical incident technique to elicit indicators of high and low quality nursing care from patients and their nurses. *Journal of Advanced Nursing*, 17, 590–600.

Orlikowski, W. J. (2010). Practice in research: Phenomenon perspectives and philosophy. In D. Goldsorkhi, L. Rouleau, D. Seidl & E. Vaara (Eds.), *Strategy as practice* (pp. 23–33). Cambridge: Cambridge University Press.

Parry, K. W. (2002). Hierarchy of Abstraction Modelling (H.A.M.) and the psychometric validation of grounded theory research. *International Journal of Organisational Behaviour*, 5(5), 180–194.

Parry, K. W., & Hansen, H. (2007). The organizational story as leadership. *Leadership*, 3(3), 281–300.

Parry, K. W., & Kempster, S. J. (2014). Love and leadership: Constructing follower narrative identities of charismatic leadership. *Management Learning*, 45(1), 21–38.

Parry, K. W., & Meindl, J. R. (2002). Models, methods and triangulation: Researching the social processes in our societies. In K. W. Parry & J. R. Meindl (Eds.), *Grounding leadership theory and research: Issues, perspectives and methods*, pp. 199–221. (Leadership Horizons series, J. Meindl, series editor). Greenwich, CT: Information Age Publishing.

Pawson, R., & Tilley, N. (1997). *Realistic evaluation*. London: Sage.

Preskill, H. (1996). The use of critical incidents to foster reflection and learning in HRD. *Human Resource Development Quarterly*, 7(4), 335–347.

Reckwitz, A. (2002). Towards a theory of social practices: A development in cultural theorizing. *European Journal of Social Theory*, 5(2), 243–263.

Rouleau, L. (2005). Micro-practices of strategic sensemaking and sensegiving: How middle managers interpret and sell change every day. *Journal of Management Studies*, 42(7), 1413–1441.

Rouleau, L. (2010). Studying strategizing through narratives of practice. In D. Goldsorkhi, L. Rouleau, D. Seidl & E. Vaara (Eds.), *Strategy as practice* (pp. 258–272). Cambridge: Cambridge University Press.

Schatzki, T. R. (2005). The sites of organizations. *Organization Studies*, 26(3), 465–483.

Schatzki, T. R., Knorr Cetina, K. & Von Savigny, E. (2001). *The practice turn in social theory*. London: Routledge.

Schulz, K. P., & Geithner, S. (2010). Individual and organizational development as interplay: An activity oriented approach. *German Journal of Research in Human Resource Management*, 24, 130–151.

Sinha, P., & Jackson, B. (2007). A dramaturgical inquiry into sensemaking and sensegiving processes during an organisational crisis. Paper presented at the Academy of Management Meeting, Philadelphia, PA.

Sjostrand, S. E., Sandberg, J., & Tyrstrup, M. (2001). *Invisible management: Social construction of leadership*. London: Thompson Learning.

Snell, R. S. (1999). Obedience to authority and ethical dilemmas in Hong Kong companies. *Business Ethics Quarterly*, 9(3), 507–526.

Takoever, V., & Kempster, S. (2014). The reappearing practice of leadership. 12th International Studying Leadership Conference, Rome, 12–14 December 2013.

Tjosvold, D., & Weicker, D. (1993). Cooperative and competitive networking by entrepreneurs: A critical incident study. *Journal of Small Business Management*, January, 11–21.

Vygotsky, L. S. (1978). *Mind in society: The development of higher psychological processes*. Cambridge, MA: Harvard University Press.

Woods, P. (1993). *Critical events in teaching and learning*. London: Falmer Press.

Yin, R. K. (1994). *Case study research: Design and methods*. London: Sage

13

DOING LEADERSHIP-AS-PRACTICE DEVELOPMENT

David Denyer and Kim Turnbull James

From leader development to leadership development

Organizations continue to invest substantial time and resources in leadership development. Business schools and other providers offer hundreds of in-house/customized and open enrolment executive programs on leadership as well as executive coaching for leadership. Although framed as *leadership* development, we argue that the focus of these programs is predominantly on improving the capabilities of managers and on nurturing new leaders. Thus, most leadership development is currently *leader* development (Day, 2000; Day, Fleenor, Atwater, Sturm & McKee, 2014). What Bennis (2007) has described as the Leadership Tripod (leader, followers, and shared goals) provides the underpinning for much leadership development activity, which explicitly or implicitly reflects a leader-centered ontology, in other words, focused on the traits, styles, actions, and competencies of the individuals who have been formally assigned leadership roles or have potential to become leaders.

If leadership is understood as residing in people (as leader-centered "entities") or on the dyadic relationship between leader and followers, then it follows that leader development should focus on *who* leaders need to be. Given that the historical basis for leadership has largely been developed through the stories of individual leaders "who grab our attention" (Ladkin, 2010, p. 11) and notions of heroism (Gronn, 2002), leader development programs often focus on developing in (ordinary) people something that some (extraordinary) leaders "have." As such, leader development emphasizes personal growth—values, qualities, and behavioral styles that make for "good" leaders, including profile, status, position, power, and top-down/administrative leadership practices (Uhl-Bien & Marion, 2009). Although learners may explore their personal, historical, and cultural conceptions of leadership on leader development programs, they are rarely invited to challenge these deeply rooted assumptions about leadership or afforded the opportunity to explore new constructions of leadership-as-practice. Walking into many classrooms, one can see the leadership/management distinction written on flip charts and these virtually always state that leaders provide vision or that leadership provides a strategy that cascades through the organization, leaders are inspirational, etc. As these assumptions shape the way organizational members perceive, act, and evaluate leadership, the result of leader development is that individuals often leave programs with the idea that they must be inspiring, visionary, connected to people in transformational relationships, more emotionally intelligent, and so on, rather than being equipped to deal with the complex, collaborative, cross-boundary, adaptive work in which they are increasingly engaged (Heifetz, 2009; Heifetz & Linsky, 2002; Uhl-Bien, Marion & McKelvey, 2007).

Leader development programs are often driven by competency frameworks, specifying an "underlying characteristic of an individual that is causally related to effective or superior performance in a job" (Boyatzis, 1982, p. 21). Consequently, leader development provides individuals with methods for assessing their performance and developmental needs against skills and characteristics that have been pre-determined as leading to success in their organizations, with outcomes being measured, often through 360-degree feedback, in terms of suitability for promotion. Competency thinking tends to be oriented towards "fixing the faults of individuals" so that they can individually perform better as leaders (Turnbull James & Ladkin, 2008). This "fixing" may involve increased self-awareness, skill, and competency enhancement, reflective practice, and depth personal development to unlearn unhelpful attitudes and behaviors to access greater inherent personal potential (Turnbull James & Ladkin, 2008). There are a number of problems with competency thinking, which stem from the processes of reduction and fragmentation (Carroll, Levy & Richmond, 2008). Bolden and Gosling (2006, p. 147) argue that competencies impose structure, predictability, and constraint at the expense of vitality, life, originality, and distinctiveness that is inherent in leadership. Thus, competencies do not provide "a sufficiently rich vocabulary" for the complex, diverse, and connected nature of leadership (2006, p. 158). Competencies based on past experiences and success may not be relevant and appropriate for the future (Carroll et al., 2008), and with competency-based programs people are sent away to learn their leadership (Raelin, 2007), resulting in individuals acting and performing in isolation to others and context (Carroll et al., 2008). Too many leader development initiatives rest on the assumption that one size fits all and that the same group of skills or style of leadership is appropriate regardless of location, organizational culture, or mandate (Carroll et al., 2008). This is problematic, for example, when universal competencies developed in multinational organizations may not fit or be understood by local managers who hold a completely different conception of leadership (Wang, Turnbull James, Denyer & Bailey 2014).

An alternative to leader development is based on our entering a post-heroic leadership age (Fletcher, 2004; Gronn, 2002), whereby leadership is " ... viewed

as a widely dispersed activity which is not necessarily lodged in formally designated leaders … " (Parry & Bryman, 2006, p. 455). Rather than looking for
leadership in people, we need to look for leadership in organizational practice.
The acts of leading can take on multiple directions, transcend formal hierarchies,
and involve multiple actors. From this perspective, actors, regardless of hierarchical position can enact practices that are traditionally viewed as leader behaviors or acts of followership. Rather than focusing on dyadic influence, leadership
can also be viewed as "dynamically changing networks of informally interacting
agents" (Uhl-Bien et al., 2007, p. 302). Leadership occurs in the "space between"
individuals (Lichtenstein et al., 2006). It is a "social influence process through
which emergent coordination (e.g., evolving social order) and change (e.g., new
approaches, values, attitudes, behaviors, ideologies) are constructed and produced" (Uhl-Bien, 2006, p. 667). Consistent with Weick's (1979) call to focus on
organizing processes as opposed to *organizations*, leadership-as-practice addresses the
processes of *leading* rather the characteristics of *leaders*. However, it is not enough
to understand simply what leaders do (Hosking, 1988, p. 147); instead, we must
examine how practices are performed and their meaning expressed by examining
the "influential acts of organizing that contribute to the structuring of interactions and
relationships." L-A-P is concerned with how leadership is produced, how goals are
accomplished, and the practices (acts, activities, and interactions) that are undertaken as actors "get on" (Chia & Holt, 2006, p. 647) with the work of leadership.

Construing leadership-as-practice requires a different approach if there are
multiple actors undertaking leadership practices, working collectively in the situation and over time. Such an approach acknowledges and makes central the fluidity,
interrelatedness, and complexity of leadership. It requires us to bring the "-ship"
back (Grint, 2010) into leadership development. This new leadership development agenda poses significant challenges for those (providers, clients, learners)
whose mind-set is leader development (Carroll et al., 2008). In the following
section we develop a set of principles that can guide but not prescribe what might
be required for developing leadership-as-practice development (LaPD).

Principle 1: Reviewing and renewing the leadership concept held by learners and their organizations

Every organization has embedded unconscious assumptions about leadership.
These assumptions have been termed the *leadership concept* (Probert & Turnbull
James, 2011). In LaPD learners are encouraged to engage in more critical reflection to review and/or renew their shared leadership concept (James & Burgoyne,
2001). LaPD involves learners in addressing collectively Ladkin's ontological
question of "what kind of phenomenon is leadership?" (Ladkin, 2010, p. 3). This
is a fundamental starting point because the way we know leadership " … provides clues about where we might usefully look for it" (Ladkin, 2010, p. 16).
LaPD examines the leadership concept by asking who, or what, is doing

leadership, where and when? Addressing these questions reveals that leadership resides in a dynamic system rather than a single leader. LaPD acknowledges that the work of leadership is distributed far and wide in an organization and that middle- and lower-level employees engage in leadership practices (Spillane, 2004). LaPD recognizes that leadership is a social process that is as much lateral across a range of individuals connected with each other in practice as it is vertical from top managers to a cadre of followers (Pearce & Conger, 2003). LaPD encourages diversity and involves multiple team members in stimulating discussion about differing views of the same processes (Crevani, Lindgren & Packendorff, 2010). LaPD broadens and redefines the *who* is engaged in leadership by exploring leadership in different sites and different organizational roles. Taking the *practice* of leadership as the object of analysis (Gronn, 2002) helps detach leadership from personality (Raelin, 2007) and focuses attention on the interactional and social rather than the rational, objective, and technical aspects of leadership (Carroll *et al.*, 2008). LaPD involves mindset work (Carroll *et al.*, 2008) because underlying assumptions (Alvesson, 1996) and established patterns (Plowman *et al.*, 2007) about the work of leadership are surfaced and questioned, helping learners appreciate that leadership occurs in a complex, indeterminate, and relational world (Carroll *et al.*, 2008).

Principle 2: Surfacing and working with leadership processes, practices, and interactions

LaPD takes a relational orientation and starts with processes and not persons, and views leadership as made in the *doing* (Hosking, 1988). LaPD explores what, where, how, and why leadership work is being organized and accomplished (Raelin, 2003). It focuses on "leadership processes, practices and interactions" (Crevani *et al.*, 2010, p. 78) and normal everyday activities. LaPD examines how these develop over time, the conditions and relations that lead to their emergence, and their effects including the moral, emotional, and relational aspects (Raelin, 2003). LaPD may address "concertive actions," that Gronn (2002) describes as spontaneous collaboration patterns and the intuitive understandings that emerge between colleagues. Thus, LaPD supports what Shotter (2006) calls "witness"-thinking or the meta-competencies to help people understand how to apprehend the immanent conditions when interacting and learning with others in the workplace (Raelin, Chapter 1, this volume).

LaPD explores how leadership functions are performed collectively, such as setting a mission, actualizing goals, sustaining commitment, and responding to changes (Parsons, Bales & Shils, 1953). LaPD also focuses on leadership outcomes such as achieving a collective sense of direction and committing to the adaptive work of the organization and its purpose through alignment of system and processes to support these (Drath *et al.*, 2008). Rather than being directed and controlled, LaPD recognizes that leadership practices often take place "on the hoof" (Chia & Holt, 2006, p. 643), involving "skilled, improvised in-situ coping"

(Chia, 2004, p. 33), "skilled improvisations" (Weick, 1996), "practical coping" (Chia & Holt, 2006), and dialogue and collaborative learning (Raelin, 2008). LaPD also pays attention to leadership practices in "ordinary work" and "ordinary habits" (Carroll *et al.*, 2008, p. 369), "the everyday" (de Certeau, 1984), "unheroic work" (Whittington, 1996, p. 734), "mundane activities" (Alvesson & Sveningsson, 2003a, p. 1435) and "nitty-gritty details" (Chia, 2004, p. 29) of leadership work.

The focus of LaPD is on how and to what extent these practices are performed as much as by who performs them (Raelin, 2007). LaPD focuses on the language used to convey these interactions to generate a deeper understanding of leadership in context. It is especially important to identify not only what actions are taken, but to explore with learners why in some situations practices manifest as "extra-ordinarized" leadership practices (Alvesson & Sveningsson, 2003a, p. 1435), whereas in others the claimed characteristics of leadership seemingly dissolve and disappear (Alvesson & Sveningsson, 2003b).

Principle 3: Working in the learners' context on their organizational problems and adaptive challenges

LaPD acknowledges the complexity of the context in which leadership must function and adapt (Uhl-Bien *et al.*, 2007). The relationship between leadership and context is not static, but is constantly shifting and changing (Cilliers, 1998). Leadership is "embedded in a complex interplay of numerous interacting forces" (Uhl-Bien *et al.*, 2007, p. 302). Context is not "an antecedent, mediator, or moderator variable; rather, it is the ambiance that spawns a given system's dynamic" (Uhl-Bien & Marion, 2007, p. 187). Therefore, LaPD is deeply embedded and originates out of the context and the challenges that people in the organization face *collectively*. LaPD focuses on "social sites in which events, entities, and meaning help compose one another" (Schatzki, 2005, p. 480). LaPD explores leadership work as a "lived" experience rather than a "reported" experience (Samra-Fredericks, 2003). Rather than learning about leadership, LaPD focuses on "managers' real problems" (Whittington, 2004, p. 62) and explores "the scene of everyday action" (Chia, 2004, p. 30). LaPD is experiential, interactive, situated, embodied, sustained, and involves relational activities that create a new kind of engagement with others and the world. Certain sites may be more conducive than others for LaPD. For example, LaPD might engage learners in addressing wicked problems (Grint, 2005), adaptive challenges (Heifetz 1994), or complex, collaborative, cross-boundary work (Uhl-Bien *et al.*, 2007), which may offer the opportunity to uncover the essential work of leadership. In responding to complex challenges, learners need to think about leadership as interventions in a system and practices that produce adaptive capability. Complex adaptive challenges focus attention on roles, relations, and practices in a specific organizational context, and require conversations and learning with people who share that context. In LaPD change is not achieved through the implementation of a known process (Kotter, 1996), but requires the disruption of existing patterns and experimentation to enable emergent futures (Plowman & Duchon, 2008). As noted earlier, leadership may also emerge in mundane, everyday social actions, especially in instances that call for a change in direction.

LaPD involves asking the right questions not providing the right answers (Grint, 2005; Heifetz, 1994) and creating the conditions for the emergence of innovative and creative responses to problems in the face of adaptive needs of the organization (Heifetz & Laurie, 1997). This involves directing attention to the issues (Heifetz, 1994), "reading" complex dynamics and seeing interconnections, injecting ideas and information, fostering interconnectivity and creating linkages (Uhl-Bien *et al.*, 2007), as well as "counter-moves, altered or new strategies, learning and new knowledge, work-around changes, new allies, and new technologies" (Uhl-Bien *et al.*, 2007, p. 303). These practices constitute leadership because they involve "intentional, local acts of influence to create change to enhance the viability of the organization" (Uhl-Bien & Marion, 2007, p. 638). Adaptive work, generates "small 't' transformational change" (Heifetz & Laurie, 1999, p. 11) through a combination of reflection (internalizing) and mobilization (engaging relationally and socially). Van Velsor and McCauley (2004) echo the need for interdependence and learning together, suggesting that interdependent groups often need to identify emerging organizational problems and pull together across boundaries to work on shared challenges. LaPD works with the tensions and paradox created by the entanglement of both adaptive and administrative leadership practices (Uhl-Bien & Marion, 2007). This may mean understanding what kind of enabling practices are required through sense-making of the current leadership balance between administrative and adaptive leadership and of the "entanglement" of administrative and adaptive leadership in the organization, the historical positioning of the organization and its capabilities (Uhl-Bien, 2006).

Principle 4: Working with the emotional and political dynamics of leadership in the system

Although a degree of tension is needed to provoke change, any heightened emotionality needs to be contained within productive ranges (Krantz, 2001) to create the conditions for adaptive responses (Heifetz & Linsky, 2002). Organizational systems create tensions and anxiety when those with authority acknowledge that they do not have the answers (Grint, 2005), when staff begin to appreciate that the solution to problems is going to take a long time to construct and will require constant effort to maintain (Grint, 2005). If unaddressed in LaPD, anxiety can occur in the "not knowing," as the political dynamics of power, influence, and competition are unleashed. As such, leadership is often so difficult to achieve that even where learners consider it appropriate and even necessary, they may be very unwilling to attempt it (Grint, 2005). In LaPD support is given to people working collectively with these organization dynamics.

A systems psychodynamics approach provides one framework for exploring how the leadership practices in the organization can generate high levels of anxiety and how they can be reduced. It focuses on how these dynamics impact some groups or individuals, and how the emotional and political dynamics in the system as a whole need to be addressed if better practices are to be established and maintained. The advantage of the systems psychodynamic approach is that the learning is about the self in role and in relation to the system. This allows a wider and deeper view to focus on what is involved in the problem and how it can be solved (Armstrong, 2005; Gould, Stapley & Stein, 2001; Huffington, 2006). LaPD theorizes individuals in ways akin to Fletcher's (2004) "self-in relation." From this perspective individuals are linked to one another "into an interdependent, symbolic, tacit, unconscious, and collusive nexus in which their interactions and shared fantasies and phantasies create and represent as one the group-as-a-whole" (Wells, 1985, p. 114). A systems psychodynamic perspective allows for the examination of fine-grained group dynamics and offers a useful approach to understanding what happens in complex systems when traditional leadership is less dominant (Fitzsimons, Turnbull James & Denyer, 2011). Furthermore, the systems psychodynamic tradition has an established educational methodology, Group Relations, which can be introduced into management programs (James, Jarrett & Neumann, 1998). This learning methodology is experiential and allows learners to learn about the unconscious emotional dynamics present in groups and organizations.

LaPD recognizes that politics are inherent in organizational life as organizations are pluralist involving many different interest groups (Arroba & James, 2005; Baddeley & James, 1987). As the assumptions about the tight control of traditional leadership are loosened and the importance of collective action to shape and disrupt organizational agenda is heightened, the focus on politics in LaPD becomes even more essential. Leadership has to be achieved without the politicking and Machiavellian politics people imagine being essential while incorporating the natural political dynamics that occur as people interact to achieve individual and mutual goals. LaPD emphasizes integrity and provides a practical framework to develop political wisdom. Baddeley and James (1987) suggest two essential practices: *Reading* the context, which can be done collectively as well as individually, and *Carrying* personal concerns so that the focus can be on organizational challenges and ways of intervening to nudge change by bringing in dissident or less heard voices, networking, and using collaborative effort.

Doing LaPD: Collaborative leadership learning groups (CLLGs)

We do not provide the four LaPD principles as a blueprint for all leadership development activity. Neither do we believe that they should apply to every leadership-learning event. This is because it may prove impossible to engage all four principles depending on the depth, length and brief for the leadership development work. For example, a short program may not be able to move beyond reviewing and renewing the leadership concept held by learners and their organizations (principle 1), without focusing attention on leadership processes, practices, and interactions, embedding learning in context by addressing directly emergent organizational challenges, and helping learners cope with the emotional and political dynamics of leadership. However, some leadership development interventions can be designed in a way that provides learners with the experience of working collaboratively on organizational challenges in ways that allow for the emergence of leadership processes, practices, and interactions, and confronting learners with the emotional and political dynamics of leadership.

Collaborative leadership learning groups (CLLGs) are particularly suited to addressing all four LaPD principles. Whereas action learning groups tend to focus primarily on the organizational challenge and individual or group learning about the organizational challenge, in CCLGs the focus is on learning about collaboration and shared leadership practices. In CLLGs solving the problem is a by-product of effective collective action. CLLGs are anchored in practice, bringing together learners who can identify and work together on the challenges they face collectively. Some general learning objectives for the program may be described to help scope and focus the intervention but the precise learning outcomes cannot be predetermined because learners decide collectively on what they hope to accomplish to achieve their mission. LaPD becomes a mechanism for the collaborative identification, formulation, and resolution of shared organizational learning needs. Learners commit to one another's learning and are mutually accountable for the learning outcomes. The program experience is a valuable learning environment in which many aspects of organizational learning can be incorporated through reflection on the experience as it unfolds.

Collaborative leadership learning groups create what Heifetz and Laurie (1997) refer to as a "holding environment," a "safe" site to explore the tensions, difficult experiences, and emotions involved in leadership. Learners attempting to work together can engage in a process to address a complex problem and are required to cope with political power plays or anxieties about the task. The role of the tutors is critical in LaPD because they raise appropriate questions, highlight issues, supply relevant materials, and pay careful attention to the dynamics of the group when they meet. LaPD is *not* "content/theory free" and is not just purely sense-making and reflection on collective participant experiences, but introduces an element of inquiry whereby learners and tutors collectively search for potential solutions to the problem or issue to be addressed. Accessing relevant information may take place through reviews of existing literature, expert inputs, or visits to organizations with a good reputation in the field. Thus, CLLGs achieve learning by integrating three forms of knowledge (James, Mann & Creasy, 2007):

1.   knowledge that the learners themselves bring, their accumulated understanding, and insights and leadership challenges from prior experience;

2.   practical and theoretical public knowledge, which might serve to frame, support, illuminate, or challenge participants' assumptions and thinking;
3.   knowledge that is collaboratively constructed or developed through the practices, processes, and interactions in the program.

A particularly powerful form of LaPD encourages learners to facilitate the formation of collaborative leadership learning groups in their organization to help address the organizational issue while helping the learners appreciate how to help develop a learning environment for others. Learners on the program receive support from tutors, but in parallel they work to facilitate CLLGs in their own organizations thereby creating distributed leadership patterns and leading learning (Turnbull James, Mann & Creasy, 2007). Figure 13.1 shows how LaPD can be achieved through CLLGs.

Example of LaPD 1: Program for a major housing association in the UK

We turn next to a description of several examples of LaPD in action. The first case takes place in a major housing association in the UK (Turnbull James, 2011). The start point was typical of most requests to tender: the specification was very

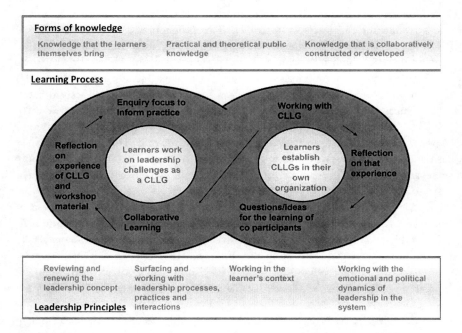

FIGURE 13.1 Leadership-as-practice development and collaborative leadership learning groups

traditional, *leader* development. However, the Executive Group, with support from the tutor team, recognized that they needed solutions to real organizational challenges and that they needed simultaneously to shift the culture and re-think how they did business, rather than simply up-skill their managers. The aims emerged as the generation of collaborative and shared leadership to create more engagement and innovation within the organization. This purpose coalesced as the executive top team realized that there was only a limited amount of change that they could personally direct and that traditional top-down leadership was not the approach that would work in their very challenging competitive context. The tutor team helped the organization to realize that what they proposed entailed deep levels of collaboration requiring social and emotional fluency. The program was designed to combine development work tailored to this purpose while at the same time providing a hard business edge. In this case collaborative leadership learning groups were chosen as the mechanism for learning about and establishing shared leadership practices while changing a traditional hierarchical organization.

The program was reframed as the establishment of a Leadership Academy, signaling that it was not just "a course." It was designed initially as a three-day residential module in which learners would work in collaborative learning groups and engage in learning events that would enhance their capacity for interacting with each other to learn collaborative leadership practices. The residential module used a variety of methods from depth psychology, music, and theatre, and a safe environment was established to facilitate deep learning. Seeded into the module were the organizational projects around which learners were to collaborate. The projects were carefully set up to be related to the organization's five-year strategic plan and to bring people from different parts of the organization to work together. The initial workshop was followed by three facilitated one-day events so that learners could work in their collaborative leadership learning groups. Where this differs from commonly used projects and action learning sets in leader development is that the focus of the program, supported by the organization's Executive Group, was *how to do collaborative work and establish collaborative leadership practices*. The project outcomes were regarded as a by-product of the group learning work.

The early phases of the program were challenging. Initially, the Executive Group itself had to work out how the culture needed to change to support collaborative working in the organization. There was a critical moment when the Executive Group suddenly realized that they were central to the success of the program (not as is often the case, where in many customized programs the Executive Group's role is to pay the bill and assess the program outputs). They realized that *they* would to have to let go and give learners on the program space to do more. *They* would have to adapt their leadership practices and do it differently if this was going to be a reality for the whole organization. Consequently, the Executive Group was the first cohort selected for the program, followed by the top 20 senior managers, then the rest of the management group in subsequent cohorts (targeted at the top 250 out of about 1200 in the organization). Each cohort had a sponsor who was part of the Executive Group. The sponsor conducted brief-ings, spent a day during their residential with the cohort, and then followed the group all the way through. Each project (four collaborative learning groups per cohort) had a project sponsor whose role was *to model collaborative and shared lea-dership practices for their project group*. The commitment of the CEO was absolutely crucial and remained so for the life of the Academy, lasting several years.

The learning from the first three cohorts was published and distributed in the organization. As the program evolved and much project work relating to funda-mental strategy had already been done, rather than engage in less important pro-jects, later cohorts worked on embedding shared and distributed leadership into their part of the organization. Lessons were also published for internal circulation. The outputs were evidence of the impact the program had on the organization as a whole. In addition, a range of evaluation methods were used, including an evaluation at the end of the three-day workshop, facilitated meetings, exchanges with managers yet to attend but observers of others' change, review meetings, and a "House Values" exercise with 300 staff, where the meaning of shared and collaborative leadership for them was explored. Over a year after the pro-gram, ten Leadership Academy "graduates" were developed through a formal process to become CLLG facilitators themselves. A further 100 team leaders attended a two-day program designed to increase their capability in colla-borative learning practices. The focus of the selected projects was innovation and enhancing the organization's reputation as a thought leader in its Sector.

Example of LaPD 2: A global services company

The second case is an ongoing program with a services company working in 32 countries across Europe, Asia, and the Americas, with plans to expand its Asian market. The company has grown through acquisition and has local companies owned by the parent company in the EU, working successfully all over the world. However, as it is headquartered in the EU, all these countries need to comply with corporate governance rules emanating from the parent company home country and with the banking and financial rules and compliance require-ments (the client also provides financial services), which have become more rig-orous in the EU and must now be applied to the local organization. It is a classic problem for international organizations that must think and act both locally and globally. The local companies are very entrepreneurial which is why they have been acquired. They have global clients who do not want local creative solutions but want the same service wherever they operate. To stay alive, the local orga-nizations need to be adaptive to local competition. One example of the tensions this creates is in the area of pricing, where in some regions charging European prices would put them out of business. Another key leadership challenge is gen-erational: they have traditional long-serving executives, particularly in the head-quarters, whose experience and expertise are crucial but who are failing to keep up with digital aspects of the business and who have traditional ideas regarding the exercise of leadership. The company is concerned that it will not retain the younger, entrepreneurial managers it needs for the future.

The request to tender for a leadership program was refreshingly open: they asked for a creative approach that would embrace multiple learning methods including project work. Although providing a list of desired outcomes, there was no specification of how to achieve these. The drive behind the program was to bring people together to make sense of real issues, develop learning around these in the classroom, and bring in expertise from faculty/experts who could help them learn about latest thought leadership specifically in relation to these issues. The design that emerged incorporated residential modules that enabled cohorts to come from around the globe to work together face-to-face, as well as networked online learning and collaborative leadership learning groups. The networked learning element was a key feature and allowed people from across the organization to come together for significant conversations about the organizational strategy, about understanding their context in terms of economic and social trends, and about creating an understanding of how business needs to be done differently as complexity increases. Learning began before the face-to-face sessions through dedicated webinars linking faculty, executives, and learners, and online conversation spaces and materials were made available through the provider's Knowledge Interchange—an extensive library of videos, exercises, readings, e-learning modules, expert inputs, and executive interviews, which had been developed over more than a decade. Learners identified their own personal preferences and assumptions by completing online questionnaires that were used to identify and raise self-awareness of what strengths they bring to new ways of working and what they might need to be aware of in themselves if they are to embrace collaborative working practices. Each cohort had "business sponsors" (higher level senior executives) whose role was to raise the visibility and profile of the program outputs and the learners—a powerful incentive for the learners.

The first residential module focuses on developing collaborative practices within the program's project teams and challenging and extending learners' existing leadership concepts. Learners work experientially on dialogue and inquiry, applying these to their group work. They work on contracting in the group to engage in collaborative practices and collective learning and explore how this may be counter-cultural either organizationally or nationally, and the implications for them of working in this new way. During this module they work face-to-face with their executive coach. The coaches are selected because they bring an organizational context approach (this is explored more extensively in the executive coaching section below). This means they work from the perspective of what is going on in the organization that impacts how people take up their roles, work together, or manage the boundaries around the work they are doing.

The residential is followed by project work in regional groups (to take account of time zones and travel for online and face-to face-activity) on key strategic imperatives for the business over a six-month period. For this they receive further executive coaching and group consultation from their executive coach. The executive coach works with all members of the group, observing the group in action because their remit is to help the group and its members learn to adopt new collaborative leadership and learning practices, not just personal growth. The strategic projects stretch learners as they develop thought leadership for the organization. The project outputs, in terms of business proposals or changes, are considered a by-product or added bonus of learning about collaborative leadership practices.

Doing LaPD: Executive coaching

Executive coaching is increasingly used in conjunction with open or customized executive development programs or as a stand-alone leadership development process. In the example of LaPD 2 above, coaching was an important element of a broader LaPD program and was used as a vehicle for managing and containing new uncertainties and anxieties that emerge through exposure to the project, through the requirement to develop new leadership practices, and through the extended personal exposure to headquarters senior executives. The focus of the coaching is very much on the business system and the dynamics emerging as change unfolds and on how individuals experience these and relate to the collective learning experience. For example, learners confront resistance and group dynamics that might undermine desired change, how they can contribute to the projects, and how they can take this back to their home workplace. The focus is not on personal development but in developing in role and in context.

Stand-alone executive coaching can also be a powerful approach to LaPD. The term, executive coaching, covers a wide range of methods, approaches, and underlying assumptions, although these are not always made explicit either in the matching of coach and coachee or in executive coaching contracts. The importance of making these explicit for the purposes of leadership development can be demonstrated by a piece in *The Huffington Post* (La Bier, 16/8/13), which describes a Stanford Business School survey that found that two-thirds of CEOs want coaching but do not seek it. The danger is that often CEOs think executive coaching is "remedial" but it can also increase self-awareness as a basis for leadership effectiveness. This is a popular conception but may be insufficient given the kind of leadership practices we are arguing need to be developed today.

Although executives often engage executive coaches upon a new appointment to help them take up their new roles, and expect to learn skills and to gain personal growth (i.e., leader development) with their coaching work, many also engage a coach when there are challenges that seem intractable or inexplicable. For example, they may be well established in a role and something goes wrong, or they find that a political approach they developed for a previous political situation is no longer effective. Executive coaching, more obviously than many other types of leadership development interventions, works in context and with real workplace challenges. However, LaPD makes several requirements of coaching that are less familiar. The coach must be able to challenge the idea that the problem to be addressed in the coaching sessions is the coachee. The coach must also understand that it is not personal emotional sensitivity alone that is required in their coaching role but an ability to relate the issues the client brings to the emotional and political dynamics operating in the wider organizational system. Thus the coaching work is understood as triadic rather than dyadic—the coach, the coachee, and the organization are all "present" in the room (Armstrong, 2005; Campbell & Huffington, 2008). A further challenge for executive coaching is that often the coachee is "left" with the coach "to sort out" and return "fixed" to the system. This was particularly important in the example of executive coaching for the LaPD to be described in the example below where the coach needed to manage the relationship with the sponsor of coaching carefully, in this case the Director, avoiding collusion with the sponsor's diagnosis of the problem and managing feedback about the outcomes of the coaching work.

Example of LaPD 3: Coaching for a senior executive team member

This is a composite case in order to fully preserve the anonymity of the individuals concerned. The organization was a global professional services firm and gave director-level roles only to those in the required grade (a personal not job grade). This meant that Directors were often in charge of functions of which they had little prior experience and so needed to rely very heavily on their team members' expertise. Team members were themselves senior executives with international responsibilities and reputations as experts. Directors needed to feel that they were well briefed and that they could rely on team members to make sure that, as Director, they did not make a legal or policy blunder that would have external and internal repercussions. The coachee was one team member in such a Directorate. The impetus for coaching arose from a critical appraisal with the Director. Some criticisms, although legitimate, were surprising and more typical of someone at a junior level in the organization and appeared on the surface to be quite trivial. However, these led the boss to question this team member's leadership capability.

The organizational problems could be seen from different perspectives, for example failure to attend a monthly team meeting seen from the Director's viewpoint as a lack of commitment to the team. From the coachee's point of view, this was explained by being on an important business trip relevant to his organizational role. Other complaints seemed more personal. For example, failure to be able to get weekend cover for eldercare to attend a "voluntary" weekend team building event in another country was described as though the boss thought the coachee should have left a vulnerable person to fend for himself. Six months later, the boss still viewed it as evidence of lack of team commitment. It seemed important to the coach to get below the surface criticisms and understand what was going on in relation to the team as a system, rather than just in the boss/coachee relationship or in terms of personal leader development for the coachee.

Although some of the complaints appeared trivial, the coach also repeatedly offered data that emerged during the coaching sessions about the legitimacy of other complaints. Because of the perceived unfairness of at least some of the complaints, the coachee was worrying about them in detail rather than treating them as a potential source of data to explore his leadership practice and the dynamics operating in the team. It became clear that some kind of psychological splitting was occurring: the boss had become "all bad" to the coachee and the coachee was "all bad" to the boss. The coachee found it hard to look at the whole feedback (good and bad) or to explore how this "all good/all bad" dynamic also reflected the dynamics of the team. The boss appeared to have "favorite children" among the direct reports, while simultaneously putting emphasis on the idea of a team and collaborative working practices. Some team members were clearly emerging as perceived "all good" team members. They kept him informed, made him look on top of things, never left him to deal with queries from other Directors at his level about activities he was unaware of or could not answer. The collaborative practices required for leadership in this team were obvious to the external coach, but the anxieties operating in a system in which the Director's personal, hierarchical "leader as out in front" concept was challenged and this created complex authority relations. By focusing on dyads (as if the team were made up of a number of good or bad one-to-one relationships rather than group relations), he found a scapegoat and further exacerbated the natural difficulties of embracing collective team practices.

One aspect of collaborative, shared, and distributed leadership that is seldom addressed is the nature of lateral relations in hierarchical institutions. An understanding of these dynamics has something to offer LaPD beyond those in traditional organizational structures. One lens through which to think about lateral relationships is that of familial sibling relationships. Indeed, it could be argued that leadership comes as much from lateral as vertical processes in organizations (Armstrong, James & Huffington, 2004). This is explored by Huffington and Miller (2008) and Mitchell (2003), who argue that understanding sibling dynamics is central to understanding the challenges and experiences that moving to new leadership practices engenders. This was a fruitful lens for coaching in this case and suggested some of the team dynamics that needed to be addressed and which were not amenable to working with leader competences or personal development.

Discussion

Aren't we already doing LaPD?

Traditional leader development may involve something that resembles or claims to be LaPD. However, while these interventions may support learning from different ontological assumptions and produce different learning outcomes (Raelin, 2006), they are often used within a traditional leader development agenda without deep consideration for the different learning that is required for LaPD. What can be provided in *any* leader development program can be extremely innovative and involve activities such as retreats, outdoor development activities, using methods originating from theatre, depth psychology, psychometrics, experiential learning, traditional case studies and lectures, simulations, arts-based methods, shadowing executives, action learning groups, stretch assignments and high profile projects, executive coaching and mentoring. Yet, facilitators and tutors on leader development programs are often professionally deeply immersed in personal transformation processes. The result is often an unhelpful melding of perspectives and approaches. For example, we have heard tutors say that they are going to teach a class about adaptive leadership *style*. We are also continually frustrated by program designers who place LaPD sessions immediately after leader development sessions that might involve something like a psychometric test. It is unreasonable to expect learners to be able to switch rapidly between vastly different perspectives on leadership.

There are also a number of learning activities that are regularly used in traditional leader development programs that address organizational challenges that learners work on collectively. The program might involve collective activity, but in leader development it would be used to identify the development needs of learners by providing personal feedback on how individuals assumed the leader role. Action learning, stretch assignments and strategic projects, executive coaching, inter-modular application work, for example, all address real-life challenges that positional leaders face in the organization, yet the focus is usually on producing leaders who can better resolve these challenges once they return to work. Traditional leader development programs, even those that include activities such as international assignments, coaching and/or mentoring, rarely question "what is leadership" except through an individual and frequently competency-based lens. Learners may *learn about* collaborative action and collective learning through these processes, but it is not often explicit how this relates to the concept of leadership that people carry away from the program or how this changes the leadership culture and practices of the organization as a whole.

In traditional leader development the teacher, as an expert, is often assumed to have knowledge to offer that is to be transferred to the mind of the learner. The focus is on the transfer of learning (learn now and apply later)—working with problems from the workplace during the program and taking that work back to the workplace to work with others who share the problem but are not on the program. Traditional leader development may also focus on the leadership practices required to produce desired outcomes, yet the agenda usually results in the collation and sharing of a prescribed set of actions, that is it slips into the styles/competency trap. As argued earlier, LaPD is not a question of deliberately developing a leader style or acquiring a set of generalized capabilities that can be transmitted from one individual to another.

Is it time to throw out the baby and the bathwater?

Given that many development programs fail to produce managers with the right capabilities to exploit business international opportunities (Ghemawat, 2012) and cope with the complex, collaborative, cross-boundary, adaptive work in which they are increasingly engaged (Uhl-Bien *et al.*, 2007), is it time to abandon leader development for LaPD?

There are two key reasons why we warn against dismissing entirely the notion of leader. First, while LaPD broadens and redefines the *who* is engaged in leadership and focuses attention on the interactional and social, *individuals* are sent to leadership development programs and these individuals often do need to develop skills such as self-awareness and a clearer understanding of their personality to appreciate how they can better relate to others and work effectively in the system. Learners on leadership development programs may also have formal leadership positions and roles that cannot be dismissed. In leadership development, learners require significant individual support to manage the mindset shift (Carroll *et al.*, 2008) involved in renewing their leadership concept (Probert & Turnbull James, 2011) and to manage expectations projected onto them relating to traditional notions of leader. Changing the leadership concept heightens feelings of vulnerability, simultaneously removing the apparent, if illusory, protection afforded by more traditional, hierarchical structures. Leadership development also needs to work with the emotional challenges entailed when learners exercise their own authority on a wider organizational front to address organizational challenges (Huffington, James & Armstrong,, 2004). In short, a move away from traditional leadership has emotional costs (Huffington *et al.*, 2004) that need to be recognized and worked through at an individual level to embed new leadership practices.

Second, the purpose of any leadership development program is carefully negotiated over time between the provider organization and the client. Where program purchase is seen as a procurement process, LaPD may be hard to deliver because the brief is too often specified around competencies. The provider has a context that influences what type of learning opportunity it can offer, for example expectations of market and the purchaser's previous encounters with the provider. The purchaser's context also influences what can be provided, such as their assumptions about what is needed (client and participant may not be same people), their history and current situation, the type of leadership development to which they are accustomed, the sponsor and funding arrangements for the learning. The four principles offered in this chapter may guide the negotiation of the learning design with purchasers but our experience is that they rarely share an understanding of some of the new thinking on leadership, and it is often extremely difficult to challenge and shape deeply held assumptions about leadership during a procurement process.

Existing LaPD programs also can be derailed in cases where the tutor team fails to constantly address the sponsors and other stakeholders' traditional notions of leader and leader development. In example LaPD 2 above, the headquarters' sponsors of the program wanted to find comfort in the familiar process of structuring and specifying how things will work precisely in the program and what they can expect to get in return. Having agreed to a collaborative process with many emergent features, the sponsors felt the need to turn it back into a more traditional program. The provider program directors had to work very carefully with this emotional and highly political dynamic, respecting the discomfort and anxiety the program raises for the organization's sponsors. While this is an important part of the organization's learning, navigating these dynamics requires experienced and skilled consultants as client managers and program directors, who are able to work with organizational learning rather than just program design.

Conclusion

In this chapter we have offered a critique of traditional leader development and competency thinking, and argue that LaPD requires a significant departure from traditional approaches to leader development offered by providers such as business schools. We have proposed four principles for LaPD that are consistent with the perspective that leadership is co-constructed through acts, activities, and interactions embedded within the situation in which it takes place. We suggest that collaborative leadership learning groups and executive coaching can support LaPD. The three case examples of LaPD show how these practices inform pedagogy, learning design, and interactions with learners. We argue that LaPD creates tensions between the expectations held by clients and learners about "desirable" leader traits, styles, and competencies, and the leadership practices required to cope with the complex, collaborative, cross-boundary, adaptive work in which they are increasingly engaged. We highlight the critical role played by program tutors and program directors who need to understand how to support learning from a leadership-as-practice (L-A-P) perspective with its different ontological assumptions and learning outcomes, and manage the emotional and highly political dynamics LaPD programs raise for both learners and sponsors.

Acknowledgements

Our thanks go to our colleagues, Dr. Hilary Harris, Lester Coupland, and Jayne Brown who generously shared their experiences as Executive Development

Directors and their program designs with us, providing case study detail that elaborates the approaches described in the chapter. Many thanks also go to Clare Huffington: the Executive Coaching section draws on previously co-authored papers, her conference paper on sibling dynamics co-authored with Sarah Miller, and the case example was developed from conversations we have held over an extended period reflecting on our own coaching experience to inform and develop our own coaching practices.

References

Alvesson, M. (1996). Leadership studies: From procedure and abstraction to reflexivity and situation. *Leadership Quarterly*, 7(4), 455–485.

Alvesson, M., & Sveningsson, S. (2003a). Managers doing leadership: The extra-ordinarization of the mundane. *Human Relations*, 56(12), 1435–1459.

Alvesson, M., & Sveningsson, S. (2003b). The great disappearing act: Difficulties in doing "leadership". *Leadership Quarterly*, 14(3), 359–381.

Armstrong, D. (2005). *Organization in the mind: Psychoanalysis, group relations and organisational consultancy*. London: Karnac Books.

Armstrong, D., James, K., & Huffington, C. (2004). The emotional costs of distributed leadership. In C. Huffington, D. Armstrong, W. Halton, L. Hoyle, & J. Pooley (Eds.), *Working below the surface: The emotional life of contemporary organisations*. London: Karnac.

Arroba, T., & James, K. (2005). Reading and carrying: A framework for learning about emotion and emotionality in organisational systems as a core aspect of leadership development. *Management Learning*, 36(3), 299–316.

Baddeley, S., & James, K. (1987). Owl, fox, donkey, sheep: Political skills for managers. *Management Education and Development*, 18(Spring), 3–19.

Bennis, W. G. (2007). The challenges of leadership in the modern world: An introduction to the special issue. *American Psychologist*, 62(1), 2–5.

Bolden, R., & Gosling, J. (2006). Leadership competencies: Time to change the tune? *Leadership*, 2(2), 147–163.

Boyatzis, R. E. (1982). *The competent manager: A mode for effective performance*. New York: John Wiley and Sons.

Campbell, D., & Huffington, C. (2008). *Organizations connected: A handbook of systemic consultation*. London: Karnac Books.

Carroll, B., Levy, L., & Richmond, D. (2008). Leadership as practice: Challenging the competency paradigm. *Leadership*, 4(4), 363–379.

Chia, R. (2004). Strategy-as-practice: Reflections on the research agenda. *European Management Review*, 1, 29–34.

Chia, R., & Holt, R. (2006). Strategy as practical coping: A Heideggerian perspective. *Organization Studies*, 27(5): 635–655.

Cilliers, P. (1998). *Complexity and postmodernism: Understanding complex systems*. London: Routledge.

Crevani, L., Lindgren, M., & Packendorff, J. (2010). Leadership, not leaders: On the study of leadership as practices and interactions. *Scandinavian Journal of Management*, 26(1), 77–86.

Day, D. V. (2000). Leadership development: A review in context. *Leadership Quarterly*, 11(4), 581–613.

Day, D. V., Fleenor, J. W., Atwater, L. E., Sturm, R. E., & McKee, R. A. (2014). Advances in leader and leadership development: A review of 25 years of research and theory. *Leadership Quarterly*, 25(1), 63–82.

de Certeau, M. (1984). *The practice of everyday life*. Berkeley, CA: University of California Press.

Drath, W. H., McCauley, C. J., Palus, C. J., Van Velsor, E., O'Connor, M.G., & McGuire, J. B. (2008). Direction, alignment, commitment: Toward a more integrative ontology of leadership. *Leadership Quarterly*, 19, 635–653.

Fitzsimons, D., Turnbull James, K., & Denyer, D. (2011). Alternative approaches for studying shared and distributed leadership. *International Journal of Management Reviews*, 13(3), 313–328.

Fletcher, J.K. (2004). The paradox of post-heroic leadership: An essay on gender, power, and transformational change. *Leadership Quarterly*, 15, 647–661.

Ghemawat, P. (2012). Developing global leaders. *McKinsey Quarterly*. Available at www.mckinsey.com/insights/leading_in_the_21st_century/developing_global_leaders (accessed 29 September 2015).

Gould, L. J., Stapley, L. F., & Stein, M. (Eds.) (2001). *The systems psychodynamics of organizations*. New York and London: Karnac Books.

Grint, K. (2005). Problems, problems, problems: The social construction of "leadership". *Human Relations*, 58(11), 1467–1494.

Grint, K. (2010). *Leadership: A very short introduction*. Oxford: Oxford University Press.

Gronn, P. (2002). Distributed leadership as a unit of analysis. *Leadership Quarterly*, 13, 423–451.

Heifetz, R. A. (1994). *Leadership without easy answers*. New York: Belknap.

Heifetz, R. A. (2009). *The practice of adaptive leadership: Tools and tactics for changing your organisational world*. Boston: Harvard Business Press.

Heifetz, R. A., & Laurie, D. L. (1999). Mobilizing adaptive work: Beyond visionary leadership. In J. Conger, *et al.* (Eds.), *The leader's change handbook*. San Francisco: Jossey-Bass.

Heifetz, R. A., & Laurie, D. L. (1997). The work of leadership. *Harvard Business Review*, 75(1), 124–134.

Heifetz, R. A., & Linsky, M. (2002). *Leadership on the line: Staying alive through the dangers of leading*. Boston: Harvard Business School Publishing.

Hosking, D. M. (1988). Organizing, leadership, and skilful process. *Journal of Management Studies*, 25(2), 147–166.

Huffington, C. (2006). Executive coaching—A contextualised approach to coaching. In H. Brunning (Ed.), *Executive coaching: Systems psychodynamic perspective*. London and New York: Karnac.

Huffington, C., James, K., & Armstrong, D. (2004). What is the emotional cost of distributed leadership? In C. Huffington, D. Armstrong, W. Halton, L. Hoyle, & J. Pooley (Eds.), *Working below the surface: The emotional life of contemporary organizations* (pp. 67–82). London: Karnac.

Huffington, C., & Miller, S. (2008). Where angels and mere mortals fear to tread: Exploring sibling relations in the workplace. *Organisation and Social Dynamics*, 8(1), 18–37.

James, K., & Burgoyne, J. (2001). *Leadership development: Best practice guide for organisations*. Report for the Council for Excellence in Management and Leadership.

James, K., Jarrett, M., & Neumann, J. (1998). Group dynamics and unconscious organizational behaviour. In R. G. Milter, J. E. Stinson & W. H. Gijselaers (Eds.), *Educational innovation in economics and business III*. Dordrecht: Kluwer Academic Publishers.

Kotter, J. P. (1996). *Leading change*. Boston: Harvard Business Press.

Krantz, J. (2001). Dilemmas of organizational change: A systems psychodynamic perspective. In L. Gould, L. Stapley & M. Stein (Eds.), *The systems psychodynamics of organizations* (pp. 133–156). London: Karnac.

Ladkin, D. (2010). *Re-thinking leadership: A new look at old questions*. Cheltenham: Edward Elgar.

Lichtenstein, B., Uhl-Bien, M., Marion, R., Seers, A., Orton, J. D., & Schreiber, C. (2006). Complexity leadership theory: An interactive perspective on leading in complex adaptive systems. *E:CO Emergence: Complexity and Organization*, 8(4), 2–12.

Mitchell, J. (2003). *Siblings: Sex and violence*. Cambridge: Polity Press.

Parry, K. W., & Bryman, A. (2006). Leadership in organizations. In S. R. Clegg, C. Hardy, T. B. Lawrence, & W. R. Nord (Eds.), *The Sage handbook of organization studies* (2nd edition). London: Sage.

Parsons, T., Bales, R. F., & Shils, E. A. (Eds.) (1953). *Working papers in the theory of action*. New York: Free Press.

Pearce, C. L., & Conger, J. A. (2003). *Shared leadership: Reframing the hows and whys of leadership*. Thousand Oaks, CA: Sage.

Plowman, D. A., Solansky, S., Beck, T. E., Baker, L., Kulkarni, M., & Travis, D. V. (2007). The role of leadership in emergent, self-organization. *Leadership Quarterly*, 18(4), 341–356.

Plowman, D. A., & Duchon, D. (2008). Dispelling the myths about leadership: From cybernetics to emergence. In R. Marion, M. Uhl-Bien, & P. Hanges (Eds.), *Complexity theory and leadership: Leadership dynamics in the knowledge era* (pp. 129–154). Greenwich, CT: Information Age Publishing Inc.

Probert, J., & Turnbull James, K. (2011). Leadership development: Crisis, opportunities and the leadership concept. *Leadership*, 7(2), 137–150.

Raelin, J. A. (2003). *Creating leaderful organizations: How to bring out leadership in everyone*. San Francisco: Berrett-Koehler.

Raelin, J. A. (2006). The role of facilitation in praxis. *Organizational Dynamics*, 35(1), 83–95.

Raelin, J. A. (2007). Toward an epistemology of practice. *Academy of Management Learning and Education*, 6(4), 495–519.

Raelin, J. A. (2008). *Work-based learning: Bridging knowledge and action in the workplace*. San Francisco: Jossey-Bass.

Samra-Fredericks, D. (2003). Strategizing as lived experience and strategists' everyday efforts to shape strategic direction. *Journal of Management Studies*, 40(1), 141–174.

Schatzki, T. R. (2005). The sites of organizations. *Organization Studies*, 26(3), 465–484.

Shotter, J. (2006). Understanding process from within: An argument for 'withness'-thinking. *Organization Studies*, 27(4), 585–604.

Spillane, J. (2004). Towards a theory of leadership practice: A distributed perspective. *Journal of Curriculum*. Available at www.tandfonline.com/doi/abs/10.1080/0022027032 000106726 (accessed 27 September 2015).

Turnbull James, K. (2011). *Leadership in context: Lessons from new leadership theory and current leadership development practice*. London: The Kings Fund.

Turnbull James, K., Mann, J., & Creasy, J. (2007). Leaders as lead learners: A case example of facilitating collaborative leadership learning for school leaders. *Management Learning*, 38(1), 79–94.

Turnbull James, K., & Ladkin, D. (2008). Meeting the challenge of leading in the 21st Century: beyond the deficit model of leadership development. In K. Turnbull James &

J. Collins (Eds.), *Leadership learning: Knowledge into action* (pp. 13–34). Basingstoke: Palgrave.

Uhl-Bien, M. (2006), Relational leadership theory: Exploring the social processes of leadership and organizing. *Leadership Quarterly*, 17(6), 654–676.

Uhl-Bien, M., & Marion, R. (2007), *Complexity leadership: Part 1: Conceptual foundations (PB): Conceptual foundations Pt. 1 (Leadership Horizons)*. Greenwich, CT: Information Age Publishing.

Uhl-Bien, M., & Marion, R. (2009). Complexity leadership in bureaucratic forms of organizing: A meso model. *Leadership Quarterly*, 20(4), 631–650.

Uhl-Bien, M., Marion, R., & McKelvey, B. (2007). Complexity leadership theory: Shifting leadership from the industrial age to the knowledge era. *Leadership Quarterly*, 18(4), 298–318.

Van Velsor, E., & McCauley, C. D. (2004). Introduction: Our view of leadership development. In C.D. McCauley, & E. Van Velsor (Eds.), *The Center for Creative Leadership handbook of leadership development* (2nd edition) (pp. 1–22). San Francisco: Jossey-Bass.

Wang, L., Turnbull James, K., Denyer, D., & Bailey, C. (2014). Western views and Chinese whispers: Re-thinking global leadership competency in multi-national corporations. *Leadership*, 10(4), 471–495.

Wells, L. Jr. (1985). The group-as-a-whole perspective and its theoretical roots. In A. D. Colman, & M. H. Geller (Eds.), *Group relations reader 2*. A.K. Rice Institute.

Whittington, R. (1996). Strategy as practice. *Long Range Planning*, 29(5), 731–735.

Whittington, R. (2004). Strategy after modernism: Recovering practice. *European Management Review*, 1, 62–68.

Weick, K. E. (1979). *The social psychology of organizing* (2nd edition). Reading, MA: Addison-Wesley.

Weick, K. E. (1996). Drop your tools: An allegory for organizational studies. *Administrative Science Quarterly*, 41(2), 301.

INDEX

59–61, 66; *see also* dialogue;
sensemaking; understanding
intersubjectivity: as a complement to
subjectivity in achieving democratic
change, 85; intersubjective inquiry, 10;
in L-A-P, 8, 10, 223–4, 237–8; the of
the practice approach, 3, 6; the ontology
of, 52–54; versus subjectivity, 54
interviews: as a complement to
observations, 92, 244; as a means of
researching individual identity, 97–9,
108; as a means of studying individuals
in their natural context, 32, 108; as a
source of data, 97, 118, 242, 247–8,
251–2, 273; focus group, 192, 194;
narrative, 32, 254, 255; as performances
or constructs, 98
intra-action 5, 12–13, 51, 151, 166, 203

Jackson, Brad 13–14, 33, 36, 242–57
James, William 147, 148
judgment: aesthetic, 29; ethics and, 75, 81;
identity and, 107; the influence of
anticipation on, 136–7; the made by a
leader, 75; non-judgmental dialogue,
180, 191; as the product of human
interactions, 132, 136–7

Kelly, S. 201, 205–7, 216
Kempster, Steve 13–14, 33, 36, 242–57
knowledge: as a basis for shared social
order, 5, 32, 80–81, 200; as an attribute
of the charismatic leader, 75; as a
product of interaction, 7, 14, 73, 99,
179, 185–6; as a product of practice, 60,
72, 112, 248; assumptions regarding,
52–53, 173, 186, 232–4, 277–8;
autoethnography as a means of
communicating, 255; in CLLGs,
269–70; embodied, 192–3; the
inadequacy of during crisis, 5; the
investigator as interpreter of, 141, 144,
152; the post-structuralist interpretation
of, 234; power and, 13, 233–5, 238; the
problematics of, 52–53; the production
of, 24, 34, 44–45, 46, 164, 224, 238–9;
propositional, 186; scientific, 164; the
spectator theory of, 164

language: Bakhtin on the dialogical
approach to, 144; the categorizing
tendency embedded within, 141; the
embodiment of leadership through, 5,

26–7, 111, 205, 224, 230, 266; Foucault
on, 235; gender and, 227, 229–30,
235–6, 237; hermeneutics and, 54, 59;
language games, 2, 181–2; the liberal-
humanist view of, 235; the metaphor,
134, 136, 181; in post-structuralist
thinking, 232–3; representationalism
versus performativity, 162–3, 164–8,
172; the study of by L-A-P researchers,
8, 9, 35, 53, 97, 174, 225; subjectivity
and, 235–7; understanding and, 65,
136–7, 144, 147, 162–3; utterances, 137,
181; versus process ontology in defining
reality, 165; Wittgenstein on, 136–7,
147, 181–2
Latour, Bruno: on hybrid agency, 115, 163,
173; on immutable mobiles, 119, 124–5,
166; on sociomateriality, 51, 115,
117–18
leadership: adaptive, 266–7; after-the-fact,
148–9; artifacts as identifiers of, 101–2;
authentic, 55–58; before-the-fact, 148,
149–53; Critical Leadership Studies
(CLS), 9, 83, 224, 226–7, 239; Critical
Management Studies (CMS), 226;
entitative, 23, 25, 26; the ephemerality
of, 144, 216; the ethics of, 65–66;
feminist post-structuralist goals in
redefining, 232–3, 235–6; gender and,
227–34; the generative qualities of, 73;
good-enough, 150–1; the Graph Project
example of, 119–25; historical
assumptions concerning, 223, 227, 229,
232; and identity, 97–9; the influence of
routine on, 106–7, 173–4; the influence
of spatial configurations on, 106–7, 127;
the leader-practitioner, 12, 29, 37,
161–2, 171, 173, 174; the occurrence of
in situ, 11, 53, 111–17, 124, 126, 265;
organizing as a fundamental function of,
27, 113; practitioners, practice, and
praxis of power, 29, 172–3; processual,
developmental models of, 8, 11, 70–72,
113–18, 149–50, 171–2; situational or
contingency, 21, 24, 25; the
understanding of, 5, 8, 10, 12–13, 22,
70–74, 111
leadership-as-practice (L-A-P): as a
co-construction, 31–2; the activities of,
5, 6–7, 64–65, 97, 100–1, 106–7;
as a democratic process, 11, 51, 73–74,
78–80, 81–85, 169, 238; as a
hermeneutic unity, 141–8; as an

CPSIA information can be obtained
at www.ICGtesting.com
Printed in the USA
FFOW03n1300240316
22626FF